MARX AND FREUD
IN LATIN AMERICA

MARX AND FREUD IN LATIN AMERICA

Politics, Psychoanalysis, and Religion in Times of Terror

BRUNO BOSTEELS

VERSO

London • New York

First published by Verso 2012
© Bruno Bosteels 2012

1 3 5 7 9 10 8 6 4 2

Verso
UK: 6 Meard Street, London W1F 0EG
US: 20 Jay Street, Suite 1010, Brooklyn, NY 11201

www.versobooks.com

Verso is the imprint of New Left Books

ISBN-13: 978-1-84467-755-9

British Library Cataloguing in Publication Data
A catalogue record for this book is available from the British Library

Library of Congress Cataloging-in-Publication Data
Bosteels, Bruno.
Marx and Freud in Latin America : politics, psychoanalysis and
religion in times of terror / by Bruno Bosteels.
p. cm.
Includes index.
ISBN 978-1-84467-755-9 (hardback)
— ISBN 978-1-84467-847-1
(ebook)
1. Latin American literature—History and criticism—Theory, etc.
2. Socialism and culture—Latin America. 3. Psychoanalysis and
culture—Latin America. 4. Marx, Karl, 1818-1883—Influence.
5. Freud, Sigmund, 1856-1939—Influence. 6. Psychology and —
Latin America. I. Title.
PQ7081.B676 2012
860.9'98—dc23
                                        2012018123

Typeset in Sabon by Hewer Text UK, Ltd, Edinburgh
Printed and bound in the US by Maple Vail

For Lucas Emiliano and Manuel Santiago

In memorium Raf Bosteels (1939–2012)

CONTENTS

ACKNOWLEDGMENTS

Having been fortunate to be able to present most ideas for this book in graduate seminars, workshops, and public lectures too numerous to mention here, I am grateful to those who invited me to do so and hope that they see at least part of this work as a collective effort.

I want to thank the friends and colleagues who have supported this particular project over the past few years: Etienne Balibar, John Beverley, Sebastian Budgen, Gerardo Calderón, Alejandro Cerletti, Raúl J. Cerdeiras, Philippe Cheron, Joshua Clover, Walter Cohen, Jonathan Culler, Pedro Erber, Evodio Escalante, Irene Fenoglio, Federico Finchelstein, Jean Franco, María Antonia Garcés, Soren García, Carlos Gómez Camarena, Horacio González, Mitchell Greenberg, Peter Hallward, Patty Keller, Richard Klein, Stathis Kouvelakis, John Kraniauskas, Nacho Maldonado, Robert March, Frida Mateos, Rodrigo Mier, Alberto Moreiras, Tim Murray, Gabriela Nouzeilles, Edmundo Paz Soltán, Ricardo Piglia, Nelly Richard, Willy Thayer, Alberto Toscano, Miguel Vatter, Geoff Waite, Gareth Williams, and Slavoj Žižek. Daniel Bensaïd, Andrea Revueltas, and León Rozitchner have passed away since I started writing this book, which now has the added function of rendering a modest homage to them. A transatlantic hug also goes out to my entire family in Belgium.

Simone Pinet is the one who made me finish this book, but this should not be held against her. Without her love and intelligence, I am nothing.

In light of what is discussed in them, especially in terms of the rebellion against the father, I dedicate these pages to my sons Lucas Emiliano and Manuel Santiago.

My own father did not live to see this book in print, but his memory will always be with me.

PREFACE

The least that may be said today about Marxism is that, without attenuating prefixes such as "post" or "neo," its mere mention has become an unmistakable sign of obsolescence. Thus, while the old manuals of historical and dialectical materialism from the Soviet Academy of Sciences keep piling up in secondhand bookstores from Mexico City to Tierra del Fuego, almost nobody seems any longer to be referring to Marxism as a vital doctrine of political or historical intervention. Rather, in the eyes of the not-so-silent majority, Marx and Marxism have become things of the past. In the best of all scenarios, they simply constitute an object for nostalgic or academic commemorations; in the worst, they stand accused in the world-historical tribunal of crimes against humanity. "Guevarists, Trotskyists, libertarians, revolutionary syndicalists, radical third worldists, and anti-Stalinist communists have all been sent back to the dock to appear before the prosecutors of 'really-existing' capitalism in the great trial of communism," Olivier Besancenot and Michael Löwy write in their recent proposal to retrieve the figure of Ernesto Guevara. "This is a trial that places executioners and victims, revolutionaries and counter-revolutionaries side by side. Not to accept capitalism is a crime in itself."[1] And while the same fate has not befallen the works of Freud and his followers, even in their case hardly anyone can keep a straight face when remembering the attempts to weld together the Marxist and psychoanalytical notions of praxis—respectively, the political revolution and the talking cure—into a combined Freudo-Marxism.

Not only have the scientific credentials of psychoanalysis come under increasing attack but so too has the idea of an emancipatory potential behind the discovery of the unconscious. Even on purely therapeutic grounds, the virtues of psychoanalysis seem to have been trumped by the pharmaceutical industry. In 1993, *Time* magazine thus famously was able to put the Viennese doctor on its cover alongside the rhetorical question "Is Freud dead?" Yet, as Anthony Elliott

---

1. Olivier Besancenot and Michael Löwy, *Che Guevara: His Revolutionary Legacy*, trans. James Membrez (New York: Monthly Review Press, 2009), 9.

admonished, "Despite the fluctuating fortunes of psychoanalysis, Freud's impact has perhaps never been as far-reaching," albeit now for reasons that are more political than clinical. "In a century that has seen totalitarianism, Hiroshima, Auschwitz and the prospect of a nuclear winter, intellectuals have demanded a language able to grapple with culture's unleashing of its unprecedented powers of destruction. Freud has provided that conceptual vocabulary."[2] Beyond providing a far-reaching, if also gloomy, diagnostic of the human condition as well as an intriguing conceptual vocabulary that has penetrated everyday use, however, the question is still very much open as to whether Freud's work might also enable us to envision the radical transformation of our current political situation in ways reminiscent of the promise behind the legacy of Marx and Marxism.

Álvaro García Linera, the current vice-president of Bolivia under Evo Morales, in an important text from 1996 written from prison, where he was being held in maximum security conditions on charges of subversive and terrorist activity—a text titled "Three Challenges for Marxism to Face the New Millennium," and included in the collective volume *The Arms of Utopia: Heretical Provocations in Marxism*—describes the situation as follows:

> Yesterday's rebels who captivated the poor peasants with the fury of their subversive language, today find themselves at the helm of dazzling private companies and NGOs that continue to ride the martyred backs of the same peasants previously summoned . . . Russia, China, Poland, El Salvador, Nicaragua, Communist and socialist parties, armed and unarmed "vanguards" without a soul these days no longer orient any impetus of social redemption nor do they emblematize any commitment to just and fair dissatisfaction; they symbolize a massive historical sham.[3]

With regard to the destiny of Marx's works and the politics associated with them, however, something else appears to be happening as well. The story is not just the usual one of crime, deception, and betrayal.

2. Anthony Elliott, "The Force of Freud," *Times Higher Education* (November 27, 2008). For a discussion of some of the attacks on Freud, see John Forrester, *Dispatches from the Freud Wars: Psychoanalysis and Its Passions* (Cambridge, MA: Harvard University Press, 1997); and, for a noteworthy defense, Kurt Jacobson, *Freud's Foes: Psychoanalysis, Science, and Resistance* (Lanham, MD: Rowman & Littlefield, 2009).

3. Álvaro García Linera, "3 retos al marxismo para encarar el nuevo milenio," in *Las armas de la utopía: Marxismo: provocaciones heréticas* (La Paz: Punto Cero, 1996): 77. Unless otherwise indicated, all translations are my own. In the expression *vanguardias armadas y desalmadas*—literally "armed and soulless vanguards"—García Linera is punning on the word *desarmadas*, "unarmed" or "disarmed." He may also be alluding here to Jorge G. Castañedas's influential book *La utopía desarmada: intrigas, dilemas y promesas de la izquierda en América Latina* (Buenos Aires: Ariel, 1993), with which Castañedas, at one point the author of a biography of Ernesto Guevara, settled his accounts with the Left and prepared his move into the neoliberal camp as Mexico's secretary of state under the presidency of Vicente Fox, who in 2000 allowed the conservative Partido de Acción Nacional (PAN) to break with seventy-one years of single-party rule by the Partido Revolucionario Institucional (PRI).

There are whole generations who know little or nothing about those "rebels of yesteryear," and much less understand how they would have been able to "captivate" the impoverished peasants and workers with the "fury" of their language.

On the one hand, all memory seems to have been broken, and many radical intellectuals and activists from the 1960s and '70s—for a variety of motives that include guilt, shame, the risk of infamy, or purely and simply the fear of ridicule if they were to vindicate their old fidelities—are accomplices to the oblivion insofar as they refuse to work through, in a quasi-analytical sense of the expression, the internal genealogy of their militant experiences. Thus, the fury of subversion remains, unelaborated, in the drawer of nostalgias, with precious few militants publicly risking the ordeal of self-criticism. What is more, the situation hardly changes if, on the other hand, we are also made privy to the opposite excess, as a wealth of personal testimonies and confessions accumulates in which the inflation of memory seems to be little more than another, more spectacular form of the same forgetfulness. As in the case of the polemic about militancy and violence unleashed in Argentina by the recent epistolary confession of Óscar del Barco ("*No matarás*: Thou shalt not kill"[4]), we certainly are treated to a heated debate, but what still remains partially hidden from view is the politico-theoretical archive and everything that might be contained therein, in terms of relevant materials for rethinking the effective legacy of Marx and Marxism in Latin America. And we could argue that the

---

4. Most of the documents have been collected in Spanish in the volume edited by Pablo René Belzagui, *No matar: Sobre la responsabilidad* (Córdoba: Del Cíclope/Universidad Nacional de Córdoba, 2008). In English, see the translation of Óscar del Barco's original letter and the accompanying dossier with responses by leading intellectuals in *Journal of Latin American Cultural Studies* 16: 2 (2007): 111–82. Some of the most provocative replies to del Barco do not appear in this special dossier in English. See, for example, the answer from León Rozitchner, "Primero hay que saber vivir: Del Vivirás materno al No matarás patriarcal," originally published in *El Ojo Mocho* 20 (Spring 2006), as well as the debate between Elías Palti, "La crítica de la razón militante: Una reflexión con motivo de *La fidelidad del olvido* de Blas de Santos y el 'affaire del Barco'," and Horacio Tarcus, "Elogio de la razón militante: Respuesta a Elías J. Palti," *Políticas de la memoria* 8–9 (Summer 2009). In Spanish, these later interventions have been gathered in the follow-up volume edited by Luis García, *No matar: Sobre la responsabilidad. Segunda compilación de intervenciones* (Córdoba: Universidad Nacional de Córdoba, 2010). More generally, the overload of memoirs and testimonies about the militant past of the 1960s and 1970s has been commented upon by Beatriz Sarlo, *Tiempo pasado: Cultura de la memoria y giro subjetivo. Una discusión* (Buenos Aires: Siglo Veintiuno, 2005); by Omar Basabe and Marisa Sadi, *La significación omitida: Militancia y lucha armada en la Argentina reciente* (Buenos Aires: Catálogos, 2008); and by Hugo Vezzetti, *Sobre la violencia revolucionaria: Memorias y olvidos* (Buenos Aires: Siglo Veintiuno, 2009). For a wider variety of perspectives, see also the essays collected in Horacio González, ed., *La memoria en el atril: Entre los mitos de archivo y el pasado de las experiencias* (Buenos Aires: Colihue, 2005); in Cecelia Vallina, ed., *Crítica del testimonio: Ensayos sobre las relaciones entre memoria y relato* (Rosario: Beatriz Viterbo, 2009); and in María Inés Mudrovcic, ed., *Pasados en conflicto: Representación, mito y memoria* (Buenos Aires: Prometeo, 2009).

same is true, though with less spectacular effect because oblivion also has been more spontaneous, of that strange hybrid of Freudo-Marxism in Latin America.

How to go against the complacency that is barely concealed behind this bipolar consensus, with its furtive silences on the one hand and its clamorous self-accusations on the other? In the first place, we should insist on something that we know only too well when it comes to domestic appliances, but that we prefer to ignore when we approach the creations of the intellect—namely, the fact that everything that is produced and consumed in this world bears from the start a certain expiration date, or the stamp of a planned obsolescence. Theories do not escape this rule, no matter how much it pains scholars and intellectuals to admit it. As a secondary effect of this obsolescence, however, we should also consider the possibility that novelty may be nothing more than the outcome of a prior oblivion. As Jorge Luis Borges remarks in the epigraph to his story "The Immortal," quoting Francis Bacon's *Essays*: "Solomon saith: *There is no new thing upon the earth.* So that as Plato had an imagination, *that all knowledge was but remembrance*; so Solomon giveth his sentence, *that all novelty is but oblivion.*"[5] This grave pronouncement applies equally to the products of criticism and theory. Here, too, all novelty is perhaps but oblivion.

In fact, the history of the concepts used in studies of politics, art, literature, and culture as well as their combination in what we can still call critical theory today appears to be riddled with holes that are very much due to the kind of silence mentioned above—a not-saying that is partly the result of voluntary omissions and partly the effect of unconscious or phantasmatic slippages. Forgetfulness, in other words, is never entirely by chance, nor can it be attributed simply to a taste for novelty on the part of overzealous artists or intellectuals in search of personal fame and fortune. After all, as the Situationist Guy Debord had already observed more than twenty years ago, in his *Comments on the Society of the Spectacle*, itself a reflection upon his book from twenty years before: "Spectacular domination's first priority was to eradicate historical knowledge in general; beginning with just about all rational information and commentary on the most recent past." And, about the events of 1968 in particular, Debord adds: "The more important something is, the more it is hidden. Nothing in the last twenty years has been so thoroughly coated in obedient lies as the history of May 1968."[6] If today, more than forty years after the original publication of *The Society of the Spectacle*, the vast majority of radicals from

5. Jorge Luis Borges, "El inmortal," *El Aleph* (Madrid: Cátedra, 1995), 7. The epigraph appears in English in the original. See Francis Bacon, "Of Vicissitude of Things," in *Essays, Civil and Moral*, ed. Charles William Eliot (New York: P. F. Collier & Son, 1909–14).
6. Guy Debord, *Comments on the Society of the Spectacle*, trans. Malcolm Imrie (London: Verso, 1988): 13–14.

the 1960s and '70s dedicate mere elegies to the twilight of their broken idols, those who were barely born at the time can only guess where all the elephants have gone to die while radical thinking disguises itself in one fancy terminology after another, each more delightfully innovative and invariably pathbreaking than the previous novelty. Thus, instead of a true polemic, let alone a genealogical work of counter-memory, what comes to dominate is a manic-depressive oscillation between silence and noise, easily coopted and swept up in the frenzied celebrations in honor of the death of communism and the worldwide victory of neoliberalism.

The current appeal of cultural studies, for example, beyond its official birthplaces in the Frankfurt and Birmingham Schools, is inseparable from a process of oblivion or interruption whereby critics and theorists seem to have lost track of the once very lively debates about the causality and efficacy of symbolic practices—debates that until the late 1960s and early '70s were dominated by the inevitable legacies of Marx and Marxism. In the United States, where these legacies never achieved a culturally dominant status to begin with, any potential they might have had was further curtailed by the effects of deconstruction, whose earlier textual trend was then only partially compensated for both by deconstruction's own turn to ethics and politics and by its short-lived rivalry with new historicism. As for Latin America, if we were to ask ourselves in which countries the model of cultural studies, or cultural critique, has achieved a notable degree of intellectual intensity and academic respectability, the answers—Argentina, Chile, Brazil—almost without exception include regions where the military regimes put a violent end to the radicalization of left-wing intellectual life, including a brutal stop to all public debates about the revolutionary promise of Marxism, while in other countries—Mexico or Cuba, for instance—many authors for years might seem to have been doing cultural criticism already, albeit *sans le savoir*, like Molière's comedian, perhaps because in these cases the influence of Marxism, though certainly also waning today, has nevertheless remained a strong undercurrent.

In Latin America, the reasons for amnesia are if possible even more complex. Not only has there been an obvious interruption of memory due to the military coups and the onslaught of neoliberalism but, in addition, this lack of a continuous dialogue with the realities of the region can already be found in the works of Marx and Freud themselves. In fact, we could say that the history of the relation of Marx and Freud to Latin America is the history of a triple *desencuentro*, or a three-fold missed encounter.

In the first place, we find a missed encounter already within the writings of Marx. Thanks to José Aricó's classic and long out-of-print study, *Marx y América Latina*, now finally reissued, we can unravel the possible reasons behind Marx's inability to approach the realities of Latin America with even a modicum of sympathy. His infamous attack on Simón Bolívar (whom Marx in a letter to Engels labels "the most dastardly, most miserable and meanest of blackguards"[7]) or his and Engels's notorious early support for the US invasion of Mexico (about whose inhabitants Marx, in another letter to his collaborator, wrote: "The Spanish are completely degenerate. But a degenerate Spaniard, a Mexican, is an ideal. All the Spanish vices, braggadocio, swagger and Don Quixotry, raised to the third power, but little or nothing of the steadiness which the Spaniards possess"[8]) are indeed compatible with three major prejudices that Aricó attributes to Marx: a belief in the linearity of history; a generalized anti-Bonapartism; and a theory of the nation-state inherited, albeit in inverted form, from Hegel, according to which there cannot exist a lasting form of the state without the prior presence of a strong sense of national unity at the level of bourgeois civil society—a sense of unity and identity whose absence or insufficiency, on the other hand, tends to provoke precisely the intervention of despotic or dictatorial figures à la Bonaparte and Bolívar. In this sense, the three prejudices are intimately related: it is only due to a

---

7.   Karl Marx, Letter to Friedrich Engels (February 14, 1858), in Karl Marx and Friedrich Engels, *Collected Works*, vol. 40 (Moscow: Progress Publishers, 1963), 266. Spanish version quoted in José Aricó, *Marx y América Latina*, 2nd edn (Mexico City: Alianza Editorial Mexicana, 1982), 116. As part of Aricó's vast effort at divulging the classics through the journal and book series of *Pasado y Presente*, Marx and Engels's dispersed writings on Latin America have been collected in a single volume in Spanish as Karl Marx and Friedrich Engels, *Materiales para la historia de América Latina*, ed. Pedro Scaron (Mexico City: Siglo Veintiuno, 1979). This volume should be read in conjunction with Karl Marx, *Imperio y colonia: Escritos sobre Irlanda* (Mexico City: Siglo Veintiuno, 1979) and *Escritos sobre Rusia*, 2 vols. (Mexico City: Siglo Veintiuno, 1980). The English edition of Karl Marx and Friedrich Engels, *On Colonialism: Articles from the* New York Tribune *and Other Writings* (New York: International Publishers, 1972), has also been translated in this same important collection of "Cuadernos Pasado y Presente" as *Escritos sobre el colonialismo* (Mexico City: Siglo Veintiuno, 1973). For a study of this editorial project and Aricó's contribution to Marxism and Gramscianism in Latin America, see Raúl Burgos, *Los gramscianos argentinos: Cultura y política en la experiencia de Pasado y Presente* (Buenos Aires: Siglo Veintiuno, 2004). The recent republication of Aricó's study also comes with a lengthy new preface from the hand of Horacio Crespo, "El marxismo latinoamericano de Aricó," in José Aricó, *Marx y América Latina* (Buenos Aires: Fondo de Cultura Económica, 2010), 9–48. See also the introductions by Horacio Crespo, "Córdoba, *Pasado y Presente* y la obra de José Aricó: una guía de aproximación," and Alicia Rubio, "Crisis y creación: Apuntes para una historia de la revista *Pasado y Presente*" in the facsimile edition of the journal put online by the Argentine CeDInCI (Centro de Documentación e Investigación de la Cultura de Izquierdas en Argentina). Aricó's own take on the importance of Gramscianism can be found in the articles collected in *La cola del diablo: Itinerario de Gramsci en América Latina* (Buenos Aires: Siglo Veintiuno, 2005).
8.   Karl Marx, Letter to Friedrich Engels (December 2, 1854), in Karl Marx and Friedrich Engels, *Collected Works*, vol. 39 (Moscow: Progress Publishers, 1983), 504. Spanish version quoted in Aricó, *Marx y América Latina*, 39. A much earlier selection of statements about Mexico culled from the works of Marx and Engels—including the two letters just quoted— can be found in Domingo P. de Toledo y P., *México en la obra de Marx y Engels* (Mexico City: Fondo de Cultura Económica, 1939). For a discussion, see Jesús Monjarás-Ruiz, "México en los escritos y fuentes de Marx," *Nueva Sociedad* 66 (May–June 1983): 105–11.

supposedly linear conception of history that all countries must necessarily pass through the same process of political and economic development in the formation of a civil society sufficiently strong to support the apparatuses of the state.

One paradox alluded to in Aricó's study, however, still deserves to be unpacked in greater detail. Especially in his final texts on Ireland, Poland, Russia, or India, after 1870, Marx indeed begins to catch a glimpse of the logic of the uneven development of capitalism, which could have served him as well to reinterpret the postcolonial condition of Latin America. "From the end of the decade of the 1870s onward, Marx never again abandons his thesis that the uneven development of capitalist accumulation displaces the center of the revolution from the countries of Western Europe to dependent and colonial countries," writes Aricó. "We find ourselves before a true 'shift' in Marx's thinking, which opens up a whole new perspective for the analysis of the conflicted problem of the relations between the class struggle and the national liberation struggle, that genuine *punctum dolens* in the entire history of the socialist movement."[9] Henceforth, Marx not only explicitly rejects the interpretation that would turn his analysis of capitalist development into a universal philosophy of history, applicable to any and all national situations; he also acknowledges the possibility that in so-called backward, dependent or colonial countries socialism may come about through a retrieval of pre-capitalist forms of communitarian production in superior conditions. If, in spite of this paradigm shift, provoked by his reflection on the supposed backwardness of cases such as Ireland or Russia, Marx is still unable to settle his accounts with Latin America by critically re-evaluating the revolutionary role of peripheral countries, this continued inability would be due, according to Aricó, to the stubborn persistence of Marx's anti-Bonapartist bias and his unwitting fidelity to the legacy of Hegel's theory of civil society and the state.

In his painstaking study of Marx's complete oeuvre from the point of view of the national question in peripheral countries, *On Hidden Demons and Revolutionary Moments: Marx and Social Revolution in the Extremities of the Capitalist Body*, García Linera nevertheless raises two objections to Aricó's interpretation. First, the Bolivian theorist accuses his Argentine comrade, exiled in Mexico, of proceeding too hastily to accept the absence of a massive or even national-popular capacity for rebellion in Latin America. According to García Linera, Marx himself never ceases to insist, against his allegedly regressive Hegelian baggage, on the importance of mass action, whereas Aricó would somehow be seduced by the autonomy of the political and the direct revolutionary potential of the state. The "blindness" or

---

9. José Aricó, *Marx y América Latina*, 65 and 68. I develop this hypothesis in my reading of José Martí in Chapter 1.

"incomprehension" of Marx toward Latin America, then, would be due to the lack of historical sources and reliable studies on the indigenous rebellions that had shaken the region since at least the end of the eighteenth century. "This is the decisive factor. In the characteristics of the masses in movement and as a force, their vitality, their national spirit, and so on, there lay the other components that Aricó does not take into account but that for Marx are the decisive ones for the national formation of the people," affirms Linera. "There exists no known text from Marx in which he tackles this matter, but it is not difficult to suppose that this is because he did not find any at the time of his setting his eyes on America."[10] The missed encounter between Marx and Latin America, therefore, would be due not to the lingering presence of Hegelianisms so much as to the fact that "this energy of the masses did not come into being as a generalized movement (at least not in South America); it was for the most part absent in the years considered by Marx's reflections."[11] In other words, it would be Aricó, not Marx, who misjudges the Latin American reality due to a blinding adherence to Hegel.

In fact, García Linera goes so far as to suggest that the supposed "not-seeing" on the part of Marx is the result of a "wanting-to-see" on the part of his most famous and prolific interpreter from Argentina: "The terrain on which Aricó places us is not that of the reality or that of Marx's tools for understanding this reality, but rather the reality that Aricó believes it to be and the tools that Aricó believes to be those of Marx."[12] In the final analysis, however, even for García Linera it cannot be a matter of denying the unfortunate missed encounter, or

---

10. Álvaro García Linera, *De demonios escondidos y momentos de revolución: Marx y la revolución social en las extremidades del cuerpo capitalista* (La Paz: Ofensiva Roja, 1991), 252. For a slightly different assessment of Aricó's interpretation, see Jorge Larraín, "Classical Political Economists and Marx on Colonialism and 'Backward' Nations," in Bob Jessop and Russell Wheatley, eds, *Karl Marx's Social and Political Thought: Critical Assessments* (New York: Routledge, 1999), vol. 6, 164–95. On the question of Marxism, colonialism, and indigenism in Latin America, see also José Carlos Mariátegui, *Seven Interpretive Essays on Peruvian Reality*, trans. Marjory Urquidi (Austin: University of Texas Press, 1971); Jorge Abelardo Ramos, *El marxismo en los países coloniales* (Cochabamba: Editorial Universitaria Universidad Mayor de San Simón, 1970); and Alberto Saladino García, *Indigenismo y marxismo en América Latina* (Toluca: Universidad Autónoma del Estado de México, 1983). In more recent years, the argument for the decolonization of knowledge and the critique of Eurocentrism has gained much momentum in Latin America thanks to the work of Aníbal Quijano, Enrique Dussel, Fernando Coronil, and Walter Mignolo. See, in particular, Walter Mignolo, "El pensamiento des-colonial, desprendimiento y apertura: un manifiesto," in Catherine Walsh, Álvaro García Linera and Walter Mignolo, *Interculturalidad, descolonización del estado y del conocimiento* (Buenos Aires: Del Signo, 2006), 83–123. On the problem of Eurocentrism, see also Carlos Franco's more extensive response to Aricó's essay in *Del marxismo eurocéntrico al marxismo latinoamericano* (Lima: Centro de Estudios para el Desarrollo y la Participación, 1981).
11. García Linera, *De demonios escondidos y momentos de revolución*, 252.
12. Ibid., 250.

desencuentro, between Marx and Latin America. To the contrary, in a recent lecture titled "Marxismo e indianismo" ("Marxism and Indigenism"), García Linera in turn speaks himself of a *desencuentro* between two revolutionary logics—the Marxist and the indigenist— before providing an overview of the different factors that hampered their finding a middle ground throughout most of the twentieth century, all the way to the tentative promise of a possible re-encounter among a small fraction of indigenous intellectuals in the last decade, especially in the Andean region: "Curiously, these small groups of critical Marxists with the utmost reflective care have come to accompany, register, and disseminate the new cycle of the indigenist horizon, inaugurating the possibility of a space of communication and mutual enrichment between indigenisms and Marxisms that will probably be the most important emancipatory concepts of society in twenty-first-century Bolivia."[13]

Following Aricó's example in the case of Marx, we could elaborate a similar critique of the missed encounter between Freud and Latin America. Georges Politzer, in his 1928 *Critique of the Foundations of Psychology*—a work that would take three-quarters of a century to be translated into English but that was widely read and discussed in Spanish-speaking countries—already tried to unmask some of these prejudices. Politzer thus criticizes Freud's "fixism," which tends to give his thought an idealist-metaphysical rather than a concrete-historical bent. As the Argentine psychoanalyst José Bleger concludes after giving an overview of Politzer's writings on Freud,

> We can observe two fundamental limitations: the first is that the key in the development of normal and pathological behavior turns out to be libidinal fixations and in this way the emphasis is put on the repetitive element, so that evolution becomes an epigenesis; the second limitation is a consequence of abstraction: to the extent that psychoanalytic theory becomes more abstract and replaces human realities with forces, entities, instances, the criterion of evolution becomes lost, in favor of a "fixism" of metaphysical allure.[14]

---

13. Álvaro García Linera, "Marxismo e indianismo," available online at cornell.edu/video. This is the inaugural lecture for the conference "Marx and Marxisms in Latin America," which took place at Cornell in September 2007 under the auspices of the journal *Diacritics*. A different version appears as "Indianismo y marxismo: El desencuentro de dos razones revolucionarias," in Pablo Stefanoni, ed., *La potencia plebeya: Acción colectiva e identidades indígenas, obreras y populares en Bolivia* (Buenos Aires: Prometeo Libros/CLACSO, 2008), 373–92, quotation at 391–2. I delve further into the archive of García Linera's writings on Marxism, the national question, and the state, especially from the militant period before his term as Vice-President, in Bruno Bosteels, *The Actuality of Communism* (London: Verso, 2011), 225–68.

14. José Bleger, *Psicoanálisis y dialéctica materialista: Estudios sobre la estructura del psicoanálisis* (first edition 1958; second edition Buenos Aires: Paidós, 1963), 88–9. Georges Politzer's *Critique des fondements de la psychologie*, first published in 1928 by Rieder, became even more influential upon its reissuing in 1968 by Presses Universitaires de France.

This might begin to account for some of Freud's more glaring blindnesses with regard to the world outside of Western Europe, particularly the New World.

In fact, even if he saw himself as the Columbus of the unconscious, the founder of psychoanalysis never refers specifically to the realities of Latin America—at least not beyond his personal and anthropological interest in pre-Hispanic artifacts, and especially his fascination with the culture of the Bolivian coca leaf. There are, to be sure, a number of eyebrow-raising assertions similar to what Marx or Engels have to say early on about Mexicans, as when Freud refers metaphorically to the unconscious, in his paper of the same title from 1915, by speaking of the mind's "aboriginal population"—or again, elsewhere, of the "dark continents."[15] And in Freud's case, too, we could try to systematize the underlying prejudices, aside from a certain metaphysical fixity of concepts, which lead to such affirmations: the universalist trend of his interpretation of evolution, with identical stages for all of humanity; the correspondence between the phylogenetic and the ontogenetic aspects of development, which leads to the utilization of metaphors of primitivism above all with reference to neurosis and the early stages of infanthood, as in his 1913 text *Totem and Taboo,* significantly subtitled *Some Points of Agreement between the Mental Lives of Savages and Neurotics*; and the Lamarckian faith in the possibility of the hereditary transmission of acquired traits, which likewise renders superfluous the study of other or earlier cultures beyond the confines of modern Western Europe. "These assumptions," as Celia Brickman notes, "did not invalidate the potential of psychoanalysis, but their presence lent

---

In English, see Politzer, *Critique of the Foundations of Psychology*, trans. Maurice Apprey (Pittsburgh: Duquesne University Press, 1994). In addition to this work, Bleger also comments on two other crucial texts by Politzer: the first, "Un faux contre-révolutionnaire: Le Freudo-marxisme," *Commune* (November 1933); and the second, "La fin de la psychanalyse," written under the pseudonym Th. W. Morris, when Politzer was already mobilized on the war front, and published in 1939, the year of Freud's death, in the newly founded Marxist journal *La Pensée*, where it would be reissued in 1955. See Bleger, "Georges Politzer: La psicología y el psicoanálisis," first published in 1955 in Brazil, and included in *Psicoanálisis y dialéctica materialista*, 29–62.

15. See Celia Brickman, *Aboriginal Populations of the Mind: Race and Primitivity in Psychoanalysis* (New York: Columbia University Press, 2003); and Ranjana Khanna, *Dark Continents: Psychoanalysis and Colonialism* (Durham: Duke University Press, 2003). While they are no match for Marx and Engels's *Materiales para la historia de América Latina*, Freud's *Cocaine Papers* (New York: Stoneville, 1973), translated into Spanish under the title *Escritos sobre la cocaína* (Barcelona: Anagrama, 1980), nonetheless show an impressive familiarity with the cultural, ethnographic, religious, and medicinal issues surrounding the coca leaf in Latin America. In fact, I would suggest that we read these Freudian texts by taking a clue from Marx: if religion, as the principal form of ideology for Marxism, is the opium for the people, then conversely could we not read treatises on opium or cocaine as surreptitious theories of ideology? This hypothesis certainly works for other texts, such as Charles Baudelaire's *Artificial Paradises*, which not surprisingly culminates in the phantasmagoric (re)creation of the self as God.

credence to readings of psychoanalysis that could perpetuate and seemingly legitimate colonialist representations of primitivity with their
associated racist implications, in much the same way that psychoanalytic representations of femininity were able to be enlisted for some
time as an ally in <u>the subordination of women</u>."[16]

And yet, we might as well invert the conclusion to be drawn from
Freud's prejudices. The fixed, timeless, and phylogenetically inherited
nature of the unconscious, even while being modeled upon evolutionary
schemes of development from, and regression to, primitivism, could thus
be read as a radical subversion of the superiority of the West: "Supposedly
primitive behaviors were seen to lurk not only in the pathological and in
the past, but in the everyday customs and in the great cultural institutions
of modern European civilized public and private life," Brickman is quick
to add. "In the end, we are all more or less neurotic; we are all more or less
primitive; we are all saurians among the horsetails."[17] Or, to make the
same point in the words of Ana, the sickly artist-character from José
Martí's novel *Lucía Jerez*: "Of wild beasts I know two kinds: one dresses
in skins, devours animals, and walks on claws; the other dresses in elegant
suits, eats animals and souls, and walks with a walking stick or umbrella.
We are nothing more than reformed beasts."[18] Similarly, Freud writes in
The Interpretation of Dreams: "What once dominated waking life, when
the mind was still young and incompetent, seems now to have been
banished into the night—just as the primitive weapons, the bows and
arrows, that have been abandoned by adult men, turn up once more in the
nursery."[19] What we could infer from this, aside from a conventional
gender portrayal, is the possibility of a truly revolutionary—rather than
merely evolutionary—awakening of that which lies dormant in the present.
This possibility resembles the way in which Marx imagines his task as a
radical thinker in a letter to Arnold Ruge:

> It will become evident that the world has long possessed the dream of some-
> thing, of which it has only to be conscious in order to possess it in reality. It
> will become evident that it is not a question of drawing a great mental divid-
> ing line between past and future, but of *realizing* the thoughts of the past.
> Lastly, it will become evident that mankind begins no *new* work, but
> consciously brings its old work to completion.[20]

---

16. Brickman, *Aboriginal Populations of the Mind*, 51.
17. Ibid., 89.
18. José Martí, *Lucía Jerez*, ed. Carlos Javier Morales (Madrid: Cátedra, 1994), 133. For a
Marxist-inspired analysis of this novel, see Chapter 1, below.
19. Sigmund Freud, *The Interpretation of Dreams*, quoted in Brickman, *Aboriginal
Populations of the Mind*, 84
20. Karl Marx, letter to Arnold Ruge (Kreuznach, September 1843), included in "Letters from
the *Deutsch-Französische Jahrbücher*," in Karl Marx and Friedrich Engels, *Collected Works*, vol.
3 (Moscow: Progress Publishers, 1975), 144 (translation modified; here and in every instance to
follow, the emphatic italics appear in the original). For a further development of this peculiar
interpretation of the dream and its awakening, see also Chapter 3, below.

What is more, in Freud's case, too, we come across an interesting paradox similar to Marx's tardy discovery of the logic of uneven development. As the late Edward Said showed in his lecture *Freud and the Non-European*, not only might we expect Freud to have arrived at a critique of the ideological notion of primitivism, based on his own experience with the ideologies of racism and anti-Semitism in Europe which forced him to seek refuge in London and eventually brought him back for a visit to America—"Little do they know we are bringing them the plague," Freud is famously said to have proclaimed when, just a little over 100 years ago he first disembarked, with Carl Jung and Sándor Ferenczi, in New York, perhaps still secretly comparing himself to Columbus, only now in terms of the discoverer's epidemic effects. But, furthermore, the later so-called "social" or "culturalist" works of Freud, above all *Group Psychology and Analysis of the Ego, Civilization and Its Discontents* and *Moses and Monotheism*, also contain radical concepts of the structural lack of adaptation of the human species and the presence of a kernel of non-identity at the heart of every identity, including that of the Jewish faith, which could have brought the founding father of psychoanalysis to the point of questioning the effects of his own limited historicism and the temptations of Eurocentrism. "For Freud, writing and thinking in the mid-1930s, the actuality of the non-European was its constitutive presence as a sort of fissure in the figure of Moses—founder of Judaism, but an unreconstructed non-Jewish Egyptian none the less," proposes Said. "Yahveh derived from Arabia, which was also non-Jewish and non-European."[21] Had he applied this radical principle of non-identity to other non-European cultures, our discoverer of the unconscious also could have had more than just a metaphorical connection to Latin America.

In addition to these missed encounters between Marx and Latin America, or between Freud and Latin America, we also have to take into account the obstacles that stand in the way of a proper articulation between Marx and Freud themselves. These are the obstacles that the various attempts at formulating some type or other of Freudo-Marxism have tried to overcome—to varying and, in the eyes of many, highly questionable degrees of success—from the earliest efforts by Wilhelm Reich and Otto Fenichel, via the parallel yet unfortunately

---

21. Edward W. Said, *Freud and the Non-European* (London: Verso, 2003), 42. Said sees in Israel's policy toward Jewish identity the exact opposite of Freud's final work: "What we discover is an extraordinary and revisionist attempt to substitute a new positive structure of Jewish history for Freud's *insistently* more complex and discontinuous late-style efforts to examine the same thing, albeit in an entirely diasporic spirit and with different, decentring results" (46). The classical interpretation of Freud's relation to Judaism in general and to the figure of Moses in particular is Yosef Hayim Yerushalmi, *Freud's Moses: Judaism Terminable and Interminable* (New Haven: Yale University Press, 1991). In the Latin American context, compare Betty Bernardo Fuks, *Freud y la judeidad: la vocación del exilio* (Mexico City: Siglo Veintiuno, 2006).

non-synchronous tracks of the likes of Herbert Marcuse or Erich
Fromm in the Frankfurt School in the 1950s and 1960s, and French
thinkers such as Jean-François Lyotard, or the combination of Gilles
Deleuze and Félix Guattari, who in the 1970s threw Nietzsche into the
Marx-Freud mix, all the way to the recent work of someone like Slavoj
Žižek who, rather than a Freudo-Marxist, would have to be considered
a proponent of Lacano-Althusserianism by way of Hegel. In Latin
America, though this too tends to be forgotten, there also exists a fasci-
nating tradition in this regard—from the presence of Fromm in Mexico
between 1950 and 1973 or the establishment of a psychoanalytical
community between 1961 and 1964 in a Cuernavacan monastery by
the soon-to-be-excommunicated Benedictine monk of Belgian origin,
Gregorio Lemercier, via the collective project for a Freudian Left spearheaded throughout much of the region, from Uruguay to Argentina to
Mexico, by the Jewish-Austrian exile Marie Langer (co-founder of the
Argentine Psychoanalytical Association) who described her own trajectory as a journey "from Vienna to Managua" under the Sandinistas),
all the way to the Sartrean-inflected Lacanianism of Oscar Masotta in
Argentina, or the Brazilian Suely Rolnik's schizoanalytical collabora-
tions with Guattari.[22]

---

22. For a detailed overview of the various trends and schools in Freudo-Marxism from
Wilhelm Reich up until the Frankfurt School, including their students, critics and interlocutors
in Latin America, see the richly documented bibliography in Guillermo Delahanty,
Psicoanálisis y marxismo (Mexico City: Plaza y Valdés, 1987); and Víctor Raggio, *Marxismo
y psicoanálisis: Medio siglo de desencuentros* (Montevideo: Ediciones de la Banda Oriental,
1988). A good sample of the Freudian Left in Latin America can be found in Marie Langer,
ed., *Cuestionamos: documentos de crítica a la ubicación actual del psicoanálisis* (Buenos
Aires: Granica, 1971); and, more recently, Alejandro Vainer, ed., *A la izquierda de Freud*
(Buenos Aires: Topía, 2009). See also Felipe Campuzano, *Izquierda freudiana y marxismo*
(Mexico City: Grijalbo, 1979); and compare with Paul A. Robinson, *The Freudian Left*
(New York: Harper & Row, 1969), trans. in Argentina as *La izquierda freudiana: Los
aportes de Reich, Fromm y Marcuse* (Buenos Aires: Granica, 1971; second edition Buenos
Aires: Gedisa, 1973). To my knowledge, Erich Fromm's role in the dissemination of
psychoanalysis and a Frankfurt-style Freudo-Marxism in Mexico has yet to receive the
critical attention it deserves, and the same is true for the truly continental role of Marie
Langer. For the latter's autobiography, see Marie Langer (with Enrique Guinsberg and Jaime
del Palacio), *From Vienna to Managua: Journey of a Psychoanalyst*, trans. Nancy Caro
Hollander (London: Free Association Books, 1989). Another important figure is the German
exile Igor A. Caruso, several of whose works were translated and became highly influential
in Latin America, including *Psicoanálisis dialéctico: aspectos sociales del psicoanálisis
personal*, trans. Rosa Tanco Duque (Buenos Aires: Paidós, 1964); and *El psicoanálisis,
lenguaje ambiguo: estudios dialécticos sobre teoría y técnica psicoanalíticas*, trans. Armando
Suárez (Mexico City: Fondo de Cultura Económica, 1966). Aside from the collection
"Biblioteca de Psicología," started by Fromm for Fondo de Cultura Económica, there is also
the left-leaning publishing house Siglo Veintiuno, with major seats in Mexico and Argentina,
which from the 1970s published many texts in this tradition, including translations of
European critical theorists as well as original studies by Latin American psychoanalysts. See,
above all, the following collections: Armando Suárez, ed., *Razón, locura y sociedad* (Mexico
City: Siglo Veintiuno, 1978); Salvador Millán and Sonia Gojman de Millán, eds, *Erich
Fromm y el psicoanálisis humanista* (Mexico City: Siglo Veintiuno, 1981); Víctor Saavedra,

Here, I should admit, we might be victims of amnesia to the second degree. Indeed, as I realized only recently, already in *Social Amnesia: A Critique of Contemporary Psychology from Adler to Laing*, the historian of Western Marxism Russell Jacoby ironically enough began with a critique of obsolescence that is strictly speaking identical to the one I am advocating here. "In the name of a new era past theory is declared honorable but feeble; one can lay aside Freud and Marx—or appreciate their limitations—and pick up the latest at the drive-in window of thought," Jacoby writes, with great sarcasm: "The intensification of the drive for surplus value and profit accelerates the rate at which past goods are liquidated to make way for new goods; planned obsolescence is everywhere, from consumer goods to thinking to sexuality."[23] Nowhere does the dilemma posed by this obsolescence make itself felt more clearly than in the case of the debates surrounding attempts to amalgamate a certain Freudo-Marxism. The difficult task of articulation in this context consists in avoiding a purely external relation of complementarity between the social and the psychic, the collective and the individual, the political and the sexual. "The various efforts to interpret Marx and Freud have been plagued by reductionism: the inability to retain the tension between individual and society,

---

La promesa incumplida de Erich Fromm (Mexico City: Siglo Veintiuno, 1994); and the translation of Helmut Dahmer, *Libido y sociedad: Estudios sobre Freud y la izquierda freudiana*, trans. Félix Blanco (Mexico City: Siglo Veintiuno, 1983). On the role of the psychoanalytical experiment in the Benedictine monastery in Cuernavaca, see Juan Alberto Litmanovich Kivatinetz, *Las operaciones psicoanalíticas gestadas al interior del monasterio benedictino de Ahucatitlán, Cuernavaca, Morelos (1961–1964)* (PhD thesis, Universidad Iberoamericana, 2008). In Argentina, aside from the work of León Rozitchner, which I discuss in Chapters 4 and 5, see also the earlier writings of José Bleger, *Psicoanálisis y dialéctica materialista: estudios sobre la estructura del psicoanálisis* (Buenos Aires: Paidós, 1963); Elías Castelnuovo, *Psicoanálisis sexual y social* (Buenos Aires: Claridad, 1966); and Enrique Pichon Rivière, *El proceso grupal: del psicoanálisis a la psicología social* (Buenos Aires: Nueva Visión, 1975). On the work of Oscar Masotta, a contemporary and one-time collaborator of Rozitchner's in the journal *Contorno*, see Germán García, *Oscar Masotta y el psicoanálisis del castellano* (Barcelona: Argonauta/Extensión Freudiana, 1980); Carlos Correa, *Operación Masotta* (Buenos Aires: Interzona, 2007); and the articles in Marcelo Izaguirre, ed., *Oscar Masotta: El revés de la trama* (Buenos Aires: Atuel/Anáfora, 1999). In English, see Philip Derbyshire, "Who Was Oscar Masotta? Psychoanalysis in Argentina," *Radical Philosophy* 158 (2009): 11–24. Masotta's work as an art critic and theoretician has attracted more attention in English, with a good selection being available in Inés Katzenstein, ed., *Listen Here Now! Argentine Art from the 1960s: Writings of the Avant-garde* (New York: MOMA, 2004), 154–222. Suely Rolnik's work with Guattari is only now beginning to be translated into English. See above all Félix Guattari, *Molecular Revolution in Brazil*, ed. Suely Rolnik, trans. Karel Clapshow and Brian Holmes (New York: Semiotext(e), 2008), originally published as *Micropolitica: Cartografias do desejo* (São Paolo: Vozes, 1986). See also Rolnik's dissertation, *Cartografia sentimental: transformações contemporâneas do desejo* (São Paolo: Estação Liberdade, 1989).

23. Russell Jacoby, *Social Amnesia: A Critique of Contemporary Psychology from Adler to Laing* (Boston: Beacon Press, 1975), 3–4. See also the farcical effect of the disjunction at the heart of certain Freudo-Marxisms, eloquently staged by the Chilean playwright Marco Antonio de la Parra, as I briefly discuss in Chapter 8, below.

psychology and political economy," Jacoby remarks, before proposing what he calls a dialectical counter-articulation, inspired by the example of the Frankfurt School: "Critical theory does not know a sharp break between these two dimensions; they are neither rendered identical nor absolutely severed. In its pursuit of this dialectical relationship it has resisted the two forms of positivism that lose the tension: psychologism and sociologism."[24] Marxism and psychoanalysis can be articulated, in other words, only if the articulation at the same time retains the antagonistic kernel that defines the core of their respective discourses.

Through the critique of amnesia and oblivion, however, we should not come to overestimate the importance of memory either. History and memory, too, whether in personal memoires, nostalgic reminiscences, or public apostasies, have today become commodities that risk concealing more than they may be able to reveal. Nor should we ignore the recent past by resorting exclusively to the alleged orthodoxy of the founding texts of Marxism and psychoanalysis. "The critique of sham novelty and the planned obsolescence of thought cannot in turn flip the coin and claim that the old texts—be they of Marx or Freud—are as valid as when written and need no interpretation or rethinking," warns Jacoby. "To the point that the theories of Marx and Freud were critiques of bourgeois civilization, orthodoxy entailed loyalty to these critiques; more exactly *dialectical* loyalty. Not repetition is called for but articulation and developments of concepts; and within Marxism—and to a degree within psychoanalysis—precisely against an Official Orthodoxy only too happy to freeze concepts into formulas."[25] Whence the need not just for remembrance to break the spell of amnesia, but also for a form of active forgetting to avoid the commodification, or what we might also call the becoming-culture, of memory.

As Gilles Deleuze posits in "Five Propositions on Psychoanalysis," a text from 1973 included in the posthumous collection *Desert Islands and Other Texts*,

> In the end, a Freudo-Marxist effort proceeds in general from a return to origins, or more specifically to the sacred texts: the sacred texts of Freud, the sacred texts of Marx. Our point of departure must be completely different: we return not to the sacred texts that must be, to a greater or lesser extent, interpreted, but to the situation as is, the situation of the bureaucratic apparatus in psychoanalysis, which is an effort to subvert these apparatuses.[26]

At the most fundamental level of our theoretical and quasi-ontological presuppositions, this means that the articulation of Freudianism with

---

24. Jacoby, *Social Amnesia*, 74, 77.
25. Ibid., 10, 11–12.
26. Gilles Deleuze, "Five Propositions on Psychoanalysis," *Desert Islands and Other Texts, 1953–1974*, ed. David Lapoujade, trans. Michael Taormina (New York: Semiotext(e), 2004), 276.

Marxism must proceed by undoing the developmental logic that would be common to both. Deleuze adds:

> In Marxism, a certain culture of memory appeared right at the beginning; even revolutionary activity was supposed to proceed to this capitalization of the memory of social formations. It is, if one prefers, Marx's Hegelian aspect, included in *Das Kapital*. In psychoanalysis, the culture of memory is even more apparent. Moreover, Marxism, like psychoanalysis, is shot through with a certain ideology of development: psychic development from a psychoanalytic point of view social development or even the development of production from a Marxist point of view.[27]

To deconstruct this ideology of memory and development, we might even be able to find an unexpected resource in the very notion of the missed encounter that is said to define the relation of Marx and Freud to Latin America.

Indeed, there is still a third perspective from which we might tackle our problem—namely, by taking the logic of the *desencuentro* itself as a key to understanding the emancipatory nature of the contributions made by Marxism and psychoanalysis and then using this key to approach the realities of Latin America. The founders of these discourses, to be sure, intended their work to be read as laying the foundation for new sciences, respectively, of history and of the unconscious. However, what these sciences at bottom encounter, despite their subsequent fixation and positivization, is something that does not belong to the realm of hard facts so much as it signals a symptomatic interruption of all factual normality:

> Marx sets out, absolutely, not from the architecture of the social, deploying its assurance and its guarantee after the fact, but from the interpretation-interruption of a symptom of hysteria of the social: the uprisings and parties of the workers. Marx defines himself by listening to these symptoms according to a hypothesis of truth regarding politics, just as Freud listens to the hysteric according to a hypothesis regarding the truth of the subject.[28]

If Marxism and psychoanalysis can still be called scientific against all odds, it is not because of the objective delimitation of a specific and empirically verifiable instance or domain of the social order—political, psychic, or libidinal economies—but because they link a category of truth onto a delinking, an unbinding, or a coming-apart of the social bond in moments of acute crisis. Even if the new discourse he is commending does not amount to a philosophical worldview, Freud is

---

27. Ibid., 277. Deleuze himself proposes a dosage of active forgetfulness and underdevelopment to counter the effects of the culture of memory and development supposedly shared by Marxism and psychoanalysis. I develop the implications of this standpoint in the first half of Chapter 4, in my analysis of Tomás Gutiérrez Alea's 1968 film *Memorias del subdesarrollo* (*Memories of Underdevelopment*).
28. Alain Badiou, *Peut-on penser la politique?* (Paris: Seuil, 1985), 20.

quite explicit about the importance of the category of truth for psycho-analysis. "I have told you that psychoanalysis began as a method of treatment," he tells his audience in his *New Introductory Lectures on Psychoanalysis*, "but I did not want to commend it to your interest as a method of treatment but on account of the truths it contains, on account of the information it gives us about what concerns human beings most of all—their own nature—and on account of the connections it discloses between the most different of their activities."[29] Freud immediately goes on to tackle the question about the problematic status of psychoanalysis as a worldview and as a science, before concluding, as is only to be expected, by engaging in a brief polemical dialogue with Marxism.

This dialogue is indeed to be expected, insofar as the notion of truth that both Marx and Freud can be said to uphold does not refer to a stable reality to be uncovered with the objectivity of a positive or empirical science, nor is the discourse for which they lay the foundation the result of a purely philosophical self-reflection. Rather, truth here is tied to a certain experience of the real that interrupts and breaks with the normal course of things. More so than as positive sciences or as philosophical worldviews, therefore, the discourses of Marx and Freud are better seen as doctrines of the intervening subject. "Even though psychoanalysis and Marxism have nothing to do with one another—the totality they would form is inconsistent—it is beyond doubt that Freud's unconscious and Marx's proletariat have the same epistemological status with regard to the break they introduce in the dominant conception of the subject," Alain Badiou writes in *Theory of the Subject*: "'Where' is the unconscious? 'Where' is the proletariat? These questions have no chance of being solved either by an empirical designation or by the transparency of a reflection. They require the dry and enlightened labour of analysis and of politics. Enlightened and also organized, into concepts as much as into institutions."[30]

The commonality between Marx and Freud, in other words, lies in their willingness and ability to propose the hypothesis of a universal truth of the political or desiring subject in answer to the crises of their time—whether these are the uprisings of the 1840s to which Marx and Engels respond in *The Communist Manifesto* with the hypothesis of an unheard-of proletarian capacity for politics, or the hysteric fits and outbursts that spread like wildfire through *fin-de-siècle* Vienna to which Freud responds with his hypothesis regarding the universality of a certain pathological subject of desire—as in his "Fragment of an

29. Sigmund Freud, "Lecture XXXIV: Explanations, Applications and Orientations," in *New Introductory Lectures on Psychoanalysis*, trans. James Strachey (New York: W. W. Norton, 1965), 138.
30. Alain Badiou, *Theory of the Subject*, trans. Bruno Bosteels (London: Continuum, 2009), 280.

Analysis of a Case of Hysteria," better known as Dora's case. A certain logic of the missed encounter, as structural-historical antagonism or as constitutive discontent, would thus be the ultimate "truth" about politics and desire that is the conceptual core of the respective doctrines of Marx and Freud.

These two figures, however, did not merely follow vaguely comparable or parallel tracks in the direction of a radical kernel of antagonism. Rather, the true insight behind the various attempts at amalgamating a form of Freudo-Marxism derives from the hypothesis that the questions of political, economic, and libidinal causality that the work of these two thinkers poses also mutually, yet without any neat symmetry, presuppose each other. As the Argentine León Rozitchner writes in *Freud y el problema del poder* (*Freud and the Problem of Power*), a book whose title should not hide the extent to which it puts Freudian psychoanalysis in dialogue both with Marxism and with the theory of war of Carl von Clausewitz,

> I think that the problem at issue is the following: on one hand we have the development of state power since the French revolution to this day—whether capitalist or socialist—and, at the same time, the emergence of a power of the masses which with ever more vehemence and activism has begun to demand participation in it. This access gained by those who are distanced from power all the while being its foundation presents us with a need linked to the search for the possible efficacy as well as the explication of the failure in which many attempts to reach it culminated: the need to return to the subjective sources of that objective power formed, even in its collective grandeur, by individuals. Trying to understand this place, which is also individual, where that collective power continues somehow to generate itself and at the same time—as is all too clear—to inhibit itself in its development. In short: What is the significance of the so-called "subjective" conditions in the development of collective processes that tend toward a radical transformation of social reality? Is the condition of radicality not determined precisely by deepening this repercussion of the so-called "objective" conditions in subjectivity, without which politics is bound to remain ineffective?[31]

Such would be, in the broadest possible terms, the long-term presuppositions that undergird the search for an articulation between psychoanalysis and Marxism.

After all, as Rozitchner also observes, Marx had already pointed out this unity of the subjective and the objective, as opposed to the usual opposition between the "merely" internal and the "merely" external. Especially in the notebooks from 1857–58 known as the *Grundrisse: Foundations of the Critique of Political Economy*, speaking of the objectification of labor, which turns individuals immediately into social

---

31. León Rozitchner, *Freud y el problema del poder* (Buenos Aires: Losada, 2003), 11–12. The five chapters in the first part of this book, subtitled "Más allá de la cura individual" ("Beyond the Individual Cure"), were first presented in the early 1980s as seminars at the UAM (Universidad Autónoma Metropolitana) in Xochimilco, Mexico City.

beings, Marx writes: "The conditions which allow them to exist in this way in the reproduction of their life, in their life's process, have been posited only by the historic economic process itself; both the objective and the subjective conditions, which are only the two distinct forms of the same conditions."[32] Conversely, in *Group Psychology and Analysis of the Ego*, Freud famously starts out by insisting that to speak of a social psychology is perhaps more redundant than truly insightful, insofar as the unconscious is always already socialized through and through: "In the individual's mental life someone else is invariably involved, as a model, as an object, as a helper, as an opponent; and so from the very first individual psychology, in this extended but entirely justifiable sense of the words, is at the same time social psychology as well."[33] This also means that power and repression are not simply external to the subject; instead, they feed on what we otherwise consider to be our innermost idiosyncrasy. For Rozitchner, this paradox of the subjective inscription of power is ultimately what psychoanalysis, as an intervening doctrine which is not restricted to the therapeutic space of the couch in the consultation room, strives to uncover: "It is the emergence, beyond censorship and repression, of significations, lived experiences, feelings, thoughts, relations, drives, etc., present in our subjectivity, very often without their having reached consciousness, but actualized in objective relations, which break with that stark opposition that the system has organized in ourselves as though it were—as in some way it is—our own."[34]

Of course, this relation of mutual presupposition between the psychic-libidinal and the politico-economic should not serve to hide the profound asymmetries between the two. Marxism and psychoanalysis do not simply complement each other by filling the gap in their neighbor's discourse. Nor should the invocation of what Freud calls overdetermination, as a feature supposed to be common to both fields, lead us to ignore the shifting priorities variously given to one instance or the other—the socio-historical or the psychic—by the different followers of Marx and Freud. Indeed, the question of knowing which

---

32. Karl Marx, *Grundrisse: Foundations of the Critique of Political Economy (Rough Draft)*, trans. Martin Nicolaus (London–New York: Penguin, 1973), 832. See also Rozitchner, *Freud y el problema del poder*, 136.

33. Freud, *Group Psychology and Analysis of the Ego*, trans. James Strachey (New York: W. W. Norton, 1959), 3. In the end, though, Freud appears to want to reinscribe the social into the psychic as it unfolds in the family: "Our expectation is therefore directed towards two other possibilities: that the social instinct may not be a primitive one and insusceptible of dissection, and that it may be possible to discover the beginnings of its development in a narrower circle, such as that of the family" (5). On the other hand, and in order better to understand Freud's reception in Latin America, for instance in the work of Rozitchner, it is important to recall that Freud's term translated in English as "group psychology," namely, *Massenpsychologie*, is usually translated in Spanish far more appropriately as *psicología de masas*, or "mass psychology."

34. Rozitchner, *Freud y el problema del poder*, 34–5.

would be determining in the final instance is still open, and the chapters that follow certainly do not claim to answer this question definitively. The aim is rather to dwell on the tensions of the struggle between the subjective and the objective, between the psychic and the historical, precisely as struggle, as combat and as transaction. "*Transaction*: objective-subjective elaboration of an agreement, the result of a prior struggle, of a combat in which the one who will become subject, that is, the I or the ego, is not that sweet angelical being called child, such as the adult imagines it, which would come to be molded with impunity by the system without resistance," Rozitchner insists. "If there is transaction, if the I is its locus, there was a struggle at the origin of individuality: there were winners and losers, and the formation of the subject is the description of this process."[35] Indeed, it is with an eye on studying the intricacies of such a struggle that I turn in the following pages to a small corpus of texts and artworks from Latin America.

More so than as a work of commemoration, not to mention nostalgia, I envision the studies that follow as exercises in a kind of counter-memory, not unlike the installation *The Wretched of the Earth* from the Argentine photographer Marcelo Brodsky. This installation includes a series of books that its owner—like so many students and intellectuals in the mid-1970s when the military junta in Argentina considered all such books potential proof of subversive activity that could lead to imprisonment, torture, and death—decided to bury in her backyard, where almost twenty years later they were dug up by her two adult children. Although time and the elements have eaten away at the books to the point of making them nearly unrecognizable, most readers familiar with the literature from the period will be able to discern that among the books on display in Brodsky's installation are Spanish translations of Frantz Fanon's *The Wretched of the Earth* (*Los condenados de la tierra*), Louis Althusser's *For Marx* (*La revolución teórica de Marx*), a collection of essays by Erich Fromm, Herbert Marcuse, André Gorz, and Víctor Olea Franco (*La sociedad industrial contemporánea*), as well as a totally disheveled and nearly coverless copy of *Materialismo histórico y materialismo dialéctico* (*Historical Materialism and Dialectical Materialism*), with texts by Althusser and Badiou, published in the book series *Pasado y Presente* edited by José Aricó. In a handwritten letter accompanying the installation, the original owner explains that, since she no longer remembered where exactly she had buried the books, her two sons had to dig several holes over the course of four days before finding the "treasure." She adds: "The screams of joy from our kids contrasted sharply with the image of the destroyed books and everything they represented."[36]

---

35.   Ibid., 20–1.
36.   Nélida Valdez, Letter of July 20, 1999, included in the installation of Marcelo Brodsky, *The Wretched of the Earth*. I would like to give special thanks to Marcelo Brodsky for giving me permission to use an image from this installation for the cover of this book.

Much of what I hope to do with the studies included in the present book can be said to consist in an effort to dig similar holes and tell the story of what happened with those works and others like them that were censored, forgotten, buried, or destroyed since the mid-1970s, in sharp contrast to the time in the late 1960s and early 1970s when many of them still represented obligatory reading materials for students, writers, intellectuals, militants, and artists alike. This effort in constructing an archive of counter-memory concerns not only the books that were actually buried and, in some cases, disinterred: what happened, for example, between the coup of 1976 in Argentina, when the books listed above were abandoned to the criticism of worms, and the supposed return to democracy during which, in 1994, they were brought back into broad daylight and exhibited to the public? Counter-memory also concerns the ideas, dreams and projects that were otherwise forced to find a more figurative hiding place in the inner recesses of the psychic apparatus of their original readers and proponents.

The questions that I have in mind are similar to the ones that León Rozitchner asks of Óscar del Barco, for instance, regarding the long period of silence that separates his recent epistolary confession in "Thou Shalt Not Kill" from the historical acts of violence for which—forty years later—he offers his loud *mea culpa*. "Are we sure that one can pass, just like that, from one theory to another, from one concept to another?" asks Rozitchner. "So then what happened to our body, to our imagination, to our affects?"[37] Del Barco may well have found a way to abandon Che Guevara's deadly model of guerrilla warfare in favor of a post-metaphysical ethics of respect for the other inspired by Emmanuel Levinas. Yet he does not touch upon the subjective roots—both psychical and corporeal—of this seemingly purely theoretical shift. Nor does he clarify the personal coherence, or lack thereof, behind the decisions of those who were militants then and are anti-militants now. "But beyond the act of personal contrition that allows them to put their lives back together, what really matters, for us, is that these facts, which they did not assume, remained congealed like hard cores, or black holes, in the collective consciousness. They determined the past which for us is this future—the future past—that we are living today."[38] What remains in the shadows thus involves the motives, illusions, dreams and misprisions by which the subject becomes part of a historical truth that is still in the making. Where did the guilt, the shame, the anxiety, the rage, the pain, or the fear of death go to hide during all those years—before erupting into a loud confession that revolves around a Judeo-Christian commandment? In part following

---

37. Léon Rozitchner, "El espejo tan temido," in *Acerca de la derrota y de los vencidos* (Buenos Aires: Quadrata/Biblioteca Nacional, 2011), 33.
38. León Rozitchner, "Primero hay que saber vivir. Del *Vivirás* materno al *No matarás* patriarcal," in *Acerca de la derrota y de los vencidos*, 57.

Rozitchner's approach, the point of the exercises of genealogical counter-memory that I am proposing here is not to retrieve such subjective
elements by inserting them into a nostalgic re-objectification of the
past, but rather to reactivate their silent and still untapped resources
for the sake of a critique of the present. "If at the time one had assumed
as a social responsibility that which later underwent a metamorphosis
and became a purely individual guilt," Rozitchner continues, "one
might have permitted the creation of something which fashionable
thinking today calls an *event*, and thus the creation of a new meaning
that would vanquish the determinism that marked us all."[39] Along
these lines, incidentally, what in European theory and philosophy is
called an "event" or "act" will also receive a rather different—
frequently polemical—interpretation thanks to the confrontation with
the conceptual trajectories behind similar notions in Latin America.

Given this critical and theoretical orientation, my project is only indirectly related to the many "left turns" in the recent political history of
Latin America, where at he start of 2010 we had democratically elected
center-left, left-populist, or self-proclaimed socialist governments in
power in at least eleven countries. "Two centuries after the wars of independence, one century after the Mexican Revolution, half a century after
the Cuban Revolution, the new mole has re-emerged spectacularly in the
continent of José Martí, Bolívar, Sandino, Farabundo Martí, Mariátegui,
Fidel, Che and Allende," writes Emir Sader, borrowing the famous mole-
metaphor from Hegel and Marx. "It has taken on new forms in order to
continue the centuries-old struggle for emancipation of the peoples of
Latin America and the Caribbean."[40] This circumstance, which constitutes the favorite topic for sociologists and political scientists writing
about Latin America today, certainly contributes to the recent resurgence of interest in the intellectual and ideological debates of the 1960s
and 1970s. Testimonies and anthologies thus proliferate, as do the often
state-sponsored facsimile republication of books and even entire runs of
left-wing journals. For the most part, though, the rich documentary and
testimonial literature that has come out of the different left turns has yet
to produce an equivalent intensification in the overall critical analysis
and theoretical elaboration of Marxism and psychoanalysis in Latin
America—a collective project to which I hope to make a small contribution in the case studies that follow.

---

39. Ibid., 81.
40. Emir Sader, *The New Mole: Paths of the Latin American Left* (London: Verso, 2011),
xi. Aside from numerous special issues of journals such as *Latin American Research Review*,
the secondary literature on the "left turns" in Latin America continues to grow exponentially.
See, among others, Marc Saint-Upéry, *El sueño de Bolívar: El desafío de las izquierdas
sudamericanas*, trans. María José Furió (Barcelona: Paidós, 2008); Maxwell A. Cameron and
Eric Hershberg, eds, *Latin America's Left Turns*, special issue of *Third World Quarterly* 30.2
(2009); and Jorge G. Castañeda and Marco A. Morales, eds, *Lo que queda de la izquierda:
Relatos de las izquierdas latinoamericanas* (Mexico City: Taurus, 2010).

The present book thus seeks to reassess the untimely relevance of certain aspects of the work of Marx (but also of Lenin and Mao) and Freud (but also of Lacan) in and for Latin America, with select case studies drawn from Mexico, Argentina, Chile, and Cuba. Starting from the abovementioned premise that Marxism and Freudianism strictly speaking are neither philosophical worldviews nor positive sciences, but rather intervening doctrines of the subject respectively in political and clinical-affective situations, I argue in the chapters of the book that art and literature—the novel, poetry, theater, film—no less than the militant tract or the theoretical treatise, provide symptomatic sites for the investigation of such processes of subjectivization. I will discuss almost none of the major recognized figures behind the various Communist (Marxist-Leninist, Trotskyist, Guevarist, Maoist) parties in Latin America—such as Julio Antonio Mella in Cuba, José Carlos Mariátegui and Víctor Raúl Haya de la Torre in Peru, Farabundo Martí and Roque Dalton in El Salvador, Vicente Lombardo Toledano in Mexico, René Zavaleta Mercado and Guillermo Lora in Bolivia, Marta Harnecker in Chile, Cuba and Venezuela, Luis Carlos Prestes or Caio Prado Júnior in Brazil, Luis Emilio Recabarren or Salvador Allende in Chile, Rodney Arismendi in Uruguay, or Aníbal Ponce and Otto Vargas in Argentina.[41] Nor do I have any pretension—or the

---

41. Individual studies of major Marxists and national histories of the different Communist parties in Latin America are legion, and I will not try to list them all here. For a detailed but still far from exhaustive bibliography, see Harry E. Vanden, *Latin American Marxism: A Bibliography* (New York: Garland, 1991). The most important anthologies of Latin American Marxist thought are *El marxismo en América Latina* (Buenos Aires: Centro Editor de América Latina, 1973); Luis E. Aguilar, ed., *Marxism in Latin America* (rev. edn, Philadelphia: Temple University Press, 1978); and Michael Löwy, ed., *El marxismo en América Latina: Antología, desde 1909 hasta nuestros días* (rev. edn, Santiago de Chile: LOM, 2007). The most recent theoretical—rather than historico-political—overviews and reassessments include Sheldon B. Liss, *Marxist Thought in Latin America* (Berkeley: University of California Press, 1984); Pablo Guadarrama González, *América Latina: Marxismo y postmodernidad* (Santa Clara, Cuba, and Bogotá: Universidad Central de Las Villas and Universidad INCCA de Colombia, 1994); Pablo Guadarrama González, ed., *Despojados de todo fetiche: Autenticidad del pensamiento marxista en América Latina* (Santa Clara, Cuba, and Bogotá: Universidad Central de Las Villas and Universidad INCCA de Colombia, 1999); Raúl Fornet-Betancourt, *Transformaciones del marxismo: Historia del marxismo en América Latina* (Mexico City: Plaza y Valdés/Universidad Autónoma de Nuevo León, 2001); Néstor Kohan, *Marx en su (tercer) mundo: Hacia un socialismo no colonizado* (Buenos Aires: Biblos, 1998), *De Ingenieros al Che: Ensayos sobre el marxismo argentino y latinoamericano* (Buenos Aires: Biblos, 2000), and *Con sangre en las venas: Apuntes polémicos sobre la revolución, los sueños, las pasiones y el marxismo desde América Latina* (Mexico City: Ocean Sur, 2008); Horacio Tarcus, *El marxismo olvidado en Argentina: Silvio Frondizi y Milcíades Peña* (Buenos Aires: El Cielo por Asalto, 1996); José Sazbón, "Marx y marxismo," in *Historia y representación* (Buenos Aires: Universidad Nacional de Quilmes, 2002), 15–189; Agustín Cueva, *Entre la ira y la esperanza y otros ensayos de crítica latinoamericana* (Buenos Aires: CLACSO/Prometeo, 2007) and Stefan Gandler, *Marxismo crítico en México: Adolfo Sánchez Vázquez y Bolívar Echeverría* (Mexico City: Fondo de Cultura Económica, 2007). See also Atilio A. Boron, Javier Amadeo and Sabrina González,

wherewithal—to retell the official history of the different national affil-
iates of the International Psychoanalytical Association (IPA), many of
which are gathered in overarching organizations such as the FEPAL, or
Federación Psicoanalítica de América Latina (Psychoanalytic Federa-
tion of Latin America, formerly known as COPAL, or Coordinating
Committee of Psychoanalytic Organizations of Latin America).[42] My
justification for not taking this canonical route is twofold: first, because
large parts of the history of the reception of Marx and Freud in their
national and institutional venues have already been published; and,
second, because the heretical treatments of Marxism and Freudianism
in literary, artistic, and critical-theoretical form are often far more

eds, *La teoría marxista hoy: Problemas y perspectivas* (Buenos Aires: CLACSO, 2006); and
the special issue on *Marxismo e izquierda en la historia de Latinoamérica*, guest-edited by
Carlos Aguirre for *A Contracorriente: A Journal on Social History and Literature in Latin
America* 5: 2 (Winter 2008).

42.   In the dissemination of Freudianism in Latin America, the Argentine national audience
and its members in exile for obvious reasons are the best served, with excellent studies by
Hugo Vezzetti—*La locura en Argentina* (Buenos Aires: Folios, 1983), *Freud en Buenos Aires,
1910-1939* (Buenos Aires: Puntosur, 1989; second edn, Universidad Nacional de Quilmes,
1996), and *Aventuras de Freud en el país de los argentinos: De Ingenieros a Enrique Pichon-
Rivière* (Buenos Aires: Paidós, 1996); Mariano Ben Plotkin, *Freud in the Pampas: The
Emergence and Development of a Psychoanalytic Culture in Argentina* (Stanford: Stanford
University Press, 2001) and *Argentina on the Couch: Psychiatry, State, and Society, 1880 to
the Present* (Albuquerque: University of New Mexico Press, 2003); Germán García, *La
entrada del psicoanálisis en la Argentina: obstáculos y perspectivas* (Buenos Aires: Altazor,
1978), and *El psicoanálisis y los debates culturales: ejemplos argentinos* (Buenos Aires:
Paidós, 2005); and Juan de la Cruz Argañaraz, *El freudismo reformista, 1926–1976: en la
literatura y la medicina, la política y la psicología* (Córdoba: Brujas, 2007). In Mexico, aside
from the exiles Erich Fromm, Igor A. Caruso, and Marie Langer, other key figures include
Armando Suárez and the Argentine exiles Néstor Braunstein, Ignacio Maldonado, and
Armando Bauleo. See, among others, José Perrés, *El nacimiento del psicoanálisis: Apuntes
críticos para una delimitación epistemológica* (Mexico City: UAM-Xochimilco/Plaza y
Valdés, 1988); Néstor Braunstein, *Por el camino de Freud* (Mexico City: Siglo Veintiuno,
2001); José Luis González, "Notas para una historia del psicoanálisis en México en los años
setenta," in Armando Suárez, ed., *Psicoanálisis y realidad* (Mexico City: Siglo Veintiuno,
1989); Raúl Páramo-Ortega, *Freud in Mexiko: Zur Geschichte der Psychoanalyse in Mexiko*
(Munich: Quintessenz, 1992); Guadalupe Rocha Guzmán, "Las instituciones psicoanalíticas
en México: Un análisis sobre la formación de analistas y sus mecanismos de regulación" (MA
thesis, UAM-Xochimilco, México, 1998), *Acheronta: Revista electrónica de psicoanálisis* 14
(2000), available online at acheronta.org; and Rubén Gallo, *Freud's Mexico: Into the Wilds
of Psychoanalysis* (Cambridge: MIT Press, 2010). In Chile, see Roberto Aceituno, *Los
retornos de Freud* (Santiago: Palinodia, 2006). The recent issue of *Estudios Interdisciplinarios
de América latina y el Caribe*, in which Chapter 8 of this book was originally published, is
devoted to the question of *Psychoanalysis North and South/Psicoanálisis Norte y Sur*, and is
guest-edited by Federico Finchelstein. See also the special first issue of the Mexican journal
Vigencia del psicoanálisis 1: 1 (2005), available online at encuentropsicoanalitico.com,
which includes papers presented at events in Colombia, Costa Rica, and Mexico. For general
overviews, see León Grinberg, Marie Langer and Emilio Rodrigué, eds, *Psicoanálisis en las
Américas: El proceso analítico. Transferencia y contratransferencia* (Buenos Aires: Paidós,
1968); and Moisés Lemlij and Dana Cáceres, eds, *Psicoanálisis en América Latina* (Lima:
FEPAL/IPA, 1993).

acutely aware of the shortcomings and the as-yet-untapped resources of Marx and Freud in and for Latin America. Besides, I might add that, just as I do not discuss any of the major intellectuals of the different Internationals linked to the legacies of Marx and Freud, so too most of the figures discussed in this book are absent from the extant histories of the reception of Marxism and psychoanalysis in Latin America—the principal exception in this last regard being the Cuban writer and freedom fighter José Martí.

To be sure, not all ten chapters of this book combine, or even seek to combine, equal parts from both Marxism and psychoanalysis. None aim to refer the works under discussion either to some prior orthodoxy or to some longed-for univocity based on these two discourses. Some chapters even discuss texts such as a series of pulp-fiction detective novels that may appear at first sight to be only remotely related to the topic of Marx and Freud in Latin America. In each case, however, I attempt to tease out a theoretical framework from the texts themselves, to the point where an author who is the object of analysis in one chapter can become the methodological reference point with which to analyze the objects of study in another. In fact, if there exists a standard against which I would like this book to be measured, aside from a penchant to go against the grain of accepted readings, it would be the idea of breaking down the traditional lines of demarcation between object and subject, criticism and theory, or literature and philosophy. Marxism and psychoanalysis, in this sense, serve as jumping-off points toward a renewed understanding of what I would gladly call "critical theory"—an intellectual practice for which criticism is not simply an ancillary qualification of theory but instead refers back to the specific tasks of close reading, as in literary or film criticism.[43] Finally, at key points in this book and again at the very end, politics and psychoanalysis enter into dialogue with religion not only by way of a historical critique of Christianity or of the role of liberation theology in Latin America, but also through a brief return to "On the Jewish

---

43.   One of the most interesting recent projects in this regard is the creation of 17, *Instituto de Estudios Críticos*, named after the original street number of the Frankfurt School and directed in Mexico City by the Lacanian psychoanalyst Benjamín Mayer Foulkes. On its website, this Institute defines "critical studies" as follows:

> As the outcome of the contributions made by those three masters of suspicion that are Freud, Nietzsche, and Marx, as well as by their contemporary intellectual inheritors, critical studies are concerned with social and cultural life. They distinguish themselves by their commitment to the events of their time and by their inter, trans, or postdisciplinary nature and their orientation with regard to three principal topics: subjectivity, language, and hegemony. Not only do they deal in innovative ways with inherited objects of knowledge, they also produce a critical inventory of traditional forms of knowledge and practice while tracing new lines of interrogation.

This definition seems perfectly appropriate for what I am calling "critical theory" as the approach used in this book, except to say that I do not include Nietzsche.

Question"—that is, to Marx's text, as well as to some of the broader issues surrounding the question of religion whereof echoes can still be heard in the many writings by and on Freud such as *The Future of an Illusion*.

There is yet a third reason why I sidestep all discussion of the orthodox traditions of Marxism and Freudianism in Latin America—namely that, chronologically speaking, all the works analyzed in this book (again with the exception of José Martí's writings) belong to a period in the latter half of the twentieth century marked by the internal crisis and critique of orthodox Marxism, and a concomitant revision of, and critical return to, Freud. If Martí is part of this book, it is because his chronicle on the occasion of Karl Marx's death on March 14, 1883, especially when read in conjunction with Martí's only novel, his 1885 *Lucía Jerez* (also known as *Amistad funesta*), anticipates a number of principles—in particular the logic of uneven development and the melodramatic responses that this logic often seems to elicit—that will recur in subsequent articulations of culture, politics, and psychoanalysis in the second half of the twentieth century, when we gradually cross beyond a post-revolutionary horizon. The events of 1968 clearly mark a threshold along this trajectory, and their influence can therefore be felt throughout the book. Thus, José Revueltas, thrown in jail by the government of President Gustavo Díaz Ordaz for his alleged role as intellectual instigator behind the revolt of this watershed year in Mexico, constitutes one of the book's central theoretical reference points, together with the work of the Argentine Freudo-Marxist León Rozitchner. More specifically, Revueltas's 1964 novel *Los errores* (*The Errors*) and his posthumous *Dialéctica de la conciencia* (*Dialectic of Consciousness*), written in the 1970s in the Lecumberri prison, are analyzed in Chapters 2 and 3 in terms of a critique of Stalinism and the ethico-theoretical revision of Marxism. Together with a little book by Paco Ignacio Taibo II, Revueltas's interpretation of the events of 1968 is also read in Chapter 6 as a counterpoint to Octavio Paz's poem about the massacre that took place in Tlatelolco on October 2, 1968—a poem that Paz sent to the cultural supplement of the magazine *Siempre!* right after the massacre, while at the same time submitting his resignation as the ambassador for Mexico in India to President Díaz Ordaz. Rozitchner's little-known book *Moral burguesa y revolución* (*Bourgeois Morality and Revolution*), on the other hand, provides an important subtext for the Cuban filmmaker Tomás Gutiérrez Alea's 1968 movie *Memorias del subdesarrollo* (*Memories of Underdevelopment*), which I study in Chapter 4 in conjunction with Gutiérrez Alea's own *Dialéctica del espectador* (*The Viewer's Dialectic*). Rozitchner's work in Freudo-Marxism in general, and his critique of Christianity in particular through the reading of Augustine's *Confessions* in his 1997 book *La Cosa y la Cruz* (*The Thing and the Cross*), constitutes the topic of Chapter 5.

Subsequent chapters, by contrast, inquire into the melancholy paths of the post-1968 Left. Chapter 7 provides an analysis of the Maoist legacy in the writings of the Argentine novelist and critic Ricardo Piglia, especially his 1975 novella "Homenaje a Roberto Arlt" ("Homage to Roberto Arlt"), included in *Nombre falso* (*Assumed Name*). This analysis leads to a critique of the political economy of traditional concepts of art and literature that persist even within the revolutionary Left, from Bakunin to Lenin to Trotsky. In Chapter 8, I read the play *Feliz nuevo siglo Doktor Freud* (*Happy New Century, Dr Freud*), which the Mexican playwright Sabina Berman in 2000 devoted to a reworking of Freud's famous Dora case, in light of the question of cultural democratization and the emancipatory potential of psychoanalysis. In Chapter 9, the series of nine novels (ten if we include *Muertos incómodos*, or *The Uncomfortable Dead*, coauthored with Subcomandante Marcos from the EZLN or Ejército Zapatista de Liberación Nacional) that, between 1976 and 1993, Paco Ignacio Taibo II structured around his hardboiled detective Héctor Belascoarán Shayne, are interpreted as contributions to a narrative history of the Left in Mexico. In Chapter 10, through an analysis of the novels *Plata quemada* (*Money to Burn*) by Ricardo Piglia and *Mano de obra* (*Labor Power or Manual Labor*) by the Chilean Diamela Eltit, I discuss the recurrent temptation of seeking a radical anarchistic alternative, often figured as the gift of a giant potlatch, to the crisis of neoliberalism and the formation of that new world order which Michael Hardt and Antonio Negri famously describe as Empire in their book of the same title—a book which was widely circulated and debated in the Southern Cone, especially around the time of the economic crisis of December 2001 in Argentina. Finally, the Epilogue revisits a question that runs through each of the previous chapters as seen in particular through the twin matrices of melodrama and the crime story—namely, the shifting relationship of hierarchy between ethics and politics that resulted from the moralization of political militancy among the post-1968 Left.

MARTÍ AND MARX

Martí on Marx

Neither Saint-Simon, nor Karl Marx, nor Marlo, nor Bakunin. Instead, the reforms that are best suited to our own bodies.
José Martí, La Nación, *February 20, 1890*

If Marx fails to see any revolutionary potential in the realities of Latin America, overshadowed as these would be by the constant temptation of despotism due to a lagging or insufficient development of civil society, we should hasten to add that the misunderstanding often turns out to be reciprocal. Think of "Honores a Karl Marx, que ha muerto" ("Tributes to Karl Marx, who has died"), a well-known but strangely under-studied chronicle by the Cuban writer and independence fighter José Martí, written when he resided in New York and worked as a foreign correspondent for, among others, the Argentine daily newspaper *La Nación*. This chronicle has been acknowledged as being "a first pillar in the reception of Marxism in the strict philosophical sense in Latin America."[1] In it, Martí focuses on a commemorative event that took place on March 19, 1883 in the Great Hall at the Cooper Union in Manhattan, marking the occasion of Marx's death five days earlier.

Of this quite extraordinary chronicle, officially dated March 29, 1883 by its author and published in *La Nación* on May 13 and 16, 1883, I wish in the first place to single out the curious *mise-en-scène*. Martí, as he had done the previous year with Oscar Wilde, indeed invites his distant readers to become the virtual spectators of a scene to which he appears to have been a personal eyewitness. "Ved esta gran sala. Karl Marx ha muerto," writes Martí—"Look at this great hall. Karl Marx has died"—repeating the visual interpellation just a few lines later: "Ved esta sala."[2] What we are invited to look at, for obvious reasons, is a

1. Raúl Fornet-Betancourt, *Transformaciones del marxismo*, 28. See also Horacio Tarcus, *Marx en la Argentina: Sus primeros lectores obreros, intelectuales y científicos* (Buenos Aires: Siglo Veintiuno, 2007), 121. A month earlier, as Tarcus discusses, *La Nación* had in fact already published a detailed intellectual and political portrait under the title "Karl Marx: Fundador de la Internacional" (see Tarcus, *Marx en la Argentina*, 119–20).
2. José Martí, "Honores a Karl Marx, que ha muerto," part of the chronicle published in the form of a letter to *La Nación*, "Carta de Martí," in *Obras completas* (Havana: Editorial Nacional de Cuba, 1963), vol. 9, 385–97. The most recent English translation appears as "Tributes to Karl Marx, who has died," in José Martí, *Selected Writings*, ed. and trans.

velorio a cuerpo ausente—that is, a wake in the absence of the deceased's corpse. Of that famous Karl Marx whom the resolutions of the "impassioned assembly" in the end proclaim to be "the most noble hero and the most powerful thinker of the working world," we will have obtained only the effigy or figure, by way of a large crayon portrait standing behind the back of the speakers: "Look at this hall. Presiding over it, wreathed in green leaves, is the portrait of that ardent reformer, uniter of men of different nations, tireless and forceful organizer."[3]

Around this absent corpse, not to say ghost, Martí describes how there gathers a whole collective scene of men and women who respectfully take turns to invoke and pay tribute to some aspect or other of the figure of Marx. The void of the dead man's body thus seems to be filled, as if compensated for by a surfeit of affectivity ranging from anger to awe. Through this public display of affect, the Great Hall of the Cooper Union in New York City becomes first and foremost the stage for a concrete example of what Martí considers the true labor of the coauthor of *The Communist Manifesto*—namely, his role as a political organizer, rather than the pursuit of scientific ambition displayed in *Capital*—a project of which the Cuban writer in any event only seems to have a vague idea at best, and which would not begin to be translated into Spanish until 1895, the year of Martí's death, when the Argentine Juan B. Justo began his version of the first volume of Marx's *Das Kapital*. "The International was his work, and men of all nations are coming to pay tribute to him," writes Martí, but not without immediately offering the following judgment, adopting a slightly paternalistic, gendered tone that will come back toward the end of the chronicle: "The multitude, made up of valiant laborers the sight of whom is touching and comforting, displays more muscles than adornments, more honest faces than silken scarves."[4] All of this, incidentally, is framed in something that we might call a moral

---

Esther Allen (New York: Penguin, 2002), 130–9. In addition to the two prior English publications of (parts of) this chronicle cited by Esther Allen, a two-page version was also published as "On the Death of Karl Marx," which opens the anthology, Luis E. Aguilar, ed., *Marxism in Latin America* (Philadelphia: Temple University Press, 1978), 102–3. For an official commentary from socialist Cuba, see Armando Hart Dávalos, "Martí y Marx, raíces de la revolución socialista de Cuba," in *Camino a lo alto: Aproximaciones marxistas a José Martí* (Havana: Editorial de Ciencias Sociales, 2006), 324–53. See also the brief commentary by Luis Alvarenga, "El humanismo de Marx desde la perspectiva de José Martí," which appears in *El marxismo hoy: una lectura crítica a 140 años de* El Capital, a special monographic issue of *Estudios Centroamericanos* 707 (2007): 849–53. For original newspaper coverage of the meeting at the Cooper Union, see the documentation gathered in Philip S. Foner, ed., *Karl Marx Remembered: Comments at the Time of His Death* (San Francisco: Synthesis Publications, 1983), esp. 83–111. This selection also includes a brief excerpt from Martí's chronicle.

3.   Martí, "Honores a Karl Marx, que ha muerto," 389, 388; "Tributes to Karl Marx," 132–3, 131.

4.   Ibid. (translation modified).

aesthetic, or an ethics of the beauty of work, based on a normative and transcendentalist idea of nature, inspired by Emerson. "Work makes men beautiful. The sight of a field hand, an ironworker, or a sailor is rejuvenating. As they grapple with nature's forces, they come to be as fair as nature."[5]

Despite this attempt at a natural-organicist aestheticization of the world of workers, Martí's chronicle never ceases to respond adversely to the great labor of Marx as a militant political organizer. Up to half a dozen times, Martí repeats the same reproach that Marx and his followers in the first International seek to accomplish their noble ends with wrong or misguided means: "Karl Marx has died. He deserves to be honored, for he placed himself on the side of the weak. But it is not the man who points out the harm and burns with generous eagerness to remedy it who does well—it is the man who advocates a mild remedy."[6] If this first formulation remains suspiciously convoluted, to the point of blurring the line between the good and the bad ways of remedying a wrong, the following phrasing does little to clear up the confusion. "To set men against men is an appalling task," writes Martí, without clarifying whether this is what he sees Marx and his followers as doing or whether he is merely describing the daunting aspect of what they, like any other human being for that matter, are up against: "The forced bestialization of some men for the profit of others stirs our indignation. But that indignation must be vented in such a way that the beast ceases to be, without escaping its bonds and causing fear."[7] A third phrasing seems necessary in order to dispel all doubts regarding the main thrust of Martí's objection against Marx. This formulation, furthermore, is absolutely crucial if we keep in mind not only the Hegelian prejudice that, according to José Aricó, would have kept Marx from properly understanding the Latin American realities, but also a certain ideological image of women and the limited role that Martí attributes to them in the process of social transformation:

> Karl Marx studied the means of establishing the world on new bases; he awoke the sleepers and showed them how to cast down the cracked pillars. But he went very fast and sometimes in darkness; he did not see that without a natural and laborious gestation, children are not born viable, from a nation in history or from a woman in the home.[8]

Social change, even or especially when revolutionary in nature, would thus by necessity have to follow the various stages of a seemingly natural process, without allowing it to become hurried or premature. Or, sticking to the same metaphor, we might say that the difference between

---

5. Ibid.
6. Ibid.
7. Ibid.
8. Ibid.

Marx and Martí lies in the fact that, for the Cuban writer, the gestation and birth of a nation in history, like that of a child at home, should be able to do without the force or violence that, for the author of *Das Kapital*, is "the midwife of every old society which is pregnant with a new one."[9]

Martí subsequently repeats the same criticism three more times, referring not just to Marx himself but also to his acolytes, the members and sympathizers of the International Working Men's Association whose militant activists he sees gathered in the Great Hall that Monday evening in New York City. About the fellow countrymen and women of "a certain Lecovitch," who speaks to them with Babelic confusion in English, German, and Russian, the Cuban exile says: "But no, these impatient, generous men, defiled by wrath, will not be the ones to lay the foundations of the new world: they are the spur, and serve their purpose, like the voice of conscience that might fall asleep, but the long sharp steel of a horseman's goad is of little use as a founding hammer."[10] About the German communist-anarchist John (Johann) Most, he says that his "right hand carries no balm with which to heal the wounds inflicted by his left." Finally, about the meeting in general, Martí adds one last overarching note of condemnation: "Music is heard and choirs ring out, but it is not the music of peace."[11]

The reasons for Martí's missed encounter with the internationalist politics of Marx would thus seem to be clear enough. According to this hero of Cuban independence and long-time resident in the belly of the monster from the North, Marx would have been the Apostle of the religion of hatred instead of love, and of war instead of peace. In fact, here we would do well to recall that Martí frames his account of the commemorative event for Marx between two strange vignettes: he thus begins his chronicle by portraying the difference between the workers' movements in America and in Europe, and he quickly follows his account of the Marx memorial by evaluating the possible decision of Columbia University in New York City either to open its doors to female students or else to create a separate undergraduate college for women, as would eventually come to pass in 1889 with the foundation of Barnard College.

---

9. Karl Marx, *Capital*, vol. 1, trans. Ben Fowkes (London: Penguin, 1976), 916. Later, in his well-known analysis of the Paris Commune, Marx is capable of suggesting a more natural process, or at least of leaving out the role of the midwife. "The working class did not expect miracles from the Commune," he writes on this occasion. "They have no ideals to realize, but to set free the elements of the new society with which the old collapsing bourgeois society itself is pregnant." See Karl Marx, "The Civil War in France," in *Political Writings, Vol. 3: The First International and After*, ed. David Fernbach (London: Penguin, 1992), 213. I discuss the implications of this view of the logic of change in Chapter 7 of Bruno Bosteels, *Badiou and Politics* (Durham, NC: Duke University Press, 2009), 227–49.

10. Martí, "Honores a Karl Marx, que ha muerto," 388; "Tributes to Karl Marx," 132 (translation modified).

11. Martí, "Honores a Karl Marx, que ha muerto," 389; "Tributes to Karl Marx," 132, 133.

Evidently, even though in most extant editions these parts are left out, there is a close connection between the two sections that immediately frame Martí's chronicle and the central part about the commemorative event at the Cooper Union in honor of Marx. Indeed, in talking about the contrast between the tactics of workers from the Old and New Worlds, Martí does no more than prepare the ground in anticipation of his reproach that Marx would have fomented hatred instead of love amid the working class:

> The future must be conquered with clean hands. The workmen of the United States would be more prudent if the most aggrieved and enraged workmen of Europe were not emptying the dregs of their hatred into their ears. Germans, Frenchmen, and Russians guide these discussions. The Americans tend to resolve the concrete matter at hand in their meetings, while those from abroad raise it to an abstract plane. Good sense and the fact of having been born into a free cradle make the men of this place slow to wrath. The rage of those from abroad is roiling and explosive because their prolonged enslavement has repressed and concentrated it. But the rotten apple must not be allowed to spoil the whole healthy barrel—though it could! The excrescences of monarchy, which rot and gnaw at Liberty's bosom like a poison, cannot match Liberty's power![12]

In a number of chronicles from the same period, Martí would time and again reiterate this distinction in organizational style between the workers' movements in Europe and in America. Still in the same letter-chronicle from March 29, 1883, in another segment usually not included in reproductions of his account of the Marx memorial, he restates the notion that the Europeans who arrived in New York filled the minds of workers in the United States with the morals of hatred and resentment. He does this with his usual rhetorical flair after comparing the disproportionate numbers of people in attendance at different events taking place around the time in the United States:

> Some twenty thousand people went to the funeral of the pugilist; to the ball of a Vanderbilt, who is a Rothschild in this part of America, a thousand gallant men and ladies; and ten thousand men with restless hands, coarse outfits, irreverent hats and inflamed hearts, went to applaud the fervent multilingual orators who excite the sons of labor to war, in memory of that German with the silky soul and iron fist, the most famous Karl Marx, whose recent death they honor.[13]

Martí, then, can almost be said to want to take the class struggle out of Marxism. Instead of communism, he defends the common sense and calm pragmatism of the new republic's civic tradition and

---

12. Martí, "Honores a Karl Marx, que ha muerto," 387–8; "Tributes to Karl Marx," 131.
13. Martí, "Cartas de Martí," in *Obras completas*, vol. 13, 245. Though part of the same chronicle-letter to *La Nación*, this segment of Martí's text is printed separately, among the portraits of North Americans (*Norteamericanos*), in the edition of his *Obras completas* that I am using in this chapter.

representative political system. "As Rubén Darío asserted, if there was a certain peculiarity, an exceptional gift, or virtue in Martí, it expressed itself in his literary writing. His political ideas, however, remained always within the Hispanic American republican canon," affirms Rafael Rojas, the author of a recent biography of Martí. "Brief and solemn forms, succinct and respectable republican representations: herein lies the discreet, primordial republicanism of José Martí."[14] Coming from the hand of an exiled intellectual who would die on the battlefield for the independence of Cuba, Martí's words of condemnation for Marx sound strange only if we ignore the profound admiration that the Cuban writer feels at the same time for the political achievements made possible in the United States, his temporary homeland, through the right to vote and the freedom of expression. The Old World, by contrast, remained steeped in the century-long legacy of monarchy and despotism. Thus, in a letter to *La Nación* on September 5, 1884, Martí also writes: "Boats filled with hatred come from Europe: they should be covered with boats full of balsamic love."[15] Any direct transfer of political ideas and organizational tactics from the Old to the New World, therefore, must be considered at best misguided, and at worst disastrous.

A couple of years later, in the first of two famous chronicles about the trial of the anarchists from the Haymarket incident in Chicago whose martyrdom we commemorate in all parts of the world—except, paradoxically, in the United States, where the events happened in the first place—as May Day, Martí similarly talks about those ideologues who come to the New World from Europe, "mere mouthpieces through which the feverish hatred accumulated over centuries among the working people in Europe comes to be emptied out over America," and he compares them yet again unfavorably to the style of political association in the New World:

> They recommended barbarous remedies imagined in countries where those who suffer have neither the right to speak nor to vote, whereas here the unhappiest fellow has in his mouth the free speech that denounces evil and in his hand the vote that makes the law that shall topple it. In favor of their foreign language, and of the very same laws they blindly ignored, they managed to obtain large masses of followers in cities where lots of Germans are employed: in New York, Milwaukee, Chicago.[16]

---

14. Rafael Rojas, "José Martí and the First Cuban Republicanism," *Essays in Cuban Intellectual History* (New York: Palgrave Macmillan, 2008), 9, 18. Rojas further claims that this minimal republican mold helps explain the easy assimilation of Martí's thought by the most heterogeneous postcolonial political actors, both in Cuba and in Miami. See also Rafael Rojas, *José Martí: la invención de Cuba* (Madrid: Colibrí, 2000); and compare with the official points of view from socialist Cuba, in *Siete enfoques marxistas sobre José Martí* (Havana: Editora Política, 1978).

15. Martí, "Cartas de Martí," in *Obras completas*, vol. 10, 80.

16. José Martí, "El proceso de los siete anarquistas de Chicago," *Obras completas*, vol. 11, 56. This letter-chronicle, also published in *La Nación*, where it appeared on October 21,

It would take another year, in a new chronicle on the trial, conviction, and execution of four of the Chicago anarchists, for Martí to change his attitude dramatically. This shift in attitude can be explained by the fact that, in the meantime, the social struggle in this great nation, between general strikes, escalating trade-unionist demands, police brutality and violent repression, had shortened the distance in style between the workers' movements in Europe and America. "This republic, in its excessive worship of wealth, has fallen, without any of the restraints of tradition, into the inequality, injustice, and violence of the monarchies," Martí observes on this occasion about his host country. And later, he is even more direct—"America, then, is the same as Europe!"—so that the use of violence as an inevitable last resort (what is sometimes referred to as "the red terror," though for the period in question "the red and black terror" would have been a more appropriate appellation given the mixture of communist and anarchist ideas) might now seem justified: "Once the disease is recognized, the generous spirit goes forth in search of a remedy; once all peaceful measures have been exhausted, the generous spirit, upon which the pain of others works like a worm in an open wound, turns to the remedy of violence."[17]

With regard to the merit of giving women entrance to the university, on the other hand, the mixed feelings and doubts that Martí expresses in his letter-chronicle on the death of Marx convey the extent to which the ideal of organic social change as both harmonious and natural—born however laboriously "from the bosom of a nation in history" no less than "from the bosom of a woman in the home"—presupposes the tender collaboration of the "feminine soul" in its most retrograde and misogynistic aspect:

1886, bears the date of September 2, 1886 as the time of its purported composition. However, as Ernesto Mejía Sánchez has recently documented, it was first published, with only slight variations, in the Mexican newspaper *El Partido Liberal*, on September 10, 1886, with August 22, 1886 as the listed date of composition. See José Martí, *Nuevas cartas de Nueva York*, ed. Ernesto Mejía Sánchez (Mexico City: Siglo Veintiuno, 1980), 213.

17. José Martí, "Un drama terrible," *Obras completas*, vol. 11, 335, 337–8. Translation into English as "Class War in Chicago: A Terrible Drama," *Selected Writings*, 199–200. This second chronicle about the tragic events of the Chicago Haymarket bears the date of November 13, 1887. It was published first in Mexico in *El Partido Liberal*, December 27, 29 and 30, 1887; and then in Argentina in *La Nación*, on January 1, 1888, with the same listed date and place of "N.Y., November 13, 1887." For an analysis of the dramatic shift in perspective between these chronicles, see José Cantón Navarro, *Algunas ideas de José Martí en relación con la clase obrera y el socialismo* (Havana: Instituto Cubano del Libro, 1970), 59–76; Philip S. Foner, "José Martí and Haymarket," *Haymarket Scrapbook*, ed. Dave Roediger and Franklin Rosemont (Chicago: Charles H. Kerr, 1986), 215–6; Roberto Fernández Retamar, "A un siglo de cuando José Martí se solidarizó con los mártires obreros asesinados en Chicago," *Valoraciones martianas* 232 (1988): 59–70; and Susana Rotker, *The American Chronicles of José Martí: Journalism and Modernity in Spanish America*, trans. Jennifer French and Katherine Semler (Hanover: University Press of New England, 2000), 99–100.

No one looks askance on the toughening of the feminine soul, for that is the outcome of the virile existence to which women are led by the need to take care of themselves and defend themselves from the men who are moved by appetite. Better that the soul be toughened than that it be debased. For there is so much goodness in the souls of women that even after having been deceived, plunged into despair, and toughened, they still exude a perfume. All of life is there: in finding a good flower.[18]

We could say that in Martí's argument there occurs, first, a displacement from politics to morals, or from the struggle of the "poor" to the plight of the "weak."[19] (Incidentally, this displacement would be reversed much later, in Fidel Castro's imprecise recollection of Martí's chronicle on the Marx memorial.) As one Martí scholar observes, "Social conflicts are now eminently moral problems. Their solution must be sought after, not in the change of the social system but in the creation of a moral conscience, generous and just, which would harmonize, without partialities, the interests of all."[20] But then, secondly, especially through the framing vignettes, there occurs an additional reinscription of the question of moral conscience in the sentimental context of "love" and "hatred" in the bosom of the home.

This movement from politics to morals and from the public realm to the private space of the family, of course, is the exact opposite of what happens at the start of *The Communist Manifesto*, where the relation between man and woman—as opposed to freeman and slave, patrician and plebeian, lord and serf, or guild-master and journeyman—precisely does not figure among the doublets enumerated to exemplify the fact that, for Marx and Engels, the history of all hitherto existing society is the history of class struggles. Rather, for Martí, the questions of gender and the relations among the sexes in the final instance appear to trump the issue of the class struggle in rather conventional ways. "Impurity is so terrible that it can never be voluntary," the Cuban writer says, still with reference to what he calls the feminine soul: "An educated woman will be purer. Yet how painful it is to see how the habits of a virile life gradually change these beauteous flowers into flowers of stone! What will become of men on the day when they can no longer rest their heads on a warm, female bosom?"[21] Thus, the romantic and organicist image of the reproduction of love at home reasserts its power over Martí's attitude to what he perceives to be the problematic role of women in

---

18.   Martí, "Honores a Karl Marx, que ha muerto," 392; "Tributes to Karl Marx," 133.
19.   Both categories had actually been invoked in the discourse of the first speaker at the Cooper Union meeting, Victor Drury, who said: "We have met to regret the death of one of those men who, although not in the acceptation of some a workingman, has at least aided the workingmen of the world to fight the greatest battle that was ever fought in the world, and that is the battle of the weak and the poor against the rich," in *Karl Marx Remembered*, 93.
20.   Raúl Fornet-Betancourt, "José Martí: vida y opción política," *Aproximaciones a José Martí* (Aachen: CONCORDIA, 1998), 26–7.
21.   Martí, "Honores a Karl Marx, que ha muerto," 392; "Tributes to Karl Marx," 136.

general in the social struggle, just as the emphasis that he puts on love prevents him from embracing the organizational methods of Marx's followers in the New World.

Marx in Martí

If Marx doesn't hold the key to the pan-American dilemma, maybe a dusted-off, postcolonial José Martí does.
Juan Flores, Foreword to Román de la Campa, Cuba on My Mind: Journeys to a Severed Nation

However, this does not necessarily mean that we are left with purely negative, missed encounters between Marx and Latin America, or between Marx and Martí. On the contrary, as I began arguing above, the logic of the failed or missed encounter, as *desencuentro*, can be considered one name among others for the unequal development of capitalism in its global phase. This could even open up the space for a renewed appreciation of the idea of the encounter, not as a euphemism for the discovery and subsequent colonization of Latin America but in the sense in which the late Louis Althusser used the term to configure what he called the "underground current" of an "aleatory materialism," based on random encounters, as opposed to the supposed determinism and stagism of traditional, dogmatic, or vulgar understandings of dialectical and historical materialism.[22] Marxism would then become the name for a mode of thinking of the missed encounter as such, now understood as the thought of unlinking or of the constitutive lack at the heart of the social link—that is, the structurally uneven development of society under the historical conditions of capitalism. This would enable us to imagine a posthumous dialogue between Marx and Martí.

After all, especially starting in the 1870s, Marx also began to formulate a series of hypotheses regarding the notion of uneven development that enabled him to generalize a logic of contingency and unevenness for the entire capitalist world, and not only for the so-called peripheral, backward, semi-capitalist, or colonial countries. As we have seen, Marx never fully took advantage of these hypotheses in order to take a fresh look at Latin America. However, making up for this absence, we can find a strange set of indications that go in the same direction in the writings of Martí.

If I may be allowed a play on words, the issue before us at this point no longer concerns the absent corpse of Marx, but the absence of his

---

22. See Louis Althusser, "The Underground Current of the Materialism of the Encounter," in *Philosophy of the Encounter: Later Writings, 1978–1987*, ed. François Matheron and Oliver Corpet, trans. G. M. Goshgarian (London: Verso, 2006), 163–207. In Spain and Latin America, as in many other parts of the world, this posthumous text has become the object of much recent discussion. See, for example, the detailed study by Pedro Fernández Liria, "Regreso al 'campo de batalla,'" in his edition of Louis Althusser, *Para un materialismo aleatorio* (Madrid: Arena Libros, 2002), 73–125.

corpus in Martí's work: How much, or which parts, of Marx's published oeuvre could Martí have read during his years in New York? What did he actually read? Did he ever consult *The Communist Manifesto*, perhaps in the English translation that was available as early as 1850? Or did he perhaps manage to get a hold of the cheap edition of the *Manifesto* that was prepared with financial contributions gathered precisely during the commemorative event of 1883 at the Cooper Union? How much did Martí know, if anything, about this text of which we recently celebrated the 160th anniversary? And how informed was he about the critique of political economy in *Das Kapital*, about which a number of speakers at the Cooper Union already raved so eloquently? Did he ever consult the popular summary of the book prepared by the German Johann Most with the help of Marx himself, or the English-language pamphlet version translated by Otto Weydemeyer and published in 1875 in Hoboken, New Jersey—just a stone's throw away from Martí's residence in New York City?[23]

Even Fidel Castro, in a recent autobiographical interview with Ignacio Ramonet, confesses to a certain wise ignorance in this regard. Or, at least, he cleverly transposes his own supposed ignorance by attributing it to the specialists of Martí's work. "He had apparently read a little Marx, because in his works he talks about him. He has two or three magnificent phrases, when he mentions Marx, and one of them, I remember now, is 'Given that he took the side of the poor, he deserves honour.' And like that one, there are other phrases that praise Marx," says Fidel, surreptitiously putting the "poor" back in the place of the "weak," and ignoring the fact that almost all references to Marx in Martí's complete works (depending on the edition used, this amounts to four or five references) are actually negative ones, similar to the one used as an epigraph to the present chapter. Promptly, though, the Cuban leader adds his doubts about the matter:

> I'm not certain whether even the experts in Martí's thought know what [Martí] knew about Marx, but he did know that Marx was a fighter on the side of the poor. Remember that Marx was fighting for the organization of workers, founding the Communist International. And Martí certainly knew that, even though those debates centred almost exclusively on Europe, and Martí of course was fighting for the independence of a colonized, slaveholding country [in another hemisphere altogether].[24]

---

23. See *Karl Marx Remembered*, 88–9, 279; and Philip S. Foner, "Marx's *Capital* in the United States," *Science & Society* 31 (1967): 461–6. For the extracts, see Johann Most, *Kapital und Arbeit: ein populärer Auszug aus "Das Kapital" von Karl Marx* (1873), with several contemporary re-editions—for instance, the one edited by Hans Magnus Enzensberger (Frankfurt am Main: Suhrkamp, 1972); and in Spanish, *Capital y trabajo: extracto popular de "El Capital" revisado y reelaborado por Marx y Engels*, trans. Manuel Arboli Gazón (Mexico City: Extemporáneos, 1974); and Karl Marx, *Extracts from The Capital of Karl Marx*, trans. Otto Weydemeyer (Hoboken, NJ: F. A. Sorge, ca. 1875).

24. Fidel Castro with Ignacio Ramonet, *My Life: A Spoken Autobiography*, trans. Andrew

In reality, no matter how much the leaders of the Cuban revolution may regret this, we have no palpable proof that Martí would have been directly familiar with any of Marx's texts. Martí's references not only consist of open or coded criticisms, but also speak exclusively of Marx's work as a political organizer, without mentioning any of his publications. However, we do have at our disposal an unexpected source for comparison, this time literary in nature—namely, the only novel written by Martí, *Lucía Jerez*, also known by the earlier title *Amistad funesta* (Baneful Friendship), under which Martí, writing under the pseudonym Adelaida Ral, first published the novel in nine installments, between May 15 and September 15, 1885, in the New York biweekly *El Latino-americano*. In certain parts of this novel, in fact, the Cuban writer almost seems to be summarizing, word for word, the logic of revolutionary social change that we find in so many of Marx's classical statements, which since then have been buried under a mountain of glosses both orthodox and heretical.

We can also read in the second chronicle on the trial of the Chicago anarchists, in which Martí already looked with much more sympathy upon the ideological work of Bakunin's followers: "They do not understand that they are only a wheel in the social mechanism and that in order for them to change the whole mechanism must be changed."[25] The logic of this great mechanism or *engranaje* is what Martí himself, in *Lucía Jerez* as well as in many of his best-known chronicles and essays, including the "Prologue to Juan Antonio Pérez Bonalde's *Poem of Niagara*" and most famously "Our America" describes as the production of structural disjunctions, maladjustments, or dismemberments at all levels of social life—from the dress code of the youth that no longer corresponds to the distinction of their soul, all the way to the

---

Hurley (NewYork: Scribner, 2008), 153–4. Fornet-Betancourt suggests, in *Transformaciones del marxismo*, that Martí may have been more familiar with utopian-socialist and anarchist thought, and that he actually seemed to favor Bakunin over Marx. In this regard, Martí's experience in Mexico City between 1875 and 1876 seems to have had a formative effect on him. "Indeed, it is highly illuminating for the purposes of this work to see how Martí, who had had the chance to witness the discussion of socialist utopian ideas in Mexican working-class circles around 1876, insists precisely on the need to differentiate and clarify theoretically the very term of socialism," Fornet-Betancourt writes: "This fact must be underscored because it is a strong argument in favor of the thesis which holds that Martí knew much more about the socialist currents of his time than what is explicitly stated in his writings" (28–9). An interesting coincidence in this regard links Martí to the historiographical work of Paco Ignacio Taibo II: the latter indeed is the editor of a collection of writings from the era about the strike of the hatmakers or *sombrereros* in Mexico City, about which Martí wrote a sympathetic chronicle. See Martí, "Beneficio de los sombrereros en huelga," first published in *Revista universal* 131 (June 10, 1875), included in the anthology *La huelga de los sombrereros: México 1875*, ed. and with an introduction by Paco Ignacio Taibo II (Mexico City: Centro de Estudios Históricos del Movimiento Obrero Mexicano, 1980), 68–71. For exhaustive documentation on Martí's Mexican connection, see also the materials gathered in *Martí y México*, ed. Luis Ángel Argüelles Espinosa (Mexico City: UNAM, 1998).
25. Martí, "Un drama terrible," 338.

radical upset, or the sudden turnabout, caused by the lack of adaptation between the level of economic development and the attendant social, political, and cultural relations.

Here is how the narrator describes the situation in a high-sounding didactic aside in *Lucía Jerez*:

> These times of ours are disjointed, and with the collapse of the old social barriers and the refinements of education, there has come into being a new and vast class of aristocrats of intelligence, with all the needs of appearance and rich tastes that follow from it, without there having been any time as of yet, in the rapidity of the turnabout, for the change in the organization and distribution of fortunes to correspond to the brusque alteration of social relations, produced by the political liberties and the vulgarization of knowledge.[26]

In Martí's text, this logic of uneven development, based on a structural lack of correspondence, in the first place affects the life of intellectuals in Latin America:

> Since with our Spanish American heads, filled with ideas from Europe and North America, we find ourselves in our countries in the manner of fruits without a market, like excrescences of the earth that weigh down on it and disturb it, and not as its natural flourishing, it so happens that those who possess intelligence, which is sterile among us due to its ill guidance, finding themselves in need of making it fertile so as simply to subsist, devote it with exclusive excess to the political battles, in the noblest of cases, thus producing an imbalance between the scarce country and the political surfeit; or else, pressured by the urgencies of life, they serve the strong man in power who pays and corrupts them, or they strive to topple him when, bothered by needy newcomers, the same strong man withdraws his abundant payment for their baneful services.[27]

Thus, the very "baneful" or "ill-fated" nature of the mysterious "friendship" alluded to in the novel's original title, *Amistad funesta*, would somehow be related to the disastrously imbalanced outcomes of uneven development. Indeed, the only other two references in the novel to the element of *lo funesto* also allude to the effects of a structural maladjustment. Juan Jerez is thus said to "have given in, in his life filled with books and abstractions, to the sweet necessity, which is so often baneful, of squeezing against his heart a little pale hand, this one or that one, it mattered little to him; he saw in womanhood the symbol of ideal beauties more so than a real being."[28] And about

---

26. José Martí, *Lucía Jerez*, ed. Carlos Javier Morales (Madrid: Cátedra, 1994), 145. After decades of relative silence about Martí's only novel, which was not attributed to him until 1911, there has been an explosion of critical interpretations in recent years, most of them focused on gender representations in the text.

27. Martí, *Lucía Jerez*, 117.

28. Ibid., 118. For a lucid analysis of the element of *lo funesto* in terms of gender and genre (in Spanish, *género* can refer to both), see Marcela Zanin, "El género funesto," in Mónica Bernabé, Antonio José Ponte and Marcela Zanin, *El abrigo de aire: Ensayos sobre literatura*

Pedro, the dandyish figure whose physical attractiveness is matched only by his arrogance, we are told that he "saw in his own beauty, the baneful beauty of a lazy and ordinary man, a natural title, that of a lion, over all earthly goods, including the greatest among them, which are its beautiful creatures."[29] But, for the narrator, this is only another example of "that rich beauty of a man, graceful and firm, with which nature clothes a scarce soul."[30] Friendship and love, among other phenomena, become baneful or fatal in Martí's novel precisely due to such maladjustments between the ideal and the real, between physical beauty and moral scarcity, between the life of the mind and the life of the heart, or between the paucity of bourgeois-civil society and the surfeit of politics.

Some of the fragments quoted above, in particular the first one, obviously recall the famous Preface to the 1859 *Contribution to the Critique of Political Economy*, in which Marx sums up the theoretical and methodological presuppositions of his work in preparation for *Capital*. Though famous to the point of saturation, this passage deserves to be quoted at length once more, if for no other reason than to highlight the striking terminological proximities and no less striking discrepancies when compared to Martí:

> In the social production of their existence, men inevitably enter into definite relations, which are independent of their will, namely relations of production appropriate to a given stage in the development of their material forces of production. The totality of these relations of production constitutes the economic structure of society, the real foundation, on which arises a legal and political superstructure and to which correspond definite forms of social consciousness. The mode of production of material life conditions the general process of social, political and intellectual life. It is not the consciousness of men that determines their existence, but their social existence that determines their consciousness. At a certain stage of

---

cubana (Rosario: Beatriz Viterbo, 2001), 85–102. The "baneful" aspect of friendship or desire, of course, could also be read as a reference to a line from book V in Virgil's *Aeneid*, which reads: "Quae lucis miseris tam dira cupido?" (What is this so deathly desire that these wretched ones have for light?) and which inspired the title of Pierre Klossowski's *Such a Deathly Desire*, ed. and trans. Russel Ford (Albany: State University of New York Press, 2007). As Klossowski's translator explains: "*Dira*, when personified [*Dirae*] is the Latin name for the Furies, the goddesses of revenge, and so can be translated as *fearful* or *awful*, but it also originally derives from the language of portents and omens and so carries the sense of *ill-omened*, *foreboding*, or *dreadful*" (ibid., 124); and about the French translation, which is equivalent to the Spanish *funesto*, he adds: "Klossowski's choice for rendering *dira*, *funeste* (from the Latin *funestus* meaning *deadly* or *calamitous*) dates from the fourteenth century and is an adjective that attaches to something that causes or is somehow concerned with death . . . In literary language it can often carry the sense of *sinister*. Here it is rendered as *deathly* rather than *deadly* because the desire is for mortal life, of which death is a moment" (ibid., 125). More so than for any other character in Martí's novel, these connotations are all relevant for understanding the case of Lucía.

29. Martí, *Lucía Jerez*, 129.

30. Ibid., 130.

development, the material productive forces of society come into conflict
with the existing relations of production or—this merely expresses the same
thing in legal terms—with the property relations within the framework of
which they have operated hitherto. From forms of development of the
productive forces these relations turn into their fetters. Then begins an era
of social revolution. The changes in the economic foundation lead sooner or
later to the transformation of the whole immense superstructure. In studying
such transformations it is always necessary to distinguish between the material transformation of the economic conditions of production, which can be
determined with the precision of natural science, and the legal, political,
religious, artistic or philosophic—in short, ideological forms in which men
become conscious of this conflict and fight it out.[31]

A similar passage about methodology can already be found in *The
Communist Manifesto*, which Martí may or may not have been able to
read, or at least hear about, during his years in New York City:

> We see then: the means of production and of exchange, on whose founda-
> tion the bourgeoisie built itself up, were generated in feudal society. At a
> certain stage in the development of these means of production and of
> exchange, the conditions under which feudal society produced and
> exchanged, the feudal organization of agriculture and manufacturing indus-
> try, in one word, the feudal relations of property became no longer
> compatible with the already developed productive forces; they became so
> many fetters. They had to be burst asunder; they were burst asunder. Into
> their place stepped free competition, accompanied by a social and political
> constitution adapted to it, and by the economic and political sway of the
> bourgeois class.[32]

Finally, toward the end of *Extracts from The Capital by Karl Marx*, the
forty-two-page pamphlet that Martí may have read in Weydemeyer's
translation, this logic of radical social change is applied to the fate of
capitalism itself:

> The privileges of capital now become fetters to the mode of production
> which has risen with them and through them. The contradiction of the
> means of production and the socialization of labor arrive at a point where
> they become incompatible with their capitalistic frame. *It will be burst.*
> *The death-knell of the capitalistic private property is sounded. The appro-*
> *priators of strange property will be expropriated.* Thus the individual
> property will be *re-instated*, but on the basis of the acquisition of the
> modern mode of production. *There will arise an amalgamation of free*
> *labor, which will collectively own the earth and the means of production*
> *created by labor.*[33]

31. Karl Marx, Preface, *A Contribution to the Critique of Political Economy*, trans. S. W.
Ryananskaya, ed. Maurice Dobb (New York: International Publishers, 1970), 20–1.
32. Karl Marx and Friedrich Engels, *The Communist Manifesto*, ed. A. J. P. Taylor (New
York: Penguin, 1967), 85.
33. Marx, *Extracts from The Capital*, 42. This extract corresponds to Chapter 32, "The
Historical Tendency of Capitalist Accumulation," in Marx, *Capital*, 929.

If we limit ourselves to this conceptual juxtaposition without bringing up questions of form, there are already two important points of disagreement that immediately catch the eye. For Martí, first of all, there is no linear relation of causality between what, in light of the fragments from Marx, has come to be known as the base and the superstructure. On the contrary, political freedom and the democratization of knowledge, for example, can also come about prior to—or without—a corresponding transformation at the level of bourgeois-civil society or political economy. In fact, this is precisely the problem that besets the newly emergent nations in Latin America, where formal or political independence has not been matched by economic, social, or ideological independence. But there also appears to be a second, as yet understated or implicit disagreement in Martí's phrasing, the consequences of which are, if possible, even more portentous for the interpretation of Marxism. This second disagreement has to do with the presupposition, which Marx and Martí at first sight would appear to share in common, that normally there exists an underlying harmony or correspondence between base and superstructure, or between the productive forces and the social relations of production with their legal, political, religious, and ideological superstructure: a correspondence interrupted only during times of revolutionary upheaval, but otherwise firmly asserted— or so it seems—as a regulative ideal by both Marx and Martí. And yet, contrary to the initial appearance of a shared presupposition, no sooner do we take a closer look at the peculiar literary-aesthetic formulation of this ideal in *Lucía Jerez*, as opposed to Martí's more famous statements such as his prologue to Pérez Bonalde's *Poem of Niagara*, than we have to come to the conclusion that all such presuppositions of harmony or correspondence turn out to be inoperative, if not for the capitalist world in general then at least in the specific context of Latin America.

What I wish to underscore in relation to Martí's novel is not just the surprising proximity to certain phrasings from Marx's canonical texts so much as the literary form and generic structure adopted therein. *Lucía Jerez*, or *Amistad funesta*, in fact constitutes a sentimental romance that ends in nothing less than the violent destruction of all the ideals of natural or harmonious development for which Martí, in his chronicle about the death of Marx, thought he could still count on the support of the feminine soul. The melodrama of ill-fated friendship and unrequited love thus ends with the brutal assassination of Sol—the adolescent orphan whose physical beauty at the same time is supposed to embody the moral ideal as well—at the hands of her friend and potential rival or lover Lucía Jerez. Juan Jerez, on the other hand, never manages to fulfill his historical role as the story's organic intellectual, his dream of becoming a man of letters—more specifically, a lawyer— at the service of the poor indigenous peasants. To be sure, like Marx, whom Martí does praise in his chronicle as "a man consumed with the desire to do good," and who "saw in everything what he bore within: rebellion, the high road, combat," Juan Jerez, too, seems destined for a higher moral mission: "Juan Jerez's was one of those unhappy souls that can only do what is grand and love what is pure."[34] And yet, in the end, his obsession with righting the wrongs of the whole universe, his nostalgia for the heroic grandeur of epic deeds, and his well-nigh masochistic sense of duty lead him to an attitude of the "beautiful soul" whose only proof of moral integrity is that it is inversely proportionate to the sordidness of the world in which, despite everything, he is forced to circulate. "Everything on this earth, in these dark times, tends to degrade the soul: everything from books and paintings to business and affects," to the point of provoking "the luminous illness of the great souls, reduced to petty chores by their current duties or the impositions of chance."[35]

Melodrama's genre and gender conventions thus are put into play as the experimental ground for testing and interrogating the brusque alteration of social relations produced in Latin America by the newfound political liberties and the vulgarization of knowledge for which there has not been any corresponding change in the economical distribution of fortunes. "Melodrama links the crisis of modernity to desire and to the body, aside from facilitating an investigation into the processes of representation," as Francine Masiello writes in a groundbreaking study, using Martí's *Lucía Jerez* as one of her examples. "To put this still more radically, I propose that it is impossible to narrate the chaos of the *fin de siècle* in Latin America *without* melodrama."[36] The typical family romances such as *Amalia* by the Argentine José Mármol or *María* by the Colombian Jorge Isaacs that had served as "foundational fictions" for the joint construction of nation and narration in Latin America thus begin to come apart at the seams in the violent dislocations that give *Lucía Jerez* its melodramatic structure.

On the one hand, Martí's novel renders explicit the presuppositions behind the shift from politics to morals, which we saw was implicitly

34. Martí, "Honores a Karl Marx, que ha muerto," 388; "Tributes to Karl Marx," 132; and *Lucía Jerez*, 119.

35. Martí, *Lucía Jerez*, 115, 125.

36. Francine Masiello, "'Horror y lágrimas': Sexo y nación en la cultura del fin de siglo," *Esplendores y miserias del siglo XIX: Cultura y sociedad en América Latina*, ed. Beatriz González Stephan, Javier Lasarte, Graciela Montaldo and María Julia Daroqui (Caracas: Monte Ávila/Equinoccio/Ediciones de la Universidad Simón Bolívar, 1995), 460. For a canonical study of the kind of national-familial romance that is thus being subverted, see Doris Sommer, *Foundational Fictions: The National Romances of Latin America* (Berkeley: University of California Press, 1991). This approach is continued and extended to the analysis of *Amistad funesta* or *Lucía Jerez* in, among others, María Fernanda Lander, *Modelando corazones: Sentimentalismo y urbanidad en la novela hispanoamericana del siglo XIX* (Rosario: Beatriz Viterbo, 2003); and Patricia Lapolla Swier, *Hybrid Nations: Gender Troping and the Emergence of Bigendered Subjects in Latin American Narrative* (Madison: Fairleigh Dickinson Press, 2009).

at work in his chronicle about Marx. Using a regionally inflected meta-phor for a view that we otherwise would associate with vulgar Marxism, the narrator in yet another didactic digression tells us how, just as the mind's well-being depends on the health of the stomach, so too the secret to a happy and well-ordered nation-state is to be found in the economy of the hacienda:

> A well-ordered hacienda is the base of universal happiness. In nations or in homes, it is in love—even the most unblemished and secure—that we must search for the cause of the many upheavals and disruptions that project darkness or ugliness upon them, when they are not the cause of separation, or even death, which is another form of separation: the hacienda is the stom-ach of happiness. Husbands, lovers, persons who still have to live and who desire to prosper: put some order in your hacienda![37]

On the other hand, in the story's actual unfolding, *Lucía Jerez* violently tears apart the amorous and familial bonds that the text's numerous didactic asides place at the origins of social and political harmony. Not surprisingly, moreover, the misogyny that we found barely hidden in Martí's chronicle in honor of Marx now comes to the foreground in the evaluation of Lucía's potential attraction to Sol. Lesbianism indeed appears as the ultimate threat to Martí's peculiar moralization of poli-tics: the epitome of women's autonomy from the constraints of family, reproduction, and heterosexuality. This is why the ultimate example of a "baneful friendship" within the fictive universe of *Amistad funesta*, as *Lucía Jerez* was first known, can be said to lie in the fatal attraction between two women or, even more forcefully, in the unrequited and ultimately murderous love of one woman for another. It is also why Lucía's friendship seems to be driven by such a strong sense of the destructive potential of love, as even some of the earliest commentators were quick to point out.[38]

Finally, aside from causing major critics such as the Cuban Cintio Vitier to speak of a "case" in the clinical-pathological sense, Lucía's desire is also a slap in the face of would-be organic intellectuals such as Juan Jerez, who is thus reduced to a state of utter inaction in which even the ideal of personal abnegation appears merely as a desperate and ultimately unsuccessful attempt to disguise powerlessness under the cloak of high-minded morality. Whence the peculiar combination of boastful martyrdom and self-sacrificing Quixotry:

> There was in him a strange and violent need for martyrdom, and if, because of the superiority of his soul, he had great difficulty finding friends who would esteem and stimulate his mind, he who felt more of a need to give

---

37. Martí, *Lucía Jerez*, 145.

38. See Enrique Anderson Imbert, "La prosa poética de José Martí. A propósito de *Amistad funesta*," in Manuel Pedro González, ed., *Antología crítica de José Martí* (Mexico City: Publicaciones de la Editorial Cultura, 1960), 106.

himself—since deep down he did not love himself at all and saw himself more as a property to others that he kept in deposit—gave himself over as a slave to anyone who seemed to love him or understood his delicate nature and wished nothing but good upon him.[39]

Whatever the reader makes of this strangely hysterical staging of desire in *Lucía Jerez*, the fact remains that the ideals of harmonious development are here allowed completely and unabashedly to fall apart. In spite of the deep reluctance about the genre to which he publicly confesses and which probably explains why he signs his "bad little novel" or *noveluca* under a female pseudonym, Martí almost seems to welcome the narrative constraints of the melodramatic format as a space in which he can work against the pressures put on him everywhere else by the strict normativity of his moral and political outlook.

As we will see in the following chapters, this melodramatic orientation will have great repercussions for the imagination of the political Left in Latin America throughout much of the twentieth century. In fact, together with the detective novel, melodrama seems to be one of the most tempting and recurrent forms for thinking politics today. In order to understand this, the traditional argument, according to which the melodramatic struggle over good and evil provided much-needed moral anchorage in the midst of the great social and political upheaval that shook Western Europe after the French Revolution, will have to be extended and transposed onto those more recent times of ours that are post-revolutionary in the much more radical sense of having lived through the decline and fall of the very idea of the revolution itself. "Even literature confronts the theme of the institutional revolution (for many the revolution betrayed) through melodrama or mythification," as Carlos Monsiváis writes in an important essay, "Mexico 1890–1976: High Contrast, Still Life," included in *Mexican Postcards*: "In melodrama dominant morality is extenuated and strengthened, governed by a convulsive, shuddering faith in the values of poetry."[40] On the other hand, in the pre-revolutionary context of Martí's *Lucía Jerez*, as Marx and Engels also keenly intuited in their commentary

---

39. Martí, *Lucía Jerez*, 119. For the description of *el caso Lucía*, see Cintio Vitier, "Sobre *Lucía Jerez*," in *Crítica cubana* (Havana: Letras Cubanas, 1988), 500–16.
40. Carlos Monsiváis, "Mexico 1890–1976: High Contrast, Still Life," *Mexican Postcards*, ed. and trans. John Kraniauskas (London: Verso, 1997), 21. John Kraniauskas is right on the mark when, in his "introduction," he makes this into the major theme of this chronicler's work: "Much of Monsiváis's work may be thought of as investigating melodrama—not just as a genre, but as the product of an uneven and transcultural modernity in Mexico—as if it were something like what Raymond Williams has called a 'structure of feeling' (as formulated in *Marxism and Literature*)" (xvii). Or, as Peter Brooks writes: "We may legitimately claim that melodrama becomes the principal mode for uncovering, demonstrating, and making operative the essential moral universe in a post-sacred era," in his *The Melodramatic Imagination: Balzac, Henry James, Melodrama, and the Mode of Excess* (New Haven: Yale University Press, 1995), 15.

from *The Holy Family* on *The Mysteries of Paris* by one of the subgenre's most celebrated founders, Eugène Sue, and as Althusser would
confirm much later in a central text in *For Marx*, melodrama provides
an ideal speculative space in which to elaborate and experiment with
the multiple effects of uneven development as the logic of the missed
encounter—whereby the latter can be read not only as the result of
Marx's defective knowledge about Latin America, nor only as the tacti-
cal and strategic error for which Martí selectively yet also consistently
reproaches Marx, but rather as the very structure of the capitalist mode
of production.

Through a melodrama complete with a violently unhappy ending in
the form of a murderous *passage à l'acte*, we thus arrive at the negation
of all the regulative ideals of natural and harmonious development
modeled upon the family or the hacienda. We could even take this
argument one step further by arguing that in his only novel Martí, too,
begins to catch a glimpse of the logic of the violently uneven development of modernity, just as Marx did a few years earlier in his writings
on Ireland, India, or Russia. Thus, in light of *Lucía Jerez*, we would
have to conclude that for Martí—in the realm of narrative experimentation perhaps no less than for a radical reading of Marx that could
find inspiration in Freud's and Lacan's psychoanalysis—there is not,
nor can there be in the current circumstances, any correspondence or
adaptation between base and superstructure, or between the social
relations of production and the economic distribution of fortunes and
productive forces.

This is also, incidentally, the conclusion arrived at by someone like
Slavoj Žižek, in his foundational book *The Sublime Object of Ideology*:

> How do we define, exactly, the moment—albeit only an ideal one—at which
> the capitalist relation[s] of production become an obstacle to the further
> development of the productive forces? Or the obverse of the same question:
> When can we speak of an accordance between productive forces and
> relation[s] of production in the capitalist mode of production? Strict analysis
> leads to only one possible answer: *never*.[41]

A strict interpretation of psychoanalysis thus would turn a historical
obstacle into an inherent one that can never be overcome. In all the
hitherto existing history of humankind, then, there would be no agreement except in disagreement, no harmony except in conflict, and no
encounter except in a missed encounter.

In fact, a similar conclusion had already been reached in *For Marx*
by Althusser, for whom "the great law of unevenness suffers no exceptions," for the simple reason that it appears to be a universal law of the
development of any social formation whatsoever:

---

41. Slavoj Žižek, *The Sublime Object of Ideology* (London: Verso, 1989), 51–2.

This unevenness suffers no exceptions because it is not itself an exception: not a derivative law, produced by peculiar conditions (imperialism, for example) or intervening in the interference between the developments of distinct social formations (the unevenness of economic development, for example, between "advanced" and "backward" countries, between colonizers and colonized, etc.). Quite the contrary, it is a primitive law, with priority over these peculiar cases and able to account for them precisely in so far as it does not derive from their existence.[42]

This primitive or originary fact of unevenness would help explain why the discoveries of Marx and Freud, even more so than with Columbus's, have been compared with the upheavals caused by the Copernican revolution. Just as Marxism shows that "the human subject, the economic, political or philosophical ego, is not the 'center' of history," so does strict analysis show that "the human subject is decentered, constituted by a structure that, too, has a 'center' solely in the imaginary misprision of the 'ego,' that is, in the ideological formations in which it 'recognizes' itself."[43] And yet, when the decentering effects of unevenness are thus posited as insuperable facts, as primitive laws, or as quasi-ontological conditions of being as such, do we not also lose out on the potential for change that would seem to be the outcome of uneven development for Marx and Martí? Does this potential for radical change, including a change in the mechanism of the whole existing social structure itself, necessarily depend on the positing of an ideal of natural harmony and organicity to be established or restored—with everything that such a restorative ideal entails, for example, in terms of the exorcism of violence, including domestic violence, which then always threatens to come back with a vengeance, as in Martí? Alternatively, does the potential for change depend on a humanist appeal to subjective freedom, allegedly disavowed in the structuralist account of uneven development? Is the humanism of the young Marx then necessarily the only answer to an Althusserian-inspired interpretation of Marxism? These are some of the fundamental theoretical questions—regarding the limits of nature and structure,

---

42. Louis Althusser, *For Marx*, trans. Ben Brewster (London: Verso), 212. For a canonical reading of the notion of uneven development from Marx to Trotsky, see Michael Löwy, *The Politics of Combined and Uneven Development: The Theory of Permanent Revolution* (London: Verso and NLB, 1981). This book has recently been reissued (Chicago: Haymarket Books, 2010), except for Part II that deals, among other regions, with Latin America and in particular with Cuba. See also Samir Amin, *Unequal Development: An Essay on the Social Formations of Peripheral Capitalism* (New York: Monthly Review Press, 1976). Of late, political scientists also have retrieved uneven development as a useful key in the theorization of international relations. See the debates in *Cambridge Review of International Affairs* 22 (2009).

43. Louis Althusser, "Freud and Lacan," in *Writings on Psychoanalysis: Freud and Lacan*, ed. Olivier Corpet and François Matheron, trans. Jeffrey Mehlman (New York: Columbia University Press, 1996), 31.

determinism and freedom, humanism and anti-humanism—that will continue to be raised in art and literature in the form of melo-dramatic oppositions, as witnessed in the novel to which I turn in the next chapter.

2

MARXISM AND MELODRAMA

The Double Intrigue

What the bourgeoisie and proletariat, middle class and lumpenproletariat look for throughout the length and breadth of the culture industry, and find without knowing it, or without needing to know it, is a systematic understanding of society unified and transfigured by melodrama.

Carlos Monsiváis, Mexican Postcards

Any discussion of *Los errores* (*The Errors*), the sixth and last novel by José Revueltas (if we except *El apando*, a short narrative whose generic nature remains unstable but which in any case hardly qualifies as a novel), published in 1964, must take as its point of departure the structural tension between its two storylines: that of the social outcasts and lumpen, with its prostitutes, pimps, small criminals, and circus artists; and that of the Communist Party, with its militant workers, its cadres, and its ideologues, as well as its typical class enemies, such as the usurer or the fascist police.[1] In itself, the contrast between these two sides of the story already carries great potential for melodrama, and in fact the entire novel breathes the feuilleton-like atmosphere of the genre, mixing elements of farce, the comedy of errors, the morality tale, and the popular theater. But we should avoid any premature judgment as to the exact value of these melodramatic elements within the context of Revueltas's literary work or political thought, since they fulfill various functions all at once.

On one hand, there can be no doubt that the sheer persistence of the criminal underworld—the *inframundo* or *bajo mundo*—left to its own devices far removed from the high-sounding debates among leaders and intellectuals of the Party, serves the effect of brutally unmasking

---

1. Other critics who have commented upon the double intrigue in *Los errores* include Christopher Domínguez Michael in his essay "Lepra y utopía," included in the excellent critical anthology *Nocturno en que todo se oye: José Revueltas ante la crítica*, ed. Edith Negrín (Mexico City: Era, 1999), 61–80; and Vicente Francisco Torres, "*Los errores*: Un sistema de vasos comunicantes," ibid., 139–48. The former writes: "Revueltas once again brings together the underworld with the world of militancy. These are the two halves of the rotten orange of marginality and when they are sealed together they create a perfect vacuum" (66); and the latter: "The two stories, the two worlds that make up the novel that we are discussing, are not exactly parallel, since they frequently join each other and weave in and out of one another all the way to conclude in what the author calls a 'blind knot'" (139).

the latter's hypocrisy, not to say its utter historical inexistence in Mexico, as Revueltas had discussed it two years earlier in his *Ensayo sobre un proletariado sin cabeza* (*Essay on a Headless Proletariat*). In this sense, we might say that, for the Mexican author, there will not exist a genuine communist party unless it finally includes those members of the underworld whom orthodox Marxism had always excluded under the denigrating term of "lumpenproletariat."[2] In spite of their enormous curiosity for the genre of melodrama, especially the work of Eugène Sue, about whom they write several eloquent pages in *The Holy Family*, Marx and Engels only rarely show a comparable appreciation for the group of marginals that typically are the genre's protagonists. "Marx and Engels do not spare their invectives with respect to the latter," Ernesto Laclau comments, referring to the lumpenproletariat, in his recent book *On Populist Reason*, before he recalls how Marx speaks in this regard of "the scum of society," whereas Engels uses even stronger language: "This rabble is absolutely brazen . . . Every leader of the workers who uses these scoundrels as guards or relies on them for support proves himself by this action alone a traitor to the movement."[3] And yet, with the help of Peter Stally-brass, Laclau goes on to demonstrate how, even in Marx's perspective, the lumpenproletariat appears after all as a key reference for the articulation—this time contingent and hegemonic, not deterministic, in nature—of any and all emancipatory politics. This perspective is further confirmed in Revueltas's *Los errores*.

Precisely insofar as it lacks any stable social inscription, the lumpen constitutes something like an ideal term of heterogeneity from which to articulate a political identity without essentialisms. This is how Frantz Fanon understood it, long after Marx, in a fragment from *The Wretched of the Earth* in which he would appear to offer an anticipation of the whole gallery of characters that populate the pages of *Los errores*:

> The lumpenproletariat, once it is constituted, brings all its forces to endanger the "security" of the town, and is the sign of the irrevocable decay, the gangrene ever present at the heart of colonial domination. So the pimps, the hooligans, the unemployed, and the petty criminals . . . throw themselves

---

2. José Revueltas, *Ensayo sobre un proletariado sin cabeza*, ed. Andrea Revueltas, Rodrigo Martínez and Philippe Cheron (Mexico City: Era, 1980), 36. This essay on the history of the *mediatización* or "cooptation" of the Mexican revolution by the bourgeois state is in dire need of a sustained critical re-evaluation. For an excellent start, see Martín Juárez (aka Pablo Langer Oprinari), "Aportes para una lectura crítica de *Ensayo sobre un proletariado sin cabeza*," *Revista Estrategia Internacional* (2005). For a brief intellectual biography of Revueltas in English, including the eventful history of his multiple expulsions from the Mexican Communist Party, see Roberto Crespi, "José Revueltas (1914–1976): A Political Biography," *Latin American Perspectives* 22 (1979): 93–113. In Spanish, compare "Autobiografía," in José Revueltas, *Las evocaciones requeridas*, ed. Andrea Revueltas and Philippe Cheron, vol. 2 (Mexico City: Era, 1987), 267–86.
3. Ernesto Laclau, *On Populist Reason* (London: Verso, 2005), 144.

into the struggle like stout working men. These classless idlers will by militant and decisive action discover the path that leads to nationhood . . . The
prostitutes too, and the maids who are paid two pounds a month . . . all
who turn in circles between suicide and madness, will recover their balance,
once more go forward and march proudly in the great procession of the
awakened nation.[4]

In *Los errores*, of course, we are a far cry from such an awakening of
the lumpenproletariat to the solution of its troubles. The worlds of
misery and of communist militancy do not really meet in this novel,
except in crime and the repression of crime. Even so, it would seem as
if this entire underworld, by its sheer physical presence, were loudly
proclaiming the void of a duty, like the task of an ethical or moral revision of really existing communist politics. The party, the narrator
seems to tell us through all the classless characters gathered in his text,
should also include the latter as the true motor of history, far from the
preachings about history as the "objective" history of the class struggle, according to the hefty manuals from the Soviet Academy.

The gesture of converting the lumpen, by way of the genre conventions of melodrama, into an integral part of the world as presented in
Los errores would thus have to be read as a denunciation of communist
politics—a criticism no less ferocious or peremptory for belonging to
the space of fiction—that is intimately tied to Revueltas's political
activism. Historically, moreover, melodrama has always been the genre
of preference for the staging of this formless mass of poor people,
beggars, and prostitutes. To be more precise, one of the interpretive
keys to understand the success of melodrama, not just as a literary
genre but as a cultural matrix in a much broader sense as well, depends
on the possibility that, through this genre or matrix, the so-called
populace or scum succeed in incorporating themselves into a people,
and the people in turn may embody itself as the—modern, urban and,
as we will see, post-revolutionary—masses:

> The stubborn persistence of the melodrama genre long after the conditions of
> its genesis have disappeared and its capacity to adapt to different technologi-
> cal formats cannot be explained simply in terms of commercial or ideological
> manipulations. One must continually pose anew the question of the cultural
> matrix of melodrama, for only with an analysis of the cultural conditions can
> we explain how melodrama mediates between the folkloric culture of the
> country fairs and the urban-popular culture of the spectacle, the emerging

---

4. Quoted in Laclau, *On Populist Reason*, 150–1. In Latin America, the question
regarding the social, economic, and political status of the lumpenproletariat of course
continued to be an urgent matter well into the 1960s and 1970s. See, for instance, André
Gunder Frank, *Lumpenburguesía: Lumpendesarrollo. Dependencia, clase y política en
Latinoamérica* (Barcelona: Laia, 1972). A whole history is waiting to be written about the
destiny of this category, whose potential for melodrama is certainly not foreign to the success
of one of its descendants today—namely, the multitude as defined by Antonio Negri and
Michael Hardt and, more ambivalently, by Paolo Virno.

mass culture. This is a mediation which, on the level of narrative forms, moves ahead through serial novels in newspapers, to the shows of the music hall and to cinema. And as we move from film to radio theatre and then to the *tele-novela*, the history of the modes of narrating and organizing the *mise-en-scène* of mass culture is, in large part, a history of melodrama.[5]

The story of *Los errores* obviously traverses many of these scenes and, due to its heightened theatricality, its comical effects, and its moral polarizations, it resembles nothing more than the old feuilleton or the contemporary farce. The novel takes advantage of the whole structural matrix of melodrama so as to re-launch the dream of a social revolution that would really subsume the rabble and mass of all those who, from the most ruinous lumpen to the disenchanted intellectual, do not count in the eyes of the high command of the Party.

On the other hand, however, we also ought not to forget that Revueltas himself, in *Ensayo sobre un proletariado sin cabeza*, refers to the small-time leaders of the Mexican Communist Party as "lumpenprole-tarian" in a purely condescending way, speaking of the "crisis of the split" that began toward the end of 1961, "again provoked, against independent opinions, by the national leadership of the PCM, made up of the same lumpenproletarian political gangsters that ejected us from the PCM in that monstrous usurpation of party sovereignty (fake dele-gates, nonexistent representations, hidden documents and so on and so forth) that was the 13th National Convention."[6] This sarcastic mention suggests that Revueltas, with regard to the lumpenproletariat, is perhaps not so distant from the denigrating orthodoxy of Marx and Engels. In *Los errores*, furthermore, the narrator refers ironically to the populism hidden behind the rhetorical invocation of the lumpen on behalf of one of his characters, the party boss Patricio Robles: "On certain occasions, he liked to use certain lumpenproletarian phrases common among pool players and gamblers, in the belief that this would give his words a nuance, a touch reminiscent of his origin as the man of the people that he had been."[7] Thus, we also cannot exclude the possibility that a similar motivation, albeit ironically, may determine the use of certain phrasings and invocations of the lumpenproletariat on the part of Revueltas.

---

5. Jesús Martín Barbero, *De los medios a las mediaciones: Comunicación, cultura y hegemonía* (Barcelona: Gustavo Gili, 1987), 131–2; in English *Communication, Culture and Hegemony: From the Media to Mediations*, trans. Elizabeth Fox and Robert A. White (London: Sage, 1993), 119. On melodrama as a cultural matrix, see the articles included in the special volume, Hermann Herlinghaus, ed., *Narraciones anacrónicas de la modernidad: melodrama e intermedialidad en América latina* (Santiago: Cuarto Propio, 2002). Gareth Williams also brilliantly reads the figure of the Mexican comedian Cantinflas in terms of melodrama, in *The Mexican Exception: Sovereignty, Police, and Democracy* (New York: Palgrave Macmillan, 2011), 65–86.

6. Revueltas, *Ensayo sobre un proletariado sin cabeza*, 36.

7. José Revueltas, *Los errores* (Mexico City: Era, 1979), 275.

In any case, we should underscore the fact that the strong melodramatic overtones of *Los errores* derive not only from the structural contrast between the two storylines of the novel, with all that this contrast entails in terms of the critique of the notion of the party, but also from the internal development of each one of these stories. This is, after all, the true lesson of the Marxist notion of uneven development for someone like Althusser as well: "The whole history of Marxist theory and practice confirms this point. Marxist theory and practice do not only approach unevenness as the external effect of the interaction of different existing social formations, but also within each social formation," as we may read in *For Marx*. "And within each social formation, Marxist theory and practice do not only approach unevenness in the form of simple exteriority (the *reciprocal action* of infrastructure and superstructure), but in a form organically *internal* to each instance of the social totality, to each contradiction."[8]

The New Life

He thought about his savings, about using all of them, without sparing a cent, in order to construct that new life—unexpected, miraculous, finally the peace and quiet—that they would live together, Mario Cobián and she, as husband and wife.

José Revueltas, Los errores

The two worlds that only precariously cohabit in *Los errores* are in similar ways marked by an internal disjunction. It is this disjunction that really defines the text's melodramatic nature. What is at stake, therefore, is not so much the history or the social function of the genre so much as its formal structure: a dual, or Manichaean structure, which tends to oppose good and evil, justice and injustice, ethics and corruption, in a pseudodialectical opposition—an opposition that is dialectical only in appearance. This is because the notions of good, justice, and salvation, due to the extreme dualism in which they are portrayed, do not genuinely enter into contradiction with the otherwise no less patent realities of evil, injustice, and exploitation. In the final analysis, there is no true contradiction, only the projection of good conscience onto real conditions of existence. This projection continues to depend on old ideological elements, such as religion, which have nothing in common, really, with the life of the underworld in the name of which melodrama speaks. "In this sense, melodrama is a foreign consciousness as a veneer on a real condition," Althusser writes in a brilliant discussion of Brecht and Bertolazzi's theatre. "The dialectic of melodramatic consciousness is only possible at this price: this consciousness must be borrowed from outside (from the world of alibis, sublimations, and lies of bourgeois morality), and it must still be lived as *the* consciousness of a condition

---

8. Althusser, *For Marx*, 213–4.

(that of the poor underworld) even though this condition is radically foreign to the consciousness."[9] Several features considered typical of melodrama, such as the rhetorical excess of moralizing polarities, can best be explained if we start from the disjuncture that serves as their structural base.

Within the first storyline, that of the underworld, the disjuncture expresses itself above all through the desire for a "new life"—that is to say, a total break with everything that defines the present of the subjects in question. Though the same holds true for several other characters, this desire for an absolute break is particularly clear in the case of the couple made up of Mario Cobián ("El Muñeco") and Lucrecia ("Luque"). Mario, especially, dreams obsessively of "that new life that he proposed to lead, of that break with himself, with his past, with the whole inferno";[10] he wants to be somebody, dreaming that "for once that I am going to make it big in my life,"[11] and above all, he wants to stop being El Muñeco. Concretely, the dream of a new life, so typical of any melodrama, is translated in *Los errores* into the ideal of a perfect, almost sacred love. For Mario, this would mean getting Luque out of prostitution, cutting all ties to the past in order finally to take the leap toward a completely new existence:

> This new existence was so extraordinary, it meant so much for both of them, that Mario would offer it to her, well-rounded, clean, and finished in all its details, similar to a true blessing fallen out of the sky, so that Lucrecia might embark upon it without the slightest obstacle, easy-going, natural, grateful, like something that had to be in this way and not in any other way.[12]

The vocabulary, as is often the case in melodrama, is borrowed from religion, or from what Marx and Engels, in their discussion of Eugène Sue in *The Holy Family,* had called *"theological* morality."[13] This can easily be understood insofar as, with the exception of suicide or the dream of ending it all—also quite common between Mario and Lucrecia—only the beyond of a pure and sacred ideal can be adequate to the desire to leave behind, once and for all, the world of injustice below. "Lucrecia was sacred, a sacred and pure ideal," Mario thinks: "Lucrecia was sacred, sacred, sacred. The new life."[14] And later: "For sure she

---

9. Louis Althusser, "The 'Piccolo Teatro': Bertolazzi and Brecht. Notes on a Materialist Theatre," in *For Marx*, 139 (translation modified).
10. Revueltas, *Los errores*, 16.
11. Ibid., 23.
12. Ibid.
13. Karl Marx and Friedrich Engels, *The Holy Family*, in *Collected Works*, vol. 4 (Moscow: Progress Publishers, 1975), 201. In a letter to his daughter Andrea written from the Lecumberri prison, José Revueltas promises to get her a clean copy of *The Holy Family* while she is studying in Paris with Henri Lefebvre, since his personal copy is one that he constantly has had with him and covered with notes. See Revueltas, *Las evocaciones requeridas*, vol. 2, 229.
14. Revueltas, *Los errores*, 26–7.

will never ever leave me, once she knows how happy we'll be with the new life I'm going to give her."[15] Once again, the melodramatic nature of such wishes depends on the fact that what is being sought is a degree of purity that is such that, in comparison, the real world can deliver only a series of disillusionments and deceptions. Meanwhile, however, the real conditions of existence remain intact precisely because they do not enter into a process of genuine transformation. Rather, the melodramatic structure of the desire for the new life only increases the false contrast between the dream of purity, on one hand, and the world of misery, on the other.

Freedom and Automatism

This is where I stand—how I would love to be: an ethical monster without empathy, doing what is to be done in a weird coincidence of blind spontaneity and reflexive distance.

Slavoj Žižek, The Monstrosity of Christ

The desire to "succeed" or "make it big" (*dar un golpe*) in life can also be read as a pathetic, well-nigh existentialist search for an authentic "act" of freedom. This theme of the act, as we will see in detail below, is actually a constant concern of the later Revueltas.[16] In *Los errores*, though, we can already begin to perceive to what extent the logic of the act encloses an insuperable paradox. On one hand, it is certainly true that a genuine act, if accomplished, would be proof of the human capacity for autonomy. Thus, Mario discovers with an "abyssal and sweet delirium" that he can be somebody, do something, become the "only true but invisible protagonist" of his own history, "in the same way that a magician brings incredible and marvelous things out of nowhere"—something which would seem to constitute a true moment of existential revelation: "A nebulous discovery of his own person: I have done *something*, me, the one who finds himself here, between the old boxes of the attic."[17] On the other hand, each genuine act seems to bring the individual to a point where it is not he or she but the objective course of things that decides in his or her stead. In this way, the human being, far from giving evidence of autonomy by acting independently, rather becomes a kind of automaton at the mercy of a plan or an order beyond its will.

To decide and to let another decide for oneself, in this sense, would be two sides of the same coin. In the case of Mario, the discovery of "being *somebody*" in the sovereign act is barely distinguishable from

---

15. Ibid., 112.
16. See also the commentary on the "profound act" (*acto profundo*) in Philippe Cheron, *El árbol de oro: José Revueltas y el pesimismo ardiente* (Ciudad Juárez: Universidad Autónoma de Ciudad Juárez, 2003), 271–86.
17. Revueltas, *Los errores*, 19–20.

the suspicion, equal parts voluptuous and delirious, of being "handed over" or "surrendered" to a chain of events beyond his control: "This is how events occurred, the anesthesia provided by a sovereign act, foreign and distant, the world, life, which linked him up with their chains without belonging to him, and which sunk their teeth in his flesh that nevertheless was his flesh, his hand, the hand of Mario Cobián."[18] What the subject feels at this point of exchange between act and necessity is the happiness of belonging to a cause greater than him- or herself. This is the pleasure of deciding as a way of letting oneself be decided, so crucial for the good functioning of all ideological interpellation: "The voluptuousness of not belonging to oneself, of being handed over, of not responding for oneself, of letting oneself be led from one side to the other, who knows whereto."[19] Here, as in a Möbius strip, the most sovereign activity, when it continues long enough in the same direction, all of a sudden turns into the highest degree of automated passivity. Revueltas's novel, among many other achievements, also represents an impeccable narrative investigation into the logic of such paradoxes surrounding the act, freedom, and the objective destiny of things.

Various characters in *Los errores* on both sides of the intrigue indeed seem to be going through similar moments of crisis, between the anxiety and the pleasure of knowing themselves to be ruled by a destiny that is beyond their individual will. "Elena," the ex-circus artist (whose nickname is a pun on *el enano*, "dwarf," as a homonym for *Elena-no*, "not Elena"), for example, yearns to exercise his freedom and break completely with his boss and supposed friend "El Muñeco." Locked up in a tiny suitcase, lying in wait for the right silence in order to jump out and rob the moneylender don Victorino's shop, he momentarily suffers from delusions of grandeur and imagines himself capable of anything and everything: "But today he would not allow Mario Cobián to take advantage of him in any way. El Suavecito was not going to allow himself to be mocked. He decided to complete the first part of the theft. The moment to act had come: and it was up to him, to Elena. It was his moment."[20] Thus, the moment of absolute freedom arrives:

> The dwarf felt the full sensation of a happy, unlimited freedom, which he could express in whatever way he wanted, shouting out loud. So he did: a scratchy, ululating, savage scream, like a drunk Mexican. Absolute, aggressive, untainted freedom . . . Nothing less than that, absolute freedom . . . [all this] was his own determination, free and sovereign, the imposition of his own destiny over things, and not the other way around.[21]

---

18. Ibid., 31.
19. Ibid., 39.
20. Ibid., 157.
21. Ibid., 181–2.

"Elena," at the same time that he feels himself capable of being "the absolute author of his deeds and their irrefutable judge," also experiences the uncannily painful and pleasant feeling of becoming an automaton under the yoke of some other—whether this other is fate or "El Muñeco"; but this sensation is actually indistinguishable from that other, "incomparably terrifying" one, which produces in him "a naked pleasure, without skin, without instruments: the sensation of infinity," leading to the "paroxysm of a form of happiness both mad and atrocious."[22] What happens precisely is that the fascination with the act—with getting his moment—coincides with the desire for abandonment—for forming part of a plan larger than himself.

Thus, the dwarf feels "an unspeakable contact" with the mandate emanating from the other, "to the point of emptying himself out completely in the void, without being aware of anything."[23] It is by purely and simply obeying orders that the desire of the subject reveals itself to be a desire of and for the other, a desire to which he submits himself as "an abandoned puppet."[24] Instead of being the agile acrobat of his own freedom, this ex-circus artist discovers that he is merely the docile automaton of a destiny that on all sides exceeds and controls him. And something similar happens not only to "La Magnífica"— "Why did she feel pushed liked an automaton to say exactly that which she had promised to keep quiet about?"[25]—but also, in anticipation of the second storyline, to the linotypist who, at the time of setting the manifesto of the Central Strike Committee (Comité Central de Huelga) "seemed like a somnambulant puppet that was being handled by someone from afar with the precision of a chess-player."[26] In all these cases, the act defines the linkage between an individual and the plane of the supra-individual, in a constitutive oscillation between freedom and automatism, between blind spontaneity and reflexive distance, between one's own will and the impersonal chain of inevitability.

Mario's example once again offers the best summary of the paradoxes of the act:

> Mario felt that the earth was slipping away from under his feet. Why did things take this absurd and arbitrary turn, as in a grotesque nightmare? The plan did not unfold in conformity with what he had foreseen, it took paths of its own, invented resources, linked distant events, anticipated situations, even though it was not really different from the plan itself. To the contrary, materials and things that belonged to him, that were included in him in order to become realized, took on a destiny and chose an occasion on their own account, appearing in a new light, as in an enchanted mirror in which they looked at themselves as they had always wanted to see themselves and

22. Ibid., 184.
23. Ibid., 20.
24. Ibid., 26.
25. Ibid., 128.
26. Ibid., 139.

not in the way they were at the point defined by that personal human will. Mario could not have these thoughts or considerations for himself, but he guessed behind everything the existence of a deceitful and sly move, not devised by anyone in particular, but of which he made himself the victim— God knows why, or moved by whom?[27]

Here Mario in effect appears to be "the Puppet" (El Muñeco) in a false setup, a nightmarish and absurd plan that is also at the same time secretly attractive. The plan that he seeks to accomplish is simultaneously an enchanting mirror in which he recognizes himself not as he is, but as he would like to appear. We might also say that the mirror returns to him an image—an imaginary identity—of his self in the analytical sense of the term, his ideal ego rather than his ego ideal. This is why abandoning himself to the plan, with all its incomprehensible whims included, turns out to be so delirious and painfully sweet. The most objective elements, a destiny woven from strange and alien forces, at the same time seem to communicate with the most intimate materials of the subjective realm, the innermost drives of one's own being. Thus, we can feel ourselves to be free and authentic in the midst of the most complete alienation.

Politics and Affectivity

Here, incidentally, we come upon one of the most striking aspects of *Los errores*. The whole point is to unravel the affective and corporeal burden that constitutes the material base without which no power could inscribe itself in a lasting way at the heart of the subject. In my view, the most outstanding passages in Revueltas's novel, stylistically speaking, are those devoted to tracing the ubiquitous circulation of rage, hatred, and resentment as the indispensable anchoring points that mark the subordination of a body to power, violence and exploitation—an exploitation which, in this way, turns out to be a kind of self-exploitation, or a servitude that is at least in part voluntary.

"Where there is oppression, there is resistance," people used to say at the time of *Los errores*, in an allusion to a famous dictum from Mao Zedong. In fact, what a novel like this one suggests is that, unless we capture where power—through affectivity and the subject's psychic and libidinal economy—inscribes itself onto the body, we also will fail to activate the mainspring of effective resistance. This vast lesson, which Revueltas appears to distribute throughout the didactic parts of nearly all his narrative oeuvre, constitutes at the same time the premise of theoretical investigations on the part of contemporary figures. For instance, in "La izquierda sin sujeto" ("The Left Without a Subject"), a programmatic essay from 1966 published in the important Argentine journal *La rosa blindada* and reprinted in the Cuban journal

---

27. Ibid., 114.

Pensamiento crítico, the slightly younger Rozitchner laments precisely the inability of the orthodox Left to think through the subjective aspect of politics other than in terms of a purely negative or ideological supposition that we would be dealing with the "merely" subjective. "I hold that without subjective modification, without the elaboration of truth in the total situation in which the human subject participates, there exists no objective revolution," writes Rozitchner. Later, he adds:

> If the transition from the bourgeoisie to the revolution appears as a necessity that emerges from within the capitalist regime itself, then this rational necessity must be read by grasping those sensible human elements therein that are also necessary and made it possible, and that both dogmatism and left-wing opportunism abstract as unnecessary: they read the rationality of the process all the while leaving out, as irrational, that which they are not capable of assuming or modifying: the subject itself, they themselves.[28]

Revueltas, by contrast, submerges all his characters precisely in this sensible and affective zone that makes alienation possible as self-alienation.

Los errores, in this sense, presents among other things a detailed physiology and psychic economy of power. The novel uncovers the affective life of resentment, rage, jubilation, and melancholy in whose web the human being remains trapped, quite literally, qua subject. "Affect," in other words, is not here a mere synonym for emotion but rather the name for the residue in the body left behind by the inscription of an individual in an incorporeal, social, or political process, which articulates both power and resistance. Affect would be the mark

---

28. León Rozitchner, "La izquierda sin sujeto" (1966), included in the anthology *Las desventuras del sujeto político: Ensayos y errores* (Buenos Aires: Ediciones El Cielo por Asalto, 1996), 55, 66. This essay is also reissued in the anthology, Néstor Kohan, ed., *La rosa blindada: una pasión de los '60* (Buenos Aires: Ediciones La Rosa Blindada, 1999), 275–307. I discuss Rozitchner's work in detail in the second half of Chapter 4 and throughout Chapter 5. Here, however, I should voice two doubts with regard to the framing of the discussion on affectivity. The first comes from Rozitchner himself, when in his doctoral thesis on the subject of Max Scheler, the latter is said to "find support in an affective, *sensible materiality*, which thus constitutes the maximum materiality of which spiritualism is capable in its attempt to justify the unmovable limits of the partiality of its world," even though Rozitchner immediately afterwards follows up this comment with an admission: "Not without tragedy, that is, the insoluble drama that condemns us to the sad acceptance of a reality which, precisely for us, it is a matter not only of suffering but also of transforming," in León Rozitchner, *Persona y comunidad: Ensayo sobre la significación ética de la afectividad en Max Scheler* (Buenos Aires: Eudeba, 1962), 14. The other doubt, or an anticipation thereof, comes from the hand of Jacques Lacan, who in one of his earliest writings warns against the risk of "utter intellectual stagnation" and "scholastic abstractions" represented by the notion of affectivity—"a catchword that came in very useful for a while to help advanced psychiatry avoid a number of issues." Quoted in Elisabeth Roudinesco, *Jacques Lacan: An Outline of a Life and a History of a System of Thought*, trans. Barbara Bray (Cambridge: Polity Press, 2005), 103–4. The question would be whether, in the final analysis, affectivity—now a fashionable topic again among the followers of Spinoza, Gilles Deleuze or Antonio Negri—is not a slippery slope toward the impoverished "ethical turn" that I will discuss at the end of this chapter and in the Epilogue.

of a subjectivization, the trace of the passage of a subject through a process of fidelity to a truth or its betrayal. Thus, to give but one example, the text reveals to us "the opaque drunkenness of a searching and artificial rage, similar to the little dosages of a narcotic that lightens the presence of things by making them innocent and faraway," a rage which nonetheless can also and at the same time open up a place for a new sense of justice, beyond the misery that provokes so much rabid despair: "A rage which immediately becomes honest—after inflicting the first whiplash—and full of a muffled and passionate justice."[29] Revueltas possesses a relentless, painfully eloquent and lucid honesty in uncovering the most recondite and perverse hideouts where power latches onto affectivity.

The affects that most insidiously circulate through the universe of Revueltas's narrative—rage, fear, and hatred, not to mention the desperate yearning for justice—all serve to link the individual to a supra-individual ideological cause. Don Victorino, the moneylender about to fall prey to an attempted robbery on behalf of the communists, considers that such a linkage offers a point of commonality that he shares not only with his accomplices in the Anticommunist Mexican League, such as Nazario Villegas, but also with his most feared class enemies, among whom we find one of his own employees, the communist infiltrator Olegario Chávez. The following sentence also offers us a good sample of Revueltas's quite unique and inimitable style—for who else, aside from Martí, can sustain for over a dozen lines a single sentence without losing its dialectical cadence and fluency?

> If he had felt capable of kneeling down before Nazario—don Victorino thought, precisely because of the secret generosity of his impulse, without fear that he would interpret it as abject behavior, it was so that a gesture of such desperate eloquence would make him understand, all of a sudden, the way in which he, don Victorino, appreciated the situation not only with respect to his own person but also, above all, insofar as in this person, in his concrete and individual destiny, there lay condensed the logic, the reason, the justice—and also the tribulations and impiety—of the cause for which both of them fought, a condensation whose discovery (barely ten minutes before, when don Victorino began to measure the magnitude of the threat represented by Olegario Chávez by his side as a communist spy) was a kind of common patrimony, an appalling common responsibility, that both had to grasp and share in everything new, radical, and unusual that it would require from their lives.[30]

Something in Olegario Chávez, for this same reason, ends up seeming curiously seductive to don Victorino. Despite the hatred each of them feels for the other, both men ultimately operate in identical ways,

---

29. Revueltas, *Los errores*, 37.
30. Ibid., 159.

devoting their lives to a cause in which they simultaneously recognize their most profound and personal vocation. Thus, still according to don Victorino,

> The communists had signaled him and nobody else, in the same way in which Judas had chosen Jesus; in the same way in which Judas had destined Jesus, inevitably, to bear witness. Both had ended up being entwined and sentenced from the beginning by the same destiny and the same fear, the fear that overcomes those who know themselves in a way to be in possession of the truth: of both sides of the truth. Above all, this is what Olegario was to don Victorino: the presence in which he contemplated himself, the inexorable and hoped-for justification of his life, of his history, of his form of being the way he was and of the reason for that vital, superhuman, and impious violence, out of spite for the mediocrity, pettiness and hatred in the midst of which he had always had to live, solitary, strong, and disdainful.[31]

The communist traitor, in this sense, plays a fundamental role in the psychic economy of his archenemy, the proto-fascist usurer don Victorino:

> Olegario Chávez plays next to him, from the point of view of the communist plans, a very special role of transcendence . . . quite the opposite of a vulgar spy or provocateur. Neither his conduct, nor the fundamental traits of his character, displayed the slightest deceitfulness: he was frank, straightforward to the point of insolence and rudeness, if one wanted, but by no means deceitful, by no means was he a type who would play with marked cards. His tactic of open, frank, and frontal attack, for this very reason, revealed the truly singular perspective of his goals.[32]

Above all, what we begin to glimpse in this impeccable narrative exposition is the way in which a certain dogmatism, on the part of communists no less than of their class enemies, nurtures itself with the full spectrum of human affectivity. With this critique of the subjective logic of dogmatism and authoritarianism, however, we already find ourselves at the center of the second intrigue in Revueltas's novel.

Rethinking the Twentieth Century

The nineteenth century announced, dreamed, and promised; the twentieth century declared it would make man, here and now.
Alain Badiou, The Century

The twentieth century did not exist. Humanity made a huge leap into the void from the theoretical presuppositions of the nineteenth century, through the failure of the twentieth century, to the dark beginning of the twenty-first century in August of 1945, with the atomic explosions of Hiroshima and Nagasaki.
José Revueltas, Dialéctica de la conciencia

---

31. Ibid., 160.
32. Ibid., 160–1.

Aside from its melodramatic plot line pitting the lumpenproletariat of prostitutes and pimps against the fascistoid anticommunists, *Los errores* in a second and parallel story presents a narrativized judgment regarding the dogmatic excesses of Stalinism and its nefarious effects in the rest of the world, including in the Mexican Communist Party. In this sense, the novel participates in a much larger self-evaluation of the twentieth century, in which we could also include Alain Badiou's *The Century* or, closer to Revueltas's home, parts of Bolívar Echeverría's *Vuelta de siglo*.[33] In fact, Badiou once commented to me that he had planned originally to include a chapter on Mexico in *The Century*. I am not sure what events (texts, artworks, political sequences) would have been summoned in this chapter, which for better or for worse remained in the drawer of good intentions. What I do know is that *Los errores* had already asked, forty years earlier, some of the same questions that drive Badiou's project in *The Century*. In particular, Revueltas's novel gives us important insights into the potential destiny of a whole jargon of finitude when it is combined with an antitotalitarian, antidogmatic, left-wing revisionism. A central place in this combination is reserved, as we will see, for our human capacity for error—our human finitude— reconceived as the essential truth in Hegel's dialectic.

Revueltas, like Bertold Brecht in his play *The Decision*, to whom Badiou devotes a chapter in *The Century*, is concerned above all with the interpretation that history has in store for the great events in the international expansion and perversion of communism. Its main prob- lem is addressed in an odd parenthesis, in which the narrator for once seems indistinguishable from the author's own voice:

> (One cannot escape the necessity of a *free and heterodox* reflection about the meaning of the "Moscow trials" and the place they occupy in the definition of our age, of our twentieth century, because we true communists—whether members of the party or not—are shouldering the terrible, overwhelming task of being the ones who bring history face to face with the disjunctive of having to decide whether this age, this perplexing century, will be designated as *the century of the Moscow trials* or as *the century of the October revolution*.)[34]

Revueltas leaves us no clear verdict in this regard. Was the twentieth century criminal or revolutionary? The disjunctive remains open throughout *Los errores*, since there is also no single character capable of occupying the organizing center of consciousness that we might attribute to its author. Critics such as Christopher Domínguez Michael, after expressing their dismay at Revueltas's "far-fetched and immoral" hypothesis regarding the Moscow trials, are quick to add how much they lament the fact that Revueltas could have suggested some kind of

---

33.   Alain Badiou, *The Century*, trans. Alberto Toscano (Malden: Polity Press, 2007); and Bolívar Echeverría, *Vuelta de siglo* (Mexico City: Era, 2007).
34.   Revueltas, *Los errores*, 222–3.

dialectical justification of sacrifice and terror: "Revueltas takes the liberties of a novelist with regard to history and, in his enthusiasm for the Hegelian triads, he converts Bukharin's tortured mind into a precise and chilling dialectical synthesis."[35] In reality, the text is far more ambiguous; and it even stages this ambiguity itself by providing several characters with a split conscience.

Thus, we find examples of an analysis of the problem in terms of the corrupting nature of power with regard to historical truth. This is the case of Olegario:

> The Moscow trials in this sense—Olegario had told himself from that moment on—present an entirely new problem for the conscience of communists: the problems of power and historical truth split off and grow apart, to the point where they become opposed and violently exclude one another in the arena of open struggle. Meanwhile, the historical truth, in the margin of power, becomes invalidated, without support, and without any recourse other than *the power of truth*, in opposition to everything *the truth of power* represents in terms of compulsive force, repressive instruments, propaganda means, and so on. This is when one must uncover and demonstrate in any way possible the fact that power has entered into a process of decomposition that will end up poisoning and corrupting society as a whole.[36]

Other arguments leave open the possibility that it may still be too early at this point in the history of the twentieth century to judge the situation in the USSR. That humanity, being still too alienated, or else—metaphysically speaking—being merely mortal, cannot exclude the future vindication of sacrifice. Precisely to the extent to which truth must inscribe itself concretely in the time and space of a specific situation, there exists no absolute vantage point from where it may be judged once and for all:

> It certainly must be repeated: truth is concrete in time and in space. It must be kept quiet or said in conformity with strict relations but never, for any concept or reason whatsoever, outside of these relations. We must see the facts with the desolate and intrepid courage of human beings, for this is why we are communists. The lapses, the injustices, and even the crimes that our cause has incurred are crimes, injustices, and lapses that our cause commits— no matter how pure and untouched by evil we conceive it to be—when it becomes a concrete truth for the human beings of an alienated age and time. It is the mutilated and preformed men of our time, men themselves, and

---

35.   Domínguez Michael, "Lepra y utopía," 65. Should we still add that these "Hegelian triads" are a posthumous invention in which neither Hegel nor Revueltas believed for a second, and that such "dialectical syntheses" and other phantoms of the same ilk exist only in the minds of readers such as Domínguez Michael? As a corrective, it is always useful to turn to Evodio Escalante's readings of the relation between Revueltas and Hegel—for example, in "El asunto de la inversión ideológica en las novelas de José Revueltas," in Francisco Ramírez Santacruz and Martín Oyata, eds, *El terreno de los días: Homenaje a José Revueltas* (Mexico City/Puebla: Miguel Angel Porrúa/Benemérita Universidad Autónoma de Puebla, 2007), 177–89.

36.   Revueltas, *Los errores*, 223–4.

among them the best, who become assassins by virtue of carrying in their hands the burning flame of that other concrete but more real—or in any case the only real—truth that is in fact transmissible. They will also be punished, of course, they will be punished even after their death. But in the meantime, history—and this is the case, whether we want or not, in an objective way— does not permit us to talk or denounce everything all the time: man does not find himself at the height that would allow him to resist the disenchantment of himself, let us put it that way, by the radical self-critique with which he would finally humanize himself.[37]

Finally, there seems in fact to come a moment for the justification of a heroic and sacrificial outlook on history:

> In light of this affirmation, nothing could appear for instance more impressive, more wrenchingly tremendous and beautiful, than the unprecedented sacrifice of the men who were sentenced to death in the Moscow trials, in their condition as victims consciously put on display to cover their names with ignominy, apparently an incomprehensible sacrifice, but for which it will be difficult to find even an approximate comparison in any other of the highest moments of human heroism from the past. Tomorrow history will vindicate these heroes, in spite of the errors, vacillations and weaknesses of their lives; these human beings who were able and knew how to accept the defaming stigma before the whole world, whose names are Bukharin, Piatakov, Rykov, Krestinski, Ter-Vaganyan, Smirnov, Sokolnikov, Zinoviev, Kamenev, Muralov, and so many others.[38]

All these interpretations, however, are not mutually exclusive, nor do they present a black-and-white picture of the ideological debate surrounding the Moscow trials. They sometimes invade the mind of a single character, dividing his inner sense with a terrifying uncertainty. This is the case of the communist intellectual Jacobo Ponce, who is on the verge of being expelled from the PCM—not unlike what happened, repeatedly, to Revueltas:

> The other part of his self, the other part of his atrociously divided spirit, replied to him: no, these concrete truths are only small and isolated lies in the process of a general reality that will continue its course, despite and above everything. The miseries, dirty tricks, and crimes of Stalin and his cohorts will be seen by tomorrow's communist society as an obscure and sinister disease of humanity from our time, from the tormented and delirious twentieth century that, all in all, will have been the century of the greatest and most inconceivable historical premonitions of humanity.[39]

From such ruminations, with their mixture of sinister premonition and sublime heroism, it is difficult to draw the simplistic conclusion that history, understood dialectically, would justify every possible means in the name of the communist end—or in the name of Stalin, as some of

---

37. Ibid., 198.
38. Ibid.
39. Ibid., 197–8.

Revueltas's detractors argue. Moreover, only a melodramatic imagination would define communism as a cause that is "pure and untouched by evil," to speak the language of *Los errores*, but this does not mean that we should move to the opposite extreme of the ideological spectrum so as to interpret evil as the profound truth of all militancy, which is the surest way to refute beforehand any future for the communist project.

In the final analysis, as in the quoted fragment above that seems to have given the novel its title, everything revolves around the status of errors: Is there or is there not sublation of the errors (mistakes, crimes, infamies) committed by history, in the sense of a dialectical *Aufhebung*? For those who reproach Revueltas for his blind confidence in the Hegelian dialectic, it would seem that the sheer idea of finding some sense or relevance in such errors only aggravates their criminal nature to the point of the abomination of justifying terror and totalitarianism. The problem with this indignant rejection of the possibility of sublating error, however, is that it leads to a position outside or beyond the history of communism. It interprets the errors as a definitive refutation of communism as such, in order henceforth to assert the cause of post-communism, or even anti-communism pure and simple. The Moscow trials, in this sense, play a role comparable to that of the Gulag, as described for the West by Aleksandr Solzhenitsyn, by leading to a defense of democratic liberalism as the only remedy against the repetition of radical Evil—that is, against the threat of so-called "totalitarianism," with its twin faces of Nazism and communism: Hitler and Stalin.

For Revueltas, as for someone like Badiou, the task consists in thinking the crimes from within the politics of communism, and not the other way around—not so as to ratify the facts with the stamp of historical inevitability, but so as to formulate an immanent critique that at the same time would avoid the simple abandonment of communism as such. "I would not want you to take these somewhat bitter reflections as yet more grist to the mill of the feeble moralizing that typifies the contemporary critique of absolute politics or 'totalitarianism,'" warns Badiou in his own Hegelian reading of the function of violence and semblance in the Moscow trials: "I am undertaking the exegesis of a singularity and of the greatness that belongs to it, even if the other side of this greatness, when grasped in terms of its conception of the real, encompasses acts of extraordinary violence."[40] What seems to be happening today, however, is a tendency to interrupt or, worse, to foreclose in anticipation any radical emancipatory project in the name of a new moral imperative—key to the "ethical turn" that globally defines the contemporary age from the 1980s onward, including within the so-called Left—which obliges us above all, if not exclusively, to avoid the repetition of the crime.

---

40. Badiou, *The Century*, 53.

Beautiful Souls

Morality is impotence in action.
Karl Marx and Friedrich Engels, The Holy Family

With *Los errores*, Revueltas may have become the unwitting accomplice of contemporary nihilism, which consists precisely in defining the Good only negatively by way of the need to avoid Evil. "Evil is that from which the Good is derived, not the other way round," as Badiou writes in his diagnosis of the ethical turn. "Nietzsche demonstrated very neatly that humanity prefers to will nothingness rather than to will nothing at all. I will reserve the name nihilism for this will to nothingness, which is like a counterpart of blind necessity."[41] In particular, there are two aspects of the debate regarding dogmatism in *Los errores* that run the risk of contributing to this complicity: the theme of the ethical role attributed to the party and the metaphysical, or more properly post-metaphysical, speculation about "man" or "humanity" (*el hombre*) as an erroneous being. Both of these themes obviously are presented in the hope of serving as possible correctives to the reigning dogmatism of Stalinism, but they could easily bring the reader to the point of adopting an ideological position that lies at the opposite extreme of the one its author upheld until his death just over thirty years ago.

Revueltas, on one hand, lets Jacobo Ponce, the character nearest to his own heart as an intellectual, devote most of his energy to the task of an ethical reflection about the party's authority. "The party as an ethical notion"—such is the topic of Jacobo's classes, against the orthodoxy of the party as the vanguard of the proletariat: "The party as a superior moral notion, not only in its role as political instrument but also as human consciousness, as the reappropriation of consciousness."[42] Thus, beyond the desire for reappropriation, or perhaps thanks to this desire, the critique of dogmatic reason already entails the temptation of a curious sense of moral superiority.

At the end of the novel, in the "Blind Knot" that serves as its epilogue, Ismael reaches the same conclusion as Jacobo: "The conclusion to be derived from this, if we introduce into our study of the problem the concepts of a humanist ethics, the concepts that stem from an ethical development of Marxism, can only be the most overwhelming and terrible conclusion, especially considering the parties that come

---

41. Alain Badiou, *Ethics: An Essay on the Understanding of Evil*, trans. Peter Hallward (London: Verso, 2001), 9, 30 (translation modified).

42. Revueltas, *Los errores*, 88. The question regarding the possible relations between Marxism and morals or ethics obviously has a long history. See, in particular, the anthology of texts by Marx edited by Maximilien Rubel, *Pages choisies pour une éthique socialiste* (Paris: Marcel Rivière, 1948). In Latin America, see above all José Carlos Mariátegui, *Defensa del marxismo* (Montevideo: Librosur, 1986).

into power."[43] The conclusion in question holds that the exercise of dogmatism on behalf of the "leading brains" of the communist movement, in Mexico as much as elsewhere in the world, with its "consoling tautology" that "the party is the party," in reality involves "the most absolute ethical nihilism, the negation of all ethics, ciphered in the concept: *to us everything is permitted*."[44]

If, on the other hand, "thought and practice . . . are identified as twin brothers in metaphysics and in dogma," then it is understandable that Jacobo, in addition to an ethical inflection of the party, would also propose a philosophico-anthropological reflection about "man as erroneous being."[45] This reflection is part of the "essay" in which Jacobo has invested "close to three months of conscientious and patient labor," no doubt similar to the labor it would take Revueltas a few years later to write his own unfinished and posthumous essay, *Dialéctica de la conciencia*. Jacobo reads from this text, which again is worth quoting at length so as to get a taste of the sheer syntactical complexity of the dialectical sentence:

> Man is an erroneous being—he began to read with his eyes, in silence; a being that never finishes by establishing itself anywhere; therein lies precisely his revolutionary and tragic, unpacifiable condition. He does not aspire to realize himself to another degree—and this is to say, in this he finds his supreme realization—to another degree—he repeated to himself—beyond what can have the thickness of a hair, that is, this space that for eternal eternity, and without their being a power capable of remedying this, will leave uncovered the maximum coincidence of the concept with the conceived, of the idea with its object: to reduce the error to a hair's breadth thus constitutes, at the most, the highest victory that he can obtain; nothing and nobody will be able to grant him exactitude. However, the space occupied in space and in time, in the cosmos, by the thickness of a hair, is an abyss without measure, more profound, more extensive, more tangible, less reduced, though perhaps more solitary, than the galaxy to which belongs the planet where this strange and hallucinating consciousness lives that we human beings are.[46]

What Jacobo proposes in this "essay" can be read as a new metaphysics—or rather an anti-metaphysics—of error and equivocity, against dogma and exactitude. Indeed, if the identity of being and thinking defines the basic premise of all metaphysical dogmatism, then human conscience or consciousness (*conciencia* in Spanish meaning both) can avoid dogmatism only by accepting an infinitesimal distance, or minimal gap, between the concept and the thing conceived.

We could say that Revueltas in *Los errores* accepts the need for a revision of the Hegelian dialectic in ways that are similar to what

43. Revueltas, *Los errores*, 271.
44. Ibid.. 272.
45. Ibid., 67.
46. Ibid., 67–8.

Adorno, around the same time, proposed with his "negative dialectics," according to which no concept ever completely covers its content without leaving behind some leftover, or remnant of nonidentity: "The name of dialectics says no more, to begin with, than that objects do not go into their concepts without leaving a remainder, that they come to contradict the traditional norm of adequacy."[47] Or, to use the almost perfectly comparable words of Badiou: "To begin with, a dialectical mode of thinking will be recognized by its conflict with representation. A thinking of this type pinpoints some unrepresentable point in its midst, which reveals that one touches upon the real."[48] Much of Revueltas's intellectual work as a novelist and a theorist during the 1960s and 1970s is devoted to such a reformulation of the dialectic, as the conception of the non-conceptual or the representation of the unrepresentable.

In the case of *Los errores*, however, it is not difficult to guess where the ethics of the party and the metaphysics of error will end up. Both arguments could in fact be invoked—not without taking on airs of moral superiority—in order to stop, interrupt, or prohibit any attempt to organize politics, as well as any project of approaching the truth of consciousness. Not only would all organizational matters then be displaced onto moral issues, which could be framed in terms of honesty and betrayal, or good and evil, but, what is more, this could even lead to a position for which the knowledge of our finitude—that is, our essential nature as "erroneous beings"—would always be morally superior and theoretically more radical that any given action, which in comparison cannot but appear "dogmatic," "totalitarian," "voluntaristic," and so on. In full melodramatic mode, we would end up with the attitude of the "beautiful soul" from Hegel's *Phenomenology of Spirit*:

> It lacks the power to externalize itself, the power to make itself into a Thing, and to endure [mere] being. It lives in dread of besmirching the splendour of its inner being by action and an existence; and, in order to preserve the purity of its heart, it flees from contact with the actual world, and persists in its self-willed impotence to renounce its self which is reduced to the extreme of ultimate abstraction, and to give itself a substantial existence, or to transform its thought into being and put its trust in the absolute difference [between thought and being]. The hollow object which it has produced for itself now fills it, therefore, with a sense of emptiness. Its activity is a yearning which merely loses itself as consciousness becomes an object devoid of substance, and, rising above this loss, and falling back on itself, finds itself only as a lost soul. In this transparent purity of its moments, an unhappy, so-called "beautiful soul," its light dies away with it, and it vanishes like a shapeless vapour that dissolves into thin air.[49]

---

47. Theodor W. Adorno, *Negative Dialectics*, trans. E. B. Ashton (New York: Continuum, 1990), 5.
48. Badiou, *Peut-on penser la politique?*, 86.
49. G. W. F. Hegel, *Phenomenology of Spirit*, trans. A. V. Miller (Oxford: Oxford University Press, 1977), 399–400.

This road toward the transparent beauty of good unhappy conscience based on the wisdom of our essential finitude, now openly post-communist if not actually anticommunist, may very well have been prefigured, unbeknownst to the author, in the double proposal of a humanist ethics of the party and a metaphysics of irreducible error. The history of the 1970s and 1980s, with its peremptory declarations of the "end of ideology," the "death" of Marxism, or the "ethical turn," would end up confirming the extent to which the defense of liberal democracy, with its absolute rejection of communism-as-totalitarianism, also adopted some of the features of this same "beautiful soul" who at least knows that its inactivity protects it from the Evil incurred by anyone intent upon imposing, here and now, some Good.

Indeed, in the decades following the publication of *Los errores*, the roles of ethics and politics seem to have been inverted. When Revueltas, through Jacobo and Ismael, speaks of an "ethics of the party" or an "ethics of Marxism," ethics is still subordinated to politics, keeping the latter in check. Ethics, in other words, would provide the political process with certain practical maxims for maintaining its consistency. At the same time, there seems to be a suggestion that there exists no ethics outside the concrete thought-practice of a party, league, or group: "There is no ethics in general. There are only—eventually—ethics of processes by which we treat the possibilities of a situation."[50] Such ethical considerations, however, can also become detached from the political processes in question, even to the point of subduing all politics as such. Here, then, we enter the terrain of a moralization of politics that no longer depends specifically on any militant procedure but that instead begins to undermine the sheer possibility of such forms of practice in general. This is because the new categorical imperative and the dominant moral judgment that it enables, whether of respect for the other or of compassion for the victim, teach us that the supreme value of our time consists in avoiding at all costs the production of more sacrificial victims. "Politics is subordinated to ethics, to the single perspective that really matters in this conception of things: the sympathetic and indignant judgement of the spectator of the circumstances," writes Badiou: "Such is the accusation so often repeated over the last fifteen years: every revolutionary project stigmatized as 'utopian' turns, we are told, into totalitarian nightmare. Every will to inscribe an idea of justice or equality turns bad. Every collective will to the Good creates Evil."[51]

Revueltas, with his tireless critique of communist dogmatism, may have opened the door for those moralizing discourses that, even in left-wing variations, can barely dissimulate their strong undercurrent of vulgar anticommunism. The challenge he bequeaths to us thus consists

---

50. Badiou, *Ethics*, 16.
51. Ibid., 9, 13.

in thinking the crimes of communism without converting the inevitability of error into the melodramatic premise for a complex of moral superiority that would deny that anything good might still emerge from Marxism—let alone from Hegelian Marxism.

Hegel's finitude and its role in the evaluation of Stalinist dogmatism should be revisited from the point of view of this historical outcome. The premise of the irreducibility of error, of the insuperable nature of alienation, and of the necessary inadequacy between concept and being, indeed runs through the entire finitist tradition of reading Hegel. Thus, central to Kojève's claim that Hegel is the first to attempt a complete atheist and finitist philosophy, we already find the idea that, on the phenomenological and anthropological level, such an attempt requires a view of "man" as an essentially erroneous being for whom being and thinking are never quite adequate to one another, or at least not yet:

> Being which *is* (in the Present) can be "conceived of" or revealed by the Concept. Or, more exactly, Being *is* conceived of at "each instant" of its being. Or else, again: Being is not only Being, but also *Truth*—that is, the adequation of the Concept and Being. This is simple. The whole question is to know where *error* comes from. In order that error be possible, the Concept must be *detached* from Being and *opposed* to it. It is Man who does this; and more exactly, Man *is* the Concept detached from Being; or better yet, he is the *act* of detaching the Concept from Being. He does so by negating-Negativity—that is, by Action, and it is here that the Future (the Pro-ject) enters in. This detaching is equivalent to an inadequation (the profound meaning of *errare humanum est*), and it is necessary to negate or act again in order to achieve conformity between the Concept (=Project) and Being (made to conform to the Project by Action). For Man, therefore, the adequation of Being and the Concept is a *process* (*Bewegung*), and the truth (*Wahrheit*) is a *result*. And only this "result of the process" merits the name of (discursive) "truth," for only this process is Logos or Discourse.[52]

The ability of human errors to survive, in fact, is what distinguishes man or the human being from nature, according to Kojève:

> If Nature happens to commit an error (the malformation of an animal, for example), it eliminates it *immediately* (the animal dies, or at least does not propagate). Only the errors committed by man *endure* indefinitely and are propagated at a distance, thanks to language. And man could be defined as an error that is preserved in existence, an error that *endures* within reality.

---

52. Alexandre Kojève, *Introduction to the Reading of Hegel: Lectures on the Phenomenology of Spirit Assembled by Raymond Queneau*, ed. Allan Bloom, trans. James H. Nichols, Jr (New York: Basic Books, 1969), 144 n. 34. I have also consulted the complete French edition, *Introduction à la lecture de Hegel* (Paris: Gallimard, 1947). I am much indebted to Evodio Escalante for first putting me on the track of Kojève's Hegel in the context of my reading of *Los errores*. For Kojève's interpretation of Hegel's philosophy as atheist and finitist, see the long footnote in which he also compares Hegel to Heidegger, on the last page of the English edition (259 n. 41).

Now, since *error* means *disagreement* with the real; since what is *other* than what is, is *false*, one can also say that the man who errs is a Nothingness that nihilates in Being, or an "ideal" that is present in the real.[53]

What is more, it is only thanks to, and not in spite of, our essentially human tendency to err that truth is possible. Otherwise, without the possibility of human error, being would be mute facticity. As Kojève adds: "Therefore, there is really a *truth* only where there *has been* an error. But error exists really only in the form of human discourse."[54] Or, to use Hegel's own words from the *Encyclopedia*, in one of Adorno's favorite formulations: "Only out of this error does the truth arise. In this fact lies the reconciliation with error and with finitude. Error or other-being, when superseded, is still a necessary dynamic element of truth: for truth can only be where it makes itself its own result."[55]

For Kojève, unlike what is the case for Adorno or Revueltas, true wisdom famously will bring about the perfect adequation of being and concept in the figure of the sage at the end of history. This also means that finitude, conscious of itself, passes over into the infinite; any additional act or action, then, is superfluous. By contrast, in the absence of any ultimate reconciliation, it would appear that philosophy or theory survives only in and through error, through the gap between the concept and its object or between representation and the real, a gap that is thus not merely temporary or accidental but constitutive of the possibility of knowing anything at all. And yet, if it is indeed the case that finitude today constitutes a new dogma that—rather than rendering the act superfluous—blocks all action so as to avoid the trappings of radical evil, should we not also invert this conclusion regarding the irreducibility of error by reaffirming the identity of being and thinking in the good old fashion of Parmenides? Perhaps as nowhere else, Revueltas will explore this possibility through his own notion of the profound act, or *acto profundo*, in "Hegel y yo" ("Hegel and I"). To understand the problem for which this story appears to provide a solution, however, we will first have to

---

53. Ibid., 187.
54. Ibid., 188. We should note that there are actually two types of error in Hegel for Kojève: the inevitable erring that is part of our human condition; but also error as mistake or superable defect, as when Hegel posits the dialecticity not only of History but also of Nature: "Hegel commits, in my opinion, a grave error. From the fact that the real Totality is dialectical he concludes that its two fundamental constituent-elements, which are Nature and Man (=History), are dialectical" (212–13, n. 15). Of course, Kojève's attempt to correct Hegel's error on this score with the reference to Heidegger's ontology is precisely the gesture that prepares the current dominance of the matrix of finitude.
55. Hegel quoted in Adorno, *Hegel: Three Studies*, trans. Shierry Weber Nicholsen (Cambridge: MIT Press, 1994), 93. Adorno subsequently offers his own version of this principle: "Within the system, and in terms of the laws of the system, the truth of the nonidentical manifests itself as error, as unresolved, in the other sense of being unmastered, as the untruth of the system, and nothing that is untrue can be understood. Thus the incomprehensible explodes the system" (147).

consider Revueltas's most ambitious theoretical work, comparable to the "essay" being written by Jacobo Ponce in *Los errores*—that is, the unfinished manuscripts and notes for the posthumously published *Dialéctica de la conciencia*.

3

ON THE SUBJECT OF THE DIALECTIC

Not All Theory Is Gray

What the enormous effort put into *Dialéctica de la conciencia* suggests is first and foremost the author's conviction that perhaps not all theoretical work is dull or superfluous, despite the fact that, from personal reflections and diary entries jotted down in the heat of the moment during and right after the events of 1968 in Mexico, Revueltas seems to have been rather fond of Goethe's one-liner according to which, in comparison with the golden tree of life, all theory is but a gray and deadening undertaking. "Gris es toda teoría," without the latter half of the original sentence, "verde es el árbol de oro de la vida," in fact serves as the recurrent header for a number of these reflections, published posthumously under the title *México 68: Juventud y revolución*: "All theory is gray, the golden tree of life is green."[1] The quote, which also appears as an inscription on Revueltas's tombstone, may remind some readers of Lenin's famous witticism, written just one month after the events of October 1917 in the Postscript to *The State and Revolution*, that "it is more pleasant and useful to undertake the 'experience of revolution' than to write about it."[2] Nowadays, this downplaying of theoretical writing, whether in favor of direct experience or of life pure and simple, would no doubt sit well with many critics, especially those who would be all too happy to oppose in very similar terms the green pastures of literary and cultural studies to the drab landscape of so-called theory. And yet, in all cases we should perhaps be wary of drawing too quick a conclusion about the significance of theoretical work, or the lack thereof.

---

1. José Revueltas, *México 68: Juventud y revolución*, ed. Andrea Revueltas and Philippe Cheron (Mexico City: Era, 1978). It is José Emilio Pacheco who restitutes the complete version of Goethe's phrase, in his prologue "Revueltas y el árbol de oro," in *Las evocaciones requeridas (Memorias, diarios, correspondencia)*, ed. Andrea Revueltas and Philippe Cheron (Mexico City: Era, 1987), vol. 1, 11–12. Pacheco also expresses his surprise at finding a predilection for this phrase in "the novelist with the most theoretical mentality that ever existed" (11).
2. V. I. Lenin, *The State and Revolution*, trans. Robert Service (London: Penguin, 1992), 111.

Lenin, to begin with, is also the author of another one-liner that was constantly invoked during the worldwide sequence of events of the late 1960s and early 1970s, by anyone from Che Guevara to followers of Chairman Mao: "Without revolutionary theory there can be no revolutionary movement."[3] Like Lenin, who considered the study of Hegel's notoriously difficult *Science of Logic* no less vital a task than answering the question of *What Is to Be Done?*, most of Revueltas's work during the final years of his life, many of which were spent in captivity in the Lecumberri prison for his alleged role as one of the intellectual instigators of the 1968 student-popular movement, was devoted to what can only be described as an ongoing effort of theoretical speculation. This is particularly evident in *Dialéctica de la conciencia*. The intense intellectual labor displayed in the pages of this often obscure volume should serve as a warning that, for a theoretician, it is not necessarily the case that the neighbor's grass is always greener. Or, rather, if we are to follow in Hegel's footsteps, the grayness of theory and philosophy may well have a function all of its own—not to celebrate the eternal fountain of life, of novelty, and of rejuvenation, but to come to know *what is*, just before it turns into the massive inertia of *what was*, at the hour of dusk. "When philosophy paints its grey in grey, then has a shape of life grown old. By philosophy's grey on grey it cannot be rejuvenated but only understood," Hegel writes in the Preface to his *Philosophy of Right*: "The owl of Minerva spreads its wings only with the falling of the dusk."[4] As for linguistic obscurity, Revueltas had this to say in one of his last interviews:

What happens is something that Ernst Bloch explains with regard to the "obscure" language of Hegel: it is obscurity imposed for reasons of precision, says Bloch. We should remember that the obscure, expressed as such with exactitude, is something completely different from the clear, expressed with obscurity . . . The first is adequate precision for what is said and sayable . . . The second, pretension and dilettantism.[5]

---

3. See, for example, Ernesto "Che" Guevara, *Obra revolucionaria*, ed. Roberto Fernández Retamar (Mexico City: Era, 1963), 507; or Mao Tsetung, *Five Essays on Philosophy* (Beijing: Foreign Languages Press, 1977), 58.

4. G. W. F. Hegel, *Philosophy of Right*, trans. T. M. Knox (London: Oxford University Press, 1967), 13. We might also think of Michel Foucault when he writes, "Genealogy is grey, meticulous, and patiently documentary. It operates on a field of entangled and confused parchments, on documents that have been scratched over and recopied many times," in "Nietzsche, Genealogy, History," *Language, Counter-Memory, Practice: Selected Essays and Interviews by Michel Foucault*, ed. Donald F. Bouchard (Ithaca: Cornell University Press, 1977), 139. My thanks to Rodrigo Mier for bringing these colorful resonances to my attention.

5. Revueltas quoted by Andrea Revueltas, "Aproximaciones a la obra teórico-política de José Revueltas," *Revueltas en la mira* (Mexico City: UAM/Molinos de Viento, 1984), 98 *n*. 2. Ernst Bloch's original comment can be found in *Sujeto-objeto: El pensamiento de Hegel*, trans. Wenceslao Roces (Mexico City: Fondo de Cultura Económica, 1983), 23.

On our end, finally, the newfound resistance to, or weariness with, theory, combined with a flourishing enthusiasm for cultural studies, can at least in part be explained by a failure to absorb exactly the kind of intellectual work found in writings such as these posthumous ones by Revueltas. Perhaps, then, by returning to these writings, we receive a chance not only to resurrect a colossal but largely neglected figure in the political and intellectual history of the twentieth century, but also to make a case, over and above the wholesale assumption of the model of cultural studies, for the simultaneous foundation of a model of critical theory in, and from, Latin America. Cultural criticism and critical theory, from this point of view, do not come to stand in stark opposition so much as they can begin to operate in terms of a productive disjunction within each of the two fields—neither of which lives up to its promise without the polemical input of the other. One urgent task, in my view, consists in an unremitting effort to return to those fragmented and often forgotten discussions, such as the ones left unanswered and unfinished by Revueltas, which in this case tackle the functions of culture, ideology, and politics in the name of a certain Karl Marx.

Cogito and the Unconscious

The fundamental question, of course, remains: Which Marx? At first, the answer to this question may appear to be fairly straightforward in the case of Revueltas. *Dialéctica de la conciencia* would thus simply present us with one more variation on the theme of humanism in the so-called "young Marx," the one associated principally with the *Economic and Philosophic Manuscripts of 1844,* for whom the alienation and reappropriation of our human essence would constitute the core principle of communism. Rather than seeking to locate the source of the dialectic in the objectivity of nature, as Engels would later attempt somewhat desperately in his *Anti-Dühring*, Marx in his *Manuscripts of 1844* starts out from, and ultimately promises what it would mean to return to, the human subject as a generic being, or species-being. Such would also be the beginning and end of the dialectic adopted by Revueltas. In fact, as Jorge Fuentes Morúa amply demonstrates in his recent intellectual biography, *José Revueltas: una biografía intelectual*, the author of *Dialéctica de la conciencia* was one of the very first intellectuals in any part of the world to study and appreciate the critical importance of Marx's *Manuscripts*, which were already published in Mexico by the end of 1937, in a Spanish version that is now impossible to find, under the title *Economía política y filosofía*, translated by two exiles from Nazi Germany:

> Revueltas used *Economía política y filosofía*; we have been able to study his annotations to this book. These glosses give us insight into the questions that attracted the author's attention with greatest intensity. These interests

of a philosophical nature, which were developed in his literary, political, and theoretical texts, refer in substance to different perspectives on alienation and the situation of the human being when confronted with the development of capitalism and technology.[6]

Fuentes Morúa is thus able to follow up on his painstaking bibliographical reconstruction by reaffirming the centrality of the concepts of alienation and reification in both narrative and theoretical writings by Revueltas, tracing their influence back to the philosophical anthropology found in Marx's 1844 *Manuscripts*.

To this reading of the presence of the early Marx in Revueltas, we all know from our textbooks how to oppose the rigorous anti-humanism of the school of Althusser, Lacan, or Foucault. In fact, according to the author of *For Marx*, the very notion of a dialectic of consciousness is devoid of all meaning. "For there is no true critique which is not immanent and already real and material before it is conscious," Althusser writes on the occasion of his analysis of Brechtian theater, to which he adds the following key principle:

> If we carry our analysis of this condition a little further we can easily find in it Marx's fundamental principle that it is impossible for any form of ideological consciousness to contain in itself, through its own internal dialectic, an escape from itself, that, *strictly speaking, there is no dialectic of consciousness*: no dialectic of consciousness which could reach reality itself by virtue of its own contradictions; in short, there can be no "phenomenology" in the Hegelian sense: for consciousness does not accede to the real through its own internal development, but by the radical discovery of what is *other than itself*.[7]

In short, any dialectic would have to come to terms with the radical discovery of a certain unconscious as the real or material *other* of consciousness. Instead of the transparency of man as self-present subject, this alternative version of the materialist dialectic would posit the primordial opacity and externality of certain symbolic structures, often under the influence of a new appreciation of psychoanalysis. Indeed, if we follow Lacan, this is precisely how we might define the unconscious: "This exteriority of the symbolic with regard to man is the very notion of the unconscious."[8]

Cogito or the unconscious, the subject or the structure: in all their simplified glory, these now familiar alternatives sum up what remains perhaps the last really great politico-philosophical battle in the twentieth century—a true example, moreover, of the Althusserian notion that

---

6. Jorge Fuentes Morúa, *José Revueltas: Una biografía intelectual* (Mexico City: UAM Iztapalapa/Miguel Angel Porrúa, 2001), 157.

7. Althusser, *For Marx*, 143.

8. Jacques Lacan, "The Situation of Psychoanalysis and the Training of Psychoanalysts in 1956," in *Écrits*, trans. Bruce Fink (New York: W. W. Norton, 2006), 391.

"philosophy represents the class struggle in theory."[9] In its most extreme and vitriolic form, this polemic quickly turned out to be a *diálogo de sordos* opposing the "bourgeois humanists" who followed the young Marx of the *Manuscripts of 1844* to the "dogmatic neo-Stalinists" who stuck to the mature and scientific Marx of *Capital*. Hegel, in this context, is often little more than a codename to denounce the persistence of humanist and idealist elements in the early Marx. Both in France and abroad, as in much of Latin America, Sartre and Althusser gave this polemic the impetus of their lifelong work and the aura of their proper names. As Alain Badiou writes:

> When the mediations of politics are clear, it is the philosopher's imperative to subsume them in the direction of a foundation. The last debate in this matter opposed the tenants of liberty, as founding reflective transparency, to the tenants of the structure, as prescription of a regime of causality. Sartre against Althusser: this meant, at bottom, the Cause against the cause.[10]

There would seem to be little doubt as to where exactly in this debate, or on which side, we should place Revueltas, since he had nothing but scorn for Althusser while he constantly expressed his admiration for Sartre. In reality, however, things are not as straightforward or as clear-cut as they first appear.

In a lucid Preface to *Dialéctica de la conciencia*, Henri Lefebvre draws our attention to this very debate regarding the foundation or ground of the dialectic. He concludes by highlighting the originality of the answer given by Revueltas: "From Engels to Revueltas, there occurs not only a change in perspective and meaning but also a polar inversion. Instead of being encountered in the *object* (nature), the foundation of the dialectic is discovered in the *subject*."[11] This conclusion would seem to confirm the initial suspicion about the understanding of the dialectic in the traditional humanist terms of liberty, consciousness, and the transparency of the self. Lefebvre, however, continues his remarks by immediately insisting on the subject's internal contradictions:

> Revueltas shows that this is not an effect of language, a disorder of discourse, a residual absurdity but, on the contrary, a situation, or better yet, a concatenation of situations, inherent in the *subject* as such: by reason of the fact that it is not a substance (as is the case for Cartesians) nor a result (as is the case

---

9. Louis Althusser, *Lenin and Philosophy and Other Essays*, trans. Ben Brewster (New York: Monthly Review Press, 1971), 18. For a critical discussion of the theoretical anti-humanism of Althusser's Marxism from the point of view of Latin America, see Adolfo Sánchez Vásquez, *Ciencia y revolución: El marxismo de Althusser* (Madrid: Alianza, 1978); for a sophisticated defense, see Emilio de Ípola, *Althusser, el infinito adiós* (Buenos Aires: Siglo Veintiuno, 2007).
10. Badiou, *Peut-on penser la politique?*, 10.
11. Henri Lefebvre, "Prólogo," in José Revueltas, *Dialéctica de la conciencia*, ed. Andrea Revueltas and Philippe Cheron (Mexico City: Era, 1982), 14.

for vulgar materialists and naturalists) but a specific activity as well as a complex and contradictory knot of relations to "the other," of initiatives, memory, adhesion to the present and projects for the time to come.[12]

Clearly much more is involved in this understanding of the dialectic than either a mere change in perspective, or even an inversion between substance and subject. In fact, the subject's consciousness, reason, or self-presence is always situated in tense contradiction with its internal other: the unconscious, unreason, or negativity. This contradictory unity is precisely what defines the dialectic, as opposed to a merely logical understanding of polar opposites in an inert relation of mutual externality or antinomy. "Revueltas shows the contradictions 'in the act' according to how they operate in consciousness," Lefebvre adds, before hinting at a surprising family resemblance in this regard between Revueltas and the work of certain members of the Frankfurt School: "At certain moments Revueltas' quest comes close to Adorno's 'negative dialectics.' Most often he distances himself from it, but along a path that leads in the same direction."[13] Following this useful lead, I want to examine in more detail where this path actually takes us. Rather than seeking an approximation with Adorno, however, I will in the end suggest that the posthumous writings of Revueltas in fact show more elective affinities with the thought of Walter Benjamin.

In any event, instead of accepting the familiar schemes with which intellectual historians try to pigeonhole what they often disparagingly call "the thought of '68,"[14] we should come to grasp how subject and structure, not unlike Marxism and psychoanalysis in general, stand to each other in a relation of antagonistic articulation through the scission or separation of each of the two terms. Thus, if among later Althusserians the systematic formalization of the structure under certain conditions, which they call events, pinpoints a symptomatic blindness, or incompleteness, the presence of which already presupposes the inscription of a subject, then conversely we can expect to find remnants of the opacity of the structure, or what Sartre would have called elements of the practico-inert, in the midst of the subject's efforts at reaching consciousness. Hegel himself, in fact, had already hinted at this possibility of seeing the first role of the subject, of spirit, or of the I, not as a schoolbook example of synthesis and sublation, but as the power to split reality into the real and the unreal, the power to sunder the concrete according to the actual and the non-actual, which is but another way of expressing the force of the *other* of consciousness, of death even, *within* consciousness itself. "For it is only because the

---

12. Revueltas, *Dialéctica de la conciencia*, 14.
13. Ibid., 13–14.
14. Luc Ferry and Alain Renaut, *French Philosophy of the Sixties: An Essay on Antihumanism*, trans. Marc H. S. Cattani (Amherst: University of Massachusetts Press, 1990).

concrete does divide itself, and make itself into something non-actual, that it is self-moving. The activity of separation is the power and work of understanding, the most astonishing and mightiest of powers, or rather the absolute power," Hegel famously wrote in his Preface to the *Phenomenology of Spirit*:

> The circle that remains self-enclosed and, like substance, holds its moments together, is an immediate relationship, one therefore which has nothing astonishing about it. But that an accident as such, detached from what circumscribes it, what is bound and is actual only in its context with others, should attain an existence of its own and a separate freedom—this is the tremendous power of the negative; it is the energy of thought, of the pure "I."[15]

Rather than opposing subject and substance as two self-enclosed circles without intersection, the real task of the dialectic must therefore consist in coming to grips with the articulation of the two through the internal division of their oneness.

For Revueltas, consciousness always follows a logic of uneven development and only on rare occasions reaches moments of identity, or near identity, with the real. There is always a lag, a gap, or an anachronism, leading to spectral or phantasmatic structures of social consciousness. In a text on "The Present Significance of the Russian October Revolution," also published in *Dialéctica de la conciencia*, Revueltas repeatedly insists on this unevenness:

> What is especially important is to notice that such relations (between rational consciousness and *praxis*) are *uneven* and they act in relations of identity only in determinate *moments* of historical development (moments which, in their most elevated expression, can be counted in years). But even such identity is never absolute, since in every case, in order to act upon praxis (and convert itself into praxis), rational consciousness is mediated by *ideology* or ideologies.[16]

More often than not, reason and ideology are intertwined; in order to become practical, all truths must pass through a moment of ideology. At the same time, there are also contradictions, not just *between* consciousness and social being or practice, but *within* consciousness as such, due to the persistence of forms of division, hierarchy, and alienation within reason. In several texts from *México 68*, this process is described in terms of a divide, or a dialectical contradiction, between consciousness, or *conciencia*, and knowledge, or *conocimiento*. "Consciousness knows itself *in the act* but it ignores the nature of the known. This fact carries with it the insertion of a contradiction between consciousness and knowledge," Revueltas writes, to which he adds a long explanation:

---

15. Hegel, *Phenomenology of Spirit*, 13–14.
16. Revueltas, *Dialéctica de la conciencia*, 219.

The question turns out to be not so simple when we approach the knowledge of consciousness from the point of view of its *internal* nature, as
constant mobility and transformation, and *externally*, as contradiction
and alienation. As mobility and transformation, consciousness is always
unhappy with what knowledge provides it with. This changes what it
knows (it discovers new data and reveals what is hidden beneath its new
objectivity) but it also transforms consciousness itself and submits it to the
anxiety of absolute non-knowledge, to the extreme point where a given
impotence could turn it into an unreal consciousness. As for the external,
its externalization, consciousness is in itself and in its *other*, in the form of
religion, civil society, the state, as consciousness alienated from itself that
no longer knows itself, in this exteriorization, as individual and free
consciousness in itself. The state, religion, civil society are the consciousness of itself of *the others*, accumulated throughout time by historical
knowledge.[17]

Reason here has to come to grips with its intrinsic other. In fact, its
concrete movement is nothing but the process of its own self-splitting.
Far from singing the stately glories of spirit as self-consciousness fully
coming into its own, the dialectic tells the story of this ongoing scission
between consciousness and knowledge, as well as between cogito and
the unconscious. Such a story, which makes for an almost impossible
narrative, always involves the risk of absolute non-knowledge, irre-
trievable anxiety, or downright madness.

Finally, one important corollary of this internally divided nature
of consciousness is that, just as there lies a rational kernel even
within ideology, radical or revolutionary thought can also become
alienated into mere ideology, which it always carries with it as a
shadow. At this moment, the split nature of all elements of the dialectic is erased in favor of a false purity: ideology without reason, or
revolutionary reason without the truth of practice. "Every ideology,
without exception, reaches a point where, by virtue of its proper
nature as ideology, it must renounce all criticism, that is, the 'rational
kernel' of which it could avail itself in the periods of revolutionary
ascent, given its conditions as consciousness alienated onto a concrete
praxis."[18] For Revueltas, this last moment is precisely the one that
defines the crisis of Marxism after the death of Lenin, and even more
so after the watershed year of 1927, when the living ghost of Trotsky
started to wander in exile through much of Europe, before meeting
his untimely death in Mexico. It is also the moment, however, when
ideology lost its rational kernel, and the road was opened for a
maddening and suicidal exasperation of the conflict, which increasingly threatened to become nuclear, between the United States and
the Soviet Union.

---

17. Revueltas, *México 68*, 115.
18. Revueltas, *Dialéctica de la conciencia*, 225.

Marx in his Limits

Indeed, another way of addressing the complex question of how to situate this writer's theoretical work would be to draw out all the consequences of the otherwise unsurprising fact that for Revueltas, by the early 1970s, Marxism was caught in a deep crisis. In this sense, too, Revueltas is much closer to Althusser than either one of them—or, for that matter, any of their critics—would be willing to admit. "Marx in his Limits,"[19] the heading under which, in the 1970s, Althusser collected many of his thoughts that were to be published only after his death, could thus very well serve as a subtitle for the posthumous *Dialéctica de la conciencia* as well. Revueltas is certainly not proposing an uncritical return to some pristine orthodoxy or hidden doctrinal kernel of the early Marx. The aim is rather more contorted, as can be gleaned from the proposed plan of study that is included in the latter half of the book by way of framing its impressive range of notes, quotes, and interpretive glosses, most of them written between 1968 and 1971 in Mexico City's Lecumberri prison. If Revueltas sought to come to terms with the fundamental concepts of alienation, consciousness, and the philosophy of praxis implied in the *Manuscripts* of the young Marx, this was primarily in order to provide himself with the means to understand the dogmatic and revisionist deformations of the dialectic in the latter half of the twentieth century, at the hands of so-called vulgar, uncritical, or non-reflective Marxism. Marx's theory of alienation and ideology thus serves as a critical tool with which to analyze, and hopefully undo the effects of, the ideological alienation of Marxism itself.

Along this complex trajectory Revueltas found a symptomatic turning point precisely in the split between the early Marx and other Young Hegelians such as Bruno Bauer, Ludwig Feuerbach or Arnold Ruge. As he wrote in his "General Plan of Study": "It is a question of leading this investigation toward a clarification of the current crisis of Marxism. The point of departure for this investigation is situated at the moment of transition when Marxism discerns itself as such, separating itself from critical philosophy by extending the latter to society and its economic foundations."[20] In the operations with which critical philosophy becomes first dialectical, and then materialist, a logic of the social is contained that, once it is cut off from the concrete understanding of society as a contradictory totality, might paradoxically serve to explain the principles of its very own deformation. Revueltas finds this process at work not only in the official doctrine of Stalinism or in the inertia of many Soviet-oriented Communist parties, but also in the ideological radicalism of another typical product of the 1960s: the ultraleftist

---

19. Althusser, "Marx in his Limits," in *Philosophy of the Encounter*, 7–162.
20. Revueltas, *Dialéctica de la conciencia*, 86.

groups, or *grupúsculos*, throughout much of Europe and Latin America. One of the early titles for the main text in *Dialéctica de la conciencia* hinted precisely at this secondary aspect of the crisis of Marxism: *La locura brujular del marxismo en México (ensayo ontológico sobre los grupúsculos marxistas)*.[21] This ambitious plan to arrive at a dialectical ontology of group formations, which is much indebted to Sartre's project in his own unfinished *Critique of Dialectical Reason* (the first volume of which is significantly subtitled *Theory of Practical Ensembles*), obviously did not come to full fruition in Revueltas's notes for *Dialéctica de la conciencia*. But the reader will find long passages in which the internal crisis of critical consciousness, as explained through the notion of thought's self-alienation and disorientation, is tied to the proliferation of extreme left-wing groups, all proclaiming their fidelity to an hyper-ideological form of Marxism.

Let us look in more detail at a brief instance of this self-reflexive critique of Marxism. As a starting point, the theoretical activity of consciousness can be situated on two levels, or as two kinds of act: "To put this in the most general way, theory functions by way of two acts that belong to the same process of knowledge. First, in those who think theory and confront it with itself as abstract thought; and, second, concretely, as praxis, when it adequately, that is, in ways consistent with itself, transforms the object proposed to it."[22] Whenever this regime of consistency is interrupted, the inner necessity of the concept, from being a moving restlessness, turns into the baleful objectivity of the practico-inert. For Revueltas, it is in this gap, in this "no man's land" between a sequence of thought and its logical consequences, that the "false consciousness" of so-called vulgar or uncritical Marxism finds its niche. In a passage that is worth quoting extensively, if for no other reason than to give a sense of his idiosyncratic style, Revueltas continues:

> The internal contradictions of knowledge that are unresolved (that do not resolve themselves) in their immediate becoming, in different ways, give way to certain inevitable fissures between a proposed (that is, not yet given) sequence and its consequence within the process, which establishes a provisionally empty space, a kind of "no man's land," which interposes itself between the prefiguration of the concept and the objective reality that has not yet been conceptualized. Thus, in a true act of usurpation of the rights of rationality, "false consciousness" with its hosts occupies this "no man's land" of knowledge and declares over it its absolute dogmatic sovereignty. Such is the point where, under the protection of said sovereignty, this concrete self-sufficient form of being flourishes, self-absorbed and impermeable to questioning, that represents the false consciousness of vulgar Marxism. Hence, the examination of contradictions will allow us to clarify the fact—hidden underneath all kinds of demagogic and leftist phrases— that practice without *praxis* is nothing but a maddening sense of

21. Ibid., 15.
22. Ibid., 19.

disorientation, a loss of the magnetic pole of knowledge—which defines, however, in essence, the activity of "Marxist" groupuscles and of vulgar Marxism as a whole, from which fatally follows an objective deformation of the revolutionary processes, with the correlative succession of the great historical defeats suffered by the working class during the last decades in Mexico.[23]

We can thus observe how it is through a dialectical theory of the inherent contradictions between consciousness and its *other*, as well as of their transformation into their opposites, that Revueltas seeks to reconstruct the crisis of Marxism based on his own readings of Marx from the time of the latter's split with the Young Hegelians.

The Dialectic Revisited

Everything in this context ultimately depends on our understanding of what is meant by dialectical thinking. "The point is to be clear about the subject of the dialectic," Badiou also writes: "The dialecticity of the dialectic consists precisely in having a conceptual history and in dividing the Hegelian matrix to the point where it turns out to be essentially a doctrine of the event, and not the guided adventure of the spirit. A politics, rather than a history."[24] Thus, when Revueltas wrote to his daughter Andrea, "We must return to Hegel's *Phenomenology*, whether we want to or not,"[25] or when he wrote to her in another letter, "We have to go back openly to Hegel, to the young Marx and to political economy 'beyond' *Capital*, that is to say, to the 'ignored' Marxism, the Marxism that was bracketed for over fifty years and not only by Stalinism," his aim was still to come to a concrete understanding of the notion of the dialectic: "All the contradictions of Marxism in Mexico can be summed up as resistance to, and ignorance of, the dialectic."[26] How, then, does Revueltas define the dialectic?

Right from the beginning of *Dialéctica de la conciencia*, Revueltas may very well have seemed to echo Sartre's position, in the latter's polemic with Heidegger, that it is above all a question of man—that is, a question not of being but of the human being. In his case, however, the affirmation "Ante todo se trata de la cuestión hombre" is immediately followed by the question "Pero, en fin, ¿qué es el hombre?"—to which the author of the *Critique of Hegel's Philosophy of Right* is allowed to reply: "Karl Marx proposes to us an illuminating answer.

---

23. Ibid., 22–3. Compare with Lacan: "One could have foreseen the results, in which the imaginary, in order to rejoin reality [*réel*], must find the no man's land that provides access to it by effacing the border between them," "The Situation of Psychoanalysis," 389.
24. Badiou, *Peut-on penser la politique?*, 84.
25. José Revueltas, *Cuestionamientos e intenciones: ensayos*, ed. Andrea Revueltas and Philippe Cheron (Mexico City: Era, 1978), vol. 2, 252.
26. Revueltas, *Las evocaciones requeridas*, vol. 2, 244; and *Dialéctica de la conciencia*, 246 n. 4.

'Man is the world of men,' he says. The world of human beings—in other words, society, its modes of production, religion, the state: a changing world which has never been the same throughout its history."[27] It is at this point that the otherwise traditional, humanist, or idealist image of Hegel's method is displaced by the search for a materialist dialectic of society as a concrete and contradictory totality. How, then, can we come to *know* this apparently unknowable totality that constitutes the proper object of dialectical reason? Revueltas does not answer this last question in any straightforward manner. Instead, in the remaining pages of the full draft of his essay, he weaves the discussion in and out of three examples, which he prefers to call "cognitive anecdotes," derived respectively from the postal system, from archaeology, and from architecture.

The essential determination of society as an object of thought cannot be discerned in the immediate knowledge of the senses: "You should not look for it in the direct and immediate report of the senses but in a vast and complex set of internal relations and correlations."[28] This much larger horizon, however, remains as invisible or unknowable to our everyday thoughts and habits as the complete functioning of the postal system is for the individual who absentmindedly drops off a letter in the mail:

> Our individual has written a letter, he has "worked" on it, but he ignores the fact that this whole vast set of activities (writing, sealing the letter, buying stamps and attaching them, depositing the letter into a postbox) is inserted within a mass of *human work* that is common, general, total, constant, active, past, present, and historical in the most plastic sense of the word, this invisible matter in which the lines of communication are drawn and draw themselves, from the time when one of them discovered himself in "the others" and succeeded in inventing and emitting the first "signs of identity," a first scream, a first smoke signal, a first letter. The postal system reveals nothing to our individual, even though it allows him at least to be this human being in whom he does not yet perceive himself, but in whom he no doubt will one day come to perceive himself as soon as he assumes consciousness of it.[29]

What Revueltas is after in this, as well as in the other two passages, is not so much an orthodox, Lukácsian or Kosikian, totality as the identical subject-object of history, but rather something more along the lines of a cognitive map, or a situational understanding of the system, as defined in more recent years by Fredric Jameson.

---

27. Revueltas, *Dialéctica de la conciencia*, 25. Marx's statement can be found in his "Introduction" to the "Contribution to the Critique of Hegel's Philosophy of Law," *Collected Works*, vol. 3, 175. See also the sixth of Marx's "Theses on Feuerbach": "But the essence of man is no abstraction inherent in each single individual. In its reality it is the ensemble of the social relations," in *Collected Works*, vol. 5, 7.
28. Revueltas, *Dialéctica de la conciencia*, 28.
29. Ibid.

If we turn now to the second case, in which an archaeologist decides to employ a group of local bricklayers to help him with the task of digging up the objects on his site, a split immediately sets apart the manual labor of the diggers from the larger cultural and intellectual knowledge regarding the objects of their labor. The diggers are thus deprived of the consciousness involved in their very own labor. Revueltas insists, however, in this case even more so than in the brief example of the letter-writer, that these bricklayers now turned into anthropological laborers, too, are perhaps on the verge of a special kind of consciousness:

> Nevertheless, what happened to them in the passage from one job to the other has an extraordinary meaning. The "world of men" placed them *socially* as "anthropological laborers," in a situation where they were "on the verge of" realizing a true human form of labor, "on the verge of" converting themselves into real *human beings* and not only because of the fact—which they will have commented upon with mocking joy—of having served for some days for this "crazy guy" who contracted them for a strange and incomprehensible activity, and paid them, to boot, with an unusual generosity. They were "on the verge," yes, but this "on the verge" stayed there, suspended, without resolving itself, like a phantasmatic emanation above the anthropological work that *disappeared*, in the same way that the vagrant flames of *fuegos fatuos* float over the graves of a cemetery. However, such being "on the verge" repeats itself and remains in the labor of bricklaying to which they returned, because in a certain sense and in a new but essential form, they continue to be "anthropologists" on their job as housebuilders.[30]

Nothing ever seems to be lost for good when it comes to the consciousness of human work. For the most part, however, even while being perhaps indestructible, the common mass of generic human labor vanishes or evaporates into the depths of a spectral or phantasmatic type of memory, a collective yet transhistorical memory that is closer to the unconscious than to consciousness, and in which experiences are accumulated, preserved, and repeated from time immemorial, until those rare moments when, as in a sudden act of awakening, they re-enter the field of vision.

Freud and Lacan had already insisted on the indestructible nature of the unconscious. The memory of desire is unlike any other form or kind of memory, precisely because of the fact that nothing is ever forgotten by desire. Lacan thus recalls that Freud's discovery is very much bound up with the discovery of "the inextinguishable duration of desire, a feature of the unconscious which is hardly the least paradoxical, even though Freud never gives it up."[31] For Lacan, of course, the locus of this peculiar kind of memory is none other than a certain

30. Ibid.
31. Lacan, "The Situation of Psychoanalysis and the Training of Psychoanalysts in 1956," 391.

automatism of language itself. It is inscribed in traces, archives, bodies, and traditions as in a machine-like structure, or on a magical writing pad similar to the one famously invoked by Freud:

> There is no other way to conceive of the indestructibility of unconscious desire—given that there is no need which, when its satiation is forbidden, does not wither, in extreme cases through the very wasting away of the organism itself. It is in a kind of memory, comparable to what goes by that name in our modern thinking-machines (which are based on an electronic realization of signifying composition), that the chain is found which *insists* by reproducing itself in the transference, and which is the chain of a dead desire.[32]

Freud himself had suggested in *Totem and Taboo*—and again, even more clearly, in *Moses and Monotheism*—that the latency and partial return of repressed materials be seen as phenomena characteristic not only of the life of the individual, but of the history of the human species as well. Speaking of the difference, or gap, between the official history of Moses and the oral tradition, Freud suggests that what is forgotten nonetheless survives elsewhere: "What has been deleted or altered in the written version might quite well have been preserved uninjured in the tradition."[33] There are thus permanent traces of this history that remain, even if they were mostly warded off and repressed. Here Freud advances one of his boldest claims: "I hold that the concordance between the individual and the mass is in this point almost complete. The masses, too, retain an impression of the past in unconscious memory traces."[34] Memory here becomes both onto- and phylogenetic in ways that do not necessarily lead us back to racially coded and ideological notions of primitivism. In fact, the notion of the return of the repressed leads the psychoanalyst to the surprising conclusion that if the idea of a collective unconscious makes any sense at all, it is only because the unconscious, understood in this way, is always already collective to begin with:

> The term "repressed" is here used not in its technical sense. Here I mean something past, vanished, and overcome in the life of a people, which I venture to treat as equivalent to repressed material in the mental life of the individual. In what psychological form the past existed during its period of darkness we cannot as yet tell. It is not easy to translate the concepts of individual psychology into mass psychology, and I do not think that much is to be gained by introducing the concept of a "collective" unconscious—the content of the unconscious is collective anyhow, a general possession of mankind.[35]

---

32. Lacan, "The Instance of the Letter in the Unconscious or Reason Since Freud," in *Écrits*, 431.
33. Sigmund Freud, *Moses and Monotheism*, trans. Katherine Jones (New York: Vintage Books, 1939), 85.
34. Ibid., 121.
35. Ibid., 170.

Freud and Lacan's notion of an inextinguishable unconscious memory—despite the appearance of insurmountable conceptual distances, not to mention a certain Jungian family resemblance—is furthermore not unrelated to the notion of a species-like memory that acquires almost cosmic dimensions in the writings of Henri Bergson and, after him, with Gilles Deleuze. This is the memory of an all-embracing past, of life itself as pure recollection—a realm that is neither real nor merely possible, but actually virtual and virtually actual at all times. "What Bergson calls 'pure recollection' has no psychological existence. This is why it is called *virtual*, inactive, and unconscious. All these words are dangerous, in particular, the word 'unconscious' which, since Freud, has become inseparable from an especially effective and active psychological existence," Deleuze explains: "We must nevertheless be clear at this point that Bergson does not use the word 'unconscious' to denote a psychological reality outside consciousness, but to denote a nonpsychological reality—being as it is in itself."[36] This is memory not just as the agency of language, not even as the unwritten and obscure record of the human species, but directly as a structure of being: memory as immemorial ontology.

Far from falling for a Jungian interpretation, what Revueltas adds to this notion of an unconscious, indestructible, and quasi-ontological memory is the political question of its rude awakening. In this sense, he is certainly not the only one during the late 1960s and early 1970s to tackle the possibility of a collective popular memory. In his testimonial novel *L'Etabli* (*The Assembly Line*), the French Maoist Robert Linhart also writes: "Nothing is lost, nothing is forgotten in the indefinitely mixed memory of the working class. Other strikes, other committees, other acts will find inspiration in past strikes—as well as in ours, the trace of which I will later discover, mixed up with so many others . . ."[37] Revueltas, though, is precisely interested in the recovery of these traces,

---

36. Gilles Deleuze, *Bergsonism*, trans. Hugh Tomlinson and Barbara Habberiam (New York: Zone Books, 1991), 55–6. When Deleuze in a later work describes the event as something by which this virtual memory is actualized and brought to the surface, he uses an image very similar to the untranslatable "fuegos fatuos" from Revueltas's anecdote:

> The event subsists in language, but it happens to things. Things and propositions are less in a situation of radical duality and more on the two sides of a frontier represented by sense. This frontier does not mingle or reunite them (for there is no more monism here than dualism); it is rather something along the line of an articulation of their difference: body/language. Comparing the event to a mist rising over the prairie, we could say that this mist rises precisely at the frontier, at the juncture of things and propositions.

Gilles Deleuze, *Logic of Sense*, trans. Mark Lester, with Charles Stivale, ed. Constantin V. Boundas (New York: Columbia University Press, 1990), 24.

37. Robert Linhart, *L'Etabli* (Paris: Minuit, 1978), 132. This affirmation can be contrasted with the plea for forgetfulness and the absence of memory found elsewhere in the work of Deleuze, as I discuss in Chapter 4.

in their phantasmatic reinscription or even resurrection. What happens, in other words, with the consciousness that the bricklayers in his second anecdote were "on the verge" of acquiring? Once this spectral consciousness sinks back into the depths of a latent collective unconscious, where it will remain insistently as a virtual memory of the human species, how can such remnants be made to re-emerge? By what kind of act—whether political or theoretical?

Before we turn to the theory of the act, however, we must consider how—when the same bricklayers partake in an architect's project to build a private home, which is then sold to the homeowner—a supplementary alienation of human work takes place in the selling of property and the juridical passage of the house from the hands of the bricklayers, through the architect's plans, to the homeowner's enjoyment. Simplistic as this third and final cognitive anecdote may seem, we should nevertheless not ignore the powerful effects of alienation, here in the sense of separation and subtraction, on the general reserve of human labor:

> This alienation, which sunders the thing from the object (making it into a thing without object), radically—at the roots—affects the subject and strips him of his essence. Placed before the subtraction of *his* object into the thing, he does not cease to possess the object (given that the object will be present in some place), but he leads it astray and appears in front of that stripped thing . . . in the condition of mere amnesia, as empty consciousness, hidden from his generic I, exactly as if one said that an individual forgot where his or her house is.[38]

For Revueltas, all architecture is in fact a preemptive form of archaeology. Indeed, the task of critical reason consists precisely in an operation similar to the uncovering of an archaeology latent within every architectural structure.

As Revueltas writes in one of his more ominous passages, "Archaeology states: this piece of architecture will disappear"—not because of some vague Heraclitean awareness of the flow of time behind the rapid succession of architectural styles and fashions, "but because archaeology as such consists in thinking about and questioning (in consciousness) the how and why of the contradictions by virtue of whose antagonisms cultures and civilizations disappear."[39] In this and other passages from *Dialéctica de la conciencia*, Revueltas comes extremely close to a definition of dialectical and historical materialism that is similar to the one found in the fragments and annotated remains—the refuse and debris of modernity, as it were—taken up and reused by Benjamin in his unfinished *Arcades Project*. "Here we are of course not talking about archaeology as a scientific discipline," Revueltas explains:

---

38. Revueltas, *Dialéctica de la conciencia*, 40–1.
39. Ibid., 35–6.

We are referring, rather, to an archaeology understood as a particular form of historical consciousness, in the same sense as when we talked about architecture. Archaeology, then, appears as a *rethinking*, as the repetition in consciousness of past architectures (cultural formations and so on), and these, in turn, as determinate forms of the totality of a historical consciousness in movement, which is nothing but the movement of its self-destruction.[40]

If the task of theory is revealed in the principle that all architecture is an anticipated archaeology, this must be understood in the rigorous sense of coming to know the past labor that vanished or disappeared into the monumental presence of the present. History, seen in this dialectical sense, is not an accumulation of cultural riches so much as the large-scale vanishing of misery into the unconscious of humanity's constitutive, generic, and originary prehistory. As Revueltas writes,

> In this way, as self-historicization without rest (which never reaches quietude), history is a constant repetition of itself in the continuous mind of human beings, in their *generic* mind and unconscious *memory*—the unconscious that is first ahistorical and then historical and social—(not in the vulgar sense in which one says "history repeats itself," but as presence produced, and producing itself, within the limits of human eternity), the natural history of man that goes back over itself without end.[41]

How, then, does humanity escape from the almost mystical slumber of its general intellect and unconscious memory? Here, both Revueltas and Benjamin, like so many other Western Marxists, seem to have been inspired by a statement of principle that appears in a letter from Marx to Arnold Ruge. "Our election cry must be: Reform of consciousness not through dogmas, but through the analysis of mystical consciousness that is unclear to itself, whether it appears in a religious or a political form," Marx had written to his friend and fellow Young Hegelian: "Then people will see that the world has long possessed the dream of a thing—and that it only needs to possess the consciousness of this thing in order really to possess it."[42] Benjamin would turn this election cry into the cornerstone of his dialectical method as a materialist historian. "The realization of dream elements in the course of waking up is the canon of dialectics. It is paradigmatic for the thinker and binding for the historian," Benjamin wrote in his notebooks for *The Arcades Project*, in which he also wondered: "Is awakening perhaps the synthesis of dream consciousness (as thesis) and waking consciousness (as antithesis)? Then the moment of awakening would be identical with the 'now of recognizability,' in which things put on

---

40. Ibid., 36.
41. Ibid., 24–5.
42. Marx quoted in Walter Benjamin, *The Arcades Project*, trans. Howard Eiland and Kevin McLaughlin, ed. Rolf Tiedemann (Cambridge: Belknap Press of Harvard University Press, 1999), 467. Marx's text appears in his "Letters from *Deutsch-Französische Jahrbücher*," *Collected Works*, vol. 3, 144.

their true—surrealist—face."[43] Is this view of awakening, this "now of recognizability" as "a supremely dialectical point of rupture" or surrealist "flash," not also reminiscent of the moment when consciousness is suddenly "on the verge" of forming itself, "on the verge" of bursting into our field of visibility, according to Revueltas?

What Revueltas is seeking in his "cognitive anecdotes" would thus be an experience akin to the formation of "dialectical images" for Benjamin:

> In the dialectical image, what has been within a particular epoch is always, simultaneously, "what has been from time immemorial." As such, however, it is manifest, on each occasion, only to a quite specific epoch—namely, the one in which humanity, rubbing its eyes, recognizes just this particular dream image as such. It is at this moment that the historian takes up, with regard to that image, the task of dream interpretation.[44]

As for the imminence of this act, which is never fully present to the mind but rather lurks behind the scenes as something that is always on the verge of, or on the point of, occurring, this too is seen as a decisive aspect of the dialectical method:

> Still to be established is the connection between presence of mind and the "method" of dialectical materialism. It's not just that one will always be able to detect a dialectical process in presence of mind, regarded as one of the highest forms of appropriate behavior. What is even more decisive is that the dialectician cannot look on history as anything other than a constellation of dangers which he is always, as he follows its development in his thought, on the point of averting.[45]

The task of critical reason, then, is much closer to the interpretation of a dream than to a simple exercise of the cogito's presence of mind and nearly divine self-consciousness. Revueltas, like Benjamin, finally proposes to see the activity of thought as a secular, or profane illumination: "Consciousness, freed and bared of all divinity—in virtue as much as in vice—puts things on their feet that were standing on their head, it illuminates them, and it profanes them."[46]

Acts of Theory

In a remarkably enigmatic short story, "Hegel y yo", published in 1973 as the opening of a planned future novel or series of narratives on the same subject that would never see the light, Revueltas returned once more to this notion of the profane illumination that takes place whenever an emergent consciousness is on the verge of breaking through the

43. Benjamin, *The Arcades Project*, 464, 364.
44. Ibid., 462.
45. Ibid., 469–70.
46. Revueltas, *Las evocaciones requeridas*, vol. 1, 48.

monumental obliteration of generic human memory and work. On this occasion, he describes such moments in terms of "acts"—that is, truly "profound acts," which completely change the seemingly eternal paradigms of existing knowledge in light of a truth that is both historical and yet part of an immemorial past that runs through, and sometimes interrupts, the continuum of human history.

Despite its unfinished nature, "Hegel and I" represents a culminating moment in the long trajectory of Revueltas as a narrator and a thinker. These two activities, narration and thought, are inseparable here perhaps more so than in any of his other stories, or in most of his already quite intellectualized novels. The story, in fact, seems to take up and try to solve some of the deadlocks present in Revueltas's strictly theoretical writings from the same period, the late 1960s and early 1970s, most of which have been published posthumously by Andrea Revueltas and Philippe Cheron in volumes such as *Dialéctica de la conciencia* and *México 68: Juventud y revolución*.

"Hegel," in the story, is the nickname of a prisoner, a paraplegic who from his wheelchair exchanges anecdotes and philosophical musings with his cellmate, a thinly disguised alter ego of Revueltas himself. "It is a questioning of Hegelian philosophy, referred to the prison," the author explained in an interview: "A character who arrives in prison is a bank-robber called 'Hegel' because he robbed a bank on Hegel Street. Everyone calls him 'Hegel.' From there the narrator takes up the positions of Hegel in order to demonstrate that the prison is the state."[47] From this character, in fact, we obtain not only a theory of the state as a prison-like panopticon, but also the outline for a provocative theory of the act; or, to be more precise, a theory of the theoretical act—of what it means to reach consciousness in the act of theory.

True acts have no witnesses in history; in other words, there are no testimonies of the truly profound acts of consciousness. Rather, they belong to the silent reserve of an unconscious and immemorial recollection, the counter-memory of that which has not taken place. "The profound act lies within you, lurking and prepared to jump up from the bottom of your memory: from that memory of the non-event [*esa memoria de lo no-ocurrido*]," says "Hegel," and the anonymous narrator approves: "He's right: our acts, our profound acts as he says, constitute that part of memory that does not accept remembering, for which it does not matter whether there are witnesses or not. Nobody is witness to nobody and nothing, each one carries his or her own recollection of the unseen, or the unheard-of, without testimonies."[48]

---

47. José Revueltas, *Conversaciones con José Revueltas*, compiled by Andrea Revueltas and Philippe Cheron (Mexico City: Era, 2001), 77.
48. José Revueltas "Hegel y yo . . . ," *Material de los sueños* (Mexico City: Era, 1979), 20, 13.

Without memory, without testimony, unwitnessed yet recorded in the blank pages of a collective unconscious, profound acts are those acts that define not only a subject's emergent consciousness but this very subject as well. Subjects are local instances of such acts.

"You," or "I," according to "Hegel and I," are but the result of the profound acts of history, whether in 1968 or 1917, in 1905 or 1871—acts that forever *will have changed* the conditions of politics in history. This is not a blind voluntaristic account of the subject's capacity for action and intervention, since it is not the subject but the act that is first. The act is not our own doing so much as it is we who are the result, or the local instance, of the act. In the words of "Hegel":

> Thus, insofar as you are here (I mean, here in prison or wherever you are, it doesn't matter), insofar as you stand in and are a certain site, you have something to do with this act. It is inscribed in your ancient memory, in the strangest part of your memory, in your *estranged* memory, unsaid and unwritten, unthought, never felt, which is that which moves you in the direction of such an act. So strange that it is a memory without language, lacking all proper signs, a memory that has to find its own way by means of the most unexpected of all means. Thus, this memory repeats, without our being aware of it, all the frustrations prior to its occurrence, until it succeeds in chancing again upon the original profound act which, for this reason alone, is yours. But only for this reason, because it is yours without belonging to you. The opposite is the case: you are the one who belongs to the act, by which, in the end, you cease to belong to yourself.[49]

The act not only constitutes the brief occurrence of an identity of thinking and being, but it also would seem retroactively to redeem past errors and failures of history. I would even suggest that, through the notion of a repetition of the memory of *lo no-ocurrido*—that is, literally "the unhappened" or "the non-occurred"—Revueltas is inverting the logic of Hegel's sublation which, as Žižek frequently reminds us, amounts to a kind of *Ungeschehenmachen*, incidentally the same German term that Freud uses in his own understanding of denegation. While Hegel famously located this capacity to unmake history in the notion of Christian forgiveness, Žižek extends its field of application to include the core of Hegel's logic as a whole:

> One is thus able to conceive of *Ungeschehenmachen*, the highest manifesta-tion of negativity, as the Hegelian version of "death drive": it is not an accidental or marginal element in the Hegelian edifice, but rather designates the crucial moment of the dialectical process, the so-called moment of the "negation of negation," the inversion of the "antithesis" into the "synthe-sis": the "reconciliation" proper to synthesis is not a surpassing or suspension (whether it be "dialectical") of scission on some higher plane, but a retroac-tive reversal which means that there never was any scission to begin with—"synthesis" retroactively annuls this scission.[50]

---

49. Ibid., 20.
50. Slavoj Žižek, "Lacan—At What Point is He Hegelian?" trans. Rex Butler and Scott

For Revueltas, however, the aim of the profound acts of history is not symbolically, or at the level of the spirit, to *unmake* what *did* happen, but rather to allow that what *did not* happen be *made* to happen. Therein lies not the retroactive annihilation of scission so much as the redemptive introduction of a scission where previously none existed.

Insofar as it relates not to the actual events of the past but to the repetition of their halo of absence, the act proper has no beginning or end. "Where the devil did these things begin?" the narrator in "Hegel and I" asks himself: "It is not the things themselves that I recall but their halo, their periphery, that which lies beyond what circumscribes and defines them."[51] It is only afterwards that historians—and perhaps philosophers of history such as Hegel—can name, date, and interpret the events that are repeated but not registered or witnessed in such an immemorial act:

> It is an act that accepts all forms: committing it, perpetrating it, consummating it, realizing it. It simply is beyond all moral qualification. Qualifying it is left to those who annotate it and date it—that is, to the journalists and the historians, who must then necessarily adjust it to a determinate critical norm that is in force, whereby they only erase its traces and falsify it, erecting it into a Myth that is more or less valid and acceptable during a certain period of time: Landru, Ghengis Khan, Galileo, Napoleon, the Marquis de Sade, Jesus Christ, or Lenin, it's all the same.[52]

Revueltas himself thus responds to the acts and events of 1968 with the demand for a theory of the act that would be able to account for the process by which the frustrated acts of past revolutions and uprisings—acts of rebellion such as the railworkers' strike of 1958–59 in Mexico—are awoken from their slumber and, from being unconscious recollections of the non-event, break out of the shell of available knowledge in order to produce the categories for an unheard-of truth.

As prolonged theoretical acts, though, events cannot be seized without sacrificing their nature, unless the interpretive framework itself is attuned to reflect this very event-like nature itself. To his friends and fellow militants of May 1968 in France, for example, Revueltas sent a public letter with the following message: "Your massive action, which immediately turns into historical praxis, from the first moment on possesses the peculiar nature of being at the same time a great theoretical leap, a radical subversion of the theory mediated, deformed, fetishized by the epigones of Stalin."[53] This radical subversion in turn

---

Stephens, in *Interrogating the Real* (London: Continuum, 2007), 34. On Freud's notion of *das Ungeschehenmachen* as neurotic compulsion, see also Elisabeth Rottenberg, *Inheriting the Future: Legacies of Kant, Freud, and Flaubert* (Stanford: Stanford University Press, 2005), 78–9.

51. Revueltas "Hegel y yo . . . ," 103.
52. Ibid., 108.
53. Revueltas, *México 68*, 26.

must be theorized without losing its subversiveness in the no-man's-land of a theory without practice. Writing from his cell in Lecumberri, Revueltas asked nothing less from his fellow Mexicans. "I believe," he wrote against all odds in 1976, in a collection of essays about the massacre in Tlatelolco, "that the experience of 1968 is a highly positive one, and one that will bring enormous benefits, provided that we know how to theorize the phenomenon."[54]

---

54. Ibid., 21.

4

CAN THE NEW MAN SPEAK?

A Subject for an Object

> To build communism it is necessary, simultaneous with the new material
> foundations, to build the new man.
>
> Ernesto "Che" Guevara, "Socialism and Man in Cuba"

The watershed year of 1968 is also the year that saw the premiere of Tomás Gutiérrez Alea's movie *Memorias del subdesarrollo* (usually translated as *Memories of Underdevelopment*, but sometimes as *Memoirs of Underdevelopment*) during the opening night of the IV Pesaro Film Festival in Rome, alongside a documentary by Joris Ivens on Vietnam. Now considered a classic both nationally and internationally as well as a precursor and founding example of so-called Third Cinema, the movie repeatedly makes the top of the list of best movies of all time as selected by film critics worldwide. In Cuba, for example, the Asociación Cubana de la Prensa Cinematográfica recently voted the movie the number one feature film for the period between 1959 and 2008 in the category of "Top Ten Most Significant Cuban Films."[1] Given the director's central role in the Instituto Cubano del Arte e Industria Cinematográficas (ICAIC), which he co-founded in 1959 in one of the first acts of cultural politics in the revolutionary process in Cuba just three months after the victory of Fidel Castro's troops, this official recognition should not come as a surprise. Far more surprising is the uninterrupted international acclaim bestowed on the film since its first showings. Indeed, while initially the US government refused Gutiérrez Alea a visa to

---

1. See the inserted frame in Víctor Fowler Calzada, "Cuban Film: What's New," *ReVista: Harvard Review of Latin America* 8: 5 (Fall 2009/Winter 2010): 61. Thanks to June C. Erlick for providing me with this special issue of *ReVista* on film in Latin America. On the place of *Memorias del subdesarrollo* and Tomás Gutiérrez Alea's filmmaking in the Cuban revolutionary process, see Michael Chanan, *The Cuban Image: Cinema and Cultural Politics in Cuba* (London: British Film Institute, 1985), 236–47; Nancy Berthier, *Tomás Gutiérrez Alea et la révolution cubaine* (Paris: Cerf, 2005); and Deborah Shaw, "Tomás Gutiérrez Alea's Changing Images of the Revolution: From *Memories of Underdevelopment* to *Strawberry and Chocolate*," in Deborah Shaw, *Contemporary Cinema of Latin America: Ten Key Films* (New York–London: Continuum, 2003), 9–35. For Gutiérrez Alea's place in Third Cinema, see Mike Wayne, *Political Film: The Dialectics of Third Cinema* (London: Pluto Press, 2001), 64–67, 145–52.

accept the 1973 National Society of Film Critics award and banned *Memorias del subdesarrollo* as part of its embargo against Castro's regime, the movie has been a remarkable success outside of Cuba with both experts and general audiences alike, including in the United States. Considering the nature of its story—the self-reflective broodings of a bourgeois intellectual who, after the departure of his wife and family, decides to remain on the island in spite of his repugnance for its continued state of underdevelopment—this success begs the obvious question as to how and why both sides of the ideological spectrum could reach such fertile common ground in the appreciation of this particular movie by Gutiérrez Alea, perhaps matched only by the success of *Fresa y chocolate* (*Strawberry and Chocolate*) twenty-five years later. In this chapter I will try to address this question anew by turning to two subtexts, or paratexts, of the movie: not, as is usually done, by comparing the filmic version to the novel from which it is loosely derived, Edmundo Desnoes's *Memorias del subdesarrollo* (translated into English under the title *Inconsolable Memories*), but rather by having a closer look at León Rozitchner's *Moral burguesa y revolución* (*Bourgeois Morality and Revolution*)—a book from 1963 purchased by the protagonist Sergio in a local bookstore in Havana early in the movie, and read by him in long sequences of voice-over—together with Gutiérrez Alea's own treatise on film theory, published in 1982 under the title *Dialéctica del espectador* (*The Viewer's Dialectic*).

Gutiérrez Alea opens this last work with an enigmatic epigraph drawn from Marx's famous "Introduction" to the 1857–58 *Foundations of the Critique of Political Economy*, also known as the *Grundrisse*: "The object of art—like every other product—creates a public which is sensitive to art and enjoys beauty. Production thus not only creates an object for the subject, but also a subject for the object."[2] In Marx's original formulation, this paragraph from the *Grundrisse* continues as follows:

---

2.   Tomás Gutiérrez Alea, *Dialéctica del espectador*, ed. Miguel Barnet (Havana: Ediciones Unión de Escritores y Artistas de Cuba, 1982), 5. It has been translated into English as *The Viewer's Dialectic*, with a Prologue, by the film critic Julia Lesage (Havana: José Martí Publishing House, 1988). This translation of the title of Gutiérrez Alea's treatise, however, loses out on the interplay between spectacle and spectator in Spanish, which is why *Dialectic of the Spectator* would have been preferable. For the comparison with Edmundo Desnoes and a reader's guide to the movie in general, including a selection of reviews and early articles, the best source of critical materials remains Tomas Gutiérrez Alea and Edmundo Desnoes, *Memories of Underdevelopment/Inconsolable Memories*, introduced by Michael Chanan (New Brunswick and London: Rutgers University Press, 1990). Incidentally, Edmundo Desnoes also wrote a follow-up to his earlier book titled *Memories of Development*, which in turn was made into a movie by the young Cuban film director Miguel Coyula. While this sequel loses out on the ideological depth of Gutiérrez Alea's original movie, it also pays homage to the technical richness of the montages in *Memories of Underdevelopment*.

Thus production produces consumption (1) by creating the material for it; (2) by determining the manner of consumption; and (3) by creating the products, initially posited by it as objects, in the form of a need felt by the consumer. It thus produces the object of consumption, the manner of consumption and the motive of consumption. Consumption likewise produces the producer's *inclination* by beckoning to him as an aim-determining need.[3]

The main questions addressed in the first part of this chapter concern precisely this production of a subject for an object: What type of subjectivity does this art object, the movie *Memorias del subdesarrollo*, produce? How does this movie beckon to so many spectators from all sides of the ideological spectrum by responding to a need that only *seems* to pre-exist the film's reception, while it is perhaps part and parcel of what the art object itself consciously or unconsciously produces? Leaving aside the usual explanatory schemes resorting to sheer ideological manipulation—which, while certainly true in many cases, also strike me as insufficient—how does Gutiérrez Alea's most critically acclaimed movie, much to his growing chagrin, provoke this dialectic between production and consumption, between spectacle and spectator, or between object and subject?

The importance of these questions is in any case highlighted right from the start. Thus, in one of his first voice-overs that also serve as interior monologues, the movie's main character Sergio reflects on whether conditions in Havana have changed objectively or subjectively—if they have changed at all—as a result of the revolution. "Here everything remains the same," he first remarks, before considering the opposite hypothesis: "Yet today everything looks so different. Have I changed, or has this city changed?"[4] The uncertainty surrounding this question will continue to haunt the rest of the movie, giving rise to a multi-perspectival interrogation of the consequences of revolutionary change at the level of subjectivity. To what extent should the individual, too, undergo a transformation so as to develop into what Ernesto "Che" Guevara, in his famous speech from 1965, "El socialismo y el hombre en Cuba" ("Socialism and Man in Cuba"), first published in the Uruguayan magazine *Marcha* and then in the Cuban journal *Pensamiento crítico*, calls *el hombre nuevo*, "the new man"? In the context of an underdeveloped country such as Cuba, Guevara had announced that the process of this construction would be long and complex: "Underdevelopment, on the one hand, and the usual flight of capital, on the other, make a rapid transition without sacrifices

---

3. Karl Marx, *Grundrisse: Foundations of the Critique of Political Economy (Rough Draft)*, transl. Martin Nicolaus (London–New York: Penguin, 1973), 92. Marx, interestingly enough, goes on to mock the facile Hegelianism hidden in all such mechanical inversions of the production of consumption and the consumption of production.
4. "Continuity Script," in Gutiérrez Alea and Desnoes, *Memories of Underdevelopment*, 35–6.

impossible. There remains a long way to go in constructing the economic base, and the temptation is very great to follow the beaten track of material interest as the lever with which to accelerate development."[5] The spirit of sacrifice applies in particular to elements from the past that remain and act as obstacles to the development of the new society from within the bosom of the old: "The vestiges of the past are brought into the present in one's consciousness, and a continual labor is necessary to eradicate them."[6]

This violent language of eradication and sacrifice signals the extent to which the revolutionary process finds itself in permanent conflict with what we might call, in a dialectical inversion of Gutiérrez Alea's title, the overdevelopment of memories—that is, the stubborn persistence of vestiges of the past within the revolutionary present. It is in the context of this conflict between memory and revolution that I want to address the question of subjectivity in the process of radical social change and whether, in the movie *Memorias del subdesarrollo*, the "new man" can speak. I then want to turn to the question of whether the process of subjective change is similar to a religious experience of conversion. Moving beyond Gutiérrez Alea's film, this will finally bring me to the much larger issue of the possible relations between politics and religion as well as, more specifically, between Marxism and Christianity, brought up time and again in Rozitchner's repeated returns to the issues raised in Marx's polemical text, "On the Jewish Question."

The Development of Underdevelopment

Marxism and psychoanalysis, in two different ways, speak in the name of a kind of memory, a culture of memory, and also speak in two different ways in the name of the requirements of a development. We believe on the contrary that one must speak in the name of a positive force of forgetting, in the name of what is for each individual his own underdevelopment.
Gilles Deleuze, "Five Propositions on Psychoanalysis"

I will start by addressing the way in which the movie itself defines the condition of underdevelopment, as such a definition will immediately allow us to reflect on the work's own structure. For Sergio (played by Sergio Corrieri), underdevelopment has above all an ideological significance, signaling an inability to connect action and intention, parts and whole, the immediate and the long-term duration. "One of the things that really gets me about people is their inability to sustain a feeling, an idea, without falling apart," he comments, thinking about the recent object of his infatuation, Elena (played by Daisy Granados), whom he

---

5. Ernesto "Che" Guevara, "El socialismo y el hombre en Cuba," *Obra revolucionaria*, 630. English translation as "Socialism and Man in Cuba," in *Che Guevara Reader: Writings on Politics and Revolution*, ed. David Deutschmann (New York: Ocean Press, 2003), 216.
6. Ibid.

has picked up on the street and invited into his private apartment: "Elena turned out to be totally inconsistent. It's pure deterioration as Ortega [y Gasset] would say. She doesn't connect one thing with another. That's one of the signs of underdevelopment: the inability to connect things"—an inability whose results include a failure to accumulate experience and, by way of compensation for this failure, a tendency to depend on others to reflect on the meaning of such experience: "People aren't consistent. And they always need somebody to do their thinking for them."[7]

The irony of this purely ideological definition of underdevelopment becomes apparent as soon as the spectator reflects upon the structural disconnect that characterizes the very form of *Memorias del subdesarrollo*. A montage of documentary footage, newsreels, photographic images, and fiction, the film—like the novel discussed in Chapter 3—stubbornly refuses to provide the image of a totality that would be ordered on the basis of a single unifying center of consciousness. Even more symptomatically and as a result of the techniques of montage, between sound and image too the relation tends to be one of violent disjunction. The constant use of voice-over, for instance, purportedly relevant as meta-commentary (whether about items such as the revolutionary billboards depicting José Martí or the victory of Playa Girón, about the street scene when Sergio walks in the opposite direction of the masses on one May Day celebration, or about the television broadcasts that all accompany such commentaries), in fact never manages to produce, or never wants to produce, a correspondence between sound and sight, between the visible and the sayable. Likewise, when Sergio plays back the tapes on the reel-to-reel recorder containing the verbally abusive fights with his ex-wife now departed for Miami, all the while rummaging through her clothes and monstrously deforming his face by pulling her luxury nylon stockings over his head, the effect is nothing if not a disconnect—a lag in time coupled with a sense of spatial out-of-jointness, beckoning to be overcome beyond the screen and outside the movie theater by the spectator's intervention. This is why Sergei M. Eisenstein's technique of intellectual montage becomes so critical, as Gutiérrez Alea explains in *Dialéctica del espectador*: "Montage combinations, not only in the case of a series of images which may be arranged in an unusual relation as an incentive to discover new meaning, but also when the relations are established between sound and image (what Eisenstein described as 'audio-visual counterpoint') constitute a specifically cinematic modality of the estrangement effect."[8] *Memorias del subdesarrollo* similarly uses structural devices that its bourgeois hero would qualify as symptomatic of underdevelopment, in order to produce a subject capable of developing from them a consistent

---

7. "Continuity Script," 65.
8. Gutiérrez Alea, *Dialéctica del espectador*, 38–9; *The Viewer's Dialectic*, 46.

dialectical image, or meaningful totality. Sergio's definition of underdevelopment, then, not only applies to his own position in the face of the revolutionary process; it also serves to define the very structure of the film that recounts his gradual collapse.

In "Memories of Memories," a retrospective evaluation originally published in 1980 in the journal Casa de las Américas and also included in Dialéctica del espectador, Gutiérrez Alea makes a similar comment about the structure of the film: "The image of reality provided by Memories of Underdevelopment is a multifaceted one—like an object contemplated from different viewpoints."[9] However, the question then inevitably becomes whether any subject capable of producing such a totality does not at the same time become liable to the suspicion of representing exactly the kind of central bourgeois consciousness that the revolutionary process is meant to destroy in favor of a new understanding of the collective. "Using this multilateral perception of the object as the film's structural principle is not precisely the 'ambivalence' we have already referred to in terms of ambiguity or indetermination," the director insists, rejecting what he considers to be the misguided and ill-informed praise bestowed upon his movie by "left-liberals" such as the president of the National Society of Film Critics in the United States:

> In contrast, it is the expression of contradictions whose purpose in the film is none other than to contribute to the concerns and impulses for action that we wish to awaken in the spectator. Thus it constitutes an incentive to stand at a distance vis-à-vis the images being shown, and in this way it encourages a critical attitude, that is, a "choosing of sides."[10]

Ultimately, in the absence of a revolutionary subject within the space of the filmic, overshadowed as this space is by the views of so-called bourgeois conscience, the difficult task of this toma de partido or "choosing of sides" falls in the lap of the spectator. And yet, what the charge of ideological manipulation reveals is the fact that much of the movie's appeal lies precisely in this very absence that is the lack of a revolutionary center.

Consider for example the documentary footage, admittedly filtered through the lens of Sergio's sarcasm, from the roundtable discussion on the topic of "Literature and Underdevelopment," moderated by Salvador Bueno with the participation of René Depestre, Gianni Totti, David Viñas, and Edmundo Desnoes himself. The latter immediately becomes

9. Gutiérrez Alea, "Memorias de Memorias," in Dialéctica del espectador, 65; The Viewer's Dialectic, 74. This text, written on the occasion of the tenth anniversary of the release of the movie, is also reproduced in English in Gutiérrez Alea and Edmundo Desnoes, Memories of Underdevelopment/Inconsolable Memories. For excellent analyses of the question of technique in the movie, see, in the same volume, Julianne Burton, "Memories of Underdevelopment in the Land of Overdevelopment," 232–47.
10. Gutiérrez Alea, Dialéctica del espectador, 68; The Viewer's Dialectic, 81.

the object of the protagonist's scorn: "What are you doing up there with that cigar? You must feel pretty important because there's not much competition here."[11] This process of mockery is not unlike the way in which earlier, in a visit by Sergio and Elena to the ICAIC, Gutiérrez Alea and his director of photography Ramón F. Suárez are put in a slightly ironic light due to Sergio's distanced standpoint. What is more, at one point during the roundtable an American in the audience, Jack Gelber, also playing—or merely being—himself, intervenes to question the incompatibility of the revolution as a total rupture with the conventional format of the roundtable discussion in which there fails to be a dynamic interaction between the panelists and the public. Sergio agrees, and makes the following reflections, in one of the movie's most important voice-overs, in which he also repeats the diagnostic of underdevelopment quoted above:

> I don't understand a thing. The American was right. Words devour words and they leave you in the clouds or on the moon. A thousand miles away. How does one get rid of underdevelopment? It marks everything. Everything. What are you doing down there, Sergio? What does it all mean? You have nothing to do with them. You're alone. In underdevelopment nothing has continuity, everything is forgotten. People aren't consistent. But you remember many things, you remember too much. Where's your family, your work, your wife? You're nothing, you're dead. Now it begins, Sergio, your final destruction.[12]

During this scene, the image of Sergio walking down below in the street slowly fades into the screen, with the camera zooming in on his face to the point of blurring the image altogether, as though to suggest that the actor has now become one with the position of the spectator in front of the movie screen. We, too, are invited to fuse with this character at the point of his imminent destruction. Furthermore, instead of moving, thanks to an act of collective reappropriation, from nothing to all, as in the famous lyrics of the International ("We are nothing, let us be all"), here we witness the opposite movement from everything to nothing (from "everything" being marked by underdevelopment to "You're

---

11. "Continuity Script," 76.
12. Ibid., 77. The American in question, Jack Gelber, not only wrote an interesting play, *The Cuban Thing* (New York: Grove Press, 1968), based on his experience on the island. Earlier, in *The Connection* (New York: Grove Press, 1957) he also inaugurated the gesture of an actor who intervenes from within the audience, as he himself would do in *Memories of Underdevelopment*. Among the other participants in the roundtable on "Literature and Underdevelopment," René Depestre published *Cantata de Octubre a la Vida y a la Muerte del Comandante Ernesto Che Guevara* in a bilingual Spanish-French edition (Havana: Instituto del Libro, 1968); and Gianni Totti contributed regularly to the discussions at the annual Pesaro Film Festival in Italy. See Manuel Pérez Estremera, ed., *Problemas del nuevo cine* (Madrid: Alianza, 1971). Finally, an anecdotal link also connects two other players in this context: in 1961, José Revueltas—who also was a prolific scriptwriter for cinema— visited and taught at the ICAIC, then directed by Gutiérrez Alea.

nothing"), due to a bourgeois individual's overdevelopment of memory ("You remember too much"). "You're neither a revolutionary nor a counterrevolutionary," Elena also tells Sergio. "Then, what am I?" he insists, to which she replies: "Nothing. You're nothing."[13]

Memorias del subdesarrollo thus tells the story of the persistence of bourgeois values in the midst of the revolutionary process and it beckons the spectators to take a stand in order to destroy the remnants of that persistence in themselves. "Theoretically, in Marxism, the proletariat was never composed of (bourgeois) individuals; this was a luxury reserved for the wealthier" (such as Sergio), we might recall, using the terms of Russell Jacoby. "However, again, the very problem is that the form of individuality that prevails in the bourgeoisie is not confined to the bourgeoisie; rather it seeps into the proletariat and cripples the process of the proletariat which seeks to constitute itself as the historical subject."[14] Ultimately, then, the real object of criticism is the subject as such—that is, in the first place the spectator, and not so much the movie's hero or antihero. "From all that has been discussed so far, one can infer that it is precisely the spectator who is the target of criticism which *Memories . . .* unleashes—the spectator who lives within the Revolution, who is part of our revolutionary reality," Gutiérrez Alea insists in *Dialéctica del espectador*: "It is to these viewers that the film ought to reveal the symptoms of possible contradictions and incongruities which exist between good revolutionary intention (in the abstract) and a spontaneous and unconscious adhesion to certain (concrete) values that characterize bourgeois ideology."[15] And yet, in the absence of a positive vantage point outside of bourgeois ideology, it is always possible for the spectator to linger exclusively on the latter's destruction, rather than take the lion's leap of identifying with the revolutionary cause.

Desnoes, Gutiérrez Alea, even Fidel Castro: in spite of the director's avowed faith in the power of documentary footage as an objective counterpoint to merely bourgeois subjectivity, none of these figures really escapes ridicule as a result of the movie's exclusive rendering of Sergio's perspective. They certainly do not provide a stable foothold within the space of the movie with which the spectator might identify. This is because Gutiérrez Alea, this time drawing his lesson from Brecht's didacticism, considers identification as such to be suspicious, always susceptible of reactionary uses—even, or especially, when the cause to be identified with presents itself as revolutionary. As the director astutely observes in "Identification and Distancing: Aristotle and Brecht," an important chapter from *Dialéctica del espectador*:

---

13. "Continuity Script," 60.
14. Jacoby, *Social Amnesia*, 81–2.
15. Gutiérrez Alea, *Dialéctica del espectador*, 71; *The Viewer's Dialectic*, 84.

Some think, with the greatest of good will, that if we were to substitute a
revolutionary hero for Tarzan, we should get more people to adhere to the
revolutionary cause, but they do not take into account that the very mechanism of identification or empathy with the hero, *if it is made into an absolute*,
puts the spectator in a position in which the only thing he can distinguish are
"bad guys" and "good guys." Of course, viewers naturally identify with the
"good guys" without considering what the character truly represents. So it
is intrinsically reactionary because it does not work at the level of the viewers' consciousness; far from it, it tends to dull it.[16]

Identification, in other words, always risks becoming a melodramatic
tool for the moralization of politics—for the reduction of all antagonism to the simple opposition of *buenos y malos*. All positive
identification in *Memorias del subdesarrollo*, for this reason, is gradually undercut, deactivated, or, in the end, left blank. Instead of offering
the cathartic pleasure and pain of identification, however, the perverse
enjoyment provided by the movie, perhaps even the need that it
wittingly or unwittingly produces in the spectator, lies in the possibility
of dwelling purely and exclusively on the destruction of the old, without the construction of the new.

The authenticity of the revolution would thus be measured only by
the violence and intensity with which it destroys the elements of its
own betrayal. In this sense, the movie effectively captures the possibility that perhaps all hope is not lost for Sergio. Or perhaps it would
be more appropriate to say that, from this moment onward in the
history of the revolutionary ideal in the twentieth century, there is
hope only in loss, in the active loss and sacrificial abnegation of one's
self. Without indulging in cheap anticommunist or antitotalitarian
sentiments, Sergio's trial at the end of *Memorias del subdesarrollo* on
charges of having sexually exploited Elena, even though he is acquitted by the people's court, can in this sense be considered a miniature
equivalent of the role of semblance in the violent staging of purges as
integral to the revolutionary process during the Moscow trials.
Perhaps Sergio is even acquitted precisely because he has given proof
of his willingness to participate in the process of his own abnegation
and destruction: "I resigned myself," he says in another voice-over, "I
was going to let myself be dragged along to the end."[17] Badiou, to
explain the uncanny combination of suspicion and purification that
reigned over the Moscow trials under Stalin, similarly refers the
reader of *The Century* back to Hegel's interpretation of the role of
terror in the French Revolution.

I think the crucial point (as Hegel grasped long ago with regard to the
revolutionary Terror) is this: the real, conceived in its contingent abso-
luteness, is never real enough not to be suspected of semblance. The

16. Ibid., 35–6, 42.
17. "Continuity Script," 86.

passion of the real is also, of necessity, suspicion. Nothing can attest that the real is the real, nothing but the system of fictions wherein it plays the role of the real.[18]

More importantly, it would seem as though constant suspicion, including of oneself, were the only guarantee of authenticity. As in Sergio and Elena's visits to the ICAIC and to the Hemingway Museum, or the roundtable discussion in which famous intellectuals act as themselves, one can never be absolutely sure that one is not merely playing instead of genuinely being revolutionary and self-critical. In the absence of an objective measure, then, the only proof of integrity is the subject's willingness to submit to the spectacular theatricality of his or her own destruction. "What matters for us is the following: we are in the realm of suspicion when a formal criterion is lacking to distinguish the real from semblance. In the absence of such a criterion, the logic that imposes itself is that the more a subjective conviction presents itself as real, the more it must be suspected," Badiou writes: "In these conditions, what is the only certainty? Nothingness. Only the nothing is not suspect, because the nothing does not lay claim to any real. The logic of purification, as Hegel astutely remarks, amounts to bringing about the nothing."[19] Here begins, spectator, your final destruction, your reduction to nothing.

The Destruction of the Old Man?

Creating a new humanity always comes down to demanding that the old one be destroyed. A violent, unreconciled debate rages about the nature of this old humanity.

Alain Badiou, The Century

A similar conclusion, but this time with even broader implications for a critical history of the present moment, can be drawn from Rozitchner's book *Moral burguesa y revolución*, published in 1963 with the dedication "A mis compañeros de *Contorno*," the latter being the important Argentine journal in which the author worked alongside David and Ismael Viñas, Oscar Masotta, Juan José Sebreli, and others. This book, Rozitchner's second after his doctoral thesis *Persona y comunidad* (*Person and Community*), offers a close textual analysis and theoretical commentary on the transcripts from the hearings of the counterrevolutionaries taken prisoners after their failed attempt to overthrow Fidel Castro's regime in 1962 in Playa Girón during the battle of the "Bay of Pigs." As I have mentioned, Sergio reads long parts of this book in voice-overs combined with documentary footage from the hearings and surrounding events. Based on the transcribed

18. Badiou, *The Century*, 52.
19. Ibid., 54.

testimonies of the counterrevolutionaries themselves, this analysis tries to come to grips with what the same author in a later work would call "the limits of bourgeois individualism."[20] In fact, the book begins with the following line: "The goal of the present work is to confront the moral conceptions of the bourgeoisie and the ethics of Revolution."[21] Such would be the stark either/or choice: Bourgeois morality or revolutionary ethics? In Gutiérrez Alea's movie, however, we catch barely a glimpse of the ethics of the revolution. Instead, through the overpowering perspective of Sergio, what we witness is an impressive montage of the sarcasms, witticisms, and neurotic reflections, both accusatory and self-deprecating, of a supreme exemplar of bourgeois morality.

In fact, I would argue that *Memorias del subdesarrollo*, including its subtle mockery not only of writers and intellectuals such as Viñas and the cigar-smoking Desnoes but even—and perhaps more importantly—of Fidel Castro himself, whose dignity at the end of the movie is said to come at a very high price, marks an important stepping stone toward the complete obliteration of the other side in Rozitchner's dichotomy—that is, the ethics of revolution as opposed to bourgeois morality. This becomes even more evident from a contemporary perspective. Indeed, with the gradual waning and subsequent collapse of the revolutionary idea, there has come a period—which is "special" in a different sense from what is commonly understood under this category in post-Soviet Cuba—in which the ethical experience no longer leads from alienation, injustice, and victimization toward a new sense of revolutionary justice, but instead remains entirely within a realm—henceforth the ethical or moral realm as such—where everyone is a potential victim, and thus also a potential suspect, or an other to someone else's unforgivable sameness.

For Rozitchner, bourgeois ethics or morality (these two terms, ethics

---

20. León Rozitchner, *Freud y los límites del individualismo burgués* (Mexico City: Siglo Veintiuno, 1972). I refer the reader to the following chapter for a more detailed discussion.
21. León Rozitchner, *Moral burguesa y revolución* (Buenos Aires: Procyon, 1963), 9. An interesting anecdote links this work to the discussion of melodrama on the part of Althusser. Rozitchner, in a personal message to the author, indeed recalled how *Moral burguesa y revolución* first appeared in the *Revista de la Universidad* of Havana, where he was teaching at the time. Later he heard that in Italy a play had been produced in the Piccolo Teatro in Milan (the same theater in which Bertolazzi presented the melodrama discussed by Althusser) based on *Moral burguesa y revolución*, by a German playwright who had been visiting Cuba and whose name Rozitchner did not recall. In fact, the author is none other than Hans Magnus Enzensberger, and the play, *The Havana Inquiry*, trans. Martin Duberman (New York: Holt, Rinehart & Winston, 1974), a rip-off from Rozitchner's analysis of the hearings in *Moral burguesa y revolución*, which Enzensberger quotes only once, ironically, in the context of his discussion of the *docta ignorantia* or "wise ignorance" invoked by the prisoners in their defense. This level of plagiarism is all the more ironic insofar as Enzensberger is also the author of an important essay in which he critically analyzes the revolutionary "tourism" of Western Leftists who visit Russia or China or Cuba. See "Tourists of the Revolution," in Hans Magnus Enzensberger, *Critical Essays*, ed. Reinhold Grimm and Bruce Armstrong (New York: Continuum, 1982), 159–85.

and morality, are not kept apart in the book as neatly as Hegel's *Sitt-lichkeit* and *Moralität* but, like Badiou, Rozitchner nonetheless tends to invert the Hegelian hierarchy so as to give ethics a more positive connotation and morality a more negative one) can be perceived in the exculpatory tactics by which the counterrevolutionaries systematically seek to evade all collective responsibility, either by blaming the group when they as individuals are at fault, or else by setting themselves apart from the group when they feel worthy of praise as individuals. The result is a pseudo-dialectical opposition between the impure group and the pure individual:

> [I]n bourgeois ethics, there is nobody, as we will see, responsible concretely for the whole. Nobody takes hold of the totality of meaning of action; all appear as dislocated elements of a global meaning that nobody assumes completely: everyone refers to his own individuality when wanting to distance himself from the misery of others which (he believes) undeservedly contaminates him, or else submerges himself in the undifferentiated group when having to hide his own responsibility, and thus contaminating the others without qualms. Among them, there is no ethical sense, only a personal morality; there is not a single one who can take charge of his action and extend its meaning so as to re-encounter in it the signification of the acts taken on collectively, by including the full materiality in which they are grounded.[22]

As we have seen, precisely this inability to sustain any collective inter-human project, this historical disconnect between actions and their meaning, is seen by Sergio in the movie as a symptom—or better yet as the very definition—of what he calls underdevelopment. The problem, which others consider the movie's principal strength in the guise of its so-called ambivalence, lies in the fact that already in this movie from 1968 there seems to be no clear path, no straightforward program, not even so much as a minimal perspective available in order to overcome the condition of underdevelopment—except by negation. In other words, the space for such an overcoming is left vacant, ready to be occupied by an emancipated spectator; but, at least within the film's universe, there is no subject capable of filling the void.

For Rozitchner, in his running commentary on the transcripts from the hearings of the counterrevolutionaries, on the other hand, the solution can consist only of an ethics of collective revolutionary commitment. But already, in the early 1960s, the Argentine Freudo-Marxist was acutely aware of the dilemmas that would soon come to haunt the consciousness of politically engaged left-wing intellectuals with ever-growing intensity, all the way up to the hyper-responsible

---

22. Rozitchner, *Moral burguesa y revolución*, 17. This passage is read out loud by Sergio in *Memorias del subdesarrollo*, in an important section of the movie—the only one not accompanied by sarcastic commentaries—preceded by the intertitle "La verdad del grupo está en el asesino" ("The Truth of the Group Lies in the Assassin").

unanswerability of Gayatri Chakravorty Spivak's pivotal question "Can the Subaltern Speak?" first asked in 1988, twenty-five years after *Moral burguesa y revolución*. Rozitchner thus writes:

> This also means that our commitment, in actualizing and validating the total connection that we maintain with the world, prepares us, as thinking human beings, to receive the object in its total inter-human signification. If we were not to do so, our act of knowing would not provide us with true knowledge. Why? Because it would mean assuming that there can be someone, the I who analyzes, or the I as privileged subject, who manages at some point to evade the responsibility that in all orders of action I maintain with other human beings; precisely, that is, at the point where I dedicate myself to think *for* them.[23]

Once the suspicion sets in that one might be thinking or speaking *for* the other, if not *in the place of* the other, a new and heightened sense of ethical responsibility can always come into the picture that displaces all traditional notions of militant political commitment. In fact, I would argue that there comes a point even in *Memorias del subdesarrollo* where it seems that the destruction of the "old man" is all there is to the construction of the "new man" of socialism in Cuba, famously theorized by Che Guevara. This is not quite yet the depoliticized ethics of the other, which will take a few more years to develop; but as spectators we are already becoming enmeshed in an ethical sensibility in which the legacy of revolutionary militantism begins to live its own crisis in anticipation, by sticking to the negative act of a spectacular downfall.

Religion and Its Discontents

Thus the criticism of heaven turns into the criticism of earth, the criticism of religion into the criticism of law and the criticism of theology into the criticism of politics.

      Karl Marx, Critique of Hegel's Philosophy of Right

Sometimes even a typographical error can put us on the tracks of a significant conceptual debate. Thus, in a recent sequence-by-sequence analysis of *Memorias del subdesarrollo* in which we can already find a fine summary of *Dialéctica del espectador*, the author of the book *Moral burguesa y revolución* at one point is wrongly quoted as "Leo

---

23. Rozitchner, *Moral burguesa y revolución*, 19. For the original formulation of the question anticipated in this quotation and parodied in the title of the present chapter, see Gayatri Chakravorty Spivak, "Can the Subaltern Speak?" in Cary Nelson and Lawrence Grossberg, eds, *Marxism and the Interpretation of Culture* (Urbana: University of Illinois Press, 1988), 271–313. For a contemporary reassessment, including a revised version of Spivak's essay, see Rosalind C. Morris, ed., *Can the Subaltern Speak? Reflections on the History of an Idea* (New York: Columbia University Press, 2010).

Rozitchner."[24] Rozitchner's actual first name, though, is not even León, which is but the common Hispanized version of Leib. From Leib to León to Leo, we are thus led to ask the thorny question of whether the creation of a "new man" necessarily also implies the obliteration of the "old man" as Jewish. Or, to put this question the other way around: To what extent is the construction of a militant subjectivity, or of a new socialist or communist humanity, a process that would be constitutively Christian, if not also anti-Semitic, modeled upon examples such as Saint Paul's or Saint Augustine's? Do these examples always necessarily carry with them the burden of having to destroy the old subject within oneself? "The nub of the problem was to reject my own will and to desire yours," as Augustine writes to God in his *Confessions.* "But it was in my inmost heart, where I had grown angry with myself, where I had been stung with remorse, where I had slain my old self and offered it in sacrifice."[25] Is this problem—common to Marxism and Christianity—of the transition between the old and the new man, or between the old and the new society, necessarily a violent process of rebirth through self-sacrifice, as the religious model of the conversion seems to suggest? More generally, can religion play an emancipatory role in politics, for instance, through the example of liberation theology? Or, as Marx would seem to suggest in "On the Jewish Question," does genuinely human, as opposed to merely political, emancipation require a purely earthly perspective, and thus the extirpation of all religious remnants, whether Jewish, Christian, or otherwise, as old (particularist) impediments to the new (generic) humanity? Finally, would not Freud seem to confirm this secular perspective insofar as, in *Civilization and Its Discontents,* for example, he classifies religion, with its oceanic feeling of fusion with the universe, as a collective neurosis—one that, according to Freud in *The Future of Illusion,* humanity will be able to overcome through the progress of science?

In *Memorias del subdesarrollo,* Gutiérrez Alea alludes to some of these questions as well. He thus confronts Sergio with three lovers— whether real or imaginary—from different religious backgrounds: Elena, whose Catholic upbringing will come back to haunt him in the form of her family's accusation that he ruined her by taking her virginity; his domestic help Noemí, a born-again Christian whose story about her baptism in the river arouses Sergio's wildest fantasies, only for them to be dispelled by photographs of the actual event; and Hanna, the German-Jewish woman who fled to Cuba with her family to escape

24.   Paul A. Schroeder, *Tomás Gutiérrez Alea: The Dialectics of a Filmmaker* (New York and London: Routledge, 2002), 64. León Rozitchner's name is spelled correctly earlier in the book (30).
25.   See Book IX of Saint Augustine, *Confessions,* trans. Henry Chadwick (Oxford: Oxford University Press, 1991), 155; and *Confessions,* trans. R. S. Pine-Coffin (London: Penguin, 1961), 188. For stylistic reasons, I have adapted and blended both translations into one.

from Hitler, before moving on to New York. Such a treatment of religion, to be sure, may seem purely anecdotal—meant not to give historical and psychological depth to the characters in question, but to turn them into mere stereotypes. But in fact the issue of religion in this filmmaker's work is far more ambivalent than the creation of character types would suggest.

On the one hand, Gutiérrez Alea implies that the persistence of religious beliefs in general and of Catholicism and Protestantism in particular is an ideological remnant of an older social formation that the revolutionary upheaval has yet to eradicate in Cuba. In this respect, he follows some of the more common assumptions behind the critique of religion in Marx. After recalling how he himself was raised a Catholic, for example, the Cuban filmmaker describes in a retrospective reflection the shock he felt upon familiarizing himself with the literature of Marxism:

> How can I explain the change produced in my way of seeing things at this point? The idea of communism had seemed to me pretty similar to that of paradise. Except that the former expressed itself as a logical and rational consequence of the development of humanity, and should be reached in this life. It was no longer just a matter of "good guys" and "bad guys" but of determinate laws of development that also manifested themselves in history. Nor was it a matter of preaching the virtues of Christ so as to improve man and suppress social injustices, but of admitting that man is moved by his interests and that the economic factor is determining *in the final instance*.[26]

This discovery of the basic insights of historical materialism, adds Gutiérrez Alea, allowed him to move "from Christian preaching to revolutionary practice."[27] Between these two, the gap would be as great as that between heaven and earth, eternity and history, theology and politics, idealism and materialism, or ideology and science.

In fact, from the standpoint of the historical materialist, the problem of religion may appear to have been solved, if not dissolved, into the material conditions that alone determine its appearance. As Gutiérrez Alea also stated in an important set of theses "Sobre vivencias y supervivencias" ("On Lived Experiences and Survivals"), first published in 1979 in the journal *Cine Cubano*:

> Religion in and of itself is not the big problem, since it is not a cause but a consequence of the historical insufficiencies of the material process of production. It will therefore die a natural death on the day that this process fully inscribes itself in the dominion of humanity over itself, over social relations, and over nature. The only thing that can be effectively opposed to the religious spirit is the development of the scientific spirit and,

---

26. Tomás Gutiérrez Alea, "No siempre fui cineasta," in Ambrosio Fornet, ed., *Alea: una retrospectiva crítica* (Havana: Letras Cubanas, 1998), 18.
27. Ibid.

evidently, it already ceases to carry any weight wherever a more just society is established.[28]

This statement resembles nothing so much as a stance commonly attributed to Marx, according to which religion, whether as the opium of the people or as ideological superstructure, will wither away as a result of material changes to be effected at the level of the economic base, or infrastructure. Indeed, in a letter from 1842 to the Young Hegelian Arnold Ruge, Marx himself had written that "religion in itself is without content, it owes its being not to heaven but to earth, and with the abolition of distorted reality, of which it is the *theory*, it will collapse of itself."[29] Gutiérrez Alea's take on religion at first appears to be perfectly attuned to this narrow materialist understanding of the Marxist critique of ideology.

And yet, on the other hand, *Memorias del subdesarrollo* also uncovers an underlying affinity between Christianity and the creation of the "new man" in socialist Cuba. "What's it like?" Sergio asks Noemí, referring to her baptism, to which she answers by relating how "the minister and I go into the water. Afterwards he told me what baptism means. It symbolizes the death of sin, the resurrection of a new life."[30] Gutiérrez Alea thus insinuates a profound structural homology between the experience of religious conversion or baptism and the revolutionary construction of socialism.

After all, there are good reasons to refer Guevara's notion back to certain affirmations that apply to Christ's intervention in human history. Consider, for example, the way in which Saint Paul identifies the very passage from the old into the new with the imitation of Christ: "So if anyone is in Christ, there is a new creation: everything old has passed away; see, everything has become new!"[31] Žižek, too, for better or worse underscores the proximity in this regard between Christ and Che Guevara: "Although we should be aware of the dangers of the 'Christification of Che,' turning him into an icon of radical-chic consumer culture, a martyr ready to die out of his love for humanity, one should perhaps take the risk of accepting this move, radicalizing it

---

28.   Tomás Gutiérrez Alea, "Sobre vivencias y supervivencias: cinco respuestas," in ibid., 204.

29.   Karl Marx, quoted in Warren Breckman, *Marx, the Young Hegelians, and the Origins of Radical Social Theory* (Cambridge: Cambridge University Press, 1999), 278. For an excellent overview of Marx's treatment of religion as more than simply the ideological form or theory of a distorted reality, see Alberto Toscano, "Beyond Abstraction: Marx and the Critique of the Critique of Religion," *Historical Materialism* 18 (2010): 3–29.

30.   "Continuity Script," 51.

31.   Letter to the Corinthians, quoted in Slavoj Žižek, *The Fragile Absolute: Or, Why is the Christian Legacy Worth Fighting For?* (London: Verso, 2000), 127. For a critique of the alleged patriarchy and anti-Judaism behind this association of Christianity with the figure of the "new man" as invoked by both Žižek and Badiou, see Amy Hollywood, "Saint Paul and the New Man," *Critical Inquiry* 35 (2009): 865–76.

into a 'Cheification' of Christ himself."[32] Gutiérrez Alea, however, always shows more reservation than enthusiasm when it comes to the supposed emancipatory role that is thus attributed, by way of analogy, to Christianity. There is not only the recurrent question of the victims of this destruction of the old, including the potential anti-Semitism hidden behind the praise for Christian-revolutionary novelty. But, in Cuba in particular, any reliance on the analogy with Christianity also risks reducing the construction of socialism to a perpetuation of the political status quo for which this religion historically has provided an ideological alibi. It is for this reason that both before and after *Memorias del subdesarrollo*, in movies such as *Doce sillas* (*Twelve Chairs*), *Los supervivientes* (*The Survivors*), and *La última cena* (*The Last Supper*), this filmmaker patiently revisits the centuries-long legacy of Christianity as a near-insuperable obstacle, rather than a helpful analogon, for the creation of the new man in Cuba. "In almost all the movies that I made, the theme of bourgeois or petty-bourgeois mentality and its persistence in the first stage of the revolution has been a constant," he remarks. "It is a way of making evident those values from the old dominant ideology which we can still find, in a more or less disguised form, in all strata of our population, and which may curb the development of a new social consciousness."[33] A mere critique of religion, along the lines of what Marx and Engels in *The German Ideology* call the "critical criticism" of the Young Hegelians, is therefore insufficient. Nor will the vestiges of the old dominant ideology automatically disappear as a result of the development of the material forces and relations of production. Gutiérrez Alea explains:

> And, in reality, what always interested me is the problem of the instrumentalization of the religious spirit (in whatever form) as subjection to a specific class and, in any event, to curb the development of society. If on different occasions we alluded to this problem starting out from the Catholic religion, it is because it is what is near at hand and because in its relations to the bourgeoisie we can show with greater clarity those mechanisms that inevitably lead to hypocrisy and lies.[34]

But, if now we look beyond Gutiérrez Alea's filmography, how should we address such broad questions concerning the role of Christianity and Judaism in relation to socialism and communism, if at the same time we wish to take into account the critique of religion that can be found in the works of Marx and Freud?

---

32. Slavoj Žižek, *For They Know Not What They Do: Enjoyment as a Political Factor* (London: Verso, 2002), xlvi.
33. Gutiérrez Alea, "No siempre fui cineasta," 27.
34. Gutiérrez Alea, "Sobre vivencias y supervivencias," 204–5.

Being Jewish

Is there a divine origin to being socialist, or is it something one comes to be?
León Rozitchner, Ser judío

The hatred for Judaism is at bottom a hatred for Christianity, and it is not surprising that in the German National Socialist revolution this close connection of the two monotheistic religions finds such clear expression in the hostile treatment of both.
Sigmund Freud, Moses and Monotheism

Rozitchner tackles several of these questions in a long essay titled *Ser judío*, which can be translated as either "Being Jewish" or "Jewish Being"—incidentally the same title, *Être juif*, as the one used first by Emmanuel Levinas in 1947 and then, in a commentary on Levinas, by the French ex-Maoist Benny Lévy, after the latter, like so many members of his generation, had turned away from the militancy of his past.[35] Completed in October 1967, the month of Che Guevara's death in Bolivia, Rozitchner's essay at the same time serves as an important conceptual link between *Moral burguesa y revolución*, with its backdrop of the Bay of Pigs invasion of April 17, 1961 and the Missile Crisis of October 1962, and the events of 1968 that surround *Memorias del subdesarrollo*. The immediate context of *Ser judío*, however, is the Israeli–Arab conflict of June 1967, which brings Rozitchner again to raise the question of the place of religion—his own included—in the context of the construction of the "new man" of socialism.[36]

Ser judío begins with what are supposed to be painfully orthodox platitudes, phrased in a series of rhetorical questions. Did Marx not propose to bring down all religion from heaven to earth, from the sacred to the profane, from the infinite to the all-too-human finitude of the class struggle? Does this not imply that a leftist should subtract all his or her stubborn attachments to religion, including the Jewish religion in the case of a Jewish leftist such as Rozitchner himself? Where, then, does this leave the index of religion by which this singular subject,

35. León Rozitchner, *Ser judío* (Buenos Aires: Ediciones de la Flor, 1967). Compare Emmanuel Levinas, "Être juif," *Confluences* 7 (1947): 253–64; and Benny Lévy, *Être juif: Étude lévinassienne* (Paris: Verdier, 2003). Levinas's text has been translated into English by Mary Beth Mader as "Being Jewish," *Continental Philosophy Review* 40: 3 (2007): 205–10. For a commentary, see Annabel Herzog, "Benny Levy versus Emmanuel Levinas on 'Being Jewish,'" *Modern Judaism* 26: 1 (2006): 15–30. See also Maurice Blanchot, "Être juif," *La Nouvelle Revue Française* 116–117 (1962): 279–85, 471–6.

36. More recently, in the context of the 2009 Israeli invasion of Gaza, Rozitchner picked up again on the same issues in "Plomo fundido' sobre la conciencia judía," *Página 12* (January 4, 2009). See also his earlier text, "¿Podemos seguir siendo judíos?" *Página 12* (July 23, 2006). Several of these texts have now been collected and reissued in León Rozitchner, *Ser judío y otros ensayos afines* (Buenos Aires: Losada, 2011). These texts can be read in a fruitful dialogue with Esther Benbassa, *Être juif après Gaza* (Paris: CNRS Éditions, 2009).

like millions of others, is inscribed in a common history, a common body, and a common territory, no matter how dispersed and threatened the latter may be? What, in short, is the possible place of religion within a revolutionary socialist or communist horizon?

In *Ser judío* Rozitchner thus places the issues surrounding the Jewish religion and the Arab–Israeli conflict within the context of the problematic that Che Guevara two years earlier had outlined in terms of the construction of the "new man" of socialism, and the destruction of the "old man" that this would necessarily entail. It is this problematic that connects the question of religion to the logics of change, sacrifice, and abnegation that we find in *Memorias del subdesarrollo*. "The revolution demands the sacrifice of the negative, the incorporation into a new level of objectivity, the destruction of old belongings, the abandonment of class complicity," Rozitchner writes. "The leftist militant is the one who, given that he is inserted in a process of change, is ready to change himself."[37] In the Middle East conflict, supposedly, the left-leaning militant should therefore not hesitate to extend this same logic by standing against the imperialism of the Jewish state and in favor of Arab socialism. By contrast, those Jewish leftists who refuse to adopt this logic risk being seen as obstacles to the historical unfolding of the revolutionary process of national liberation and international solidarity. Rozitchner summarizes this last objection as follows:

> Here lies, it will then be pointed out without equivocation, the exact point where at last the lack of revolutionary modification of the Jewish leftist, his permanence in the past, the petrified kernel of non-innovation, his traditional incapacity to sacrifice what is his own and include himself fully in the movement of history. Here appears the emphasis on a divisive particularity, an uncanny difference that would thus show the persistence of a central rightist zone that has not yet been extirpated, irreducible to analysis and to the process of liberation: a counterrevolutionary kernel in the bosom of the revolutionary himself.[38]

Being Jewish, according to this objection, would be an obstacle to being leftist, the sign of a persistent counterrevolutionary attachment and the overdevelopment of divisively particularist memories. "But is this really so?" Rozitchner immediately asks. "Let us consider whether being Jewish, and recognizing oneself as such, is incompatible with being consistent with the Left."[39]

In the first place, Rozitchner suggests rather surprisingly that it is this interpretation of religion that is idealist. To demand the pure negation of the religious element leaves this element itself in the realm of a bad kind of infinity, one that is merely imaginary and transcendent, while the earth into which this same element is supposed to be dissolved

37. Rozitchner, *Ser judío*, 9.
38. Ibid., 10.
39. Ibid., 11.

acquires in turn the purely imaginary attributes of the heavenly. It means to abandon the trace of what makes human subjects into who they are, and thus to lose out on the possible index that links one subject, group, or nation to another.

> What is it that disappears forever together with this index? It is the density of the historical process that produced us; it is the reduction to pure form without content, to the one-dimensionality of a process that contains other dimensions and that, by having cast them out of ourselves, we actually do no more than cast out, without knowing it, from the world.[40]

Far from merely repeating an enlightened critique of religious ideology in the name of secular-scientific reason, a Marxist understanding of religion must therefore begin by assuming the material and historical conditions for the emergence of the religious subject itself—conditions that are never purely rational but that include the sentient rationality of affectivity, corporeality, and even territoriality. Not only is it strangely angelical to treat religion as a mere superstructure or as pure opium for the people, to be sacrificed on the altar of socialist internationalism; this scission between the real and the imaginary, between the political and the ideological, is precisely a remnant of bourgeois individualism. Rozitchner writes:

> "Being of the world," "being international": these are pretty metaphors of the Left, but without support in the body. Atheistic, they have the corporeality of angels, the tenuous spatiality of the religious heaven, a celestial ground to which the batting of wings of ideas lifts whoever believes in them, only so as all of a sudden, at the first bang, to make them descend to it and cover it up forever with its truth . . . And it is this demand not to be what we are, which appears at the crucial all-or-nothing moments, in which the other either counts as similar or is scorned as sacrificeable, it is this demand that must be signaled, despite everything, as a survival of the Right in the very bosom of the Left.[41]

The original objection from leftists against the persistence of religious elements is thus turned back upon itself. It is the demand for the destruction of all attachments to religion that is rightist, whereas the leftist answer, properly speaking, would rather consist in coming to terms with the genealogical backdrop of such attachments, whether religious or otherwise.

Being Jewish, for Rozitchner, is what he calls an index of the inhuman treatment and persecution of humanity—one that, if fully assumed, should connect with other indices such as being a worker, being black, or being a woman. These are indices of suffering, pain, and exploitation, but also indices of emancipation and rebellion that should be able to link up in an international movement of liberation.

---

40. Ibid., 48.
41. Ibid., 38, 31.

In this sense, they function as possible points of insertion of the subject into history:

> Being Jewish is my index of the inhumanity of the human, but not only of that inhumanity which weighs down on us: there is a consistency of evil in the world, there is a linkage between pain and pain, there exists an international of suffering that the hand of man inflicts on man. Thus, being Jewish can only be, coherently, the index of a meaning that keeps itself alive in history: to destroy inhumanity in all its forms of relation.[42]

Obviously, not all of these indices have the same status. "Thus, the subtraction of the worker, being as radical as it is, never reaches the extreme of that of the Jew: because the latter is not only robbed of the *things* of the world, he is not only dominated: as Jews we are denied the very *ground* of being in the world."[43] In one case, we would be dealing with the subtraction of a *mode* of being; in the other, with the destruction of *being* as such. What are the consequences of this difference, for example, between being a worker and being Jewish? Is this the same difference, to put it crudely, as that between being a worker and being Christian?

The difference in question can be measured in terms of the demands for change, negation, and destruction that it entails, as well as in terms of the historical burden carried by such demands in the twentieth century:

> One can change the *mode* of being human; ceasing to be bad in order to be good, ceasing to be a thief in order to be honest, inverting the values, ceasing to be a worker in order to be the boss. In this mode of being there is an access to another mode of being, to another mode of recognition. But there is a condition that is not a *mode* but a *being*: being black, being Jewish. To be negated for the fact of being—this experience, no matter how reduced in certain cases and no matter how profound in others—is the *minimal experience* which in each Jew, because of the fact of his *origin*, opened up for him as an enigma, as a fundamental injustice that is difficult to assimilate: being negated by an other for the fact of being what one is.[44]

Rozitchner is quick to add that there is neither hierarchy nor priority between these two levels of modes of being and being itself. "And yet I do not say that this negation that one suffers is all the negation in the world there is, nor that it is the greatest, not even the most profound among the other negations that man gave rise to among men. I only say that it is ours, that it is our most radical point of insertion into human history."[45] The issue is not to place one index or point of insertion before or higher than the other, but rather, through each one of them,

---

42. Ibid., 17.
43. Ibid., 36.
44. Ibid., 27.
45. Ibid., 28.

to reach a common cause that we might call generic. The aim, in other words, ultimately remains that of finding ways of inscribing subjectivity on a path of universal emancipation.

The question then immediately arises as to that prior decision which concerns the very discrimination between modes of being and being as such. On what grounds does one place being-Jewish in the same column as being-black or being-woman, rather than that of being-worker or being-bourgeois? As social constructivists might argue, is there not a whole affective, cultural, geographical, economic, and ideological prehistory—precisely the history of how one becomes who one is—that makes of any being, in fact, a *mode* of being? Why maintain the gap at all between the ontological and the ontic, all the while insisting that for a Jew, but perhaps not for a Christian, this gap cannot be closed: "This transformation of the ontological into the ontic, of the 'metaphysical' into the 'physical,' this transformation of the negation of being into mere negation of quality, this reduction of one's own meaning, is what the Jew cannot accomplish."[46] But did not the rebuttal of the common objections against the impediment of religion point in the direction of a general becoming-physical of all metaphysics, a becoming-finite of the infinite, and a becoming-ontic of the ontological? Why, then, preserve an exception on the side of metaphysics? If this exception is grounded in the history of persecution and genocide, should the emancipatory answer not consist in understanding the place of religion by and through history, rather than by setting up a transcendent ontology? And if, on the other hand, the retrieval of one's being is meant to bolster the links of solidarity with other beings who would similarly have retrieved and assumed their own origin, who decides which of these indices belongs on the side of the ontic and which on the side of the ontological?

In fact, the danger would appear to be twofold. There is first of all the danger of cultural relativism, in which each subject has his or her index of the inhumanity of the human, among which we can build chains of equivalence and solidarity, though none would be worth more than any other. They would all be equally other from all others, without ontological hierarchy. Conversely, however, there is also the opposite danger of setting up a transcendent standard—some ontological level of being from which all other levels must appear as merely ontic modes of being.

Marxism traditionally avoided the first of these dangers, but potentially falls into the traps of the second by setting up the category of a fundamental contradiction—namely, the class struggle—as being prior to all other contradictions. As Slavoj Žižek writes about the Marxist notion of antagonism:

---

46. Ibid., 30.

This traditional notion implies two interconnected features: (1) there exists a certain fundamental antagonism possessing an ontological priority to "mediate" all other antagonisms, determining their place and their specific weight (class antagonism, economic exploitation); (2) historical development brings about, if not a necessity, at least an "objective possibility" of solving this fundamental antagonism and, in this way, mediating all other antagonisms—to recall the well-known Marxist formulation, the same logic which drove mankind into alienation and class division also creates the condition for its abolition—"die Wunde schliesst der Speer nur, der sie schlug" ("the wound can be healed only by the spear which made it")—as Wagner, Marx's contemporary, said through the mouth of Parsifal.[47]

Insofar as Freud and Lacan also place a fundamental deadlock or discontent at the foundation of the social bond, do they too not contribute to a similar notion, against relativistic anti-essentialism, that all identity-formations hover around the kernel of a radical non-identity? Was this not Freud's message to the world when, fleeing Nazi Germany, he nonetheless decided not to cling to his cultural identity as a Jew but instead took away, as it were, the very founding figure of Jewish religion in *Moses and Monotheism*—his final work, considered by many to be his testament to humanity—by claiming that Moses was an Egyptian? This theft would then also be Freud's greatest gift, his most daring deed: "To deny a people the man whom it praises as the greatest of its sons is not a deed to be undertaken lightheartedly—especially by one belonging to that people."[48] As Edward Said indicated shortly before his death, it may have been Freud's way of indicating that even the most stubborn communal identity hides inherent limits that keep it from becoming one:

> Freud's symbol of those limits was that the founder of Jewish identity was himself a non-European Egyptian. In other words, identity cannot be thought or worked through itself alone; it cannot constitute or even imagine itself without that radical originary break or flaw which will not be repressed, because Moses was Egyptian, and therefore always outside the identity inside which so many have stood, and suffered—and later, perhaps, even triumphed. The strength of his thought is, I believe, that it can be articulated in and speak to other besieged identities as well—not through dispensing palliatives such as tolerance and compassion but, rather, by attending to it as a troubling, disabling, destabilizing secular wound—the essence of the cosmopolitan, from which there can be no recovery, no state of resolved or Stoic calm, and no utopian reconciliation even within itself.[49]

Finally, in Žižek's rather different tone, the same could perhaps be said about the contribution of Freud's heir Lacan:

---

47. Žižek, *The Sublime Object of Ideology*, 3.
48. Freud, *Moses and Monotheism*, 3.
49. Said, *Freud and the Non-European*, 54.

That is to say, Lacanian psychoanalysis goes a decisive step further than the usual "post-Marxist" anti-essentialism affirming the irreducible plurality of particular struggles—in other words, demonstrating how their articulation into a series of equivalences depends always on the radical contingency of the social-historical process: it enables us to grasp this plurality itself as a multitude of responses to the same impossible-real kernel.[50]

Rozitchner's claim, in the end, is more modest. He does not seek to turn non-identity into the metaphysical ground for an ethics of cosmopolitanism, nor does he need to refer socialism back to the non-historical kernel of some impossible-real. Instead, he asks us to delve into the origin of who we are as the contradictory index of what we are not yet; and, based on the assumption of this origin, he proposes linkages with similar traces within the ensemble of human relations. The point is to retrieve the full affective, corporeal, and historical density of one's mode of being for the sake of generic sameness. "But there is no leap from the old to the new: the *transit* from one to the other is revolution, and the *result* will be revolution," Rozitchner concludes in *Ser judío*. "For this category of the separating negation, this crazy dialectic which leaps from one domain to the other, this obstinate negation that abandons the one simply to pass on to the other, is a bourgeois scheme of thinking."[51]

What has happened since then, however, is that the ontological priority of the other, of difference or of non-identity—a priority given imponderable historical weight through reference to the Holocaust—has become the basis for an ethics of respect for this absolutely prior ground, the result of which tends to entail the complete obliteration of the very process in the construction of socialism and the "new man" that we still find in *Memorias del subdesarrollo* and *Moral burguesa y revolución*. Rozitchner's answer to this obliteration in subsequent writings of his consists in reaching back even farther into the history of subjectivity in order to understand how a logic of terror and destruction can latch on to our innermost materials—our core sentient being or the guts of our conscious reason—so as to subject us to the rule of capital and war. One way of doing so is to revisit all the implications of one of Marx's most difficult and problematic texts: his response to Bruno Bauer's "The Jewish Question."[52]

---

50. Žižek, *The Sublime Object of Ideology*, 4.
51. Rozitchner, *Ser judío*, 32, 56.
52. León Rozitchner, "La cuestión judía," in Daniel Bensaïd, Karl Marx, Bruno Bauer and Roman Rosdolski, *Volver a "La cuestión judía,"* ed. Esteban Vernik (Barcelona: Gedisa, 2011), 193–253. This is the Spanish translation of Karl Marx, *Sur la question juive*, ed. and introduced by Daniel Bensaïd (Paris: La Fabrique, 2006).

On the Christian Question

We think the "political" like Romans, i.e., imperially.
                                        Martin Heidegger, Parmenides

Rome conquered Christianity by becoming Christendom . . . Thus twenty Christian centuries were necessary to give the ancient and naked Roman idea a tunic with which to cover up its shameful parts and a conscience for its base moments. And now that idea is here, perfect and equipped with all the forces of the soul. Who will destroy it? Is it indestructible? Is it precisely its ruin that humanity has conquered with thousandfold efforts?
                                        Elias Canetti, The Human Province

"On the Jewish Question," Marx's text from 1843 published the following year in the sole issue of the *Deutsch-Französische Jahrbücher* ever to see the light, is one of those texts that we may have understood all too well. Not only has this text been buried under a mountain of accusations against its author, ranging from charges of Jewish self-hatred to outright anti-Semitism. Even authors such as the late Daniel Bensaïd, who are otherwise wholly sympathetic to Marx's arguments, often see no need to go beyond the plea for a complete secularization of all theological arguments, against the current "religious turn" among radical thinkers of Left and Right alike. Admittedly, Marx himself may seem to be arguing along these lines. Indeed, does he too not propose to bring heaven down to earth, to put the spiritual back on its material base, and to reduce the infinite to the strictly finite? "Religion no longer appears as the basis, but as the *manifestation* of secular narrowness," he writes. Or again: "We do not turn secular questions into theological questions. We turn theological questions into secular ones. History has long enough been merged in superstition, we now merge superstition in history."[53] However, merely to argue for the secularization of theology misses the whole point of "On the Jewish Question," according to Rozitchner. Worse, it confuses Marx's argument with that of its principal interlocutor, Bruno Bauer, in the original text published in German as *Die Judenfrage*— a title, incidentally, that we should perhaps translate as "The Jewish Demand" or "The Demand of the Jews." It is Bauer, not Marx, who reasons that Jews in Germany cannot be emancipated so long as they do not emancipate themselves from being Jewish. "Bauer therefore demands," in Marx's paraphrase, "on the one hand, that the Jew should renounce Judaism, and that mankind in general should renounce religion, in order to achieve *civic* emancipation. On the other hand, he quite consistently regards the *political* abolition of

---

53. Karl Marx, "On the Jewish Question," in Karl Marx and Friedrich Engels, *Collected Works*, vol. 3 (New York: International Publishers, 1975), 151.

religion as the abolition of religion as such."[54] Marx is still para-phrasing Bauer when he later writes: "The *political* emancipation of the Jew, the Christian, and in general of *religious* man is the *emancipation of* the state from Judaism, from Christianity, from *religion* in general."[55] Clearly, even for the future author of *Capital* who will delight in signaling all the "theological niceties" involved in "commodity fetishism," the argument for the total emancipation from religion cannot suffice. In fact, the abolition of religion risks leaving intact the religious—more properly Christian—core of the dominant form of modern politics—that is, it fails to touch upon the Christian core of the modern state as propounded even by Bauer and other Young Hegelians such as Arnold Ruge, Marx's friend and co-editor of the *Deutsch-Französische Jahrbücher*, with whom he would promptly break both personally and ideologically.

In his reinterpretation of "On the Jewish Question," Rozitchner draws attention to our continuing inability to come to terms with the complexities of the text, blinded as most contemporary readers undoubtedly are by Marx's constant use of ironic, not to say sarcastic language that seems all the more disturbing in the wake of the Holocaust. For Rozitchner, the point is not just to secularize religion and spirituality in the name of materialism but, rather, to travel down the road to the religious alienation that lies at the root of political and economic alienation. Why else would Marx see the need to pick up the question of religion again, if already in the so-called Kreuznach manu-script from the beginning of 1843, in a summary settling of accounts with his own Hegelianism, he had written that "the criticism of religion is in the main complete"?[56] Why else would he return to religiosity when in this same pivotal year he was already moving away from humanist themes like the freedom of the press in favor of the critique of political economy and other topics of historical materialism, such as the polemics unleashed by the question of the theft of wood?[57]

As a non-believing Jewish Freudo-Marxist who has spent much of his life as a thinker studying the origins of modern capitalism in pre-capitalist Christian subject-formations, Rozitchner is especially sensitive to the fact that the call for religious self-sacrifice that Bauer proposed to the Jews as the solution to their demand for political emancipation in Germany must have awakened painful personal memories on the part of Marx. Upon the recommendation of his father, Marx had after all been baptized at the age of six. As a Jew who had become a socially acceptable Christian, Marx had thus already traveled

---

54. Ibid., 149.
55. Ibid., 151.
56. Marx, "Contribution to the Critique of Hegel's Philosophy of Law," *Complete Works*, vol. 3, 175.
57. See Daniel Bensaïd, *Les Dépossédés: Karl Marx, les voleurs de bois et le droit des pauvres* (Paris: La Fabrique, 2007).

half the road toward complete political emancipation in the eyes of Bauer. In Marx himself, though, this experience must have left deep psychic scars. Precisely in a long letter to his father written when he was nineteen years old, shortly after arriving at the University of Berlin, young Karl would justify his career choice by explaining why he had abandoned the study of law in favor of philosophy, first idealist and then materialist. "From the idealism which, by the way, I had compared and nourished with the idealism of Kant and Fichte, I arrived at the point of seeking the idea in reality itself. If previously the gods had dwelt above the earth, now they became its centre," as Marx put it, "and like a vigorous traveller I set about the task itself, a philosophical-dialectical account of divinity, as it manifests itself as the idea-in-itself, as religion, as nature, and as history."[58] And yet, even through such a near-materialist working-through of religion as nature and as history, this loving son never seems to have fully healed from the trauma of his conversion to Christianity decided upon by his father Heinrich.

When Marx returned to the relation between politics and religion in "On the Jewish Question," according to Rozitchner he was speaking partly from the painful memory traces left in his body and soul by his forced conversion to Christianity. What this experience allowed Marx to see, perhaps in a sadly privileged way, was the extent to which there is a Christian foundation that lives on hidden at the very heart of the supposedly secular modern state. This is because the logic of secularization, as in the separation of Church and state so often invoked—whether with pride or nowadays increasing regret—in North America, presupposes a prior separation of the private and the public, symbolized in the split nature of the human being as "man," on one hand, and "citizen," on the other, in the different Declarations of the Rights of Man and the Citizen that accompany the French and American Revolutions. The real question, then, does not pertain to the difference between two religions, Jewish and Christian, according to what Bauer, in the second text to which Marx responds, calls their respective capacities for being free. Instead, for Marx, this religious difference is itself nothing more than a displaced version of the division between the private realm, in which there exists freedom of religious belief, and the public sphere, which is supposed to be the realm of politics proper and in which, as a consequence, religion should no longer have any place. But then, added Marx, this last division in turn does nothing more than prolong the Christian division of the heavenly and the earthly, the infinite and the finite. "Where the political state has attained to its full development, man leads, not only in thought, in consciousness, but in *reality*, in *life*, a double existence—celestial and terrestrial," writes Marx, with great sarcasm:

---

58. Marx, "Letter from Marx to His Father in Trier," in Karl Marx and Friedrich Engels, *Collected Works*, vol. 1 (Moscow: Progress Publishers, 1975), 18.

He lives in the *political community*, where he regards himself as *communal being*, and in *civil society* where he acts simply as a *private individual*, treats other men as means, degrades himself to the role of a mere means, and becomes the plaything of alien powers. The political state, in relation to civil society, is just as spiritual as is heaven in relation to earth.[59]

What this means is that modern politics, embodied in the state, continues to be built on the permanence of a form of subjectivity that is profoundly Christian. Or, as Rozitchner concludes: "The Christian subjective scission becomes objective and unfolds itself in that scission within the state." And this is all the more true when the latter proclaims itself to be secular: "The Christian spirit, subjective, infinite, and immanent, which had become objective, finite and transcendent in the theological Christian state, has constituted itself into the secular and political basis of the perfect rational secular state."[60]

What Rozitchner's reading makes clear is the extent to which Marx blames Bauer for failing to see the extent to which the Jewish question remains unanswerable without commenting upon the Christian question. Similarly, I might add, what even contemporary proponents of the complete profanation of politics fail to understand is the extent to which the demand of the Jews cannot be met without putting Christianity into question: "The division of man into a *public man* and a *private man*, the *displacement* of religion from the state into civil society, this is not a stage in political emancipation but its *completion*; this emancipation therefore neither abolishes the *real* religiousness of man, nor strives to do so."[61] The Christian state, which still leaves Christianity in existence as an explicit creed, as for example in the case of Germany at the time of Marx, has not yet fully perfected the transubstantiation of religion into politics. Paradoxically, this level of perfection is achieved only in the so-called secular democratic state, which Marx associates with the United States of America. Marx writes:

Political democracy is Christian in the sense that man, not merely one man but every man, is there considered a sovereign being, a supreme being: but it is uneducated, unsocial man, man just as he is in his fortuitous existence, man as he has been corrupted, lost to himself, alienated, subjected to the rule of inhuman conditions and elements, by the whole organization of our society—in short man who is not yet a *real* species-being.

59. Marx, "On the Jewish Question," 154.
60. Rozitchner, "La cuestión judía," 200. Rozitchner actually began his investigations into the contradictory links between Marxism and Christianity as early as a contribution to the journal *Pasado y Presente*, then still edited by Óscar del Barco and Aníbal Arcondo. See León Rozitchner, "Marxismo y cristianismo," *Pasado y Presente: Revista trimestral de ideología y cultura* 2-3 (July–December 1963): 113–133. This text is followed by a reply and an additional polemic in Conrado Eggers Lan and León Rozitchner, "Acerca de 'Marxismo o cristianismo'," *Pasado y Presente: Revista trimestral de ideología y cultura* 4 (January–March 1964): 322–332.
61. Marx, "On the Jewish Question," 155.

Later, he adds:

> In the perfect democracy, the religious and theological consciousness itself is in its own eyes the more religious and the more theological because it is apparently without political significance, without worldly aims, an affair of the heart withdrawn from the world, the expression of the limitations of reason, the product of arbitrariness and fantasy, and because it is a life that is really of the other world. Christianity attains here the *practical* expression of its universal-religious significance in that the most diverse world outlooks are grouped together alongside one another in the form of Christianity and still more because it does not ask that anyone should profess Christianity, but simply that he should have some kind of religion.[62]

What Marx proposed to do in "On the Jewish Question," then, was at least theoretically to retrace some of the steps that had led up to the paradoxical accomplishment of the Christian spirit in the modern secular state. The political timeliness of this proposal for the present moment should be obvious enough, provided that we are not seduced by the secularization thesis nor misled by the accusations of ubiquitous anti-Semitism. There are important theoretical as well as political lessons to be learned from Marx's youthful text. In addition to developing a Marxist theory of the subject, a contemporary reading of "On the Jewish Question" thus requires that we also reconstruct a history of modern capitalist as well as pre-capitalist forms of subjectivity, along the lines of what Rozitchner himself does in his book *La Cosa y la Cruz*, which offers a close textual reading of Saint Augustine's *Confessions* as the quintessential manual of subjection of the individual to both the Christian religion and the power of command of the Roman Empire.

In retrospect, this is an agenda for theoretical work that Rozitchner already finds in Marx's text from the *Deutsch-Französiche Jahrbücher*, perhaps deriving the task of historical genealogy from Marx's own autobiographical trajectory:

> We might think that in "On the Jewish Question" Marx expresses his own drama of transition in order to help the Jews understand—for it is they to whom he addresses himself directly toward the end of the first part—how they ought to think so as to reach an understanding of their being Jewish that would be not religious but secular. He does not want them to do what Bauer asks from them, nor what his father did. And he tells them that without rehabilitating that primordial place they will never be able to understand the secret of Christian disdain that the Jewish child experiences almost from the moment it is born; that instead of becoming Christians, or demanding that the state recognize them as citizens but only in order to continue living disdained as Jewish men and women, they ought to walk down the historical path [*desanden el camino histórico*] that took them toward the Jewish religious essence so as to find hidden, at its very base and as though lying in wait for when they wake up from the dream, the secular generic human essence that he tells them about.[63]

---

62. Marx, "On the Jewish Question," 159 (translation modified).
63. Rozitchner, "La cuestión judía," 197–198. In a long appendix to his reading of "On

Rozitchner is quick to add that Marx himself, even later in his mature work, did not bring to fruition the agenda of such a combined history and theory of political subjectivity:

> It is true, Marx does not analyze in detail the historical conditions, the "social relationships" that from historical Judaism in its determinate context led to the metamorphosis produced in the ancient popular pagan imaginary by the new Christian myth so dear to Constantine, with whom religion at its origin appears as a new technology of domination in the production of subjects appropriate for the subsistence of the Roman Empire. But contemporary Marxists cannot ignore this, as can be deduced from Marx's analysis, when they pretend to transform the consciousness of alienated political subjects by modifying only the economic relations of production, without putting into play the mythic determinations of Christianity.[64]

There are those today, like Žižek, who manage to present Christianity as a legacy still worth fighting for, or a lost cause still worth defending. For them, such a task requires a materialist reversal, whereby what otherwise appears to bask in the light of dogmatic truth all of a sudden shines forth as a "fragile absolute," summed up in Christ's exclamation on the Cross: "Oh Father, why hast Thou forsaken me?" What this cry symbolizes is in fact precisely that which resists symbolization absolutely—that is, the fact that the order of the universe is inherently incomplete, dysfunctional, non-All. "In short, with this 'Father, hast thou forsaken me?', it is God who actually dies, revealing His utter impotence, and thereupon rises from the dead in the guise of the Holy Spirit."[65] Far from simply betraying a momentary lack of faith, Jesus's cry would highlight the properly revolutionary nature of Christianity in the eyes of Žižek—in this regard also a strict follower of Chesterton, who wrote in his *Orthodoxy*: "Christianity is the only religion on earth that has felt that omnipotence made God incomplete. Christianity alone has felt that God, to be wholly God, must have been a rebel as well as a king."[66]

No matter how much we may spruce them up with examples from Hegel to Hollywood, though, all such dialectical reformulations and reversals of Christianity—including Žižek's bold reformulations of the

---

the Jewish Question," Rozitchner proposes a systematic retrieval of the Marxist notion of "generic human being," which for years has been buried under the scorn of Althusserian anti-humanism. See León Rozitchner, "Apéndice: ¿Qué pasó con el ser genérico como analizador de una sociedad?" in *Volver a "La cuestión judía,"* 230–53.

64.   Rozitchner, "La cuestión judía," 204.

65.   Slavoj Žižek, *For They Know Not What They Do: Enjoyment as a Political Factor* (2nd edn, London: Verso, 2002), liii.

66.   Slavoj Žižek, "A Modest Plea for the Hegelian Reading of Christianity," in Slavoj Žižek and John Milbank, *The Monstrosity of Christ: Paradox or Dialectic*, ed. Creston Davis (Cambridge: MIT Press, 2009), 48. For a criticism of this reading, see Bruno Bosteels, "Žižek and Christianity, or, the Critique of Religion after Marx and Freud," in Molly Anne Rothenberg and Jamil Khader, eds, *Žižek Now* (London: Polity Press, 2012).

passage from Judaism to Christianity—in the name of a newborn materialism remain, strictly speaking, at the level of a structural or
transcendental discussion of the conditions of possibility of subjectivity
as such. Even the addition of a dual focus on both the ontogenesis and
phylogenesis of the subject is not quite the same as taking into account
such profound historical complicities as the one that, according to
Marx, links the democratic form of the state to Christianity. Nor does
it suffice merely to abandon the vocabulary of the religious turn, with
all its reactionary and fundamentalist overtones, if at the same time the
very religious—and more properly Christian—foundations of the
theory of the subject are not only left untouched, but not even explicitly admitted anymore. If such a theory may properly claim to be a kind
of recommencement of the materialist dialectic, as in the case of Badiou
or Žižek, then what remains to be done will be once more closer to the
task of the historical materialist, which will also require placing politics
in a force-field between theory and history. "We therefore must reach
back from political to religious alienation in order to understand the
persistence of the religious within the political," as Rozitchner writes in
his careful commentary on "On the Jewish Question." This task is all
the more urgent today, in the wake of the so-called war on terror,
waged in the name of Western civilization against so-called fundamentalism: "We must show that the Christian essence, which 'critical
criticism' claims to have overcome, remains and is objectified in the
material social relations of the democratic secular state whose terminal
form, as Marx demonstrates, is the United States of America; and
show, moreover, how it persists to this very day."[67]

---

67. Rozitchner, "La cuestión judía," 199.

5

POLITICS, PSYCHOANALYSIS, AND RELIGION IN THE AGE OF TERROR

Are There Any Saints Left?

A curtain had fallen, my holy of holies was rent asunder, and new gods had to be installed.

Marx, letter to his father, November 10, 1837

The more saints, the more laughter; that's my principle, to wit, the way out of capitalist discourse—which will not constitute progress, if it happens only for some.

Jacques Lacan, Television

In recent years a whole spate of thinkers on the left end of the political spectrum seem to feel the need not just to engage with religion and with the persistence of a certain political theology in radical thought, but more particularly to model new forms of militantism upon the figure of the saint: from Saint Paul for Badiou and Žižek to Saint Francis of Assisi for Hardt and Negri.[1] That this is not merely a Christian debate, nor one dominated exclusively by male voices, can be seen in the fact that Hélène Cixous also turns to the image of the saint in her *Portrait of Jacques Derrida as a Young Jewish Saint*, following Derrida's rather heavy reliance on Saint Augustine's *Confessions* in his own *Circumfessions*.[2] Clearly more is at stake than a superficial coincidence; rather, the saint confronts us with a tangle of references at the intersection

---

1. Alain Badiou, *Saint Paul: The Foundation of Universalism*, trans. Ray Brassier (Stanford: Stanford University Press, 2003); Slavoj Žižek, "The Politics of Truth, or, Alain Badiou as a Reader of St Paul," in Slavoj Žižek, *The Ticklish Subject: The Absent Centre of Political Ontology* (London: Verso, 1999), 127–70; Michael Hardt and Antonio Negri, *Empire* (Cambridge: Harvard University Press, 2000), 413. To this list we could add Giorgio Agamben but his reading of Saint Paul, especially in *The Time That Remains: A Commentary on the Letter to the Romans*, trans. Patricia Dailey (Stanford: Stanford University Press, 2005), is unlike the use of the saint's reference on behalf of Badiou, Žižek, or Hardt and Negri.
2. Hélène Cixous, *Portrait de Jacques Derrida en jeune saint juif* (Paris: Galilée, 2001); and Jacques Derrida (with Geoffrey Bennington), "Circonfession," in *Jacques Derrida* (Paris: Seuil, 1991), 7–291.

between politics, religion, and psychoanalysis. In fact, insofar as saints seem to come marching in at an almost unstoppable speed, few tasks could be more urgent today than to begin unraveling this dense tangle of references. Precisely such a task is taken up in León Rozitchner's formidable book, *La Cosa y la Cruz: Cristianismo y capitalismo (en torno a las* Confesiones *de san Agustín)*, originally published in 1997.[3]

The title of this book, *La Cosa y la Cruz* (The Thing and the Cross), is most likely a pun on Hegel's famous passage from his *Philosophy of Right* in which the German philosopher proposes to read the cross or crucifixion itself as the revelation of reason in history:

> To recognize reason as the rose in the cross of the present and thereby to enjoy the present, this is the rational insight which reconciles us to the actual, the reconciliation which philosophy affords to those in whom there has once arisen an inner voice bidding them to comprehend, not only to dwell in what is substantive while still retaining subjective freedom, but also to possess individual freedom while standing not in anything particular and accidental but in what exists absolutely.[4]

By substituting the Freudian Thing (*das Ding* in German, *la Cosa* in Spanish) for Hegel's rose (*la Rosa* in Spanish), Rozitchner proposes to investigate via the example of Augustine's *Confessions* to what extent a psychoanalytical approach to religion also means tearing apart the relation of reconciliation with reality promised by Christianity. "The *Confessions* are the most ardent story of that which Augustine evokes and at the same time eludes so meticulously while telling his story, like someone who wants nothing to do with the Thing," writes Rozitchner. He continues: "Faced with this indelible and unrepresentable mark, which persecutes him as what is most desirable (and at the same time most fear-inspiring), Augustine covers it with the words of God the Father so as to pacify the anxiety that emanates from what has no name: the unnamed Thing."[5] Not even Christianity—with its construction of the divine Father in the place of his absent father and the Virgin Mary in the place of his mother Monica—will be able to pacify Augustine's anxiety over the Thing. Rozitchner's close reading of the *Confessions*, on the contrary, reveals the impossibility of ever fully recognizing the rose in the Cross, and thus unravels the promise of reconciliation suggested by Hegel's reading of Christianity.

---

3. León Rozitchner, *La Cosa y la Cruz: Cristianismo y Capitalismo (en torno a las* Confesiones *de san Agustín)* (Buenos Aires: Losada, 1997). The Introduction and Appendix 1 of this book have been translated, by Karen Benezra and Rachel Price, as León Rozitchner, *The Thing and the Cross: Christianity and Capitalism (About Saint Augustine's* Confessions*)*, *Polygraph: An International Journal of Culture & Politics* 19-20 (2008): 33–53.

4. G. W. F. Hegel, *Philosophy of Right*, trans. T. M. Knox (Oxford: Oxford University Press, 1977), 12.

5. Rozitchner, *La Cosa y la Cruz*, 34.

Moreover, far from coinciding with the examples of Badiou or Negri in their re-evaluation of Saul of Tarsus or Francis of Assisi, Rozitchner's reading of Saint Augustine also runs completely counter to the impetus behind the widespread upsurge of interest in the lives of saints. Of course, not so long ago saints were the targets of great wit and sarcasm on the part of the Left. In the diatribes that Marx and Engels directed against Saint Max (Stirner) and Saint Bruno (Bauer) in *The German Ideology*, the mere appellation immediately served a denigrating purpose. Among contemporary thinkers, even Badiou—before turning to Saint Paul as a figure of the militant without a party—still has recourse to this sarcastic usage when, in his Maoist booklet *Theory of Contradiction*, published in the mid 1970s, he attacks Saint Jean-François (Lyotard), Saint Gilles (Deleuze), and Saint Félix (Guattari) as so many left-wing "revisionists."[6] By contrast, in David Halperin's *Saint Foucault*, as in Jean-Paul Sartre's *Saint Genet* before that, the saintly reference already seems to blend, if not completely dissolve, the element of blame into a more general mixture of admiring yet still somewhat ironic praise.[7] So how did we move from denigration to praise? What has happened in more recent years so that today we are being bombarded with the lives of saints as models for militant figures of a new type?

A good starting point from which to approach this question would involve a comparison between the respective readings of Augustine's *Confessions* found in Lyotard and Rozitchner: the first, offering a posthumous and unfinished, almost hagiographic testament; and the second, a painfully dense, often repetitive, and occasionally vicious attack—an attack that would have to be qualified as "base," if it is true that, as Henri Marrou writes, "only a base mind could deny Augustine's greatness."[8] For Lyotard, Saint Augustine's *Confessions* seem to provide the occasion for an experience of near-sublime joy: "The ability to feel and to take pleasure unencumbered, raised to an unknown power—this is saintly joy. Rarely did grace take a less dialectical turn, less negativist and less repressive. In Augustine, flesh bestowed with grace fulfills its desire, in innocence."[9] Despite sharing an interest in

6. Alain Badiou, *Théorie de la contradiction* (Paris: Maspero, 1975), 72.

7. David Halperin, *Saint Foucault: Towards a Gay Hagiography* (New York: Oxford University Press, 1995); Jean-Paul Sartre, *Saint Genet: Actor and Martyr*, trans. Bernard Frechtman (New York: G. Braziller, 1963).

8. Henri Marrou, *Saint Augustine and His Influence Through the Ages*, trans. Patrick Hepburne-Scott (New York: Harper, 1962), 61. Rozitchner quotes this claim and accepts the epithet, in *La Cosa y la Cruz*, 10.

9. Jean-François Lyotard, *The Confession of Augustine*, trans. Richard Beardsworth (Stanford: Stanford University Press, 2000), 12 (translation modified). Compare with the tone of Hardt and Negri's last page in *Empire*:

There is an ancient legend that might serve to illuminate the future life of communist militancy: that of Saint Francis of Assisi . . . Once again in postmodernity we find ourselves in Francis's

the relation between grace and the flesh, Rozitchner would have to reject this interpretation almost word for word. Beyond the appearance of sheer innocence and sensuous joy, nothing could in fact be more repressive or more negative than the dialectic between death and salvation, or between grace and terror, which Rozitchner uncovers in the *Confessions*. Rather than serving as a substitute love letter, in which the divine "Thou" comes to stand in effortlessly for the beloved, as is the case for Lyotard, Augustine's text in Rozitchner's hands thus becomes the target of an incursion into hostile territory where a declining Roman Empire, making common cause with the Christian Church in a world-historical juncture best depicted in Augustine's own subsequent elaboration in *City of God*, gives rise to sinister subject formations that prepare the onslaught of capitalism several hundreds of years later. Saint Augustine, then, is not a model; he is the enemy, or at best an anti-model. "In his theological libidinal economy the saint proposed to us, from the oldest times, the most productive originary investment to accumulate sacred capital: 'By making savings on the flesh, you will be able to invest in the spirit,'" Rozitchner writes quoting Tertullian, before summing up the bold hypothesis behind his reading of the *Confessions*: "The Christian Spirit and Capital have complementary metaphysical premises."[10] Following this hypothesis, we slowly delve into the visceral depths of the subject so as to locate the place where terror and the fear of death, from the earliest experiences of the child onward, become ingrained into the material soul. In fact, without this inscription of terror in subjectivity, the user's manual for which can be read on page after page in Augustine's *Confessions*, Rozitchner claims that capitalism would not have been possible.

Marx and Freud in the Pampas

If there is a beyond of Marx, it passes through Marx, just as, if there is a beyond of Freud, it passes through Freud: we do not deny our old loves in the new ones.
        León Rozitchner, *"La crisis de los intelectuales y el marxismo"*

As a unique and loyal Freudo-Marxist who remained almost entirely unknown outside of his home country, and who until his recent death was frequently ostracized even in Argentina, Rozitchner worked for over fifty years in the domain where questions of politics and

---

situation, posing against the misery of power the joy of being. This is a revolution that no power will control—because biopower and communism, cooperation and revolution remain together, in love, simplicity, and also innocence. This is the irrepressible lightness and joy of being communist (413).

10.   Rozitchner, *La Cosa y la Cruz*, 12. For the quote from Tertullian, see the discussion in Peter Brown, *The Body and Society: Men, Women, and Sexual Renunciation in Early Christianity* (New York: Columbia University Press, 1988), 78.

subjectivity come head to head, particularly in the historical contexts of left-wing populism and guerrilla struggles, right-wing authoritarianism, military dictatorship, and the so-called transition to democracy under global neoliberalism. A thinker of untiring energy, he had also formed many generations of younger scholars, intellectuals, and activists—including militants involved in the uprisings and mobilizations in Argentina after the crisis of December 2001. And yet, a strange half-silence surrounded Rozitchner's writings during much of his lifetime. Thus, when I would ask older friends of mine about their familiarity with the work and thought of this prolific philosopher, many of them would recall for me how they learned their Freud from "the old León," whether at the university or in clandestine seminars during the Argentinean military dictatorship which forced Rozitchner into exile in Venezuela; but, until the recent effusion of posthumous homages, there was almost no public discussion of his many books. Rozitchner himself did not seem affected by this academic silencing of his work. Nor did he seek out recognition abroad by appealing to the latest fashions of theory from across the Atlantic. Even if he went to study at the Sorbonne with Lucien Goldmann and Maurice Merleau-Ponty, whose *Adventures of the Dialectic* and *Humanism and Terror* he translated into Spanish, by contrast he was always scornful of the structuralism of Louis Althusser and Jacques Lacan. To their theoretical anti-humanism and linguistic idealism, he preferred his own form of sensual, embodied, and historical materialism, summed up in the crucial book *Freud y los límites del individualismo burgués* (*Freud and the Limits of Bourgeois Individualism*), based on a detailed reading of Freud's *New Introductory Lectures on Psychoanalysis* and his "social" works *Civilization and Its Discontents* and *Group Psychology and Analysis of the Ego.*

In fact, all of Rozitchner's works, including over a dozen books, contribute to the unrelenting effort to uncover the hidden recesses in which power is capable of thriving on the terrorizing fear for, and simultaneous seduction by, the figure of authority. However, this is not merely an analytical attempt to locate the origins of power, for instance, in the structure of the superego; rather, such an analysis also marks the desired onset of an alternative democratic politics that would be able in a completely different way to elaborate these profoundly affective and bodily materials with which subjectivity is constituted. "This is the fundamental aim of all democratic politics," Rozitchner says in an important interview on "The Crisis of the Intellectuals and Marxism," to which he adds:

> I believe that this aim is present in all subjectivity, and in intellectual work, too: to defeat the limit of that which authorizes you to think and to act. If we want to think, we must confront the anxiety of death that terror decants in us so as to impede us from doing so: we must continue to think within and

against this anxiety.[11]

The aim, then, is to think terror and death dialectically—not just as universal structures beyond history, nor only as moralizing figures of evil located outside and at a safe remove from oneself, but rather as historical appearances and as subject formations that reach the core of one's very being. "A strange and paradoxical challenge" is what Rozitchner calls the task of philosophy: "To open up a distance in that which is without distance, in the fullest proximity, starting from the sentient body, alienating ourselves into that which persecutes us, but so as to transform it into its opposite."[12] Rozitchner's *La Cosa y la Cruz* seeks to open up precisely such an intimate distance at the very core of the modern subject—using the powers of alienation as a lever to undo the logic of persecution on which rests all alienation of the body politic.

We might be able to situate the book on Augustine more accurately if we adopt a basic principle that should help in understanding all of Rozitchner's work. I mean the principle of reading history *à rebours*, "against the grain," or "backwards," as Benjamin would say—namely, from the contemporary moments of dependent and global capitalism to its earliest foundations in pre-capitalist times. In fact, after he published his doctoral thesis on Max Scheler's theory of affectivity, Rozitchner's books gradually moved further back in time, so that the chronology of his publications follows an order that strangely inverts the chronology of the historical content that is their active subject-matter—from *Moral burguesa y revolución*, about the Cuban victory in Playa Girón, discussed in the previous chapter, through the key polemical essay on "The Left Without Subject," published in the important Argentine journal *La rosa blindada* and again in the Cuban journal *Pensamiento crítico*, in which he blames orthodox revolutionary thought—especially in the figure of the Peronist-Guevarist John William Cooke—for failing to conceive of the subjective roots of power, all the way to his two-volume investigation into the theory and politics of Peronism, *Perón: Entre la sangre y el tiempo: Lo inconsciente y la política* (*Perón: Between Blood and Time: Politics and the Unconscious*).[13] In this respect, the book on Saint Augustine constitutes

---

11. León Rozitchner, "La crisis de los intelectuales y el marxismo," in *Las desventuras del sujeto político: Ensayos y errores* (Buenos Aires: El Cielo por Asalto, 1996), 154–5.

12. Ibid., 176.

13. León Rozitchner, *Persona y comunidad: Ensayo sobre la significación ética de la afectividad en Max Scheler* (Buenos Aires: Eudeba, 1962); *Moral burguesa y revolución* (Buenos Aires: Procyon, 1963); "La izquierda sin sujeto," *La rosa blindada* 9 (1966), reprinted in *Pensamiento crítico* 12 (1968): 151–83; and in Rozitchner, *Las desventuras del sujeto político*, 45–75; *Perón: Entre la sangre y el tiempo: Lo inconsciente y la política*, 2 vols (Buenos Aires: Centro Editor de América Latina, 1985). Parts of the research on Perón, the military junta, and the transition to democracy have been translated into English, by Philip Derbyshire, as León Rozitchner, "Exile, War and Democracy: An Exemplary Sequence," *Radical Philosophy* 152 (November/December 2008): 41–50. For a descriptive overview of Rozitchner's work, see Sebastián Scolnik, "Notas para un materialismo argentino. Una

the point of culmination on an extended path toward a historical *longue durée*—somewhat along the lines of Michel Foucault's sweeping return from modernity to ancient Greece, which likewise passes by way of Augustine's *Confessions*, in his unfinished *History of Sexuality*.[14]

Read today, moreover, many of these writings may seem prescient. This fact can almost serve as a second hermeneutic principle to understand this philosopher's work as a whole. Rozitchner's obsessive inquiries into the roots of terror, which originally referred to the military dictatorship, nowadays indeed become timely and uncanny investigations into the terrorizing logic behind the war on terror itself. The mantle of ambivalence thus constantly shrouds previous uses of the notion of terror, which now seem to refer to the contemporary moment. No great leap of the imagination is required, for instance, to move from the books written from exile in the late 1970s and early 1980s, when Argentina was under military rule, to one of the latest books, titled *El terror y la gracia* (Terror and Grace), which includes Rozitchner's comments on the aftermath of September 11, 2001 and on the war in Iraq.[15] And a similar temporal loop already overdetermines some of the earlier books. Thus, while the investigation into Peronism was actually initiated well before the Argentinean military coup of 1976, its underlying logic regarding the continued presence of war at the heart of politics as such, presented in a daring juxtaposition of Freud, Marx, and von Clausewitz, already anticipates not only the regime of terror under the military junta but also the illusions that undergirded the later so-called transition to democracy in Argentina. It is almost as if, by a perverse counter-finality, the more we step back in time to dig up the prior origins of the power of subjection, the more history catches up with us from behind by turning the distant past into an ominous premonition of the present.

Finally, a third principle worth keeping in mind is a penchant for polemical writing. Rozitchner thus seems to have devoted most of his work to criticizing others, be they friendly opponents, useful adversaries, or full-blown enemies. This is already the case in *Moral burguesa y revolución*, as we saw in the previous chapter, if not even earlier in

---

lectura de los textos de León Rozitchner," *La Biblioteca* 2-3 (2005): 244–55. In this same issue of *La Biblioteca*, the journal of the Argentine National Library under the directorship of Horacio González, the reader will also find an extensive interview with Sebastián Scolnik, "León Rozitchner: 'El Ser se devela hablando en castellano,'" ibid., 16–33. Thanks to Miguel Maiden for passing along this last reference and for sharing his thoughts on Rozitchner with me.

14. For Michel Foucault's reading of Saint Augustine, see among others *The Use of Pleasure*, vol. 2 of *The History of Sexuality*, trans. Robert Hurley (New York: Vintage, 1990), 40 and *passim*.

15. León Rozitchner, *El terror y la gracia*, ed. Rubén H. Ríos (Buenos Aires: Norma, 2003).

Rozitchner's doctoral thesis on Scheler, whose reluctant materialism is shown to be unable to undermine the moralizing idealism of his theory of affects. But the trend to write, as it were, from within enemy territory becomes only more pronounced in response to what Rozitchner perceives as an ill-constructed compound of leftism and Peronism, and it clearly reaches its apogee in his painstaking analysis of Augustine's *Confessions*. "I did my whole apprenticeship in philosophy with people who in some cases are radically heterogeneous to me and in others extremely close: Saint Augustine, Scheler, Freud, Marx, and even Perón. Every apprenticeship is always polemical," Rozitchner explains in an interview with the Argentine Colectivo Situaciones. But this does not mean that the mistakes or shortcomings targeted in the polemic would pertain only to others. On the contrary, every criticism is also always a self-criticism: "I, with Perón, was a Peronist; with Saint Augustine, I was a Christian; I became a converted Jew with Max Scheler. With Marx, I became revolutionary, and with Freud, psychoanalyst. From all of them I have kept a remainder."[16]

The Rebellious Origin

It is always a question of continuing the dialectic, against metaphysics, which means: to give reason to the rebels, to say that they are right.
Alain Badiou, Théorie de la contradiction

A few words are in order about the substance of Rozitchner's philosophy in general—that is, his peculiar brand of Freudo-Marxism, summed up in the two books *Freud y los límites del individualismo burgués* (*Freud and the Limits of Bourgeois Individualism*) and *Freud y el problema del poder* (*Freud and the Problem of Power*).[17] Theoretically, the core of this philosophical proposal, which has remained remarkably— some would say stubbornly—consistent over the years, is twofold, combining as it does a thorough investigation into the roots of power and subjection in terror, on the one hand, with a willful retrieval of the collective potential for rebellion and subjectivization, on the other.

The first theoretical strand allows us in hindsight to posit that terror and grace are actually twin developments, which the critique of subjection therefore cannot treat as separate or mutually exclusive phenomena. For Rozitchner, terror derives from the anxiety and fear of death installed in the innermost core of the subject due to the guilt felt over

---

16. Rozitchner, *Acerca de la derrota y de los vencidos*, 128.
17. León Rozitchner, *Freud y los límites del individualismo burgués*, 2nd edn (Mexico City: Siglo Veintiuno, 1979; 1st edn 1972); *Freud y el problema del poder* (Buenos Aires: Losada, 2003). A brief discussion of Rozitchner's Freudo-Marxism can be found in the chapter "When Marx Meets Freud," in Mariano Plotkin's impressively documented *Freud in the Pampas: The Emergence and Development of a Psychoanalytic Culture in Argentina* (Stanford: Stanford University Press, 2001), 166–90.

killing or wanting to kill the primordial father. Grace, however, is merely a false solution, or a defense formation in which the origin of power and its extension into the subject's life are covered up—or, more precisely, promised an imaginary solution. Today, in fact, grace is also terror. Both terror and grace, in any event, rely on a similar logic of exception: a law beyond the law that takes hold of us because of the guilt for a crime committed prior to history; and a freedom beyond freedom based upon the suspension of the state of original sin and primordial guilt.

It is not just that terror and grace correspond to two forms of fundamentalism, one supposedly Islamic and the other Christian, competing on the stage of world history today. In fact, Rozitchner´s investigations into the place of terror in any theory of subjection, as well as his interest in the Christian model of grace, preceded by many years the events of 9/11 in the US and the ensuing war on terror. But it is also not just a matter, as it seems to be for Badiou and Žižek, of re-establishing the original link between (good) terror and revolution, from the Jacobins to Hegel. Rather, the unenviable privilege of Rozitchner's viewpoint stems from the insight that the regime of terror that is the military dictatorship in Argentina extends its reign well beyond the so-called Process of National Reorganization. Through a strange temporal loop to which I alluded earlier, the "view from the South" thus opens up a completely different perspective on the war on terror that was to be unleashed with particular violence in March 2003 during the "Shock and Awe" operation in Iraq. In fact, the Chilean 9/11—that is, Pinochet's 1973 military coup and the spectacular bombing of the presidential palace of La Moneda in the nation's capital—in this sense would be instructive of the logic of events following 9/11 in the United States.[18]

We must think through the sinister dialectical link between grace and terror, without locating the former as the gift of peace or democracy or civilization that would come *after* and *in response to* the latter as civil war or dictatorship or barbarism. "To understand the pacification we must first start from the terror that grounds it," Rozitchner writes. "War and the dictatorship are terror; but democracy is a grace that the power of terror concedes to us as a truce. Both, democracy and dictatorship, are two modalities of politics, and they constitute the alternating domain in which social contradictions are fought out."[19] Such would be the sad lesson to be drawn from the experience of the military dictatorships, which we now know amounted to the violent imposition of the reign of neoliberalism. The transition to democracy, however, did not mark a break with the underlying logic of terror. To

18.   For the lessons to be drawn from the mirroring relationships between the two 9/11 attacks, see also the interventions by Ariel Dorfman and others collected in *Chile: El otro 11 de septiembre* (New York: Ocean Press, 2003).

19.   Rozitchner, *El terror y la gracia*, 26–7.

the contrary, the democratic process continues to be grounded in this very logic, only now it is hidden or disavowed: "The dictatorship from which we come, then, is not an *accident* nor an *abnormal* fact in our political development: military terror, on the contrary, is part of the same system together with the implicit limits of democracy itself. It constitutes its founding and persistent violence."[20] Much less obvious is the answer to the question of what is to be done once the founding violence of our political order is exposed.

The difficulty in question stems from the play of dissimulation through which democracy appears as the epitome of liberty and peace, only temporarily interrupted by the abnormality of civil war and dictatorship. Insofar as this game of hide and seek is not accidental but constitutive of the democratic order, the first step necessarily requires an effort of undoing the logic of dissimulation. As Rozitchner writes,

> When democracy returns, the most important thing is to hide from civil society the violent ground from which it came, and whose terror and threat continue to maintain themselves, dissimulated but active, in the political field. But it was terror itself, in its persistence, that planted among the citizens, in each one of them, the possibility of dissimulation. Terror represses the personal place that feeds the impulses for resistance: the collective drives. Because of this it is necessary to undo this subjective trap: to keep present, in order to conjure it, the mortal threat that will emerge again when resistance appears.[21]

Several years before Naomi Klein would make this the main thesis of her book *The Shock Doctrine*, Rozitchner goes so far as to suggest that capitalism imposes a diffused "shock and awe" operation on each and every subject, in the civilized West no less than in the rest of the world—as witnessed, by way of a dark precursor, under the military regimes in the Southern Cone:

> Terror, denied in political society but always threatening, corrodes human subjectivity from within. This unconscious fear that runs through society—the terror of death in religion, which it enlivens in the face of rebellion; the terror of unemployment, of bankruptcy or of poverty in the economy; the terror of the armed forces of repression; the terror of the covering-up of those forms of knowledge that might be able to unravel this domination—is the ground on the basis of which the system negates, within each one, the very thing that it animates.[22]

Here, however, we already begin to grasp the other strand in Rozitchner's overarching theoretical proposal. In effect, his aim is never merely to uncover the originary violence of the political field per se, but rather

---

20. Ibid., 121.
21. Ibid., 122.
22. Ibid., 128–9. See also Naomi Klein, *The Shock Doctrine: The Rise of Disaster Capitalism* (New York: Picador, 2007).

to retrieve the potential for rebellion and resistance with which this violence, from time immemorial, has always had to come to terms.

This originary rebellion, for instance, of the child against the father, is precisely the moment—in the sense of constituting both a structure and an event—that Rozitchner seeks to bring to the foreground in his pivotal rereading of the myth of the killing of the primordial father in Freud's so-called "collective" writings, particularly *Totem and Taboo* and *Civilization and Its Discontents*. Unlike what happens in certain texts by Agamben, or even Žižek, the killing of the primordial father, upon this reading, is not meant to produce a radical metaphysics of the state of exception or of the death drive. It is certainly true that Freud's story, in its own way, starts with a double exception: first, because the primeval or primordial father is excepted from the universal logic of castration, and second, because the act of killing this figure functions as a "scientific myth," to use Freud's oxymoron—that is, as a purely conjectural fact outside of history that nonetheless must be presupposed as the radical condition of possibility that opens up all human history. It is, in this sense, the nonhistorical ground of all historicity. But for Rozitchner, the point is not to locate an act of originary violence that would precede history as a kind of *Ur*-crime, similar to the way in which Ernst Bloch reads the metaphysics of the detective novel in terms of the postulate of a radical crime or evil *ante rem*. This temptation may very well be inherent in Freud's story, and Rozitchner does not shy away from exploiting its pathos, as when he writes: "Conscience, and not only moral conscience, begins in a crime."[23] Nevertheless, the crucial point lies in the act of rebellion of the brothers. Theirs is an act that is both collective and geared toward a real opponent, the father; only later does this opponent become imaginary and moral, just as the relation to him becomes individualized, with the subsequent erasure of the prior collective act, through the guilt, moral conscience, and super-egoic law by which power inscribes itself into each person's subjectivity. Beyond the unmasking of originary violence, therefore, the aim is above all to restore force to the collective subject. In other words, if there is a constant effort to reach back and delve into the roots of

---

23. Rozitchner, *Freud y los límites del individualismo burgués*, 224. Here, Rozitchner is paraphrasing Sigmund Freud, *Civilization and Its Discontents*, trans. James Strachey (New York: W. W. Norton, 1989): "If this is correct, we may assert truly that in the beginning conscience arises through the suppression of an aggressive impulse, and that it is subsequently reinforced by fresh suppressions of the same kind" (92). See also Ernst Bloch, "A Philosophical View of the Detective Novel," in *The Utopian Function of Art and Literature: Selected Essays*, trans. Jack Zipes and Frank Mecklenburg (Cambridge: MIT Press, 1966), 245–64. The notion of an originary crime, Bloch argues, traveled from literature into metaphysics and, we might add, into psychoanalysis as well: "Thus the suspicion of an accursed secret *ante rem, ante lucem, ante historiam*, of a *casus ante mundum* appeared in *philosophy* as well, in a particularly conspicuous and penetrating form: that is to say, in those passages and indeed quite partisan images of a primevally conceived revolt, outlined by Franz Baader and the late Schelling" (ibid., 258). For further discussion, see Chapter 9, below.

subjection, the purpose of this return is to enable a collective form of emancipatory subjectivization.

Thus, whereas Rozitchner's discussion of the production of the disappeared, or of the use of camps and detention centers under the military dictatorship as a matrix of political power, may very well present numerous points of contact with Agamben's ongoing politico-philosophical project, we could also argue that his reading of the brothers' initial rebellion against the primordial father is the exact opposite of the central fascination—I think the word is not exaggerated—with the "Vitae necisque potestas" in *Homo sacer*. Agamben understands this as the unconditional authority of the *pater* over his sons, which also signals "the very model of political power in general," insofar as the prepubescent son, or *puer*, is originarily and immediately subject to a power of life and death on the part of the father. "There is no clearer way to say that the first foundation of political life is a life that may be killed, which is politicized through its very capacity to be killed," writes Agamben. "It is as if male citizens had to pay for their participation in political life with an unconditional subjection to a power of death, as if life were able to enter the city only in the double exception of being capable of being killed and yet not sacrificed [by their father]."[24] In Rozitchner's reading of Freud, on the contrary, the emphasis falls not on unconditional subjection but on collective rebellion; not on the power of death and life but on the power to resist death—even, if necessary, through violence:

> Civilization does not triumph over the child because, subjected from birth, the latter would prolong and extend this submission into adulthood. The child is a rebel and an aggressor and a victor; only the remorse over his triumph leads to the guilt that subsequently bends and subjects the child. It is because the child is deeply [*entrañablemente*] moral and pays with his guilt for the imaginary murder that the adult's morality, which is the true assassin, takes power over this noble sense and ratifies with its judgment an imaginary situation as if it were real.[25]

Finally, it might be useful to stress that, conceptually, the shift from the power of terror to the force of rebellion also means that the exception at the origin of humankind is not an insuperable originary or metaphysical structure, but a mixture of structural and event-like elements that can be animated and reactivated if they are acknowledged as such:

> Thus, in the originary drama there lies hidden the structural meaning of the ground of every human being: there where event (the murder) and structure (the transition from natural individuality to cultural individuation through the fraternal alliance) constitute the originary point from which all human rationality was produced. In the relation of individual to individual (between

24.   Giorgio Agamben, *Homo sacer: Sovereign Power and Bare Life*, trans. Daniel Heller-Roazen (Stanford: Stanford University Press, 1998), 88–90.
25.   Rozitchner, *Freud y los límites del individualismo burgués*, 221.

father and son), the mediating third was a collective being: the fraternal alliance. This initial moment is crucial because it is from this first opposition that, in the ambiguity of love and hatred toward the father, the point of insertion of the cultural dialectic takes shape—that is, of reason that supports itself in the flesh of the other but at the same time in the common body sketched out by the brothers, as a necessary process for one's own coming-into-being.[26]

To be sure, through the guilt and remorse felt by the brothers as well as the renunciation of instincts with which they seek to gain the love of the father who returns in the imaginary after the killing of the primordial father, consciousness or conscience (*conciencia* in Spanish meaning both) erases this origin which is collective rebellion. The result of this erasure is that the superegoic injunction and terrorizing command of the moral law appear as though they marked an absolute beginning, whereas in reality they are the result of a prolonged struggle:

> But the dead father "lives" within us as though we ourselves were made other, and now it regulates, in its interiorized form, our relations to the outside world. Except that, from being a real fact, it now appears here, in the occultation that follows the pain of death and remorse, as though also erased for the conscience that thus develops itself. It erases its origin in that other as if it lacked any genesis. Because to reanimate its origin would imply, for this first human being only, to remit itself to this first act of giving death. Thus there opened in the beginning of history itself *an anteriority to history, as if the superego that thus inaugurates it were its absolute beginning, and not a secondary moment of a real event which conscience ignores and which nevertheless is its foundation.* Conscience appears as an absolute foundation, without presuppositions.[27]

Conscience appears as an absolute foundation, or a radical first ground, only because it has forgotten or concealed the traces of the transition that brought it into existence. The real task, then, consists chiefly in the ongoing effort to reactivate a possible return to this forgotten origin. But far from remaining caught in an analytic of finitude, with its typical retreat and return of the origin as an insuperable structure of repetition, this is an effort at *desfatalización* or "defatalization"—that is, an effort to restore the force of historical possibility by reanimating the event-like structure of the process of subjectivization, whose archaic persistence does not preclude the option of reaching out for its effective supercession. Such is precisely the hope that speaks through the project of *La Cosa y la Cruz*—even though Augustine's meticulous avoidance of Oedipal identification, conflict, and guilt, as we will see, also renders unlikely the retrieval of a rebellious force from the symbolic matrix of Christianity.

---

26. Ibid., 236.
27. Ibid., 239.

Pre-Capitalist Subjective Formations

God has value only insofar as he represents Christ, and man has value only insofar as he represents Christ. It is the same with money.
    Karl Marx, *"Comments on James Mill, Éléments d'économie politique"*

Rozitchner's book on Augustine, published when the author had already reached the mature age of seventy-three, is an astonishing feat that combines a painstaking and sustained close reading with a series of wild theoretical speculations. Its claims repeat many of the ideas made in earlier works, add new ones, and correct still others, all the while anchoring them in the self-proclaimed example of a medieval saint who might well turn out to have been the first modern subject.

Why would an incredulous Jew want to write, Rozitchner himself asks from the beginning, about the *Confessions* of a Christian saint? Among the various answers, the most audacious one—certainly out-daring Max Weber's hypothesis about the ideological affinity between capitalism and Protestantism—holds that capitalism simply would not have been possible without Christianity: "Triumphant capitalism, the quantitative and *infinite* accumulation of wealth in the abstract mone-tary form, would not have been possible without the human model of religious infinity promoted by Christianity, without the imaginary and symbolical reorganization operated in subjectivity by the new religion of the Roman Empire."[28] Augustine is the paramount model of these profound transformations in the psychic economy. His *Confessions*, Rozitchner proposes, can be read as a user's manual for subjection and servitude. The complete devalorization of the flesh, of pleasure, and of the social in general, together with the newly constituted subject's submission to the rule of law and imperial order, constitute the lasting religious premises of the political sphere.

Rozitchner's project, however, does not amount a reconstruction of the possible transpositions and systematic analogies between the

---

28. Rozitchner, *La Cosa y la Cruz*, 9. Weber's well-known thesis is partially anticipated by Marx himself in *Capital*:

> For a society of commodity producers, whose general social relation of production consists in the fact that they treat their products as commodities, hence as values, and in this material form bring their individual, private labours into relation with each other as homogeneous human labour, Christianity with its religious cult of man in the abstract, more particularly in its bourgeois development, i.e. in Protestantism, Deism, etc., is the most fitting form of religion. (172)

All of Rozitchner's work starting with *La Cosa y la Cruz* consists in an attempt to explain this claim, which Marx himself does not fully develop, that Christianity is "the most fitting form of religion" for capitalism.

political and the theological. Unlike Carl Schmitt, he does not propose a political theology—even though such a concept, according to Schmitt himself, is sufficiently "polymorphous" so as to warrant its application even to *La Cosa y la Cruz*.[29] Rozitchner also does not focus on *City of God* as a student of political theology might—not even in order to invert its hierarchy in favor of the "earthly city," as Hardt and Negri propose to do in *Empire*. Rather, he chooses to concentrate on the personal itinerary in the *Confessions* that, according to him, lays the foundation for *City of God* as Augustine's grand politico-theological synthesis, written years later. Finally, a third reason for not conflating the analysis of the *Confessions* with the questions of political theology is the fact that the main discourse of which Rozitchner makes use is not juridical but psychoanalytical—Freud being a more useful reference for understanding the subjective stakes of politics than Schmitt. How, then, does this discourse affect the methodology for investigating the formation of the subject?

To describe the method of his inquiry into the origins of the long historical process of capitalist subject-formation, Rozitchner frequently uses the verb *desentrañar*, meaning "to disentangle," "to unravel," or "to clarify," but also, literally, "to bring up what was embroiled in the entrails," *entrañas* in Spanish, just as *entrañable* is often used both in the sense of "dear," "close" or "intimate" and in the sense of "soulful" or "heartfelt," but also, more literally, "from the gut" or "visceral." I would argue that this usage is symptomatic of the author's approach as a whole. Rozitchner's work indeed presents us with a psychoanalytical investigation into the core of a truly visceral materialism, or a theory of what he also calls the "rationality of the body" and the "intelligence of the flesh."[30] He uncovers the material, bodily, and affective parts of the subject that had to be eviscerated in the name of either a transcendent religion or a purely immanent reason—but only after the power of authority, of the law, and of empire had already been able to impose itself in these very same recesses that subsequently were to have been denied:

Augustine is of interest to me in this endeavor only for the apparatus of

29. Carl Schmitt, *Political Theology: Four Chapters on the Concept of Sovereignty*, trans. George Schwab (Chicago: University of Chicago Press, 2005), 36–7. For the comparison of Rozitchner's work with Schmitt's political theology, see also Eduardo Grüner, "De los síntomas del 'pensamiento crítico' (In memoriam L. R.)" (online at lateclaene.blogspot.com). For a slightly different account of the currency of political theology in our contemporary imaginary, see the work of the Brazilian philosopher Marilena Chauí, "Political Theology, Religious Fundamentalism and Modern Politics," *Radical Philosophy* 171 (January/February 2011): 27–32.

30. Rozitchner uses these expressions, for example, in *Freud y los límites del individualismo burgués*, 70, 173. In more recent years, he began speaking in terms of "*mater*ialism," stressing the maternal matrix of his history and theory of the subject. See, for example, the posthumous collection of essays, León Rozitchner, *El materialismo ensoñado: Ensayos* (Buenos Aires: Tinta Limón, 2011).

domination and war with which he constructed man's subjectivity under the insignia of love and truth. This is what continues to be relevant today. Augustine knew to find the intimate place where power vivifies and stokes emotion, arousing the most sinister phantasms to activate the body, and in that terrible hour in which the old world crumbles, yoke it to the war chariots of political and economic power.[31]

Along the path of this investigation, we obtain not only a detailed picture of how the subject, prior to becoming the flesh and fodder of capitalist accumulation, first had to become the subject of law at the time of the Christian Roman Empire's imminent collapse—that is, the sack of Rome that would mark the immediate reference point for Saint Augustine in *City of God*—but also a daring series of comparisons between Christianity and Judaism, as well as a powerful suggestion of supplementing Freud's own doctrine of Oedipal guilt and the superego law (including its origin in the killing of the primordial father, which takes its clues mainly from the Jewish God) with an interpretation of the theory of the subject derived from Christianity.

Saint Augustine For Our Times

He instructs us by his example in the art of living through an age of catastrophe.
        Henri Marrou, *Saint Augustine and His Influence Through the Ages*

Rozitchner opens *La Cosa y la Cruz* by reiterating the insufficiency of the traditional Marxist critique of religion. Insofar as Marx in *Capital*, for example, still expected the veil of religious beliefs to drop as a result of the rational development of the material conditions of everyday life, such a critique "did not reach the nucleus that is the subjective place where the most tenacious submission resides."[32] But this is exactly the place where Rozitchner wants to inscribe his own approach to the power of religion in general and of Christianity in particular. His aim is to reach a more radical understanding of the logic of social change so as to avoid the errors and shortcomings inherent in previous emancipatory projects: "A radicalized social transformation must modify that which religion has organized in the depth of every subject if we do not wish to repeat the heroic but sterile sacrifices of our recent past."[33]

For Rozitchner, religion operates by way of an expropriation that

---

31. Rozitchner, *La Cosa y la Cruz*, 16; *The Thing and the Cross*, 39.
32. Rozitchner, *La Cosa y la Cruz*, 9; *The Thing and the Cross*, 34 (translation modified). Compare Marx in *Capital*: "The religious reflections of the real world can, in any case, vanish only when the practical relations of everyday life between man and man, and man and nature, generally present themselves to him in a transparent and rational form"; and further on: "This, however, requires that society possess a material foundation, or a series of material conditions of existence, which in their turn are the natural and spontaneous product of a long and tormented historical development" (173).
33. Rozitchner, *La Cosa y la Cruz*, 9; *The Thing and the Cross*, 34.

takes place at the level of the imaginary and symbolic matrix of subjectivity—prior to, but also complicit with, the material expropriation of
the labor of already-constituted subjects, studied by Marx. In *La Cosa
y la Cruz*, he thus focuses on Christianity understood as the dominant
model for the constitution of subjectivity in the West. This model
works with psychic, mythical, philosophical, symbolic and bodily-
affective materials that are much more permanent and resilient than
the traditional critique of religious ideology as a superstructure
assumes. "Even if we accept the primacy of economic production as the
point of departure for understanding history, we must think that since
the origin of Christianity until the present day—twenty long centuries—there has not been a fundamental change either in the religious
model or in its symbolic schema."[34] With other psychoanalytic interpreters such as Pierre Legendre or Slavoj Žižek who likewise write
about religion in the wake of Freud and Lacan, Rozitchner thus shares
an interest in explaining the relative stability and symbolic efficacy of
the religious matrix of Christianity and its specific differences compared
to Judaism. In this sense, a principled atheism does not preclude, but
rather demands, a sustained inquiry into the mechanisms that account
for the long-term dominance of religious ideology in the first place:
"We don't ask if God exists. In following the experience that Augustine
relates, we seek only to grasp the recourses by which God is subjectively constructed in order to produce those effects in historical
reality."[35] But, unlike Žižek, for example, Rozitchner adopts an
approach that is more historical than strictly theoretical, and more
genealogical than purely psychoanalytical.

Rozitchner's reasons for choosing Saint Augustine's *Confessions*
rather than, say, Saint Paul's *Letters* (which, written in Greek, tend to
be the preferred object for philosophers, as can be seen today from
Badiou to Agamben) have to do with the historical context in which
the famous Bishop from Hippo developed his user's manual for
subjection for future generations as well as with the continued relevance of this historical context for our own times of terror and
regression:

> Christianity, as a religion and as a culture, continues, in the West, to occupy
> and mold the most archaic stratum, a layer always present in everyone and
> which emerges, as if novel and indispensable, at certain moments—moments
> in which a population terrorized by social, economic and political crises
> similar to the ones we are living today, withdraw into themselves. In Augus-
> tine we wish at least to glimpse the obscure logic of this emergence.[36]

Augustine's role in the history of Christianity not only coincides with

---

34. Rozitchner, *La Cosa y la Cruz*, 11; *The Thing and the Cross*, 35.
35. Rozitchner, *La Cosa y la Cruz*, 13; *The Thing and the Cross*, 36.
36. Rozitchner, *La Cosa y la Cruz*, 14; *The Thing and the Cross*, 37.

the moment when rebellion is transubstantiated into a logic of submission. It also marks the moment when politics as such is subsumed and morphed into religion. Rozitchner's reading of the *Confessions* thus seeks to come to terms with the religious roots of modern politics:

> Our aim is to understand the moment in which the politics that was rebellious and resistant to Roman imperial power was supplanted by the religion of the State through a strategy of domination; to understand how it is that through this operation it transforms an eminently political fact—the rebellion of a Jewish Jesus against the religious and imperial power—into a purely religious one—Christ, God's son resurrected who dies not for having confronted the Empire, but for purging our sins through his death.[37]

The very logic by which the initial rebellion in Augustine's life as retold in his *Confessions* will come to serve as an ever more effective leverage for submission also explains why the Christian model of subjectivity no longer allows for the same degree of emancipatory hope in *La Cosa y la Cruz* as Rozitchner still showed in *Freud y los límites del individualismo burgués*. This is because Christianity does not operate according to the same Oedipal schema for which Freud could still count on the example of Greek tragedy and Jewish law.

Oedipus in Hippo

> *Is it enough to replace the* For Marx *of Althusser with the* For Saint Augustine *of an unknown, post-Marxist, frustrated '68er—Claude Lorin to be exact—to confront the present catastrophe?*
> León Rozitchner, *La Cosa y la Cruz*

Rozitchner was fond of calling his investigation initiated in *La Cosa y la Cruz* a study in the three Oedipuses: Greek, Jewish, and Christian. In part, he meant this as a corrective to some of Freud's most central tenets, which Rozitchner believes are overly tied to a Greek and Jewish understanding of the Oedipal complex, just as he faults Lacan for not acknowledging the extent to which his own understanding of the matrix of subjectivity is actually profoundly Christian and thus strangely un-Freudian.

From pagan sinner to Christian saint, Augustine offers the model of his own personal itinerary in the construction of the "new man" needed by the declining Roman Empire and the emergent Catholic Church. "Saint Augustine dreams up and constructs the terrifying mythology later prolonged in the Christian West throughout sixteen centuries," Rozitchner writes. "The *Confessions* elaborate a new literary figure for religious conviction, a form of evangelization for the possessed: another guide for the perplexed."[38] The image of Christianity that emerges

---

37. Ibid.
38. Rozitchner, *La Cosa y la Cruz*, 21; *The Thing and the Cross*, 41 (translation

from Augustine's literary elaborations in the new genre of the confession does not correspond exactly to the passage from the religion of the Father to the religion of the Son, or from the religion of the law to the religion of love—which is how traditionally the shift from Judaism to Christianity has been described. Even Freud's explanations about identification, rivalry, and murder of the father figure, from *Totem and Taboo* to *Moses and Monotheism*, are unable to account for the novelty of the Christian myth that Augustine helped create for centuries to come. This is because, for Rozitchner, the Christian matrix of subjectivity inaugurated in the *Confessions*, far from stemming from a mortal combat of the young child with his real father, proceeds by installing a divine Father in the intimate and archaic place of the child's interiority still infused with the symbiotic love of his mother, even though she too must make place for the immaculate image of the Virgin.

From the father-son rivalry encapsulated in the Oedipus complex, we thus move into the entirely different imaginary and symbolic schema of the Holy Trinity. About this schema, built from the ground up on the basis of primeval maternal rather than paternal materials, we learn next to nothing from the psychoanalytical tradition handed down to us by Freud:

> The affective and sensuous content of the mother—as opposed to Freud's Oedipus—serves the creation of a new father. The love for the carnal body of the mother is funneled, as such, into the abstract body of words pronounced by conscience, and into the reason of Father-God. This abstract Father-God, which Augustine learns from Greek philosophy and which is the insensitive product of pure thought, in order to be something, nevertheless must be given a body with the maternal contents that had been denied.[39]

For Rozitchner, the Christian subject thus fundamentally develops on the basis of a regressive capture of the child's symbiotic love for his mother—in this case Augustine's imaginary fusion with Monica—only to go on denying and disparaging every subsequent mark of this originary affective bond on all earthly relationships, in the sole name of the divine-symbolic Father.

This entire trajectory can be summed up in a creative rewriting of the famous dictum in which Freud tried to concentrate the lesson of the psychoanalytic cure: *Wo es war, soll Ich werden*, "Where id was, there ego shall be" or "Where it was, I shall come to be."[40] According to Rozitchner's reading of the *Confessions*, this dictum would have to be rephrased as follows:

> Where she was, God-the-Father shall come. It is not that hatred is succeeded by love in order to give life to the dead father, as Freud believes following

---

modified).

39. Rozitchner, *La Cosa y la Cruz*, 42.

40. Freud, *New Introductory Lectures on Psychoanalysis*, 71.

the Jewish Oedipus that he generalizes unduly; in Christianity the son, by his amorous bond, remained clandestinely tied to the mother, and it is from within the trace of the complicit mother that he finds the materials with which to construct the new Father who, in the dissimulation, keeps them united forever.[41]

We are thus no longer operating in the realm of the traditional Oedipal schema—whether Greek or Jewish. Instead, Augustine's *Confessions* weakens and displaces the possibility of identification with the paternal law in order to build a maternal refuge from the threat of collapse and decay embodied in Alaric's hordes of barbarians invading the Roman Empire.

Instead of speaking of three Oedipuses, Rozitchner sometimes prefers to oppose the myth of Oedipus to two other founding myths: those of Moses and Christ. Augustine's *Confessions* allow him to delineate the contours of a new mechanism of subjective domination, or a new technology of control and subjugation, for which Freud's explanations about the Oedipal conflict no longer have much heuristic value:

> We believe, on the contrary, that Augustine is the one who shows us clearly the transition from one God to an altogether different one. The Greek Oedipus, and even the Jewish Oedipus, who was tragic, retains its currency only as long as patriarchal power, present in the state but found lacking, still ratifies the subjective escape route that necessarily finds support in the political power that was consolidated in its external and objective power as the Law of the father. We only know that the Roman Empire, in which this law was incarnated in the visible figure of the Emperor, had been converted into a terrorizing and despotic regime, and began to be emptied out. It then had to validate a father who would find support in the only place to which Augustine had been able to return, walking down the path [*desandando el camino*] of his life and seeking refuge within himself: the welcoming and secure atmosphere of his mother's primeval imprint. The goal was to give life to a new father from within the space of his own body, in which this inscription had been erased and displaced. The patriarchal God was emptied out into Christianity. Indeed, identification with the dead father, the figure from one's own childhood against whom one fights so as to be transformed into his equal, is excluded. This place of the father is occupied and filled with the sole contents of the mother, who encompasses everything. To the father, as concept, all that is left is the space of pure thought, of words that invoke him and give him a different body to substitute the sentient and guilty body: a body made of words.[42]

Whereas the Greek Oedipus in relation to the father involves identification, rivalry and murder, Augustine's elaboration of Jesus Christ as a model for his own saintly life proceeds by way of indifference,

---

41. Rozitchner, *La Cosa y la Cruz*, 50.
42. Ibid., 65–6. For Rozitchner, the importance of God's purely verbal or symbolic body in Christianity, as in the name of the Father, explains why Lacan is both farther removed from Freud's Greek-Jewish presuppositions than he might think and perhaps unwittingly better attuned to capture the essence of Christianity.

displacement, and the absorption of the law as the innermost resource of subjectivity itself. These are two fundamentally different schemata for dealing with the death of the father. As Rozitchner writes, "the father can be dead in two ways, at least: he can be killed imaginarily by the son, or he can die simply from sheer impotence, vanishing without leaving almost any traces as he is vanquished in the son by the maternal power"; and this fundamental difference, in turn, depends on the child's prior relation to the father while he was still alive. "It depends on how the father died for the son, on whether the latter in order to kill the father had to *identify* himself with him or whether, without any aggression whatsoever, he simply had to *imitate* him from a distance and win the staring contest," Rozitchner concludes. "In other words, it depends on whether there was confrontation, crime and guilt, or merely indifference and compassion."[43]

Instead of the Greek tragedy that in the tradition of Sophocles predominates the psychoanalytic model of subjectivity after Freud, Christianity thus would produce at best a poor parody and at worst a mere simulacrum of tragic conflict: "Augustine will convert the Greek tragedy into the Christian simulacrum, stripping it of the inevitability of death that besieges it, and transforming it into a representation devoid of drama, a parody that avoids all dramatic conflict."[44] Or perhaps we should say that Augustine's Christian subject lives through conflict only in the anti-tragic and pseudo-dialectical mode of melodrama that suits and soothes the inhabitants of the faltering Roman Empire? This would begin to explain the continued relevance of Augustine's model of subjectivity for our own time, defined by what Hardt and Negri describe as the new regime of post-statal sovereignty for which they also still propose the name of Empire. "Without showing the social and political situation in which Augustine's dilemma unfolds," Rozitchner insists, "we cannot understand the role played by the religious solution in anti-tragic periods, in which a confrontation between two opposed systems can be articulated at the level of the social consciousness of the inhabitants of the Empire."[45] But then such an articulation also describes the basic matrix of melodramatic configurations so common in our contemporary world. "Augustine thus returns to the first caesura, to the primordial division-indivision between the external and the internal which he experienced as an infant," Rozitchner further writes. "Now again, like before, everything good is inside and everything bad is outside. The archaic schema of the psychic apparatus once again comes to be installed as the adult model under the maternal dominance."[46]

---

43. Rozitchner, *La Cosa y la Cruz*, 93.
44. Ibid., 259.
45. Ibid., 265.
46. Ibid., 301. Already in *Freud y los límites del individualismo burgués*, Rozitchner had

Finally, just as the Christian matrix no longer obeys the tragic laws of the Greek Oedipus, the mythic model for the imitation of Christ that Augustine belabors in his *Confessions* also no longer corresponds to the function of the Mosaic Law. Whereas the latter operates as God's harsh external command against which there nonetheless still exists the possibility of revolt and collective historical action, the former by contrast no longer seems to provide for any rebellious leverage since all such resources have now become absorbed in the subject's dutiful obedience to a law which is, if not of his own making, then at least of his own desiring.

Rozitchner thus describes the difference between the two mythic models of Moses and Jesus in a passage that deserves to be quoted at length:

> In Moses it is not a fusion with God that comes to life in the engraving of words on stone, and not in the heart. Moses only makes himself momentarily into the human place in which the divine—the socio-historical truth—opens up a collective space for itself in which God appears and must be shown in order to be effective, coming from beyond the human itself, from high up on the mountain to be precise. There is distance between men and God; the liberated slaves feel the terror of seeing His face. There is no fusion with the father, in the way there is with the mother in the archaic origin of the child's coming-into-life. The Word is so external for the Jews that they even go so far as to eat the books in order to incarnate it; they want for it to sink into their most profound depths, but it does not emerge from within their own entrails. By contrast, Jesus, according to the Gospels transformed by Paul's doctrine and by Augustine's interpretation, does not identify but fuses with the Father of his mother by recognizing himself as his Son, he channels the maternal fusion into the God of words whereby the maternal element is transmuted into the Father.[47]

Many thinkers before Rozitchner of course have dwelled on this shift from the external to the internal law, which first would have occurred in the passage from Judaism to Christianity and supposedly repeated itself in the passage from Catholicism to Protestantism. Žižek, for one, likes to think of this shift in terms of the potentially atheist core that would properly belong only to Christianity, insofar as the gap that in Judaism separates man from God becomes transposed, in the figure of Christ on the Cross, onto a gap internal to God Himself. The Slovenian even goes so far as to claim that on this account Christianity is the only true monotheism, which at the same time functions as a radical atheism and a thorough materialism. "This is why Christianity, precisely because of the Trinity, is the only true monotheism: the lesson of the

---

repeatedly described this regressive transition to the maternal imaginary of symbiotic love on the inside and the threat of death on the outside. Only in *La Cosa y la Cruz* does he recode this melodramatic framework—without giving it this name—as essential to the matrix of Christian-Augustinean subjectivity.

47. Rozitchner, *La Cosa y la Cruz*, 298.

Trinity is that God fully coincides with the gap between God and man, that God *is* this gap—this is Christ, not the God of beyond separated from man by a gap, but the gap as such, the gap which simultaneously separates God from God and man from man."[48] In Christianity, there thus would be a double alienation at work, or a double kenosis, not only of man from God but also of God from Himself. Or, to use the more Badiouian-sounding formulation from *The Monstrosity of Christ*: "Insofar as the truly materialist axiom is the assertion of primordial multiplicity, the One which precedes this multiplicity can only be zero itself. No wonder, then, that only in Christianity—as the only truly logical monotheism—does God himself turn momentarily into an atheist."[49]

However, what Rozitchner's reading of Augustine reveals is the extent to which the addition of the adverb "momentarily" in Žižek's last formulation might turn out to be a crucial concession. What if this momentary atheism in fact quickly gives way once again to the ferocious superego demand of a God who, even in becoming finite and impotent, has never really or fully relinquished His power? What if the becoming-finite of God is merely the beginning of an ever more terrorizing power of Christian infinity? After all, the fact that God appears as finite should by no means come as a surprise, nor is it necessarily a radical atheist core hidden within the mystical shell of institutionalized religiosity. Žižek reads the self-alienation of God from Himself as a moment of radical doubt and impenetrability. He compares this in psychoanalytical terms, both to one of Freud's formulations that he quotes, among numerous other places, in *On Belief*: "What is incomprehensible within the pre-Christian horizon is the full shattering dimension of this impenetrability of God to Himself, discernible in Christ's 'Father, why did you forsake me?', this Christian version of the Freudian 'Father, can't you see that I am burning?'" and to Lacan's formulation evoked, for example, in *The Puppet and the Dwarf*: "Are we not, in the case of Christian identification, dealing with something similar? In our very failure, we identify with the divine failure, with Christ's confrontation with '*Che vuoi?*', with the enigma of the Other's desire ('Why are you doing this to me, Father? What do you want from me?')."[50] However, what if this cry is not so much the signal of God's total self-abandonment but rather, as Rozitchner suggests, the point at

---

48. Slavoj Žižek, *The Puppet and the Dwarf: The Perverse Core of Christianity* (Cambridge: MIT Press, 2003), 24.

49. Slavoj Žižek and John Milbank, *The Monstrosity of Christ: Paradox or Dialectic?*, ed. Creston Davis (Cambridge: MIT Press, 2009), 96.

50. Slavoj Žižek, *On Belief* (New York: Routledge, 2001), 145–6; and *The Puppet and the Dwarf*, 90. Contrary to Žižek's frequent invocations of Christ's final lamentation on the Cross ("Oh Father, why hast Thou forsaken me?"), Rozitchner writes: "Every man when he dies uncovers the trap into which poor Christ fell: 'Oh mother, oh mother, why hast thou forsaken me?' would be the true words" (48).

which the fragile, thrown, and mortally threatened human being becomes all the more securely sutured onto religious ideology, precisely, by way of the gap of finitude? Finally, what if it is not so much God the Father who stumbles upon the limit of his omnipotence in Christianity, but Christ who, through his exclamation of doubt on the Cross, assures that impotence serves ideologically to close the gap inherent in God?

Žižek himself is fully aware of the double-edged nature of the identification with failure, which from a reverse perspective can be seen as the recipe for an ever greater success of ideological identification. "We are one with God only when God is no longer one with Himself, but abandons Himself, 'internalizes' the radical distance which separates us from Him," Žižek also writes in *The Puppet and the Dwarf*. He continues:

> Our radical experience of separation from God is the very feature which unites us with Him—not in the usual mystical sense that only through such an experience do we open ourselves to the radical Otherness of God, but in a sense similar to the one in which Kant claims that humiliation and pain are the only transcendental feelings: it is preposterous to think that I can identify myself with the divine bliss—only when I experience the infinite pain of separation from God do I share an experience with God Himself (Christ on the Cross).[51]

We may well be far removed from the imaginary representations of religion based on oceanic feelings of divine bliss and awe-inspiring power. Yet, on the other hand, as Augustine's *Confessions* show in excruciating detail long before Kant, humiliation and pain may also come to function as the affective channels for the ever more awe-inspiring inscription of God's presence qua immanent transcendence within the fragile human body. What unites me with God is the gap that separates God from Himself; but such a logic of separation, far from revealing the atheist core of monotheism, can also be seen as an ever more pernicious incorporation of the human subject into the fold of the Christian God.

What most troubles Rozitchner in this post-Oedipal reconfiguration of Christian subjectivity is the difficulty of retrieving the moment of collective rebellion. In Augustine's *Confessions*, this difficulty becomes evident in the famous scene of the theft of pears. Here, in fact, we do have an incipient collective action—an infraction of the law in which we might read an attempted rebellion against young Augustine's father. But promptly we are transposed onto a different stage where, once again, it is the archaic scene of maternal fusion that is played out as a last imaginary resort against the threats of the outside world:

It is the intricacy of desire as profound nucleus that is actualized

---

51. Žižek, *The Puppet and the Dwarf*, 91.

and dramatized in the theft that Augustine hides and satisfies in the act of discovery—diminished but realized enjoyment. It is the commemoration of a fundamental and clandestine violation, degraded and ignored through the guilt that he still feels. In the theft the yearned-for element is actualized, but quietly. The law that is transgressed and the object that is stolen serve to evoke another scene, this time unconscious, the only one that gives us the clue to the emotion he feels in relating it. About that which the body animated in this minuscule act, consciousness knows nothing; only rumors come to it from an ancient drama, and even then only in a fragmented and displaced form.[52]

Augustine's fellow sinners in the theft of pears thus quickly vanish from the story, as do the clandestine links with the object-cause of desire that is the unnameable maternal Thing. Instead of a combat, we obtain a displacement; and instead of an act of rebellion, a guilty acquiescence to the symbolic Father-God.

Imitation without identification; indifference without confrontation; fusion without conflict; shame without guilt; melodrama without tragedy: such would be the relatively stable mechanisms of psychic power with which the modern subject tries to cope with the crumbling of patriarchal and imperial power, following the model inaugurated in the new literary experiment of Augustine's *Confessions*: "Christianity dissolves the political failure of Jesus the rebel and converts it into the social success of Christ crucified for the Empire."[53] We therefore should not be surprised to find that this model is proposed once again today and each time when an imperial order faces the threat of its imminent collapse. "Christian technology, organizer of the human mind and soul, antecedes the capitalist technology of the means of production; the former paves the way for the latter," Rozitchner posited already in 1997 at the start of *La Cosa y la Cruz*, in many ways predicting what we have come to witness even more forcefully some two decades later. "It is not by accident that when finance capitalism's abstract and monetary infinity triumphs and 'globalizes' itself, nothing less than the infinite void of Christian religion appears to fill the hole of the defeated social revolution as the only other horizon left; accomplices implicated in the spoliation of body and soul."[54]

In Search of Method

Obviously, I cannot discuss in detail all the speculative contributions of Rozitchner's *La Cosa y la Cruz*. Instead, I would like to raise three overarching questions about his work that concern the links—or, if necessary, the delinking—between politics, religion, and philosophy as inflected by psychoanalysis.

---

52. Rozitchner, *La Cosa y la Cruz*, 79.
53. Ibid., 133.
54. Rozitchner, *La Cosa y la Cruz*, 10; *The Thing and the Cross*, 35.

In one of the rare responses to Rozitchner's work published during his life, his long-time friend and fellow leftist political thinker Emilio de Ípola once accused him of presenting *un pensamiento develador*—that is, a revelatory kind of thinking aimed at unveiling or unmasking our ideological fantasies and illusions in the school of the so-called "hermeneutics of suspicion" of Marx, Nietzsche, and Freud. "The presupposition, let us call it ontological, that puts in motion the critical machine affirms simply that nothing is what it shows, seems, or says itself to be."[55] It is true that Rozitchner often claims to "expose," "uncover," or "lay bare" the innermost kernel of political power and submission which is said to be "concealed," "disavowed" or "covered-up." In this regard, he is perhaps not so different from someone like Žižek, who typically exposes the obscene scenarios of enjoyment that undergird our noble public life—even though Žižek's undying Lacanianism would be condemned by Rozitchner, who never fails to proclaim his loyalty to Freud in ways very different from Lacan's own proposed return to Freud. Here is one such instance of a methodological self-description in Rozitchner's work that might seem to justify de Ípola's objection:

> Thus we told ourselves: If we were to read Augustine and reveal the fundamental equation of his model of humanity—the "Love" and "Truth" of the divine Word that only the chosen ones hear, that which calls for the denial of the body and of the life of others as the necessary sacrifice that permits love and truth to situate themselves with impunity beyond crime—would we not also, in doing so, lay bare a cultural system that utilizes death and converts it, secretly, into an inevitable demand of its political logic? If we take this human model, considered to be the most sublime, and if we show that there, in the exaltation of the most sacred, the commitment to what is most sinister also finds a niche, will we not also, in doing so, have uncovered the obscene mechanism of Christian religious production? This is the challenge: to understand a model of being human that has produced sixteen centuries of subtle, refined, brutal and merciless subjection.[56]

---

55.   Emilio de Ípola, "León Rozitchner: La especulación filosófica como política sustituta," in *Investigaciones políticas* (Buenos Aires: Nueva Visión, 1989), 121. De Ípola also highlights two other constants in Rozitchner's method: his reliance on polemical adversaries, and his repeated denunciation of the illusions and misconceptions of an increasingly generic Left that is also supposed to function as an interlocutor. However, it is worth recalling something that this critic mentions only reluctantly at the very end of his article—namely, that he was part of a group of socialist intellectuals exiled in Mexico who, at the end of the military dictatorship in Argentina, supported the junta's claim of sovereignty over the Falkland Islands, and who were unforgivingly—and in my eyes legitimately—blasted for this show of nationalistic pride and socialist illusion in Rozitchner's book *Malvinas: de la guerra "sucia" a la guerra "limpia"* (Buenos Aires: Centro Editor de América Latina, 1985). Other co-signatories of the document by the Grupo de Discusión Socialista included José M. Aricó, Néstor García Canclini, José Nun, and Juan Carlos Portantiero. The document is reproduced in the appendix to Rozitchner's *Malvinas*, 139–153.

56.   Rozitchner, *La Cosa y la Cruz*, 10; *The Thing and the Cross*, 34 (translation modified).

A first question, then, is whether this revelatory mode of the critique of ideology, which is typical of a certain Marxist-inflected psychoanalysis in general, is also compatible with politics, or whether it may not actually forestall emancipatory transformations under the pressure of those very same subjective formations that have so forcefully been exposed in the first place. While this last possibility may to some extent affect the case of his counterpart in Slovenia, Rozitchner avoids the temptation of merely becoming enthralled by the revelation of the obscene underside of the law—merely showing or rendering its dark and gutsy entrails, as the death-driven ground of the human condition as such. Not only does he refuse to remain locked in a structural or quasi-transcendental framework; what is more, he also continues to expand the historical overdeterminations of the subject in the long run. By doing so, he has at least opened up the possibility of its real transformation.

A second question regards the links between religion and politics. In fact, the current rush to retrieve the figure of saintliness as a future model for political militantism forces us, after the caveats mentioned above, to reopen the question of political theology and its increasingly pivotal role for contemporary theories of the Left. In this context, Rozitchner's book on Augustine has the enormous virtue of exposing the extent to which the notion of political subjectivity continues to be contaminated by Christian theology:

> This is why we became interested in finding the fundament of the political in that which is most specifically religious. And we wondered whether it might truly be possible for any believer, with the content of the Christian imaginary—despite the best of intentions, and even if he or she subscribes to Liberation Theology—to create a political experience that might be *essentially* different from the politics that he or she combats. We are asking if every Christian religious fundament is not also *necessarily* a fundament of domination precisely in what is religious in it.[57]

The examples of Badiou, Negri, and Žižek reveal the real difficulty of answering the demand for a political experience, including on a subjective level, that would be *essentially* different from the one it combats. All of these thinkers, in fact, remain deeply entangled in the political theology of Christianity—unable to illustrate the militant subject except through the figure of the saint. In some cases writing several years ahead of them, Rozitchner thus seems almost directly to answer his younger colleagues: "The model offered to humanity is the martyrdom of saints, just as the saints' model is Christ's martyrdom."[58]

Faced with this dilemma, which is not merely a burden of theory but

---

57. Rozitchner, *La Cosa y la Cruz*, 11; *The Thing and the Cross*, 35 (translation modified).
58. Rozitchner, *La Cosa y la Cruz*, 332; *The Thing and the Cross*, 35.

also perhaps the result of the interiorization of a failed practice, it is certainly tempting to leave behind the politics of subjectivity altogether, based on "the intuition, which I believe to be theoretically inarticulable, that there is in us and beyond us something that overwhelmingly exceeds subjectivity, including the subjectivity of the unconscious."[59] After centuries of refined and subtle subjection, however, I also fear that any act of taking leave from the subject remains inscribed in the metaphysical grammar of subjectivity, now turned toward its sinister and abject, properly subaltern, underside—not unlike the way in which Lacan himself, I might add, envisioned a role for the analyst as a saint. The saint, then, would no longer be the source of innocent pleasure and joy, as in Lyotard; he or she would rather embody the sheer leftover, the remaining piece of dirt or debris of the analytical process: "So as to embody what the structure entails, namely allowing the subject, the subject of the unconscious, to take him as the cause of the subject's own desire," as Lacan says in one of his presentations for *Television*. "In fact it is through the abjection of this cause that the subject in question has a chance to be aware of his position, at least within the structure. For the saint, this is not amusing, but I imagine that for a few ears glued to this TV it converges with many of the oddities of the acts of saints."[60] Ultimately, the saint would embody the piece of the real that has to drop out of the picture in order for the subject—in the analytical act properly speaking—to come to terms with its self-divestiture.

Finally, a third question concerns the relation between this psycho-analytico-political theology and philosophy. In other words, what about "love" and "truth" when it is the truth itself that is the object of love? Is there not a religious element, both sublime and obscene, at the root of the philosophical as such? How, then, can we reconcile the materialist critique of religion with the pursuit of philosophy when it would not be difficult to show that, beneath every mastered truth, there lies the beaten flesh of a repressed naked body, terrorized in the name of the spirit? It is in answer to this last question that Rozitchner, who has never stopped calling himself a philosopher despite the widespread sympathies among psychoanalysts for the tradition of what Lacan called "antiphilosophy," has produced some of his most breathtaking pages. I am thinking, in particular, of the theses contained in "Philosophy and Terror" published from exile during the military regime in Argentina.

When military power ceases to hide the kernel of terror and the anxiety of death that underlies every principle of authority, the task of

59. Alberto Moreiras, *Línea de sombra: El no sujeto de lo político* (Santiago de Chile: Palinodia, 2006), 10. For a more detailed discussion of this preferred option of the non-subject, see Chapter 2 in Bosteels, *The Actuality of Communism*.
60. Jacques Lacan, *Television*, ed. Joan Copjec, trans. Denis Hollier, Rosalind Krauss, and Annette Michelson (New York: W. W. Norton, 1990), 15.

theory or philosophy can only lie in seeking out and undoing the spaces within thought where this kernel finds a way to nest itself. "At times when the contradictions and crisis deepen, as occurs now among us, we must ask ourselves about the essence of reflection, and thus about the essence of philosophy that terror, by opposing it in its answer, seeks to cut short," Rozitchner writes. "Once again: it is war that nests itself within truth, and whoever pronounces truth is, in his or her own way, a combatant."[61] Rozitchner, in a near-Adornian style, will use the powers of reflection to undo the ties that in principle bind all reflection to power and terror: "To think the conditions of truth in philosophy means to reach out within thinking human beings for the foundation where the core of terror takes refuge within them, as their own limit."[62] To think against this limit means abandoning neither the subject nor the concept, but rather to turn the power of the subject against the domination of constituted subjectivity, as well as to open up the concept to that which cannot but remain unconceptualized. Such would be, after all, the possible role of philosophy or theory in the face of terror— even, or especially, when this terror seeks refuge within the hearts of combatants who fight against it in the name of freedom and grace.

61. León Rozitchner, "Filosofía y terror," in *Freud y el problema del poder*, 245–6. An English translation, by Don Deere and Ricardo Ortiz Vázquez, is forthcoming in the journal *Theory & Event*.
62. Rozitchner, "Filosofía y terror," 250.

6

THE MELANCHOLY LEFT

A Sinister Legacy

In 68, Paco Ignacio Taibo II notes: "Today the movement of '68 is one more Mexican specter, one of the many unredeemed and sleepless specters that haunt our land."[1] Of course, the image repeats that of the specter or ghost whose haunting force runs through the first pages of *The Communist Manifesto*, an image that was taken up in turn in the 1960s by some of the most outspoken actors in the student-popular movements in the world, from the brothers Daniel and Gabriel Cohn-Bendit in France, whose *Leftism as a Remedy Against the Senile Disease of Communism* (a clever inversion of Lenin's *Leftism as a Childhood Disease of Communism*) begins with the lines "A specter haunts the world today, the specter of the students,"[2] all the way to the fragment "Un fantasma recorre México" ("A Phantasm or Specter Haunts Mexico"), which is José Revueltas's first published text on the student movement, written shortly after the massacre that took place on the Plaza de las Tres Culturas, in the Tlatelolco neighborhood of Mexico City.[3] In other words, 1968 becomes a ghost not only for its inheritors today; at the time of the events themselves, the force

1. Paco Ignacio Taibo II, 68 (Mexico City: Planeta, 1991), 9. Previously published in a much shorter version as "Fantasmas nuestros de cada día: Notas sobre la presencia del 68, veinte años después," *Casa de las Américas* 171 (1988): 96–113. The book, interestingly enough, has been translated into English by Guy Debord's habitual translator Donald Nicholson Smith, as Paco Ignacio Taibo II, '68 (New York: Seven Stories, 2004). At Harvard University, as part of a 1998 seminar on 1968 in Paris and Mexico City, the students and I completed a collective translation, which is the one that guides me in the following pages.
2. Daniel and Gabriel Cohn-Bendit, *Le gauchisme remède à la maladie sénile du communisme* (Paris: Seuil, 1968), 21. Available in English as *Obsolete Communism: The Left-Wing Alternative*, trans. Arnold Pomerans (New York: McGraw-Hill, 1968). For further discussion, I refer the reader to my "The Leftist Hypothesis: Communism in the Age of Terror," in Alain Badiou and Slavoj Žižek, eds, *On the Idea of Communism* (London: Verso, 2010, 33–66).
3. José Revueltas, "Un fantasma recorre México," in *México 68: Juventud y revolución* (Mexico City: Era, 1978), 79–84. See also Armando Bartra, "Un joven fantasma recorre el mundo: Revolución en la cultura y cultura de la revolución," a talk given at the Universidad Nacional Autónoma de México as part of the series "Desde el umbral del nuevo siglo: 1968–1998" (November 12, 1998).

of the movement already appeared as a formidable specter. It would be a mistake, however, to subsume all these uses of the spectral or phantasmatic image into a vast ontology, or hauntology of the specter, similar to that presented by Jacques Derrida in *Specters of Marx: The State of the Debt, the Work of Mourning and the New International*. Even under one and the same translucent cloak, no ghost ever presents itself twice with the same appearance. In France, for instance, immediately after the events of May–June 1968, to invoke the specter of leftism still entailed launching a double threat, certainly against the government of Charles de Gaulle but also—this time ironically, if we recall the famous first political use of the specter—against the orthodoxy of the Communist Party. In Mexico, by contrast, the gesture of conjuring up the ghost, even if it retains the charge of intimate rebellion against the regime of President Gustavo Díaz Ordaz, is not without a strong undercurrent of obstinate melancholy as a result of the repression that took place on October 2, 1968, when more than 200 students, activists and bystanders were shot by government forces. It is this violent act of military repression that, to this day, is remembered in Mexico with the words "2 de octubre no se olvida" ("October 2, we won't forget").

An event, then, appears as a ghost both for what it no longer is and for what it has yet to be. In one case, it ciphers the memory of an annihilated possibility; in the other, the glimpse of a promise that is perhaps on the verge of becoming real. Ghosts or phantasms can mark the death of the ideas from the old world, as well as announcing a new principle of life. "It is true that the old world belongs to the philistine. But one should not treat the latter as a ghost from which to recoil in fear. On the contrary, we ought to stare the ghost in the eye," Marx warned in one of his letters to Arnold Ruge, five years before the upheavals of 1848. And he ended his letter: "For our part, we must expose the old world to the full light of day and shape the new one in a positive way. The longer the time that events allow to thinking humanity for taking stock of its position, and to suffering humanity for mobilising its forces, the more perfect on entering the world will be the product that the present time bears in its womb."[4] The anchoring point for the figure of the ghost is always a break on the extreme edge where the old bears the new, either to give in to what is gestating there or else to tie it down with the threads of the past. Today, these two postures are perhaps only two sides of the same coin, one that from passing from hand to hand ends up losing its inscription forever.

---

4. Karl Marx, quoted from the Spanish translation of the correspondence between Marx and Arnold Ruge, which is one of the few versions to include Ruge's responses, in *Escritos de juventud*, trans. Wenceslao Roces (Mexico City: Fondo de Cultura Económica, 1982): 445, 450. Marx's own letters can be consulted in Karl Marx and Friedrich Engels, *Collected Works*, vol. 3 (Moscow: Progress, 1975), 133–45.

Without a doubt, this is the price the Left has to pay if it wants to survive its multiple crises. The result, however, is that today the utopian desire can no longer be opposed simply as a force of innovation to the allegedly regressive negativity of melancholy, but rather is somehow contained within the latter. It is precisely this ambivalence that marks the different trajectories of the ghost or phantasm. Thus, in the retrospective judgment of many a "sesentayochero" there are no doubt fears of an irreparable loss or defeat that is difficult to confess, but there is also a will to be faithful to an event or series of events, the political and ideological effects of which perhaps have not yet been exhausted. "It is possible that this ghost, because of its youth, still enjoys good health and that it normally comes to the rescue of our generation every time its presence is conjured up. Saint Francis of Assisi of our doubts, Saint Che Guevara of our emotions, Saint Philip Marlowe of our private investigations, Saint Jane Fonda of our anxieties," Taibo suggests. "Or at least, it created the inevitable reference point, which is useful for our sense of pride, guilt, and comparison . . . But I also confess, with difficulties, sadly [*penosamente*], that the ghost is losing its corporeity and its profile. It is becoming reduced to myth, to a collection of stubbornnesses. I've found some who even say that it never existed."[5] No radical thinker can get rid of the strange sensation that in those years something slipped out of our hands that should not have gotten away— or worse, that perhaps even before the loss was never really in our possession to begin with.

At this point, in a strange kind of originary loss, the Left takes the step from mourning into melancholy. As the Argentine novelist and critic Ricardo Piglia writes in a slightly different context, with a quote falsely attributed to Roberto Arlt that in fact belongs to Jorge Luis Borges: "Sólo se pierde lo que realmente no se ha tenido nunca" ("We only lose that which we never really had").[6] This epigraph from Piglia's collection *Nombre falso* (*Assumed Name*) could serve as a shorthand notation to portray the destiny of left-wing radicalism from the 1960s onwards. For many militants or onlookers, the various defeats of revolutionary fervor in the final instance would merely confirm, if not the end of all politics, then at least the end of modern politics, understood as being based on a substantial social link as the principle to ground a universally just community. The sovereignty of the social bond—the bond as necessary support for any subject in politics: this would be the lost object-cause of the New Left. The vanishing of this ideological principle, however, opens up an uncanny process of melancholy, comparable to an "unconscious loss," or an "unknown loss," in the words of Freud, because "one feels justified in concluding

---

5. Taibo, *68*, 9–10, 14.
6. Ricardo Piglia, *Nombre falso* (Buenos Aires: Siglo Veintiuno, 1975), 7. For further discussion of the logic behind this erroneous attribution, see Chapter 7.

that a loss of the kind has been experienced, but one cannot see clearly what has been lost, and may the more readily suppose that the patient too cannot consciously perceive what it is he has lost."[7] What is more, giving one more turn of the screw to Freud's intuition, we might suppose the original nonexistence of the lost object. The bond as a founding principle of modern politics would never have existed in reality; in fact, the idea of such a social link constitutes a phantasmatic object, so that the work of melancholy would become infinitely more complex, not to say interminable. "From this point of view, melancholy would be not so much the regressive reaction to the loss of the love object as the imaginative capacity to make an unobtainable object appear as if lost," Agamben suggests. "If the libido behaves *as if* a loss had occurred although *nothing* has in fact been lost, this is because the libido stages a simulation where what cannot be lost because it has never been possessed appears as lost, and what could never be possessed because it had never perhaps existed may be appropriated insofar as it is lost."[8] This seems to me to be the condition of large parts of the Left today, four decades after the momentous upsurge of radicalism all over the world as a case—not the only one, to be sure—of emancipatory politics. Žižek also writes, as if to echo the words from Borges that Piglia erroneously attributes to Arlt: "The crucial step that has to be taken here is to get rid of this nostalgic longing for the lost closed universe by recognizing that *we never had what we have lost*; the idyll was false from the very beginning, society was always-already ridden with fierce antagonism."[9] Thus, in painful shame or with resigned pride, not without a certain euphoria disguised as if it were the gift of a recently acquired lucidity beyond all alibis, many thinkers of the Left after 1968 became aware that they never possessed that which they nonetheless seemed to have lost. In circumstances such as these, it should not be surprising to find that many consider the very use of the opposition between Left and Right a sure sign of obsolescence.

In a wordplay whose ambiguity unfortunately survives only in Italian, as Massimo Cacciari recalls for us, we could also refer to the current state of radical political thought as a sinister Left.[10] *Das Unheimliche*, the uncanny or sinister, in the Freudian sense, alludes to

7. Sigmund Freud, "Mourning and Melancholy," in *General Psychological Theory*, ed. Philip Rieff (New York: Macmillan, 1963), 166. On mourning after 1968 in France and Italy, see Isabelle Sommier, *La violence politique et son deuil: L'après 68 en France et en Italie* (Rennes: Presses Universitaires de Rennes, 1998); and on melancholy in Mexico, Roger Bartra, *La jaula de la melancolía: Identidad y metamorfosis del mexicano* (Mexico City: Grijalbo, 1987).
8. Giorgio Agamben, *Stanzas: Word and Phantasm in Western Culture*, trans. Ronald L. Martínez (Minneapolis: University of Minnesota Press, 1993), 20.
9. Slavoj Žižek, *For They Know Not What They Do: Enjoyment as a Political Factor*, 2nd edn (London: Verso, 2002), 168.
10. Massimo Cacciari, "Sinisteritas," *Il concetto di sinistra* (Milan: Bompiani, 1982), 7–19.

the furtive return of primitive or infantile convictions, such as the belief in the life of the dead, which were supposed to have been overcome long ago. "Today we no longer believe in them, having surmounted such modes of thought. Yet we do not feel entirely secure in these new convictions; the old ones live on in us, on the lookout for confirmation," writes Freud. "Now, as soon as something *happens* in our lives that seems to confirm these old, discarded beliefs, we experience a sense of the uncanny."[11] The uncanny element that is lying in wait, in this sense, must be added to the notorious tendency toward melancholy in political thought today. These two subjective modalities, both of them for sure traversed by a phantasmatic or spectral experience, run together in the trajectory of 1968 radicalism over the past decades. In short, we can suppose that the conviction that returns, one that is intimately tied to the idea of the social bond, is precisely the belief in the possibility of a revolutionary politics. Today, there can be no doubt, this belief is considered over and done with; many will even add that it has never been more than the unreal object of a melancholic desire. And yet, what happened during the events of 1968 for a moment seemed to confirm the spectral return of those very same beliefs that were supposed to have been overcome or lost from the start. Beginning with this watershed year, a large part of the Left no longer escapes its melancholy except to live on in a sinister if not downright cynical position.

In response to this tendency, I propose to read the ghost or phantasm as a point of departure for a subjective figure of emancipatory politics. The premise behind this reading is that we must think of politics—this would be the task of a certain metapolitics—not so much as an affair that is objectively inscribed in a set of public spaces, parties, or interests, but as an immanent procedure of subjectivization. "Subjective," in other words, must be understood as referring to all that enters into the constitution of a subject. Of course, in everyday language, the term has mostly pejorative connotations when it comes to politics. It would refer to the merely personal, the individual, or the affective—all of them registers of experience normally foreclosed or considered secondary in comparison to the public, universal, or at least deliberate decisions of politics. One of the lasting consequences of the events of 1968, however, consists precisely in displacing the borders of the political so as to include the everydayness—the infra-ordinariness, so to speak—of those who are the subjects of struggles for justice. Many observers allude to this when they talk about the new role of morality, or ethics, in politics. "A task imposes itself on the students: to transform the violence against them into an ideological resistance, still rudimentary to be sure, but

---

11. Sigmund Freud, "The Uncanny," in *The Uncanny*, trans. David McLintock (New York: Penguin, 2003), 154.

assumed with the admirable consistency of the example," Carlos Monsiváis writes. "There is a novelty in this: courage and convictions turn personal impulses into acts of conscience [*tomas de conciencia*] in the face of oppression."[12] The political, in any case, defines neither a human faculty nor a social field that would have to be philosophically or objectively stabilized. By contrast, politics, when understood at the level of subjectivity, is above all a form of practiced thought. "The subjective is not linked in any way to the objective; the subjective that is unprecedented is thought," Sylvain Lazarus remarks. "In this sense, politics thought in interiority is thinking."[13] The effects of a process of subjectivization, by producing unprecedented collective truths, turn out to be strictly internal to politics as thought; they do not automatically obey any of the referents studied, for instance, in sociology or history, or even the critique of political economy. On the contrary, when we think politics from within—that is, subjectively— it can appear in the least suspected of places, including in art and poetry, many of them considered marginal or unimportant from an external or institutional point of view.

The key questions in this reading thus revolve around an understanding of the ghostly or phantasmatic as the site for an event in the midst of the cultural-political situation of 1968. What happens in the space of this opening? How does one remain faithful to the consequences of such an event? How does one think anew—subjectively—a topic as classical as the idea of justice in relation to power and culture? How—by what protocols of subjectivization—has the Left moved to its current melancholy state? And what role should we attribute in this process to the ghost or phantasm previously conjured up as the site of the event, and currently as its foreclosure? To answer these questions, habit or good manners demand that we return to the political philosophy contained in a few founding documents, so as to bring them up to date with the most recent feats in our history books. The answers, thus, would be lying in wait for us in a few wisely reinterpreted pages by Machiavelli, Tocqueville, Hobbes, Weber, or Schmitt. Sometimes, however, we must urgently break with good habits if we are to come across an event whose truth can all of a sudden sharpen its profile more vividly in the instantaneous act of writing a chronicle or a poem than in the respectable tomes of political philosophy. That is to say, as a specific condition of truth, art and

---

12. Carlos Monsiváis, "1968: Dramatis personae," in Sergio Zermeño, *México: Una democracia utópica: El movimiento estudiantil del 68* (Mexico City: Siglo Veintiuno,1978), xvi–xvii. Inspired by Alain Touraine's analysis of the French 1968, Zermeño's book is still one of the best sociological overviews of the events of 1968 in Mexico.

13. Sylvain Lazarus, *Anthropologie du nom* (Paris: Seuil, 1996), 14. This definition of the politics of subjectivization is the basis for the "metapolitics" proposed by Alain Badiou in *Metapolitics*, trans. Jason Barker (London: Verso, 2005). For further discussion, see "Whose Politics?" in Bosteels, *Badiou and Politics*, 17–33.

poetry can also anticipate some of the consequences that are immanent to a political event—without for this reason becoming confused
with it. Or at least this is the wager with which I would now like to
turn to the events of 1968 in Mexico.

Basic Banalities

Under this subheading, borrowed from the Belgian Situationist Raoul
Vaneigem, I would first like to present a series of facts and working
hypotheses whose logic informs my analysis of 1968 as part of a critical history of the present. Though apparently trivial or banal, these
facts and hypotheses, taken together, project a fairly consistent picture,
as should be obvious from other attempts at conceptualization, such as
Fredric Jameson's "Periodizing the 60s."[14] In each case, I indicate as

---

14. Fredric Jameson, "Periodizing the 60s," in *The Ideologies of Theory* (Minneapolis:
University of Minnesota Press, 1988), 178–208. See also Raoul Vaneigem, "Banalités de
base," *Internationale Situationniste* 7 (1962): 32–40; and 8 (1963): 34–47; in English,
"Basic Banalities," *Situationist International Anthology*, ed. and trans. Ken Knabb
(Berkeley: Bureau of Public Secrets, 1981), 89–100, 118–33; and, for a world-system
analysis, Immanuel Wallerstein, "1968, revolución en el sistema-mundo: Tesis e
interrogantes," in *El juicio al sujeto: Un análisis global de los movimientos sociales*,
(Mexico City: FLACSO/Miguel Angel Porrúa, 1990), 15–41. For an analysis of the
Mexican case, see Ramón Ramírez, *El movimiento estudiantil de México (julio/diciembre
de 1968)* (Mexico City: Era, 1969), vol. 1, 13–141; Jorge Carrión and Daniel Cazés, *Tres
culturas en agonía* (Mexico City: Nuestro Tiempo, 1969); Gilberto Guevara Niebla, *La
democracia en la calle: Crónica del movimiento estudiantil mexicano* (Mexico City: Siglo
Veintiuno, 1988); César Gilabert, *El hábito de la utopía: Análisis del imaginario
sociopolítico en el movimiento estudiantil de México, 1968* (Mexico City: Instituto Mora/
Miguel Angel Porrúa, 1993). Among the most famous essays are Octavio Paz, *Posdata*
(Mexico City: Siglo Veintiuno, 1970) and Carlos Fuentes, "La disyuntiva mexicana,"
Tiempo mexicano (Mexico City: Joaquín Mortiz, 1971), 147–93. Chronicles include
Carlos Monsiváis, *Días de guardar* (Mexico City: Era, 1970) and Elena Poniatowska, "El
movimiento estudiantil de 1968," in *Fuerte es el silencio* (Mexico City: Era, 1980), 34–77.
Among the numerous testimonies, I should mention Elena Poniatowska, *La noche de
Tlatelolco* (Mexico City: Era, 1971); Luis González de Alba, *Los días y los años* (Mexico
City: Era, 1971); Hermann Bellinghausen, et al., *Pensar el 68* (Mexico City: Cal y Arena,
1988); Daniel Cazés, ed., *Memorial del 68: Relato a muchas voces* (Mexico City: La
Jornada, 1993). For an overview of literary, cinematic and graphic approaches, see
Gonzalo Martré, *El movimiento popular estudiantil de 1968 en la novela mexicana*
(Mexico City: UNAM, 1998); Leopoldo Ayala, *Nuestra verdad: Memorial del movimiento
estudiantil popular y el dos de octubre de 1968* (Mexico City: J. Porrúa, 1989); Marco
Antonio Campos and Alejandro Toledo, *Poemas y narraciones sobre el movimiento
estudiantil de 1968* (Mexico City: UNAM, 1998); Ivonne Gutiérrez, ed., *Entre el silencio
y la estridencia: La protesta literaria del 68* (Mexico City: Aldus, 1998); Xavier Robles y
Guadalupe Ortega, *Rojo amanecer (Bengalas en el cielo)* (Mexico City: El Milagro/Instituto
Mexicano de Cinematografía, 1995); Óscar Menéndez, *México 68* (Mexico City:
Cooperativa de Producción Salvador Toscano, 1998); Grupo Mira, *La gráfica del '68:
Homenaje al movimiento estudiantil*, ed. Jorge Pérez Vega (Mexico City: Zurda, 1988).
The thirtieth anniversary of the events, in 1998, seems to have been particularly productive:
Sergio Aguayo Quezada, *1968: Los archivos de la violencia* (Mexico City: Grijalbo, 1998);
Raúl Alvarez Garín, *La estela de Tlatelolco: Una reconstrucción histórica del Movimiento*

much as possible the singularity of the student-popular movement in Mexico.

1. The understanding of 1968 requires a major revision of the Marxist-Leninist theory of the class struggle, according to which the masses make history but only classes organize the masses, just as politics would be the concentrated expression of economics according to a famous statement from Lenin. Instead of the party of vanguard intellectuals, the student movement proposes a series of spontaneous tactics, such as the *mitines-relámpago* (literally "meetings that strike like lightning") or "exemplary actions," based on the structure of the group, or *grupúsculo*, as the principal detonating mechanism—a concept on which the model of the *foco* of Guevara's guerrilla warfare left deep imprints, as did the Sartrean theory of the group in fusion. In Mexico, however, not all revolutionary thinkers share the global criticism of the party, even though they are witnesses to the various experiments in participatory democracy such as the *brigadas* or *asambleas* of the National Strike Council (CNH). Thus, as we saw, Revueltas in several posthumous texts from *México 68: Juventud y revolución*, still insists on the need for an authentic working-class party in the Marxist-Leninist sense, since no such party can be found in the Mexican Communist Party (PCM), let alone in Vicente Lombardo Toledano's Popular Socialist Party (PPS). Even so, starting in 1968, this theoretician of the Mexican Spartacists also expresses serious doubts about the structure of political organization as a result of the student movement. These are the typical unresolved doubts with regard to the alternative between party centralism and the *autogestión* of a council, assembly, or brigade; between direction from the outside or mobilization from below; or between the need for disciplined organization and the spontaneous capacities of the masses. The struggle, in other words, between Marx

---

estudiantil del 68 (Mexico City: Grijalbo, 1998); Héctor Anaya, *Los parricidas del 68* (Mexico City: Plaza y Valdés, 1998); Esteban Ascencio, *1968: Más allá del mito* (Mexico City: Milenio, 1998); Roberta "la Tita" Avedaño Martínez, *De la libertad y el encierro* (Mexico City: La Idea Dorada, 1998); Leopoldo Ayala, *Lienzo Tlatelolco* (Mexico City: Nuevo Siglo, 1998); Renward García Medrano, *El 2 de octubre de 1968 en sus propias palabras* (Mexico City: Grijalbo/Consejo Nacional para la Cultura y las Artes, 1998); Raúl Jardón, *1968: El fuego de la esperanza* (Mexico City: Siglo Veintiuno, 1998); Jorge Volpi, *La imaginación y el poder: Una historia intelectual de 1968* (Mexico City: Era, 1998); and Julio Scherer García and Carlos Monsiváis, *Parte de guerra. Tlatelolco 1968* (Mexico City: Nuevo Siglo/Aguilar, 1999). Ten years later, in 2008, the fortieth anniversary for the most part produced only re-editions. Significantly, among the few original takes, aside from Monsiváis's *El 68: La tradición de la resistencia* (Mexico City: Era, 2008), we find Pablo Gómez's *1968: La historia también está hecha de derrotas* (Mexico City: Miguel Ángel Porrúa, 2008). Defeat, I will argue, becomes part of the moralization of politics, which here takes the form of a melancholy Left. Compare with the argument for the French context formulated by Julian Bourg in *From Revolution to Ethics: May 1968 and Contemporary French Thought* (Montreal: McGill–Queen's University Press, 2007).

and Bakunin, or between Lenin and Rosa Luxemburg. "Even though the concept of *autogestión* was not explicitly developed as such by the Movement of the Generation of '68, it constitutes nevertheless its essential theoretical conquest," notes Revueltas. "I firmly believe that the Leninist theory of the party—as well as the theory of the state and the dictatorship of the proletariat—in light of the experiences of this second half of the twentieth century must and can be overcome."[15] The general trend of the student base, indeed, distances itself from the class struggle in the strict sense so as to approach new forms of spontaneous activism on the multiple fronts of direct democracy.

2. An understanding of 1968 likewise requires a revision of the productivist presuppositions behind socialism according to the dominant model of the Soviet Union. We can see here the combined influence of three major political sequences with a profound effect worldwide: the revolutionary victory in Cuba, the Cultural Revolution in China, and the so-called socialism with a human face of the Prague Spring. In each case, the emergence of new political actors is parallel to a strong reaffirmation of the relative autonomy of superstructural instances, aside from the economic base, following the famous dialectic of objective and subjective conditions. This is why the various struggles of 1968 are often summarized erroneously—whether in favor of the students or against them—as the rebellion of the subject against the system. In any case, the crisis of narrowly defined economic determinism is undeniable. Aside from Althusser's proposal to apply Freud's concept of overdetermination to Marxism, a genealogy of the relevant conceptual shifts would also have to include the names of Mao, Guevara, and Dubcek. Thus, in "On Contradiction," Mao observes: "True, the productive forces, practice and the economic base generally play the principal and decisive role; whoever denies this is not a materialist. But it must also be admitted that in certain conditions, such aspects as the relations of production, theory and the superstructure in turn manifest themselves in the principal and decisive role."[16] In "El socialismo y el hombre en Cuba" ("Socialism and Man in Cuba"), first published in the Uruguayan journal *Marcha* in 1965, Che Guevara noted: "To build communism it is necessary, simultaneous with the new material foundations, to build the new man and woman. That is why it is very important to choose the right instrument for mobilizing the masses. Basically, this instrument must be moral in character,

---

15. Revueltas, *México 68*, 137; and Andrea Revueltas and Philippe Cheron, eds, *José Revueltas y el 68* (Mexico City: Era/UNAM, 1998), 30. For a study of these theoretico-political developments in Revueltas, see Enrique González Rojo, "Las últimas concepciones teórico-políticas de José Revueltas," in *Revueltas en la mira* (Mexico City: Universidad Autónoma Metropolitana, 1984), 101–127.
16. Mao Zedong, "On Contradiction," in *Five Essays on Philosophy* (Beijing: Foreign Languages Press, 1977), 58.

without neglecting, however, a correct use of the material incentive."[17] Finally, in the "Action Program of the Communist Party of Czechoslovakia," published on April 5, 1968, at the onset of the Prague Spring, Dubcek's followers affirm: "The ideas according to which the edification of the new society depended solely on accelerated and extensive development of production were not combated on time"; but, henceforth, they add: "Socialism cannot mean only the liberation of the workers from the domination of class relations but [must also include] the full flourishing of personality . . . The interest in culture, both material and spiritual, not only represents a concern for the cultural front but must also become the affair of society as a whole."[18] In México, too, there is mounting resistance against the Soviet model. In the mind of Revueltas, for instance, the race for nuclear armament between the United States and the USSR, responsible for the 1962 Missile Crisis with Cuba, not only signaled the definitive sacrifice of international workers' solidarity on the altar of national interests, but was also a symptom of unilateral determinism in a different sense, insofar as the economy now came to stand under the imminent threat of destruction: "In the recent past, that which constitutes the economic base—the complex totality of relations of production—conditioned the other social, political, and ideological relations, as Engels used to say, *in the final instance*; today, by contrast, the productive relations have been converted into destructive relations that *immediately* condition the other human relations in contemporary society."[19] The Mexican Left at the time of the 1968 events, however, had only just accepted the capitalist nature of post-revolutionary society in Mexico, with large sectors still favoring the model of heavy industrialization under the influence of the global Cold War. Thus, as long as the old alliances with progressive sectors of the bourgeoisie were not excluded, the old orthodoxy of the Comintern policy remained intact. To this tendency, the students and militants oppose a revolt stemming from the sectors of education and culture, not in order to limit themselves to mere university reforms but in order to question the very social structure in which the dominance of the economy has canceled the difference between

---

17.   Ernesto "Che" Guevara, "El socialismo y el hombre en Cuba," in *Obra revolucionaria* (Mexico City: Era, 1963), 631; in English, "Socialism and Man in Cuba," in David Deutschmann, ed., *Che Guevara Reader* (New York: Ocean Press, 2003), 217 (the gender correction in "the new man and woman" for "el hombre nuevo" is obviously the translator's work).

18.   Alexander Dubcek et al., "Le programme d'action du Parti Communiste de Tchécoslovaquie," in *La liberté en sursis: Prague 1968* (Paris: Fayard, 1968), 49, 54. These lines are not included in the excerpts reprinted in English in Jaromir Navrátil, ed., *The Prague Spring 1968: A National Security Archive Documents Reader* (Prague: Prague Spring Foundation, 1998), 92–6.

19.   José Revueltas, "La enajenación de la sociedad contemporánea y el canto del cisne de Lombardo Toledano," in *México: una democracia bárbara (y escritos acerca de Lombardo Toledano)* (Mexico City: Era, 1983), 146.

socialism and imperialism, all the while undermining any claim that the Mexican Revolution would have accomplished anything other than a new repressive state bureaucracy. As Octavio Paz would write in *Posdata*: "The relation has been reversed: first the imperative was economic progress; now, in order for the latter to continue, social development—justice—is equally imperative."[20]

3. The events of 1968 throw into relief the new political role of the social. In terms of political philosophy or the theory of new social movements, this emphasis can be translated as the predominance of civil society over political society or the state. "There are no long-term objectives, only an immediate criticism, a negation of the strong and authoritarian state," writes Sergio Zermeño in his analysis of 1968 in Mexico. "The movement expresses the strengthening of civil society against the State."[21] Readings such as these, though, may have the drawback of a limited concept of the political. That is to say, the student revolt would be new in forming a social rather than a political movement only because the criteria for defining the sphere of the political continue to be defined by the seizure of power at the level of the state. By contrast, what might be needed is a different emphasis on the very political nature of the social—to be more precise, on the subjective dimension of politics itself. This should not be understood as implying the cohesiveness of the social bond—whether this cohesiveness is named the people, civil society, or simply public opinion—against the false mechanisms of official apparatuses—the parties, unions, and press tied to the state. This would merely entail replacing the old antagonism proletariat/bourgeoisie with the new one of civil society/state. The real issue, however, is not to oppose one social bond to another, let alone—in a typically melodramatic fashion—to oppose one that is intrinsically good to another that is intrinsically bad. Rather, the revolt undoes the very logic of the social bond or link so as to give way to a politics of delinking.

The whole debate about the "success" or "failure" of 1968, in France as well as in Mexico, is equivocal insofar as it continues to revolve around the capacity—or lack of capacity—of the students to forge links or alliances with other sectors of society, above all with workers and peasants. This point of view loses sight of the power of the movement to unlink society and to sunder the social bond. Prior to its fusion into a homogeneous social force, the radical emancipatory potential of a mass action might very well consist in such a capacity to divide or split the ground on which a given social order is established. Politics, then, would be social not because it starts from an objective identity whose delimitation would be the task typically assigned to the

---

20. Octavio Paz, *Posdata* (Mexico City: Siglo Veintiuno, 1970), 72.
21. Zermeño, *México: Una democracia utópica*, 51.

sociologist or political economist, but because it takes off from the opening of a gap or breach in that imaginary whole called society. "Even at the heart of the mass movement, political activity is an unbinding, and is experienced as such by the movement," affirms Badiou. He continues:

> Politics will always strive to deconstruct the bond, including the one within the mass movement, the better to detect those ramified divisions that attest to the mass-being of strictly political consciousness ... Mass politics therefore grapples with the bound consistency of parts in order to undo its illusory hold and to deploy every affirmative singularity presented by the multiple on the edge of the void. It is through such singularities, whose latent void is articulated by the event, that politics constructs the new law that subtracts itself from the State's authority.[22]

In Mexico, the first person to confirm this logic of delinking or unbinding is, not surprisingly, President Gustavo Díaz Ordaz himself. In his IV Informe Presidencial (State of the Union Address), on September 1, 1968, the Mexican head of state thus warns his people: "No podemos admitir que las universidades, entraña misma de México, hayan dejado de ser parte del suelo patrio y estén sustraídas al régimen constitucional de la nación" ["We cannot allow that universities, the very heart and soul of Mexico, have ceased being part of the fatherland and are subtracted from the constitutional regime of the nation"].[23] Indeed, what this indirect threat to the heart and soul, or literally, to the entrails of the state reveals is the extent to which political action consists, in the first place, in a subtraction from the objectivity of the state. From the point of view of the students, on the other hand, the same logic explains the central importance, in the *pliego petitorio* or list of demands, of the abrogation of articles 145 and 145bis of the Penal Code, which refer to the so-called *delito de disolución social*, or *delito político*—articles which had served for many years to repress all kinds of popular mobilization. The demand to abrogate these articles is one way of demanding the right to dissolve the official law of the existing juridical order in order to found the effective justice of a new law. The social, then, becomes political by subtracting itself from society, but only if it assumes at the same time the risk of becoming split in its turn. Indeed, if "the state obtains its force from subtracting the forces of civil society," then it is only logical that the students proceed the other way around, as César Gilabert writes: "The other option is to make politics there where it should not be made, with the aim of breaking the monopoly of the state."[24]

---

22. Badiou, *Metapolitics*, 72–4.
23. Gustavo Díaz Ordaz, IV Informe Presidencial, quoted in Anaya, *Los parricidas del 68*, 275.
24. Gilabert, *El hábito de la utopia*, 255.

4.   The events of 1968 underscore the decisive role of ideology, culture, and the practices of everyday life as integral parts of the political struggle in contemporary society. The arms of criticism matter more than the criticism of arms. "There emerges a movement that in essence is more expressive and symbolic than political," Gilabert concludes. "We should think of the movement of '68 as precipitating itself to the extreme limits of the imagination. Forced to create new means of conceiving and practicing politics, such action is the visible part of a growing process in the politicization of the everyday, as opposed to authoritarianism, and the seed for a new sociability."[25] After the time of the historical avant-gardes in the first half of the twentieth century, this is perhaps only the second time during which it makes sense to speak of a cultural politics. In fact, the entire sequence at the end of the 1960s and the early 1970s deserves to be named "cultural revolution" in a generic sense, irreducible to its singular conditions in Maoist China.[26] The history of this process, despite numerous sociological, historiographical, and philosophical accounts, to a large extent still remains to be written. From a critical perspective of the present, we can observe at least two contemporary phenomena that indicate a new approach to the question of cultural politics. In philosophy, the dialogue with the political, scientific, or artistic present continues to unfold in what we might call *critical theory*, but, precisely starting in this period, the latter term embraces a much wider variety of tendencies, such as deconstruction or hermeneutics, instead of remaining confined to the institutional context of the Frankfurt School and its exile in New York City. Literary studies, on the other hand, have also undergone a major transformation toward the domain of popular artistic expression, giving way to so-called *cultural studies*—first in the School of Birmingham, and then, above all, in the United States. In this sense, many of us who work in the fields of critical theory and cultural studies are indeed the collective inheritors of 1968.

5.   In discussions of 1968 the term "events" has become universally consolidated, not only in the academic world but also in the daily talk of journalists and historians. From this we can derive the principal hypothesis about the joint emergence of cultural studies and a renewed understanding of critical theory—namely, the hypothesis that what these domains seek to discern is precisely the possibility of thinking of a genuine event, be it in politics, in art, or in science. Indeed, if the concept of the event nowadays is key to the work of critical theory and cultural critique, then the analysis of the events of 1968 as part of such a critico-theoretical investigation amounts in fact to a rigorous self-reflection. The question thus becomes: "When, and under what

---

25.   Ibid., 156–7.
26.   See Víctor Flores Olea, "Cultura y vida intelectual," in *La espiral sin fin: Ensayo político sobre México actual* (Mexico City: Joaquín Mortiz, 1994), 102–7.

conditions, can an event be said to be political? What is the 'what happens' insofar as it happens politically?"[27] This in turn implies a double task. The question is not only: What happened? but also: How can we understand what it means to ask what happened? "We have to force ourselves to grasp the meaning of what happened in the event itself," as Michel de Certeau writes in his analysis of May 1968 in *The Capture of Speech*, originally written just weeks after the events in France. But this also requires a thorough revision of the link between the event and thought itself, insofar as each interpretation of the events "offers a more or less developed solution to the problem put before everyone: with what kind of intellectual grid, through what perspective can be grasped (or, which finally amounts to the same thing, causes to be grasped) that which resists both a mental order and a social order, namely, 'the events'?"[28] In other words, the point is not just to pick a perspective of one's choosing and apply it to the events; the events in question actually may have caused the perspective, or the intellectual grid, from which alone they can be grasped. In de Certeau's own case, the solution to this problem involves a peculiar understanding of the speech act by which the students and workers momentarily succeeded in opening up a contestatory gap or fissure in the midst of the existing order of representation, in both the linguistic and the political senses of the term. The logic of change implied in the capture of speech thus depends on the capacity for a political subject first to reveal and then actively to put to work the fact that words and things, what is said and what is done, do not agree anymore than governors and governed, teachers and students. "Speech now turned into a 'symbolic place' designates the space created through the distance that separates the represented from their representations, the members of a society and the modalities of their association," de Certeau writes. He continues:

> It is at once everything and nothing because it announces an unhinging in the density of exchanges and a void, a disagreement, exactly where the mechanisms ought to be built upon what they claim to express. It escapes outside of structures, but in order to indicate what is lacking in them, namely, solidarity and the participation of those who are subjected to them.[29]

6.   In the project for an immanent self-reflection regarding both the events of 1968 and the nature of thinking of an event as such, the Marxist critique of political economy serves at best as a way to fix the

---

27.   Badiou, *Metapolitics*, 140.
28.   Michel de Certeau, *The Capture of Speech and Other Political Writings*, trans. Tom Conley (Minneapolis: University of Minnesota Press, 1997), 43–4. For a broader commentary on the logic of change based on such an unhinging of the place of representation in the name of a utopian or heterotopian nonplace, see my "Nonplaces: An Anecdoted Topography of Contemporary French Theory," *Diacritics: A Review of Contemporary Criticism* 33: 3–4 (2003): 117–39.
29.   De Certeau, *The Capture of Speech*, 9–10 (translation modified).

event's possible site. The economic instance, then, appears as a kind of vanishing term, or absent cause, within a structural logic for thinking the different instances of a given sociohistorical totality. The latter, evidently, is the visible project of all the published work of Althusser, whose most loyal disciple in Latin America, Marta Harnecker, can be said to have had an influence similar to that of Jameson in the United States. With the Freudian concept of overdetermination, for example, a structuralist account allows the theory of the weakest link to be stretched and extended in the direction of an active putting into crisis of the conceptual chain of Marxism itself. Arrived at the point of this objective impasse, however, even this immanent critique of Marxism is unable to capture the new subjective forces, such as the students, capable of forcing a passageway through the breach. In fact, the aleatory irruption of the event would seem by definition to escape the representations of the structure. Thus, generally speaking, events never cease to be in some way indiscernible—or, perhaps, discernible only through various limit-experiences with an abruptly twisted and distorted language, forced to say the unsayable and show the unshowable.

Unlike what happened in France, where May 1968 almost immediately received a now-canonical series of interpretations from academic disciplines both old and new, in Mexico it seems as if the experience of 1968 had, by force, to pass through more experimental forms, including dozens of poems, novels, testimonies, and memoirs. Only recently, with the release of new documents, have the facts at last begun to dissipate the rumors and uncertainties that for decades continued to surround this watershed year in the history of Mexico. We might even argue that, despite Nicolas Sarkozy's recent attacks against May 1968 in France, it is in Mexico that the legacy of 1968 is still open. Our question thus becomes the following: How—aside from the historical facts—are the events of that year lived at the subjective level? And to what extent is the current disarray of the Left in large parts of the world pre-inscribed in the way events such as October 2 were subjectivized forty years ago?

7.   To capture the events of 1968, we find a whole series of experiments on the outer edges of representation where language touches upon an impossibility as the void of a given situation. In Mexico, there thus emerge new generic forms of collective testimony, inaugurated by Elena Poniatowska, as well as displacements of the traditional forms of the novel and the chronicle, especially in the direction of popular culture, in the hands of Paco Ignacio Taibo II, José Agustín, Carlos Monsiváis or José Joaquín Blanco. Taibo himself opens his little book 68 with a first chapter titled "Se explica que con cosas como éstas nunca pude escribir una novela" ("Wherein It Is Explained that with Stuff Like This I Could Never Write a Novel"), in which he sketches out, after all, something of a working method. "After twenty years—and here you can bring in

Dumas and his three musketeers or Carlos Gardel and his 'twenty years is nothing'—after twenty years, the *only* thing that works is memory. Collective memory, but also even the tiniest, saddest memory of a personal kind," he writes in 1988. "I suspect, in fact, that the one can barely survive without the other, that legends cannot be fabricated without anecdotes. That there are no countries without fairy tales lurking in their shadow."[30] In this way, everything that previously would have been excluded from the domain of politics proper for being frivolous, adventurous, trivial, fictitious, or merely anecdotal, after the fact comes to play a role similar to that of the graffiti, the handouts, or the graphic art during the events of the student-popular movement. Finally, it is in this context that we can also read the poems about 1968 in Mexico and France written by Octavio Paz.

Revolutionary Shame

In the midst of so much cult of victory, these are stories of tremendous but for this reason no less heroic defeats. Histories that have to do with tenacity, the cult of principles, politics understood as tragic and terrible morality.
                                        Paco Ignacio Taibo II, Arcángeles

One day after the massacre of October 2 in Tlatelolco, Paz composed perhaps the most famous poem about 1968 in Mexico, titled "Intermitencias del Oeste (3)" ("Intermittencies of the West (3)"), included in the collection *Ladera este* (Eastern Slope). At the time, the poet was living in India as Mexico's ambassador. From this voluntary exile, he reflects upon the revolutionary myth in a series of four poems, as so many "intermittencies" of the West in the East: two are devoted to the revolutions in Russia and Mexico, respectively, and two more to the student-popular movements of 1968 in Mexico and France. The third poem is actually based on another letter Marx wrote to Ruge just prior to the uprisings that would hit Europe in 1848. In this period, the soon-to-be coauthor of *The Communist Manifesto* was likewise living in exile, but even from Holland he felt a certain national shame for the dismal state in which Germany found itself. "The mantle of liberalism has been discarded and the most disgusting despotism in all its nakedness is disclosed to the eyes of the whole world," wrote Marx, before anticipating the skepticism of his correspondent:

> You look at me with a smile and ask: What is gained by that? No revolution is made out of shame. I reply: Shame is already revolution of a kind . . . Shame is a kind of anger which is turned inward. And if a whole nation really experienced a sense of shame, it would be like a lion, crouching ready to spring.[31]

---

30. Taibo, '68, 9.
31. Marx, *Escritos de juventud*, 441; in English, Karl Marx, "Letters from the *Deutsch-Französische Jahrbücher*," in Marx and Engels, *Collected Works*, vol. 3, 133.

History repeats itself, no doubt; but after tragedy this time it is not the turn of farce, but rather of a process of melancholy. What in the letters of Marx is still a subjective wager to revolutionize shame against the brooding skepticism of philosophers such as Ruge, in the hands of Octavio Paz becomes an ambiguous act of introspection made public to denounce the oppression suffered by the student rebellion.

"Intermittencies of the West (3)" is in fact an excruciatingly equivocal poem, in which various tendencies or trajectories are present at once. Paz sent the poem to *La Cultura en México*, the cultural supplement of the magazine *Siempre!*, where it was published after the closing ceremony of the Olympic Games in Mexico; at the same time, he submitted his letter of resignation as ambassador in India to president Gustavo Díaz Ordaz:

> INTERMITENCIAS DEL OESTE (3)
> (México: Olimpiada de 1968)
>   A Dore y Adja Yunkers
>
> La limpidez
>   (Quizá valga la pena
> Escribirlo sobre la limpieza
> De esta hoja)
>   No es límpida:
> Es una rabia
>   (Amarilla y negra
> Acumulación de bilis en español)
> Extendida sobra la página.
> ¿Por qué?
>   *La vergüenza es ira*
> *Vuelta contra uno mismo:*
>   *Si*
> *Una nación entera se avergüenza*
> *Es león que se agazapa*
> *Para saltar.*
>   (Los empleados
> Municipales lavan la sangre
> En la Plaza de los Sacrificios.)
> Mira ahora,
>   Manchada
> Antes de haber dicho algo
> Que valga la pena,
>   La limpidez.
>
> [INTERMITTENCIES OF THE WEST (3)
> (Mexico City: The 1968 Olympiad)
>   for Dore and Adja Yunkers
>
> Limpidity
> (perhaps it's worth
> writing on the cleanness
> of this page)
>   is not limpid:
> it is rage

(yellow and black
accumulation of bile in Spanish)
extended over the page.
Why?
Shame is rage
Turned against itself:
If
an entire nation is ashamed
it is like a lion crouching
ready to jump.
(The municipal
employees wash the blood
from the Plaza of the Sacrificed.)
Look now,
Stained
Before having said anything
Worth the effort,
Limpidity.][32]

Based on this poem, we can recapitulate some of the better-known protocols of subjectivization that we can find in of all of Paz's political and poetic work. The poem, obviously, is structured around a parallelism in which the image of the blood on the public square corresponds to the ink thrown onto the white page. In between these two substances, as if to mediate, there appears the bile, at once yellow and black. Together with rage or ire (*la rabia*), shame (*la vergüenza* but also *pena*) is the text's circulating term, the one that subjectively articulates politics and art. As opposed to the blood and the ink,

---

32. Octavio Paz, *Obra poética (1935–1988)* (Barcelona: Seix Barral, 1990), 429; in English, *The Collected Poems of Octavio Paz (1957–1987)*, ed. and trans. Eliot Weinberger (New York: New Directions, 1987), 225–7 (translation modified). For a commentary, see Guillermo Sheridan, "La renuncia de Octavio Paz a la embajada de la India," *Proceso* 1144 (1998): 68–70; and Jorge Volpi, *El poder y la imaginación: Una historia intelectual de 1968* (Mexico City: Era, 1998), 369–80. Paz's relation to Marx is analyzed in Xavier Rodríguez Ledesma, "La reflexión crítica de Octavio Paz sobre el marxismo y el socialismo," *El pensamiento político de Octavio Paz: Las trampas de la ideología* (Mexico City: Plaza y Valdés/UNAM, 1996), 115–272; and, more recently, in Yvon Grenier, "El socialismo en una sola persona: El espectro de Marx en la obra de Octavio Paz," in the useful collection, Anthony Stanton, ed., *Octavio Paz: Entre poética y política* (Mexico City: El Colegio de México, 2009), 211–33. Grenier writes (221–2):

> A *fundamental* contrast for Paz is the fact that Marx (and rarely the Marxists) embodies a rare combination of cardinal virtues: he was at once a rebel and (more importantly) a *writer*—avid reader of Greek tragedies, of Cervantes (see *The German Ideology*) and of Shakespeare—whose ideas (syncretically put: he was a rationalist and a romantic at the same time) transfigured the world. This singular combination of attributes deserves respect and even admiration from a man who, presumably, had the same ambitions.

Carlos Monsiváis, in a special section of *Letras Libres* 6 (April 1999) on Octavio Paz's links to the Mexican Left, praises and quotes—without respecting the italics—only those six verses from "Intermitencias del Oeste (3)" that are drawn from Marx's 1843 letter to Ruge. Paz's most praiseworthy gift to the Mexican Left thus would be an unacknowledged poem from Marx!

however, the bile apparently has nowhere to go, except inwards. This marks the moment of crouching down, or lying down in wait. It is the moment when shame becomes rage, or when rage turns inward and doubles back upon itself so as to become shame. The whole question will then be whether this turning-inward of enraged subjectivity produces an inner recoil sufficiently powerful to give way, after all, to a leap—a leap of faith or of fidelity to the event that will have been, precisely, a leap into the void, since it has no ostensible place at its disposal, no foothold either on the public square or on the poet's white page.

At this point, one of the more disconcerting analogies in Paz's work becomes apparent. The poem indeed establishes an involuntary parallelism between the official policy of erasing the traces of the violence and the poetic procedure of what Paz, in a poem from the year before ("Carta a León Felipe"), about the death of Ernesto "Che" Guevara, calls "unwriting the written," *inescribir lo escrito*:

> La escritura poética
> Es borrar lo escrito
> > Escribir
> Sobre lo escrito
> Lo no escrito
> . . .
> La escritura poética es
> > Aprender a leer
> El hueco de la escritura
> > En la escritura
> No huellas de lo que fuimos
> > Caminos
> Hacia lo que somos
> . . .
> La poesía
> > Es la ruptura instantánea
> Instantáneamente cicatrizada
> > > Abierta de nuevo
> Por la mirada de los otros
> > La ruptura
> Es la continuidad
> La muerte del Comandante Guevara
> También es ruptura
> > No un fin
> Su memoria
> > No es una cicatriz
> Es una continuidad que se desgarra
> Para continuarse
> > La poesía
> Es la hendidura
> > El espacio
> Entre una palabra y otra
> Configuración del inacabamiento.

[Poetic writing
is erasing the written
          Writing
on the written
          the nonwritten
. . .
Poetic writing is
          learning to read
the hole of writing
          in writing
Not traces of what we were
          Paths
Toward what we are
. . .
Poetry
          Is the instantaneous rupture
Instantly scarred
                    Opened anew
By the gaze of the others
                    The rupture
Is the continuity
The death of Comandante Guevara
Also means rupture
          Not an end
His memory
          Is not a scar
It is a continuity that tears apart
So as to continue itself
                    Poetry
Is the fissure
          The space
Between one word and another
Configuration of incompleteness.][33]

Paz, in this poem as in so many others, follows what is a quintessen-
tially Mallarméan procedure, based on a principle of erasure or
subtraction.[34] Words emerge only to withdraw themselves at once in
the intervals of an originary gap or void. To write means to subtract

33.   Paz, *Obra poética*, 443–4. In yet another interesting anecdotal coincidence, the personal
anthology of poetry that Che Guevara was carrying in his backpack in Bolivia at the time of
his death, a handwritten anthology in which León Felipe's poetry figures prominently
alongside that of Pablo Neruda, Nicolás Guillén, and César Vallejo, has recently been edited
by Paco Ignacio Taibo II as *El cuaderno verde del Che* (Barcelona: Seix Barral, 2007). "La
canción desesperada" ("The Song of Despair"), from Neruda's *Veinte poemas de amor y una
canción desesperada* (*Twenty Love Poems and A Song of Despair*) transcribed by Che
Guevara in his notebook, also includes the lines quoted (out of order) by Sergio in the
opening scene of *Memories of Underdevelopment*: "Es la hora de partir. Oh abandonado
como los muelles en el alba. Todo en ti fue naufragio" ("It's the time of departure. Oh!
Abandoned like the wharves at dawn. Everything in you was shipwrecked"). See Taibo, ed.,
El cuaderno verde del Che, 51.
34.   See also Alain Badiou's reading of Mallarmé with Lacan, in "The Subject under the
Signifiers of Exception," Part II of his *Theory of the Subject*, trans. Bruno Bosteels (London
and New York: Continuum, 2009), 51–110.

one word from another word. It means forever to precipitate oneself toward the fugitive moment when the already written vanishes, when presence becomes absence or lack. As a result of such abolition, the real never fully manages to represent itself; on the contrary, it is precisely that which erupts in the interstices of the representable. This is where the poetic operation appears to be analogous to a political process. The disappearance of the revolutionary figure, for instance, surely marks the site of a possible political event. If this possibility appears in a poem, it is because the process likewise gives rise to a vanishing term, similar to the incompletion or unachievement, *el inacabamiento*, that is proper to poetry according to Paz. Politics, too, would intervene in society according to a principle of delinking comparable to the writing of poetry when the latter undoes the links between words so as to establish itself in the very space of the tearing apart.

However, this is not what the poem actually does but rather what it says it does. The ease with which these texts affirm their own metapoetical principles should alert us to the fact that we are faced with a purely structural approach to the specter or phantasm. Such a perspective, whether in art or in politics, may very well expose the lack intrinsic to any given system of representation, but without exceeding the limits of a mere recognition of this lack. The spectral or phantasmatic element, then, remains as such, indefinitely suspending the protocols of delinking, instead of marking the onset of a subjective intervention. The process, in other words, may well lay bare the site of a possible event, but the latter is nowhere sustained by any subsequent fidelity. The void acts as a pathway to what we unconsciously already are, by indicating that which we lack from the start—but nobody dares to take a leap so as to affirm what we will have become.

Similarly, in the poem written after Tlatelolco, there appears a formal complicity, if nothing more, between clarity and cleanliness. In this sense, the shame that is conjured up can be read in a variety of ways. The most obvious reading attributes shame to the ambassador, if not to the Mexican people as a whole, over the government's despotic intervention against its own population. Another reading, however, would link shame to the very task of the poet who has been unable to say anything that was worth the effort—*la pena*, which can also be understood as shame in Mexican Spanish. Words themselves would provoke in the poet a sensation of being superfluous, as if all of a sudden he felt ineptitude when faced with the brutality of his government. Finally, even this poem, which is so often quoted as a preeminent example of anti-authoritarian protest in favor of the students, could also be read as saying that it was the student movement itself that did not have a chance to say anything worthwhile. The same ambiguity, in fact, reappears in the short poem in the same series from *Ladera este*, dedicated to May 1968 in France:

INTERMITENCIAS DEL OESTE (4)
(París: Les aveugles lucides)

Dans l'une des banlieues de l'absolu,
Les mots ayant perdu leur ombre
Ils faisaient commerce de reflets
Jusqu'à perte de vue.
                    Ils se sont noyés
Dans une interjection.

[INTERMITTENCIES FROM THE WEST (4)
(Paris: The Lucid Blind)

In one of the suburbs of the absolute,
Words having lost their shadow
They traded in reflections
Until the end of sight.
                    They drowned themselves
In an interjection.][35]

Paz's poems about 1968 also allude, in some way, to the limits of student activism. Perhaps the youths said nothing that was worth the effort; perhaps they drowned in a mere interjection, in anarchic outbursts and ungrammatical graffiti. To an extent, we are already in the middle of the critique of the revolutionary myth—or of the myth of the absolute—that we find in so many later essays by Paz.

Indeed, if we confront these poems from *Ladera este* with the analysis of *Posdata* ("The Other Mexico"), which Paz first presented as a series of talks in the wake of 1968 and then published as a postscript to *El laberinto de la soledad* (*The Labyrinth of Solitude*), it becomes increasingly difficult to grasp the exact sense of his outlook. On the one hand, the student movement seeks to incarnate the idea of justice in the here and now, and thus undoes the mirage of a better future promised by the different governments in Mexico: "The deeper meaning of the protest movement—not overlooking its reasons and its immediate, circumstantial aims—consists in having opposed the implacable phantasm of the future with the spontaneous reality of the now."[36] Even so, unlike Taibo or Revueltas, Paz centers most of his analysis not so much on the student activism that unfolded in the nation's capital over the course of three months, from the Colegio de San Ildefonso all the way to the Zócalo, so much as on the violent repression and massacre in Tlatelolco. In order to understand the secret reason behind this violence, he thus proposes a kind of collective psychoanalysis of the history of modern Mexico. In the course of this analysis the ghost or phantasm acquires a radically new significance. Instead of opening the search for

35. Paz, *Obra poética*, 431.
36. Paz, *Posdata*, 27; in English, "The Other Mexico," in *The Labyrinth of Solitude and Other Writings*, trans. Lysander Kemp (New York: Grove Press, 1985), 225.

effective justice, the *fantasma* now alludes to the survival of vertical hierarchies inherited from the Aztec world. Paz's analysis of repression revolves entirely around the way in which the politico-theological archetype of pre-Hispanic authoritarianism, petrified in the structure of the pyramid, returns in the present with the force of the uncanny. "The massacre at Tlatelolco shows us that the past which we thought was buried is still alive and has burst out among us. Each time it appears in public it is both masked and armed, and we cannot tell what it is, except that it is vengeance and destruction," warns Paz. "It is a past that we have not been able to recognize, to name, to unmask."[37] Such, ultimately, is the true specter that fascinates Paz. It is a complex of attitudes, beliefs, and suppositions the persistence of which constitutes the hidden face of Mexico—the "other" Mexico: the constitutive outside without which there can be no identity. Mexico is never fully self-present in the plenitude of an interior monologue, but it is always haunted by its other: "The other Mexico, the submerged and repressed, reappears in the modern Mexico: when we talk with ourselves, we talk with it; when we talk with it, we talk with ourselves."[38] We cannot even speak of a "double" of Mexico. "Its double? Which is the original and which the phantasm? As with the Möbius strip, there is neither inside nor outside, and otherness is not there, beyond, but here, within: otherness is ourselves," insists Paz, after flirting briefly with the definition of the other Mexico as a combination of both Freud's concept of the (individual) unconscious and Marx's (social) ideology: "Neither within nor without, neither before nor after: the past reappears because it is a hidden present."[39] The analysis thus unravels the antinomy of the other within the same according to a strange kind of negative dialectic, only to insist in the end on the need to recognize the principle according to which identity is never one and undivided but rather split from within by a constitutive exteriority.

According to Paz, the task to be accomplished, far from "incarnating" the "friendly ghosts" of justice to come, would consist in developing a rational "critique" of the "other" Mexico. True democracy, for example, will not come unless we pass through the analysis of the authoritarian nucleus that is immanent within it. This nucleus is the phantasm or ghost from time immemorial that we must learn how to look into the eye. "It is a Mexico which, if we learn to name and recognize it, we can someday bring to an end by transfiguring it. Then it will cease to be that phantasm that glides into reality and turns it into a blood-drenched nightmare," writes Paz, as if to recall certain phrases from Marx. "México-Tenochtitlán has disappeared, and what concerns me, as I gaze upon its fallen body, is not the problem of historical

---

37. Ibid., 40; 236.
38. Ibid., 109; 287.
39. Ibid., 111; 289.

interpretation but the fact that we cannot contemplate the cadaver face to face: its phantasm inhabits us."[40] Instead of unfolding the new world already present within the old one, analysis must first bring to light the latent past in its aspect as eternal present.

Paz never stops pointing out the impudence typical of any desire for justice to right the wrongs in this world. For him, the lucidity of the youth is inseparable from their blindness. Innocent, ambitious, even audacious, the integrity of the students should also show a little more modesty and shame. Here is how Paz puts it in the thinly disguised autobiographical poem "Nocturno de San Ildefonso" ("San Ildefonso Nocturne"), in *Vuelta (1969–1975)*:

> El muchacho que camina por este poema,
> entre San Ildefonso y el Zócalo,
> es el hombre que lo escribe:
> > esta página
> también es una caminata oscura.
> > Aquí encarnan
> los espectros amigos,
> > las ideas se disipan.
> El bien, quisimos el bien:
> > enderezar el mundo
> No nos faltó entereza:
> > nos faltó humildad.

> [The boy who walks through this poem,
> Between San Ildefonso and the Zócalo,
> Is the man who writes it:
> > This page
> Also is a dark walk.
> > Here incarnate
> The friendly specters,
> > Ideas are dissipated.
> The good, we wanted the good:
> > To right the wrong
> We didn't lack integrity:
> > We lacked modesty.][41]

The central idea in these lines inevitably recalls Hamlet's cursed cause: "The time is out of joint. O cursed spite, / That ever I was born to set it right!"[42] To right the wrong would also have been the ideal of the student movement: to maintain their integrity, without ever giving in;

40. Ibid., 113–14, 134; 291, 308.
41. Paz, *Obra poética*, 634. Regarding shamelessness or lack of modesty, compare also the statement about the theft of pears, in Saint Augustine's *Confessions*: "As soon as the words are spoken 'Let us go and do it,' one is ashamed not to be shameless" (34); and the commentary in Rozitchner, *La Cosa y la Cruz*, 98.
42. Hamlet as quoted and interpreted at length by Jacques Derrida, *Specters of Marx: The State of the Debt, the Work of Mourning, and the New International*, trans. Peggy Kamuf (New York: Routledge, 1994), 3.

not to let justice roam the country as an intangible ghost but, on the contrary, to animate its specter so as to break the wrongs of a truncated modernity. Otherwise, the idea would once again leave its soul at the level of pure promises—an anticipation of what Mexico could have been but is not yet.

For Paz, however, it increasingly appears as though searching to incarnate justice in action—his concept of revolution is no different—carries with it the seeds of its own authoritarian or bureaucratic deformation. For this reason, the poet would ever more openly support the cause of political liberalism—for instance, in *Poesía, mito, revolución* (*Poetry, Myth, Revolution*), his acceptance speech upon receiving the Alexis de Tocqueville Prize a few months after the fall of the Berlin Wall. It is the rejection of this fatal temptation within the revolutionary myth that explains Paz's barely veiled critique of 1968 in his poems and essay. The students and young militants would have lacked modesty, shame, or prudence. They would have been sinfully disingenuous, as though the excess of innocence, paradoxically, constituted proof of heightened guilt. Thus, in "Nocturno de San Ildefonso," Paz adds:

> La culpa que no se sabe culpa,
> la inocencia,
> fue la culpa mayor.

> [The guilt that does not know itself to be guilt,
> innocence,
> was their biggest guilt.][43]

Only one option remains open: to combine critical thinking in the liberal-democratic tradition with a vision of modern art. "True, criticism is not the dream, but it teaches us to dream and to distinguish between the specters and the true visions," Paz concludes. "Criticism is the apprenticeship of the imagination in its second stage: imagination cured of fantasy and resolved to confront the reality of the world."[44] By comparison, we can only infer that the student movement, or 1960s leftism in general, is the apprenticeship of the imagination in its first stage: innocent, fantasizing, sickly. Stubbornly unable to accept the frontiers of the real, but resolved to confront them with the power of the imagination. It is the desire to traverse the very specter or phantasm of a truly just society.

In the reflections from *Posdata*, too, both the student revolt and its

---

43. Paz, *Obra poética*, 635. Compare also the statement from Saint Augustine's *Confessions*: "That was a sin the more incurable for the fact that I did not think myself a sinner" (84). In the Spanish translation used by Rozitchner this line reads even more concisely: "Mi pecado realmente incurable era *no creerme pecador*" (quoted in Rozitchner, *La Cosa y la Cruz*, 228).

44. Paz, *Posdata*, 155; and "The Other Mexico," 325. See also Paz, *Poesía, mito, revolución: Premio Alexis de Tocqueville*, preceded by the speeches of François Mitterrand, Alain Peyrefitte and Pierre Godefroy (Mexico City: Vuelta, 1989).

violent repression in the end confirm the unconscious structure of Mexican history. The people capable of understanding the truth of this
recurrent structure through a collective act of analysis might even be
able to transcend the level of mere history so as to live, beyond the here
and now, in the plenitude of a time without time, in which each day is
equal to all others. While he awaits this grand day, the poet continues
to unwrite the written and the specter remains, without a genuine event,
as a reminder of that which has already occurred or has yet to occur.
The ghost or phantasm is not the point of departure for a process of
subjective intervention, but only the unconscious kernel of the whole
politico-juridical structure of the Mexican nation-state. Its apparition
uncovers the trauma of a constitutive otherness that we must recognize,
without exceeding the frame of this structure or the logic of recognition
itself. What is more, it does not remit us to the here and now of actual
circumstances but to an eternal present, latent in all of Mexican history.
The analysis is ultimately geared toward the hidden fixity of a mythical-
archetypal recurrence. Thus, with reference to the "other" Mexico, Paz
explains: "I am speaking of the real past, which is not the same as 'what
took place': dates, persons, everything we refer to as history. What took
place is indeed the past, yet there is something that does not pass away,
something that takes place but does not wholly recede into the past, a
constantly returning present."[45] The result is a structural or quasi-ontological schema: each structure, each assemblage, each complex of
presuppositions contains a blind spot—that is, a constitutive otherness
that is also its Achilles' heel: an inconsistency that is not accidental and
derivative but necessary and inherent.

Perhaps the most important aspect of 1968 in Mexico, however, is
not the fact that the repression unmasked this blind spot in the seemingly democratic appearance (though it certainly did that), but rather
the fact that students and workers tried to force the situation so as to
found a new structure, another frame of reference, or another society
(and their failure to do so does not cancel out the attempt). What seems
to be at stake for them is not just to occupy the unoccupyable empty
place, but to exceed it. Instead of merely recognizing the specter, or
even standing in awe of the ghost with a properly messianic or vision-
ary outlook, the task would be to traverse the fantasy. Such would be
the utopia of a radical emancipatory politics, as opposed to the essentially liberal-democratic critique of the political: not only to exhibit, as
a condition of possibility that is simultaneously a condition of impossibility, the maladjustment inherent in all attempts to adjust the times
that are changing, but to prescribe a sequence to found a new justice.

In Paz's work, a rupture such as that of the student movement or the
death of a revolutionary martyr seems to be radically foreign to the
banality of our everydayness. Insofar as it is not inscribed in the order of

---

45. Paz, *Posdata*, 111; and "The Other Mexico," 289.

existence except as a gap that is indicative of what we always already are in essence, the site of such breaches also does not demand to be taken over in a subjective intervention or wager. Rather, the tearing asunder of history opens up a breach in which an absolute present can take place—that is, the timeless time of an eternal recurrence, following the cyclical rhythm of a mythico-political unconscious that is perhaps more Jungian than Freudian. In "Nocturno de San Ildefonso," Paz writes:

> La historia es el error.
>   La verdad es aquello,
> más allá de las fechas,
>   más acá de los nombres,
> que la historia desdeña:
>   el cada día
> —latido anónimo de todos,
>   latido
> único de cada uno—,
>   el irrepetible
> cada día idéntico a todos los días.
> . . .
>   La verdad:
> sabernos,
>   desde el origen,
>   suspendidos.
> Fraternidad sobre el vacío.
> . . .
> Las ideas se disipan,
>   quedan los espectros:
> verdad de lo vivido y padecido.[46]
>
> [History is the mistake.
>   The truth is that which,
> beyond all dates,
>   beneath all names,
> history disdains:
>   the everyday
> —anonymous heartbeat of everyone,
>   the beat
> unique to each one—
>   the unrepeatable
> every day identical to all days.
> . . .
>   The truth:
> To know ourselves,
>   from the origin,
>   suspended.
> Fraternity over the void.
> . . .
> Ideas are dissipated,
>   only the specters remain:
> truth of the lived and the suffered.]

---

46. Paz, *Obra poética*, 635–7.

Suspended above the void, the subject of truth remains eternally out of joint. If what remains are only the specters, though, perhaps it is not because history disdains the truth of everyday life so much as because the truth of metapoetry, in the process of unwriting the written, ends up showing its disdain for the history of everydayness.

In the same year in which Paz's lectures for *Posdata* were published in Mexico City, Jacques Lacan taught a very similar lesson to his students in *L'envers de la psychanalyse* (*The Other Side of Psychoanalysis*), part of his regular seminar in Paris. Seemingly familiar with Marx's correspondence with Ruge as well, Lacan addressed the students and activists of May '68 with a typical provocation:

> You will say to me, "What's the use of shame? If that is what the other side of psychoanalysis is, we don't want any." My reply to you is, "You've got enough to open a shop." If you are not yet aware of this, then do a bit of analysis, as they say. You will see this vapid air of yours run up against an outlandish shame of living . . .

Lacan finally adds a brief explanation: "The point is to know why the students feel, like the others, superfluous [*de trop*]. It does not at all seem as though they see clearly how to get out of all this. I would like to point out to them that one essential aspect of the system is the production—the production of shame. This translates itself—into impudence."[47] Both Paz and Lacan, in a sense, suggest that the reverse side of the subversive project is the desire for a new absolute value. This desire inevitably leads to dogma or to the cult of personality. A truly lucid analysis or critique, by contrast, would broach the topic of shame without fear of touching upon a point of the impossible—that is, without fear of discovering in shame a welcome hideout (perhaps the only one after anxiety and fear itself) for the truth. The reverse side of psychoanalysis, in other words, must be the sentiment of an inescapable shame.

Based on these principles, we can now return to the melancholy itinerary of so much radical political thinking. The ghost functions

47. Jacques Lacan, *Le Séminaire, XVII: L'Envers de la psychanalyse*, ed. Jacques-Alain Miller (Paris: Seuil, 1991), 211, 220; in English, *The Other Side of Psychoanalysis*, trans. Russell Grigg (New York: W. W. Norton, 2007), 212, 190 (I have corrected the English translation, which misses out completely on the sense of superfluousness alluded to in the students' being *de trop*, "too much" or "in excess" of what is needed). See also Jacques-Alain Miller, "On Shame," in Justin Clemens and Russell Grigg, eds, *Jacques Lacan and the Other Side of Psychoanalysis* (Durham: Duke University Press, 2006), 11–28; and Joan Copjec, "May '68, the Emotional Month," in Slavoj Žižek, ed., *Lacan: His Silent Partners* (London and New York, Verso: 2006), 90–114. Here, in addition to debates within Lacanian psychoanalysis, I would refer the reader to León Rozitchner's discussion of *pudor* or "shame" (*pudeur* in French), in the chapter "Desde la perspectiva de la intimidad: el pudor," in his book on Max Scheler, *Persona y comunidad*, 247–94. On the link between shame and rage in revolutionary politics, see the recent intervention by Peter Sloterdijk, *Rage and Time: A Psychopolitical Investigation*, trans. Mario Wenning (New York: Columbia University Press, 2010).

as the analyst along this itinerary. And what it reveals is the sinister presence of a void in the very midst of the social order. It is worth quoting Marx's letters one more time. On the appearance of despotism in supposedly liberal German society, he writes to Ruge: "That, too, is a revelation, although one of the opposite kind. It is a truth which, at least, teaches us to recognize the emptiness of our patriotism and the abnormity of our state system, and makes us hide our faces in shame."[48] For the author of this letter, of course, the analysis cannot be limited to a recognition of the emptiness of despotic power; nor is it enough merely to blush or cover our faces in shame: it is also necessary to revolutionize shame itself, to exceed the empty place of power through a radical transformation of the structure as such—to take the lion's leap. However, if the emphasis falls on the lack as the essential point of the entire system; or, according to a similar logic, if authoritarianism always lies in wait as a sinister constitutive outside of all democracy precisely due to the totalitarian desire to incarnate it, then the new radical politics to come will consist in keeping firm in the shame, in the anxiety, and in the uncertainty, without giving in to the impudence of wanting to fill the empty place of power—that is, without giving in to the metaphysical temptation to give body to the ghost of effective justice. We have to be realistic, without demanding the impossible. Such is the answer with which Ruge actually anticipates today's critics of Marx, no matter whether they are followers of Lacan or of Derrida: "It is sweet to hope and bitter to give up on all chimeras. Despair demands more courage than hope. But it is the courage of reason, and we have come to the point where we no longer have the right to keep fooling ourselves."[49]

Today, the only courage of the Left, for large parts of political philosophy, consists in persevering heroically in despair—or in euphoria, which is but the other side of the same melancholy process. As Slavoj Žižek writes, "Enthusiasm and resignation, then, are not two opposite moments: it is the 'resignation' itself, that is to say, the experience of a certain impossibility, that incites enthusiasm."[50] The lion should never take the leap, but this does not keep him from roaring. With the aim of keeping the place of power necessarily inoperative or empty, it calls radical what is only the crouching, the withdrawal, or the insuperable end of politics. Turned back upon itself, shame hides many corners where it can accumulate the reserve of an inexhaustible radicalism. This is not rage accumulated before the counterattack: it is shame as the rage of defeat put at the service of a new philosophical

---

48. Marx, *Escritos de juventud*, 441; Marx and Engels, *Collected Works*, vol. 3, 133.
49. Ruge, in Marx, *Escritos de juventud*, 442.
50. Slavoj Žižek, "Beyond Discourse-Analysis," in Ernesto Laclau, *New Reflections on the Revolution of Our Time* (London: Verso, 1990), 259–60.

lucidity, foreign to all subjective wagers except the interminable critique of its own specters. To quote once more from "Nocturno de San Ilde-fonso":

> La rabia
> se volvió filósofa
> su baba ha cubierto el planeta.
>
> [Rage
> has become a philosopher
> its spit has covered the whole planet.][51]

Once yellow, then, the bile turns black. According to the theory of four humors, it does not produce rage but melancholy—that is, in strictly etymological terms, black bile.

In fact, did Freud not highlight this tendency in the melancholic subject to become philosophical, by splitting its consciousness into a critical instance capable of representing as object that other part of itself that suffers the loss—whether real or imaginary? This process rather accurately describes the philosophical trajectory of so many ex-enthusiasts of 1968. From observing defeat after the fact, it seems to be only a small step to proclaim the original nonexistence of the lost cause—or to assert that only lost causes are ever worthy of our defense.

Agamben, also writing from exile about the scandals of corruption and repentance in Italy in the 1990s, already felt the need to revise Marx's optimism. "Marx still used to put some trust in shame," he recalls. "But what he was referring to was the 'national shame' that concerns specific peoples each with respect to other peoples, the Germans with respect to the French. Primo Levi has shown, however, that there is today a 'shame of being human,' a shame that in some way or other has tainted every human being."[52] If, after Auschwitz, shame points to an insuperable human condition, and if, furthermore, those who in the past might have turned shame into a stepping stone—nations or peoples—are absent today, then it appears that the only conclusion to be drawn for any politics-to-come is a retreat, or exodus, from the very idea of revolutionizing shame. Philippe Lacoue-Labarthe and Jean-Luc Nancy, for example, invite us to rephrase political philosophy under the deliberately ambiguous programmatic title of *Le retrait du politique* (*Retreating the Political*). Summing up the various categories of the political in the concept of sovereignty, the authors launch the hypothesis according to which the "withdrawal" of the political would at the same time be a "retreatment" of politics, "above all in light of

---

51. Paz, *Obra poética*, 634.
52. Giorgio Agamben, "In This Exile (Italian Diary, 1992–94)," in *Means Without End: Notes on Politics*, trans. Vincenzo Binetti and Cesare Casarino (Minneapolis: University of Minnesota Press, 2000), 132.

the fact that what withdrew never really took place to begin with."[53] To such trends in current political philosophy, a symptomatic reading of melancholy could oppose the project for a metapolitics that could be summed up in the title of another collection of articles, this time published in Mexico: *La tenacidad de la política.* The editors explain: "Calling upon the tenacity of politics refers to resistance both in theory and in political practice in the face of the various attempts to declare its dilution, if not its end . . . Because despite the diagnosis or the desire of its extinction, politics remains, tenaciously."[54] The question, from this point of view, is not whether 1968 counts as a revolutionary "failure" or as an indirect "success," but whether its capacities for subjectivization remain active or have been exhausted in the process of becoming melancholic.

Paz's poem after Tlatelolco not only traces the path followed by many *sesentayocheros* now retired; it also announces between the lines the possible answer of a politics of tenacity. In order to avoid the complicity of the empty page with the false cleanness of the official story, this would involve not so much a figure of subtraction but one of forcing. Instead of unwriting the written, the injunction would be to write the unwritten. This is how we might read the poem about May 1968 in France. Does the diabolical force of an interjection not consist in throwing itself into the void, twisting the grammar so as to inscribe itself in the disorderly interstices of unreason within the existing order? This would have been the courage of the lion's leap: to find a foothold in the emptiness of the system so as to anticipate the new order already present in the bosom or entrails of the old one. This is also, incidentally, how the students understood one of the culminating moments of their movement when, on September 13, they marched through the streets of Mexico City during the so-called *manifestación del silencio* or "silent march"—students walking side by side with workers, peasants, unionists, office workers, and housewives, their mouths taped shut so as to prove a degree of contained rage before the jump. "This march of silence is the answer to the injustice," one of the speakers finally says. "We have begun the task of making a just Mexico, because liberty is what we are gaining every day. This page is clean and clear [Esta página es limpia y clara]."[55]

---

53. Philippe Lacoue-Labarthe and Jean-Luc Nancy, eds, *Le retrait du politique* (Paris: Galilée, 1983), 194.

54. Nora Rabotnikov, Ambrosio Velasco, and Corina Yturbe, eds, *La tenacidad de la política* (Mexico City: UNAM, 1995), 8–9.

55. Quoted in Ramón Ramírez, *El movimiento estudiantil de México* (Mexico City: Era, 1969), vol. 1, 314. In a letter to his daughter Andrea, incidentally, José Revueltas uses the same adjective, *limpio*, in its moral sense to refer to the upright, proper and respectable attitude of Octavio Paz, who went to visit him in the prison of Lecumberri. "As always magnificent, proper, honest—the great Octavio whom I hadn't seen for more or less eight years" (*Las evocaciones requeridas*, vol. 2, 217).

Even the utopia of the student movement cannot avoid the truth glimpsed with special lucidity by the melancholy trend of later political philosophies—namely, the notion that the leap takes place in the void. A political subject has no ground to stand on, no stable identity or social link; instead, the lion's leap starts precisely from anxiety, even shame, provoked by the coming apart of the social link. However, the subject exceeds melancholy by twisting shame into rage, so that something else may take place. Disorder, or the absence exposed in the previous order, *le da coraje*, in the double sense of the expression in Spanish: it produces rage or anger, but also courage, audacity, tenacity. "Anxiety means deficiency of the place, while courage is the assumption of the real by which the place is split," Badiou writes in his *Theory of the Subject*: "Courage positively carries out the disorder of the symbolic, the breakdown of communication, whereas anxiety calls for its death."[56] By uncovering the emptiness of the symbolic order, moreover, shame always runs the risk of falling into the opposite extreme, which consolidates the unchanging necessity of the structure of this lack itself. Anxiety before the specter can all too easily slip into conformism due to a secret fascination with order. Tenacity, by contrast, consists in the wager for a different order. This means writing history not from the point of view of the state, but from the subjective principle of equality that universally resists the power of the state. This makes all the difference between those who fatally privilege the massacre of Tlatelolco, now more than forty years ago, and those for whom the vitality of the movement consisted in traversing the rest of Mexico City. Paz, for instance, starts out from the order of things only to pinpoint its inherent void, the abyss in which we are left hanging in suspense; Revueltas or Taibo, by contrast, start out from the precariousness of the given order so as to track down the rare sequences of an emancipatory politics at a distance from the state.

The figure of Che Guevara turns out once more to be exemplary here. More so than the man himself, however, what a metapolitical reading enquires about is the process of subjectivization to which his figure gives birth—even, or especially, after his death. Taibo, for instance, wrote in 68:

> Che was a man who had spoken the first and last words. He had led us, from "Episodes of the Revolutionary War" to "Socialism and Man in Cuba," taking us by the hand toward a clearly understood ethical debate. His death in '67 left us with an enormous vacuum that not even the "Bolivian Diary" was able to fill. He was our number one ghost who was there and wasn't there, haunting our lives: the voice, the character, the central imperative to put everything aside and get going, the mocking dialogue, the project, the photograph that looks at you from every corner, the ever-growing and seemingly endless stream of fact and anecdote, the only way that lines

---

56. Badiou, *Theory of the Subject*, 160.

worthy of a bolero such as "total commitment" [*entrega total*] did not seem laughable. But above all, Che was a guy who was everywhere even after his death. Our dead.[57]

Here, the ghostly or spectral element marks a nonplace in the midst of the existing state of affairs. Without giving in to the fugitive gaze, the tenacious phantasm proffers a "yes" and a "no" at the same time. Insistently, it withdraws from the order that is given, whereas that which is not there, or that which is not yet there, is boldly affirmed. The ghost is everywhere, without ever being where it appears. It exists, or rather insists, for what it is not. And yet, it therefore also demands the wager of a commitment. It is the imperative of a subjective answer that would not get going [*echar a andar*] from any established identity, given the command to put everything to the side [*ponerlo todo al lado*], but that rather supports the void as the starting point for a possible universalist project. Here, in the passage in which a subject emerges from the void in the order of things toward the declaration of a new universal truth, we find summarized a brief grammar of utopian thought regarding the events of 1968. Finally, in the name of total commitment, the entire process of militancy proceeds not against the registers of popular culture, or over the heads of the people, but in an intimate dialogue with them, to the point where rumors, anecdotes, and the lyrics of a bolero can have a contagious force equal to the ubiquitous picture of Che's dead body.

This mode of proceeding from the ghostly element in a given order to the fidelity of a militant subject could serve as a model to interpret not only the role of popular culture, but also the forms of political consciousness sought at the time. This is how *fantasma*, as ghost or specter, appears in several of Revueltas's posthumous writings collected in *México 68*, and in his *Dialéctica de la conciencia*, discussed above. In "Un fantasma recorre México," for instance, Revueltas observes:

I begin to write these notes in a large and orderly room, in some house in some neighborhood in the city, today, Tuesday October 29. A house, a refuge of the friend I will call *Chronos*. *Chronos* smiles through his eyes, he is ironic and very kind. He has left me alone to write. To write . . . The fact of writing itself is weird, astounding. One doesn't know what it means, what that thing is about putting together words, in a world, an unbreathable void in which all of them seem to have been broken without daring to say what has happened, what they designate: it is not the horror but this void, this orphanhood, with so many deaths surrounding us. In reality I had started taking notes in early May, before the Movement. One day sooner or later I will reconstruct—in the ever-new light, new at every minute and every hour—of this vertiginous, changing, ungraspable life in which something

57. Taibo, '68, 16–17 (translation modified). Taibo's portrait of the role of Che Guevara for contemporary post-1968 politics compares usefully to Ricardo Piglia's portrait, in "Ernesto Guevara, rastros de lectura," *El último lector* (Barcelona: Anagrama, 2005), 103–38.

that in its time had an enormous or anxious importance afterwards seems to us unreal, dream-like, and lived in all unlikelihood, as though we ourselves were our own story, our own distant story as told by others.

"Don't you think we're a bit supernatural?, I will say one of these days to *Chronos*, "that all of us, you and I and the others are supernatural?" There is something of that in all of us, in this struggle, in this chaos in which we find ourselves, living and phantasmatic at the same time, lucid and opaque, each one a character of their own dreams and of the dreams of others: not only is it a question of loving each other; we also dream one another; the others, those who are other, are my dream, not my reality.[58]

Undoubtedly, this text is porous to the melancholy influence of loss and defeat. "It rains in all our eyes and our old familiar pieces of furniture, the portraits of mother or grandfather, are somewhere out there, in some shed," Revueltas confesses. "As though a certain melancholy felt like falling over my soul."[59] As in Taibo's judgment, however, in this fragment too there are notes of resistance against all odds: "We are caught in a time and a space that are incommensurable, personal and impersonal, devoid of number, only pure will in the raw. I feel sad and full of violence. We will vanquish. We will vanquish."[60] Participating in this conviction of victorious fidelity to the most obscure of events is the writer's awareness of being both living and phantasmatic, or ghost-like. For Revueltas, any commitment should begin precisely from such a state between dreaming and awakening, at once lucid and opaque, with which an emergent collectivity can face up to the unbreathable void of a given situation. Even Tlatelolco, more so than an irreparable loss, in this sense might name precisely the kind of forgotten labor and phantasmatic consciousness that the author seeks to grasp in his unfinished *Dialéctica de la conciencia*: the consciousness of those who were and were not there and whose gaze looks at you from everywhere; that which is "on the verge" of becoming real but which remains in suspense, unresolved, yet promises one day to become real.

When such a sinister or uncanny apparition lays bare the fundamental lack in the structure of the law, the melancholy answer tirelessly reiterates how this lack is the constitutive law of the structure itself, whereas a truly courageous answer would reply by discerning the prescriptive structure of a new law. In one case, the specter must remain as such—out of joint, sign of an insuperable maladjustment that from time immemorial has marked a messianic promise, as Derrida might say: "Of a disjointed or disjunctive time without which there would be neither event nor history nor promise of justice."[61] In the other case, something must come to pass for an event to take place, beyond the

58. José Revueltas, "Un fantasma recorre México," in *México 68: Juventud y revolución*, 79–80.
59. Ibid., 82–3.
60. Ibid.
61. Derrida, *Specters of Marx*, 170.

impasse signaled by the specter. Such would be the passage of a truly effective justice: "Justice is that by which the subject's nodal link to the place, to the law, takes on the divisible figure of its transformation, whereas the superego expressed the ferocious archaism of the fixity of the law," as Badiou notes. "More radically, justice names the possibility—from the standpoint of what it brings into being as subject-effect—that what is nonlaw may function as law."[62]

Paz's poem ultimately divides these two trajectories of the specter or phantasm. Instead of initiating the process of an interminable melancholy, the black bile can also turn shame into rage sufficient to throw the ink of an angry audacity against the page. In this sense, the activists in the student-popular movement could also have been another of the stories told by Taibo in his book *Arcángeles: Doce historias de revolucionarios herejes del siglo XX (Archangels: Twelve Stories of Revolutionary Heretics in the Twentieth Century)*: "All of them sought out the revolution and went to hell several times to find it," the author remarks. "They are gathered in this stubbornness, in their fidelity to the attempt radically to transform the planet, in their marvelous tenacity."[63] This is also, finally, the stubborn fidelity that we find in fragments such as Revueltas's "Un fantasma recorre México." Instead of remaining suspended above the void, the specter of these texts opens the space for an event and prepares the subject's leap. Perhaps this double assignment can still inspire a critique of the merely sinister state of the Left in radical political thinking today. Tlatelolco, then, would not only be the name of the place where state power exhibited its intrinsically excessive nature, as always brutally superior to the situation at hand, but it would also be the anchoring point for the tenacious search for a different "we," or a different subjective figure of equality, capable of putting a limit on the errancy of the state. Instead of expressing a morbid fascination with the massacre, this seems to me to be the universalizable hope contained in the seemingly simple words of Revueltas in *México 68*: "Un fantasma recorre México, nuestras vidas. Somos Tlatelolco . . . " ("A specter haunts Mexico, our lives. We are Tlatelolco . . . ").[64]

---

62. Badiou, *Theory of the Subject*, 159. For a more detailed analysis of this notion of nonlaw qua law or justice, see Chapter Two in my *Badiou and Politics*.

63. Paco Ignacio Taibo II, *Arcángeles: Doce historias de revolucionarios herejes del siglo XX* (Mexico City: Planeta, 1998), 12.

64. José Revueltas, "Un fantasma recorre México," in *México 68*, 83. For an alternative analysis of Revueltas's relation to 1968 in Mexico, see the conclusion to Chapter 3, above. My reading has also been expanded and developed, in close proximity to the Derridean notion of the "passive decision," in Chapter 5 of Gareth Williams, *The Mexican Exception*, 117–152.

7

IN THE SHADOW OF MAO

The Uses of Literature

Every book begins as the desire for another book, as the drive to copy, to steal, and to contradict, as envy and as overconfidence.
                    Beatriz Sarlo, Una modernidad periférica

"Homenaje a Roberto Arlt" ("Homage to Roberto Arlt"), the closing text of Ricardo Piglia's collection of short stories *Nombre falso* (*Assumed Name*), at first sight seems to revolve around the theme of plagiarism as the key to a renewed understanding of the literary. This understanding would situate the act of writing between the two extremes of originality, which turns out to be undesirable aside from being an illusion, and falsification, which becomes deliberate to the point of being an authentic duty. In fact, as other critics have suggested, the story combines not one but two figures of modern Argentine literature: not only Arlt, but also Borges.[1] The project consists in articulating the writerly modes of these two precursors in the direction of a single narrative poetics, where previously the debate had been overshadowed by the old polemic, which determined so much of Argentina's official literary history, between the groups of Boedo and Florida. Piglia would close this gap between the autonomy of the text and its social and political inscription. A new practice of storytelling that tried to demonstrate the fallacy of these oppositions, together with others such as that between commitment and vanguardism: such would ultimately have been the ambitious project made possible by the idea of plagiarism—all this, it seems, without having to exceed the limits of the literary itself, with everything this notion promises or threatens to convey.

Piglia's experiment begins by fusing the theory and practice of plagiarism in the opening epigraph to the entire collection *Assumed*

---

1. Rita Gnutzmann rightly observes that the story might as well be called "Homage to Jorge Luis Borges." See her article "Homenaje a Arlt, Borges y Onetti," *Revista Iberoamericana* 159 (1992): 446. Noé Jitrik also brings out the parallelism between Borges and Arlt, in "En las manos de Borges el corazón de Arlt: A propósito de *Nombre falso*, de Ricardo Piglia," *Cambio* 3 (1976): 84–8. A further link, precisely through Onetti, should be established with Josefina Ludmer, who uses the title "Homenaje a *La vida breve*" for one of the chapters in her book *Onetti: Los procesos de construcción del relato* (Buenos Aires: Sudamericana, 1977), a book dedicated to Ricardo Piglia, while Piglia dedicates "Homage to Roberto Arlt" to Josefina Ludmer.

Name—an epigraph attributed to Arlt when in reality it is a direct quotation from Borges: "Sólo se pierde lo que realmente no se ha tenido" ("The only things that we lose are those that we never really had").[2] Without returning to the possible interpretations of this phrase already discussed in the previous chapter, we can observe how the mere gesture of a falsely attributed quotation not only accomplishes the program of plagiarism before giving way to the story in which it will be the central theme; through the double reference, it also anticipates the hypothesis that the author will be no less indebted to Borges than to Arlt. After *Assumed Name*, of course, the project to rewrite the history of Argentine literature based on this particular combination would be a constant throughout Piglia's work not only as a writer but also as a critic and teacher, to the point where he himself for a while thought about using *Entre Borges y Arlt* (*Between Borges and Arlt*) as the title for his collection of essays that we now know in various editions as *Crítica y ficción* (*Criticism and Fiction*). "To cross Arlt with Borges," Piglia states in an interview from the 1980s, "is one of the great utopias of Argentine literature . . . Arlt and Borges are the two great Argentine writers and, in some way, all the genealogies, intrigues, and family resemblances of contemporary Argentine literature start with them."[3] Thus, what emerges in the final text of *Assumed Name* as a double rewriting of the tradition of the Argentine writer also prepares the famous debates about Arlt and Borges which would appear later in *Respiración artificial* (*Artificial Respiration*), without a doubt Piglia's most discussed book. The literary aspects that these two precursors would share most notably converge in the creative use of tradition through the ironic or parodied displacement of authorities and translations; in the delirious manipulation of quotes that are falsely or correctly attributed; in the mixture of heterogeneous genres, both high and low, narrative and essayistic; in the causality of crime and the story of its investigation; in a paranoid view of society based on conspiracy and betrayal as an heroic act beyond good and evil; and, finally, in the incorporation into the text of the reader's role as a detective, charged with the task of deciphering a crime-like enigma. All of these are obviously

---

2. Ricardo Piglia, *Nombre falso* (Barcelona: Seix Barral, 1994), 7. This Seix Barral edition is supposed to be the "definitive" one. For the English version, see Ricardo Piglia, *Assumed Name*, trans. Sergio Gabriel Waisman (Pittsburgh: Latin American Literary Review Press, 1995), 11. Borges's phrase appears in an autobiographical fragment from "New Refutation of Time," in *Other Inquisitions 1937–1952*, trans. Ruth L. C. Simms (Austin: University of Texas Press, 1964): "I cannot mourn the loss of a love or a friendship without reflecting that one can lose only what one has never really had" (177). Jorge Fornet, in "'Homenaje a Roberto Arlt' o la literatura como plagio," *Nueva Revista de Filología Hispánica* 42 (1994), also recalls another line by Borges, in the poem "1964," from *El otro, el mismo*: "Nadie pierde . . . / Sino lo que no tiene y no ha tenido / Nunca . . . " (115, n. 1).
3. Piglia in an interview with Marithelma Costa, *Hispamérica* 44 (1986): 42.

materials and techniques that put their stamp on Piglia's narrative and critical works.

So far, however, this fairly common reading, restricted to the intertextual effects of plagiarism, has been unable to account for the powerful critical and political strain of thought that inhabits the pages of "Homage to Roberto Arlt." Nor can we understand the original force of *Assumed Name* if we ignore the ideological break that separates the final text of this collection from the later project that would lead to *Artificial Respiration*. By this I mean not only the military coup of 1976 as an external historical referent, but also the change in Piglia's project that between the two texts—the first published immediately before the dictatorship, when the author together with a large part of his generation still lived in a period of revolutionary fervor, and the other at the height of the military regime—affected the history of political events as much as their repercussions for the genealogy of literature. What is lost in this change could very well be said to affect the prescriptive dimension of politics as a process of collective emancipation. This dimension's absence, however, also profoundly transforms the status of the literary act itself, opening a gap that is in fact quite difficult to bridge between the project that culminates in *Assumed Name* and the one that begins with *Artificial Respiration*.

In following the textual logic of "Homage to Roberto Arlt," my opening hypothesis holds that, in this story, two series of action and signification, the first literary and the second political, must be rigorously articulated without separating them according to an inert relation of exteriority or abandoning them to the false depth of interpretation. This hypothesis is coherent with the author's own thesis, today already a bit overused, that a story always narrates two histories—one visible and the other invisible. "A visible story hides a secret one, narrated in a fragmentary and elliptical manner," affirms Piglia. "This is not a question of a hidden meaning that would depend on interpretation: the enigma is nothing but a story that is told in an enigmatic way."[4] In light of the success this thesis has enjoyed among Piglia's critics, it is even more surprising that there has not been a reading of the final story in *Assumed Name* that has systematically applied this same principle. This story is not only a claim against literary property in the name of a new "aesthetic" of plagiarism or of intertextuality, even if we find that this claim is then adorned with anecdotes drawn from Marxism or anarchism. To the contrary, and

---

4. Ricardo Piglia, "Tesis sobre el cuento," *Formas breves* (Buenos Aires: Temas Grupo, 1999), 94–5. This text is also included in an earlier edition of his *Crítica y ficción* (Buenos Aires: Fausto, 1993), 75–7. It has been translated into English as "Theses on the Short Story," *New Left Review* 70 (July/August 2011): 63–6. The same idea, I should add, already appears in (or is taken from) Ludmer, *Onetti*, 46–8; and later, perhaps not surprisingly, in the work of a French Maoist, in Natasha Michel, "Fiction 1 et fiction 2," in *L'écrivain pensif* (Paris: Verdier, 1998), 62–5.

precisely through such anecdotes, we should also situate the story within the political frame that begins to define the "new Left" at the end of the 1960s and the beginning of the 1970s, through a redefinition of the classic problem, inherited from Marxism-Leninism, of the position of the intellectuals with regard to the party—as well as their organic relationship with the masses for whom they, as intellectuals, intend to serve as a revolutionary vanguard.

In "Homage to Roberto Arlt" we face a story that cannot be read without connecting the practice of literature with contemporary forms of political and ideological militantism. In fact, in the early seventies, this militantism carried with it, as one of its most productive forces, a devastating critique of the entire notion of "the literary" itself. Behind the visible Arlt-Borges lineage, so extensively discussed in the criticism on Piglia's *Assumed Name* and *Artificial Respiration*, there effectively lies a second lineage, at once oblique and yet secretly alluded to in "Homage to Roberto Arlt" as well as, more recently, in the novel *Plata quemada* (*Money to Burn*), which we can refer to as the invisible lineage of Brecht–Mao. In Piglia's writing, even the significance of the first lineage must be understood anew through the ideological framing of the second. Such appears to have been the programmatic intent of one of Piglia's courses, in the first semester of 1975, the same year he published the collection *Assumed Name*, at the Center for Investigations in the Social Sciences in Buenos Aires, under the title "Hypothesis for an Ideological Analysis of Literature: Arlt and Borges."[5] The author's first courses during his exile in the United States, in 1977, also appear to have revolved around the same problematic and, clearly, the theory and practice of plagiarism are to be considered part of this double analytical framework.

Piglia's use of plagiarism does not limit itself to a purely literary-juridical question, even if we include the ambiguous role of the critic within the creative text. To the contrary, by questioning the very boundaries of what is legitimate and what is not—at all levels of society, and not only in the realm of letters—the story entangles itself in an obscure ethico-political web. At other times, this more obscure effect undoubtedly would have led to discussions of "commitment" or "authenticity"; but today, after the collapse of the revolutionary project, we might perhaps reformulate this as a question of subjective "purity" or, rather, of "fidelity." This at least is what we can surmise based on the working hypothesis according to which "Homage to Roberto Arlt" should be read, beyond the alternative between Arlt and Borges, as a text profoundly marked by the ideas of Mao and Brecht.

---

5. This course, together with Emilio de Ípola's, titled "Analysis of Ideologies (Theory and Methodology)," is announced in the Argentine magazine *Los Libros* 40 (March–April 1975): 26.

The Arms of Criticism

I mean, writing is always a particular way of reading, and in order to talk of influences (that is, of approval, of inheritance, but also of theft, of plagiarism, or in the final instance, of property), I think we should rely on a theory of reading.

Ricardo Piglia, *"La autodestrucción de una escritura"*

What I propose in this chapter could also be seen as a treatise on the use of epigrams or epigraphs, be they falsely or correctly attributed. At times these are relatively autonomous phrases interpolated into the body of the text, while at others they establish authentic maxims, or rules of thought, at the beginning of a book or chapter. In each case, they serve to condense the ideology of literature as well as its critique on the part of Piglia. When asked in a recent interview about the possible authoritarian effects of such maxims, he himself explained: "Why do writers use this epigrammatic style? At one point I tried to extract from Borges's texts what I called separable ideological definitions such as, for example, 'Reality likes symmetries.' I made a list of sentences like this, and there was a Borgesian ideological dictionary."[6] Here we have another example of the creative use of plagiarism, since this idea in fact comes from the French philosopher Alain Badiou, also a Maoist at the time, who gives us a model for this kind of reading—including the expression "separable ideological statement"—in his article "The Autonomy of the Aesthetic Process," an article that Piglia included in an anthology of theoretical texts he edited, *Literatura y sociedad*, along with his own essay on the aesthetic ideas of Mao Zedong.[7]

Piglia's imaginary project would consist in demarcating all of those phrases which, as extrapolatable statements, serve to anchor a text in the ideological materials of its time. In a later version of the same theory, which appears in *Prisión perpetua* (*Perpetual Prison*), the separable ideological statements function, in the way of aphorisms or proverbs, as traces of lost events, the remains of forgotten social fictions. As one of the female characters states:

> You should view these sayings . . . as ruins of a lost story; in the proverb there persists a story that is told over and over again throughout the

---

6. See Marina Kaplan, "Between Arlt and Borges: An Interview with Ricardo Piglia," *New Orleans Review* 16 (1989): 73.

7. Alain Badiou, "La autonomía del proceso estético," *Literatura y sociedad* (Buenos Aires: Tiempo Contemporáneo, 1974). Badiou writes: "I will call 'separable ideological statement' a statement of the novelistic discourse that fulfills the following three conditions: I) It produces in and of itself a complete and independent effect of signification. II) It has the logical structure of a universal proposition. III) It is not tied contextually to any subjectivity" (106).

ages ... These phrases are ruins of lost stories and real scenes. If one were to reconstruct them, one would be able to know the history of the life form of the popular classes.[8]

In Piglia's case, a list of all of such phrases would produce not only a dictionary of ideology but also a model for the critique of literary ideology, based on a materialist theory of cultural production. Finally, there is little doubt in my mind that this hypothetical task of reconstruction, applied to the whole of a latent popular narrative which would condense itself in a proverb or an aphorism, for better or worse found an important source of inspiration in the very style of the "little red book" of quotations from Chairman Mao.

As an initial guideline for the materialist critique of literary production, we could pick up on a quotation attributed to Witold Gombrowicz with which Piglia opens his volume *Crítica y ficción*: "One should not speak poetically about poetry [*No hay que hablar poéticamente de la poesía*]."[9] From a critical position, this means that we should not submit the study of literature (in this case, poetry) to the canons of verisimilitude that in each society define what is sayable and readable, and then, within this field, what is literary (or, here, what is poetic). Even if it is sometimes (but rarely) the case that writers make for the best critics, as many of the writers themselves understandably think, the fact that some of the most famous critics also believe this is a symptom of something much more serious—namely, a tendency toward intellectual abnegation. The possible autonomy of the critico-theoretical task, however, should not be given up without resistance. For Piglia, such resistance consists in capturing the specificity of the labor of writing in relation to other forms of work, material as much as intellectual.

Art and literature are not defined purely on a formal level, but also in terms of their social function; each in its way participates in the contradictions that define society as a whole. Using the vocabulary of the period, when the revolutionary promise had yet to expire, this set of contradictions was to have been read in terms of class antagonism. This becomes especially clear if we take into account Piglia's publications in the Argentine magazine *Los Libros*, which he edited with Beatriz Sarlo and Carlos Altamirano between 1973 and 1975—a Maoist period that is indispensable in understanding the possible ideological project of *Assumed Name*. Piglia writes in one of his essays for *Los Libros*, "Mao Zedong: práctica estética y lucha de clases" ("Mao

---

8. Ricardo Piglia, *Prisión perpetua* (Barcelona: Seix Barral, 1998), 125, 131. Piglia plays with the double meaning of *sentencia* or "sentence": "That is, a saying that encloses both a conviction and a condemnation" (147–8), before he repeats the method in the words of Erika: "We ought to start from there and reconstruct the material conditions in which the sentence was produced" (124).

9. Ricardo Piglia, *Crítica y ficción* (Barcelona: Anagrama, 2001), 7.

Zedong: Aesthetic Practice and Class Struggle"): "The aesthetic effect, the ideological signification, the mode of production, the forms of distribution and consumption, the materials and instruments of work, i.e., the whole literary system is determined by class interests, and class interests determine in each case what is art and for whom (or for what) it 'serves.'"[10] The social function of literature, however, often remains hidden, dissimulated by the idea of a disinterested art that supposedly serves no extrinsic purpose whatsoever. Indeed, a society defines itself by its codes of verisimilitude that naturalize the work's meaning and guarantee the illusion of an immediate and transparent reception. "Thus, bourgeois verisimilitude means the legality of the text, its free passage, a reassurance of communication in the process of social consumption of its products," writes Sarlo in another essay for *Los Libros*. "The text 'serves' because it is verisimilar—that is, every verisimilar text has an *end*, to be read without violating its code, with the understanding that this is the *natural code*, and that for this reason there is no other naturalness except that of the text."[11] The first task of a materialist critique should thus consist in the denaturalization of meaning, which at the same time implies a reinscription of art and literature in the set of social practices.

As Brecht states in the epigraph that Piglia quotes in his essay on Mao for *Los Libros*, "Art is a social practice, with its specific features and its own history: a practice among others, connected to others."[12] This Brechtian idea, which enables a reading of art as a branch of material production, directly connects with Mao's theories of practice and contradiction. "For Mao, society is divided into three fundamental practices: the struggle over production, the class struggle, and culture and scientific experimentation," Piglia notes in "La lucha ideológica en la construcción socialista" ("The Ideological Struggle in the Construction of Socialism"), a second essay on Mao written for *Los Libros*. "Each one of these practices (economy, politics, culture) possesses, then, a specific form and its own intelligibility defined on the basis of the theory of contradiction which for Mao allows one to think the life of society in its entirety."[13] The rearticulation of these practices, keeping in mind the specificity of art and writing, would define the goal of a "political critique of culture," which is also how the magazine's new subtitle begins to read for this last period in the history of *Los Libros*. Such appears to be the only criticism Piglia considers valid, unlike its

10. Ricardo Piglia, "Mao Tse-Tung: Práctica estética y lucha de clases," *Los Libros: Para una crítica política de la cultura* 25 (1972): 22.

11. Beatriz Sarlo, "Novela argentina actual: códigos de lo verosímil," *Los Libros: Para una crítica política de la cultura* 25 (1972): 18.

12. Piglia, "Mao Tse-Tung," 22.

13. Ricardo Piglia, "La lucha ideológica en la construcción socialista," *Los Libros: Para una crítica política de la cultura* 35 (1974): 7. This is part of a special issue on *China después de la revolución cultural* (*China After the Cultural Revolution*).

journalistic deformation, which rather performs a mediating function as representative of the law of the market:

> That criticism alone is valid which, dedicated to literature, generates a concept that can be used outside of literature. Those are the critics that I am interested in, that is, when one reads only about literature while reading them, but what they say about literature produces a concept that can be used to read social processes, modalities of language, the structure of relationships.[14]

The value of literary criticism, then, depends at the same time on such a redefinition of the social field as a set of articulated practices.

Faced with the stubborn problem of the relationship between literature and society, the space of criticism becomes decentered according to the paradox of an internal exteriority. One can read literature's outside only from within the parameters that constitute its inner core. The same can be said with respect to "Homage to Roberto Arlt," in the sense that the story transcends its strictly literary frame without ever leaving it. In other words, by critically belaboring the idea of plagiarism, the story coins a series of concepts that, once they are extracted from the domain in which they operate in a privileged if not exclusive manner, are also capable of reconfiguring the modes of being of politics in what we might call its Maoist, or post-Leninist, sequence.

Finally, this critical model, which in the 1970s began to be shared by a generation of young Argentine intellectuals through journals such as *Los Libros* and *Crisis*, presupposes that the rules of inscription of a work in the system of its conditions of possibility are in some way decipherable from the very interior of its own functioning. As Josefina Ludmer suggests in answer to a questionnaire for *Los Libros*: "*The system of production of a work*—that is, its process of appropriating, transforming, and reproducing everything that constitutes it (the unconscious, language, desire, history, economy: all the 'extraliterary' stuff)—*is the work itself, its system.*"[15] In fact, the process of the

---

14. See Arcadio Díaz-Quiñones, Paul Firbas, Noel Luna and José A. Rodríguez-Garrido, eds, *Ricardo Piglia: Conversación en Princeton* (Princeton: PLAS Cuadernos, 1998), 36.

15. Josefina Ludmer "Hacia la crítica," *Los Libros* 28 (1972): 5. This is part of a special issue under the title *Para una crítica política de la cultura*, with which *Los Libros* began its second epoch. I should add that at least two of the authors of the questionnaire are members of the generation of the journal *Contorno*, to which León Rozitchner also belongs. This circumstance may play a role in the answers, in which a group of younger critics define the future task of the study of literature, opening a new space for the project of *Los Libros*. The best study of this project, with a clear explanation of its two phases between structuralism and the poststructuralist critique of ideology, is still the work of my brother Wouter Bosteels, in "Texto e ideología: Análisis discursivo de *Los Libros*: Una revista literaria argentina de los años setenta" (MA thesis, Katholieke Universiteit Leuven, 1993). For a more recent analysis, see Jorge H. Wolff, *Telquelismos latinoamericanos: la teoría crítica francesa en el entre-lugar de los trópicos* (Buenos Aires: Grumo, 2009).

transformation of those ideological materials is precisely that which, in any narration, gives rise to that second, secret story hidden within the first. Without falling into the mechanistic error, typical of certain sociologies of literature, which would consist in separating the literary and the non-literary before asking with feigned astonishment about their relation of reflection or distance, a materialist critique should understand the very separation as a result of the formative process of writing as such. As Ludmer adds, "One of the fundamental critical functions, then, is the analysis of the transformations, the processes to which all these elements are subjected, not merely as 'extraliterary facts' but as essential components of the work itself."[16] In this sense, a painstaking structural analysis does not exclude a critique of the text's place in the whole of literary ideology, but rather supposes the effective completion of precisely such a critique.

As for "Homage to Roberto Arlt," it is no exaggeration to state that absolutely everything in its structure is divided into two, as is only to be expected from a writer who at that point was still a loyal follower of Mao. The story stages a progressive logic of scission, which it applies even to the most trivial details of the plot. At the outset, the text combines the report of the narrator, an editor-critic named Ricardo Piglia, with the published version, as an appendix, of the story titled "Luba," a supposedly unpublished text that is attributed to Arlt. The report itself is divided into, on one hand, the editor's annotations about the circumstances of his discovery, and, on the other, the various notes, also transcribed by the editor, found among the materials in Arlt's workshop. These notes, in turn, contain two large projects attributed to Arlt: first, the outline of a novel about the perfect crime—namely, Lettif's murder of his wife Matilde or Lisette—and then various of Arlt's letters and lecture notes on anarchism, political economy, and other themes. It is in these notes and letters that the existence of an unpublished text is announced, the very text, it is suggested, that we will later read under the title of "Luba." Finally, all of the characters in the text appear within a dual structure whereby one dominates or manipulates the other, or at least believes himself to be superior to the other. This is the case, in the first instance, with Piglia and Kostia, Arlt's friend in whose hands the unpublished text appears for the first time; then later, with Rinaldi and Lettif, the former being the pedagogical master in the latter's criminal education; and, finally, with Enrique, the revolutionary anarchist hidden in a brothel during his flight from the police, and the prostitute Beatriz Sánchez, also known as Luba.

---

16. Ludmer, "Hacia la crítica," 5. As Badiou also observes, "In general, it is necessary to understand clearly that what the aesthetic practice 'belabors,' the generalities it transforms, cannot be heterogeneous elements: the 'raw materials' of the process of production are themselves 'already' aesthetic" ("La autonomía," 110).

This dual structure, continuously split from within, makes the plot bifurcate for the full length of "Homage to Roberto Arlt." As the assignment of a series of fixed places, however, the logic of scission acquires mobility only by unfolding itself into a dialectic of subjective forces—through a small number of internecine struggles pitting one side against another. There is something that serves as a motor, an absent cause, behind this order that assigns to every force a strict place in the hierarchical duality of the plot. What, then, is this cause—without out a doubt the true enigma of the story, its invisible core—if it is indeed the case, as would happen in any story according to Piglia, that this motor is put in the service of a secret narration?

Before anything else, the enigma has to do with the obscure reason that Kostia, after having sold what he considers to be an unpublished story by Arlt to Piglia, suddenly decides to publish it under his own name—appropriating another's text as if it were his own. Piglia, the character-narrator, indignant at this act of plagiarism that obviously robs him of the possibility of an editorial success, considers several hypotheses that might explain such an act. Among these possible explanations, let me draw attention first to the one that suggests the presence of a secret motive that appears to leave the editor perplexed while he continues assuming that the text is an Arlt original: "Was one to think, then, that Arlt himself had refused—for some reason that I did not know—its being published? In that case, why did Arlt not destroy the story? Why did Kostia save it?"[17] Then, in a footnote, the editor adds: "There was also another hypothesis that perhaps only now (when everything is finished) I can propose to myself: Arlt could have specifically asked Kostia to destroy the text. In that case, what secret did the story contain? . . . [M]ust one think that Kostia or he himself had found something in the text that prevented its publication?"[18] Finally, upon receiving a metal box full of Arlt's materials, one of them being an unfinished manuscript version of the recently discovered story, Piglia the narrator-editor notes: "Inside I found the explanation, the motive, that had made Kostia decide to publish Arlt's story with his own name."[19]

What is this secret motive that first impedes and then permits, or even imposes, the publication of the text under an assumed name? Piglia only affirms that such a motive exists, but does not tell us what it is. As a matter of fact, in a recent interview he shows his determination never to reveal the key to the enigma. Various critics, in the meantime, have arrived at the right conclusion that "Luba" is a translation of Leonid Andreyev's story "Darkness."[20] Piglia's story

17. Piglia, *Assumed Name*, 129.
18. Ibid.
19. Ibid., 131.
20. Leonid Andreyev, "Darkness," in *Visions: Stories and Photographs by Leonid*

itself had suggested this conclusion by putting the names of Andreyev and Saint Petersburg in Kostia's mouth, and by mentioning the presence of a copy of "Darkness" in the metal box that also contained the manuscript version of the story attributed to Arlt. Plagiarism would then present itself as the subversive act of the false appropriation of a translation, either by Kostia or by Arlt himself. However, since no plagiarism can be perceived as such so long as there is no legal witness to verify it, it takes the arrival of a specialized editor like the one named Piglia so that Kostia can repeat the gesture of falsification or erroneous attribution, possibly following the logic of his teacher and friend Arlt. Or, in a final hypothesis that in reality obliges the reader to leave the fictional universe presented in the pages of "Homage to Roberto Arlt," we can suppose that the translation of Andreyev's story is Piglia's own work, even if, within the plot, he attributes the text alternately to Arlt and to Kostia. In this case, the noble or sad task of representing the law with the end of detecting plagiarism would be our duty as readers of the story.

The decoding of the solution to the enigma would depend upon a few astute readers who, like latter-day detectives, would be capable of following the diverse clues left behind in the text. Behind the sequence that takes us from Piglia to Arlt by way of Kostia, one finds the melodramatic figure, long forgotten in his own country after his repudiation of the October Revolution, of Leonid Andreyev. The proper name of this Russian writer would bring to a close the series of falsifications, at last re-establishing the original rights of the author and, thanks to the painstaking work of textual criticism, the reader could consider himself the proud owner of the text's true and proper meaning. In fact, it is not without some surprise that we observe how some critics have identified themselves as the true detectives capable of resolving the enigma. Ellen McCracken, for example, insists on the need for an "avant-garde" or "postmodern" reader, similar to Julio Cortázar's "active reader" in *Hopscotch*, after years of misunderstandings about *Assumed Name*, finally to bring together all the elements that make "Homage to Roberto Arlt" a clear metafictional plagiarism of Andreyev's "Darkness." She concludes: "Piglia aims at vanguardism but cannot achieve it without patient and aggressive readers who will collaborate with him in actualizing the text's literary experimentation."[21] There is a need, then, for a

Andreyev, ed. Olga Andreyev Carlisle (San Diego: Harcourt Brace Jovanovich, 1987), 185–238. The first Spanish translation appeared in *Las tinieblas y otros cuentos*, trans. N. Tasin (Madrid: Espasa Calpe, 1920), and the story reappeared with the title "Liuba" in Argentina, in *La risa roja* (Buenos Aires: Ayacucho, 1946). For more details, see Fornet, "'Homenaje a Roberto Arlt' o la literatura como plagio," 115–19.
21. Ellen McCracken, "Metaplagiarism and the Critic's Role as Detective," *PMLA* 106 (1991): 1081. We are even witness to a struggle over who was the first to make the discovery of Andreyev as the "true" author of "Luba," while those are mocked who let themselves be had by Piglia, to the point of including "Luba" as a "real" unpublished story in a bibliography

singularly alert consciousness to break the spell of falsification. Only then would one be able to discover, finally, the truth of the story.

This solution to the enigma of plagiarism by an avant-garde reader runs the risk of losing sight of the real stakes amid so much eagerness to reveal them. "That is not the clue to the story," Piglia answers when he is confronted with the explanation that Andreyev is the true author of Arlt's text: "The clue of this attribution lies with Kostia rather than Arlt! But that is a secret I wouldn't think of revealing. I only say that there is a secret, because I like those stories that have a blind spot, that not only tell a secret but have something to hide that only a single reader in the future is going to discover."[22] Of course, I do not pretend to be this exceptional or vanguardist reader. On the contrary, for reasons that have to do with the significance of Maoism as a critique of the very idea of the vanguard, it appears that one must avoid at all costs the privileged role of representing the subject supposed to know with respect to the final story in *Assumed Name*. What is more, in what follows I want to propose two hypotheses to explain the strict neces-sity—not only literary but also political—of that blind spot at the core of the story. The first hypothesis derives from a critique of the political economy of art and literature, while the second will bring us, through the dialectic of bad conscience, to Piglia's political and ideological proposal.

Critique of the Political Economy of Art

All of us, those who write and sign our names, do it to make ends meet. Nothing else. And to make ends meet we do not hesitate in affirming that white is black and vice-versa. People are looking for the truth and we give them counterfeit money.

Ricardo Piglia, "Homenaje a Roberto Arlt"

The most effective articulation, within the text, of the literary and the political depends upon a critique of the political economy of art. As contributions to such a critique we can read not only the notes attrib-uted to Arlt on money, beauty, and revolution in the final story of *Assumed Name*, but also Piglia's own studies published in *Los Libros* and *Hispamérica* on the economy of literature, once again with special emphasis on Arlt. In both cases, the main object of attack is beauty itself as a supposedly pure aesthetic value, separate from the circuits of supply and demand and independent of the crude assigning of prices according to the abstract measure of money as the form of general equivalence: "As always, what is at stake is the—forbidden, guilty—access to beauty, and in this case language serves as the support

---

of works by Arlt. See, for example, the unfortunate case of Aden W. Hayes, "La revolución y el prostíbulo: 'Luba' de Roberto Arlt," *Ideologies and Literature* 2 (1987): 141–7.
22. Piglia, *Crítica y ficción*, 138.

for desire and for property."[23] Against this idealist interpretation of art as a free, disinterested activity, a materialist reading has been developing over the last century and a half, in practice as much as in theory, whose basic elements can also be found in the conflicting proposals of Borges and Arlt—or, at least, such is Piglia's deliberately provocative hypothesis. According to this reading, only the principles of political economy can provide an account of the aesthetic or literary act: "Changed into the commodity, the law of supply and demand seems to be the only thing that enables one, from the point of consumption, to give 'reasons' for literary production."[24] As we will see, however, this is a lesson that many intellectuals, even in the 1970s, have continued to reject—particularly when they have aspired to speak in the name of the New Left.

Stéphane Mallarmé, in a characteristic anticipation, defined the crossroads that literature faces in the modern age: "There only exist, open to mental investigation, two roads, in all, along which our need bifurcates, namely, on the one hand, aesthetics, and, on the other, political economy."[25] This affirmation, nevertheless, remains hostage to a romantic scheme that we can also call liberal-bourgeois, even if the poet assigns himself the impossible mission of carrying this scheme, through a paroxysmic return, to its neo-aristocratic limit. Mallarmé still thinks of the aesthetic as a domain—if not the last one, then possibly the promise of a new place that is still to come—ruled by the will of a pure act, diametrically opposed to any use of language as a simple means of communication. This is the magisterial gesture of the captain's arm submerging in the midst of the shipwreck of meaning. Damned or not, the poet, notwithstanding his eagerness for the advent of an active mass, is still enclosed within a model of disinterested art, supreme object of a minority action over and above the circuits of everyday sociability and universal reportage—whence the bifurcation of his programmatic vision into two irreconcilable roads.

---

23. Ricardo Piglia "Roberto Arlt: una crítica de la economía literaria," *Los Libros: Para una crítica política de la cultura* 29 (1973): 27. This article is presented as part of a book project by Piglia, *Traducción: sistema literario y dependencia*, a second article being announced under the title "La traducción: legibilidad y génesis del valor," which I have not been able to locate in subsequent numbers of *Los Libros* or anywhere else for that matter. See also Piglia, "Roberto Arlt: la ficción del dinero," *Hispamérica* 7 (1974): 25–8; and "Introducción," in Roberto Arlt, *El juguete rabioso* (Buenos Aires: Espasa Calpe, 1993), 9–27. Derived from Arlt, the critique of the political economy of literature was a much-debated topic in Argentine literary criticism just before the military coup. In addition to Piglia, the best instances remain Noé Jitrik, "Entre el dinero y el ser (lectura de *El juguete rabioso* de Roberto Arlt)," *Dispositio* 1 (1976): 100–33; and Gerardo Mario Goloboff, "La primera novela de Arlt: el asalto a la literatura," *Revista de crítica literaria latinoamericana* 1 (1975): 35–49.
24. Piglia, "Roberto Arlt: una crítica de la economía literaria," 22.
25. Stéphane Mallarmé, "Magie," in Henri Mondor and G. Jean-Aubry, eds, *Œuvres complètes* (Paris: Gallimard, 1945), 399.

Piglia, on the contrary, opens his investigation into plagiarism precisely at the inevitable crossover between these two trails—at the point where the definition of literature becomes inseparable from the economic organization of exchange in terms of the production, circulation, and consumption of not only material but also symbolic goods. The author will ultimately attempt to undermine the very foundation on which a false opposition is erected between economics and literature, as if these two concepts marked two parallel tracks, with no other contact but that of a treacherous disparagement or an ephemeral sublimation. It is only on the ruins of this liberal model that an alternative project can arise—some would call it utopian—for a true cultural politics of the Left. First, however, literature's place must be defined in a society organized around the private appropriation of work.

Borges and Arlt, in this context, can serve as abbreviations for two opposing models in the definition of the modern economy of art. According to the first model, which is nothing other than a liberal extension of the previous aristocratic perspective, art serves no purpose, but rather is a useless luxury, the aesthetic expression of a happy destiny. "Luxury is the visible commentary of a happy moment," writes Borges in his definition of metaphor—for him the quintessential element of poetic art—as luxury or adornment. "What happens is that I almost never feel worthy of these generosities."[26] To confess oneself unworthy of luxury is not a contradictory reaction, but rather confirms, while adding the guilt and repudiation of a moralizing judgment, the minority character of art—that is, the unequal access to culture, beauty, or good aesthetic taste. Art is priceless; or, better, it comes at the cost of a luxurious waste of energy. Its value is not simply opposed to the system of economic valuation, but rather constitutes itself within this system as its internal limit, its constitutive excess. Thus we can define Borges's style, to which Piglia's reading of Arlt is directly opposed: "By establishing a relation between style and luxury, he at once shows what it costs to *have* a writing style: the exercise of literature appears once again linked to expenditure, to unproductive labor without a price."[27] An idealist view of the aesthetic act erases the labor of others and of oneself that alone gives one the time necessary to dedicate oneself to art. We also read in a letter attributed to Arlt: "We cannot think if we do not have time to read, nor feel if we find ourselves emotionally exhausted; we cannot write if we do not have free time (that is to say: money to finance free time). We cannot coordinate what we do not have."[28] In Borges, all this leads, if not any longer to a metaphysics of genius,

26. Jorge Luis Borges, "Otra vez la metáfora," *El idioma de los argentinos* (Barcelona: Seix Barral, 1994), 54–5.
27. Piglia, "Roberto Arlt: una crítica de la economía literaria," 22.
28. Piglia, *Assumed Name*, 111.

then to a vision of the universe as a library—a neutral zone, far removed from manual labor, where all readers, or possibly only a few rare birds, can have access to all the shelves of universal culture.

It is true that Piglia has never carried out an economic reading of Borges's work, a vast endeavor for which we would have to return to texts such as "El espejo y la máscara" or "El Zahir."[29] Based on Arlt's work, however, Piglia lays the ground for a second model of the economy of literature, which in turn inspires a critical perspective on the first. In this model it becomes apparent how art, even when defined as luxury, conceals the inequality behind the differential access to culture: "Arlt inverts the value system of this aristocratic morality that refuses to recognize the economic determinations that rule over every reading, the class codes that decide the circulation and appropriation of literature."[30] This alternative reading targets private property itself as the motor of the artistic economy. The result is that beauty appears as a crime, based on property as the unequal expropriation of values. The economy penetrates even the most intimate of cultural values. As Piglia writes of Arlt, "Price interferes with the access to 'beauty': only the deviation of this illegal appropriation makes it possible to *have* a text. In this sense the whole situation can be read as a critique of the liberal reading: there is no place where money does not reach to criticize the value behind the price."[31] Ultimately, there exists no pure beauty, but rather the aesthetic effect is always an integral part of the economic circuit that defines society as a whole.

Following this reading of Arlt, literature would be nothing special; the so-called cultural exception does not exist, save in the function of determined social uses. As Kostia affirms in another letter in *Assumed Name*: "To imagine that literature is a specialty, a profession, seems to me inaccurate. Everyone is a writer. The writer does not exist, everyone in the world is a writer, everyone knows how to write."[32] This is perhaps another plagiarism, this time worthy of Gramsci, as we can infer from Piglia's writings in *Los Libros*: "Paraphrasing Gramsci, we could say: 'All those who know how to write are "writers," since at some point in their life they have practiced writing. What they don't do is perform the *function* of being a writer in society.'"[33] We already know that this function does not magically derive from some divine gift, but is historically inscribed in a series of material necessities. These are the conditions of production that Arlt's writing renders visible according to Piglia: "In this way, by naming that which everyone hides, he gives the lie to the illusions of an

---

29. See Bruno Bosteels, "Beggars Banquet: For a Critique of the Political Economy of the Sign in Borges," *Variaciones Borges* 30 (2010): 3–52.

30. Piglia, "Roberto Arlt: una crítica de la economía literaria," 22.

31. Ibid., 24.

32. Piglia, *Assumed Name*, 113.

33. Ricardo Piglia, "Hacia la crítica," *Los Libros* 28 (1972): 6.

ideology that masks and sublimates the unforgiving logic of capitalist production in the myth of spiritual riches."[34]

If in the politico-economic articulation of art, commerce, and money, the concepts of leisure, the gift, and guilty luxury correspond to Borges's perspective, then debt, theft, and criminal consumption define Arlt's position. In one case, beauty appears as a conspicuous expenditure of energy, a prestigious but otherwise useless luxury; in the other, the aim includes a demolishing critique of the entire economic system that is capable of integrating even unproductive expenditures, provided that its global rule still prevails. Liberal but with strong aristocratic tendencies, the first model permits the elite to extend its control, sublimating the social contradictions it is faced with; the second, with its affinities for the massive denunciation of injustices behind the alleged disinterest of art, appears to open the road to a revolutionary alternative.

For Piglia, however, in the period when he writes "Homage to Roberto Arlt," the problem is a different one: not the usual critique, on behalf of the orthodox Left, of the liberal-aristocratic model of art, but rather the tenacious persistence of this model in the very heart of the revolutionary Left. One can read this problem between the lines of an apocryphal *aguafuerte* or "etching" attributed to Arlt under the provisional title *Los jarrones de Sèvres ¿sirven de orinales?* In this "etching"—a kind of topsy-turvy Duchamp—Arlt, according to Piglia, reconstructs a small archive of affirmations about art made by revolutionary thinkers, from an admirer of Bakunin to Trotsky.

Paulino Scarfó, the Argentine anarchist assassinated by Uriburu's dictatorship in 1931 one day after the killing of Severino Di Giovanni, is quoted first as saying: "If the revolutionary masses erupted into my room set upon tearing to pieces the bust of Bakunin and destroying my library, I would fight against them to the end."[35] More importantly, Arlt, according to Piglia, also quoted a fragment by Maxim Gorky, from *Mis recuerdos de Lenin* (*Days with Lenin*), in which Gorky complains of the irreverence shown by the peasants during a conference of "rural indigents" that took place in Moscow, two years after the October Revolution. Gorky seems particularly indignant upon observing that the peasants used the urns from Sèvres as urinals. Piglia attributes this long commentary on Gorky to Arlt:

> It does not even cross his mind that the peasants were acting, without knowing it, as art critics; that is to say, they *used* the urns from Sèvres. For Gorky the urns from Sèvres are only "beautiful objects," untouchable, that everyone must "recognize" and "respect." He does not realize that those men, by pissing in the urns from Sèvres, inside the Romanov Palace, are denying that beauty is universal; they are actually opposed to the bourgeois idea of a

34. Piglia, "Roberto Arlt: una crítica de la economía literaria," 23.
35. Piglia, *Assumed Name*, 107.

beauty that is more beautiful the less useful it is (when it is not useful for anything). By using them in such a "brutal" manner (so unaesthetically) the peasants are looking at the "beautiful object" to know what purpose it serves. Beauty is untouchable: *it must be useless.* There is the entire crime: a crime against property (even if Gorky does not like it).[36]

The "etching" thus also enters into dialogue with another phrase, this time stolen from Proudhon's anarchism, which Piglia mentions as the title for Arlt's story of the "perfect crime": "Property is theft."[37] Beauty is also a theft in its appropriation of a sum of social energy with the sole end of not serving any end.

Finally, the fragment copied from Trotsky's *Autobiography* refers to an incident similar to that of the urns from Sèvres. Speaking in 1918, Trotsky observes how a revolutionary soldier rips the velvet from the seats of a first-class train car in order to make himself a pair of gaiters. Trotsky appears more compassionate than Lenin's admirer Gorky, since for Trotsky "even in such a destructive act, the awakening of personality is revealed," to which Piglia adds, still in Arlt's name: "It seems like a criticism of Gorky's comment. (Again: beauty is only valuable when one can answer what purpose it serves. How can it be used? *Who* can use it? There is no universal beauty.)"[38]

In these materials for an apocryphal *aguafuerte* by Arlt, Piglia really is outlining the Left's need for a self-critique with regard to its supposedly revolutionary concept of art, following the exemplary experience of the critique of "revisionism" during the Cultural Revolution in China. If, for chronological reasons or so as not to break the illusion of presenting us with an unpublished story by Arlt, the author completely omits Mao's name, he does bring together three of the most notorious revolutionary authorities: Bakunin (through Scarfó), Lenin (through Gorky) and Trotsky. Could it be that Mao lies in wait, behind the very absence of his proper name, as the only one who will propose valid answers to the questions that these other revolutionaries have left unanswered? In each of the three cases cited, in effect, there still survives a concept of art as a beautiful object, an imperishable value, or a spiritual luxury, whose destruction is morally infuriating. Even Trotsky, who comes closest to a critique of this concept in observing the awakening of a new class consciousness, continued for most of his life to propose a dual, or pluralist, solution to the problem of aesthetic ideology, in the style of "proletarian politics, bourgeois art."[39] The lesson that Piglia takes up from Mao, on the contrary, allows him to formulate practical answers to the interrogations that arise from the reconstructed *aguafuerte* at the end of *Assumed Name*; or, at least,

---

36. Ibid.
37. Ibid., 109.
38. Ibid., 106.
39. See Ricardo Piglia, "Notas sobre Brecht," *Los Libros* 40 (1975): 8–9.

given that there are no explicit references to the Chinese experience in this story, this is how the author summarizes the situation—in almost exactly the same terms—in his first article about Mao in *Los Libros*: "Writing for whom? From where? Who can read us? All of Mao's 'aesthetic' reflection is meant to define artistic production as a specific answer to a differentiated social demand that arises from the class struggle."[40] Piglia's idea of plagiarism also responds to these great social demands posed, according to Maoism, by artistic production.

According to the notes that Piglia attributes to Arlt, Bakunian anarchism, Leninism, and Trotskyism all share the fact that they perpetuate, within the revolutionary Left, a bourgeois or liberal-humanist conception of art as an expression of "humanity" as an essential, inalienable and eternal value; and of the artist as one gifted with sufficient "genius" so as to transcend his circumstances in favor of such an imperishable value system. Mao, by contrast, affirms exactly the opposite in a quotation that Piglia uses in his review for *Los Libros*: "There is no art above the classes."[41] The key story in *Assumed Name*, in fact, can be read as an active critique of any such conception that would elevate art above the class struggle—that is to say, as a practical realization of a negation whose theoretical version is condensed in Piglia's essays in *Crisis* and *Los Libros*: "We deny that there exists an abstract and absolutely invariable artistic measure; in every society, each class has its own political and aesthetic criteria."[42] What "Homage to Roberto Arlt" reveals, then, is the subsequent problem that consists in knowing how to continue writing under such conditions, without falling into the old traps of the aesthetics of sublimation, secrecy, or (good) bad faith.

How, then, does one avoid, not just in theory but in the practice of a different writing, the whole of literary ideology, with its basic elements of creation, genius, and the canon of absolute values? Piglia responds to this dilemma with the systematic application of plagiarism and false attribution—that is, with a practice that destroys the most obstinate of all ideologies of the literary: the cult of originality. It is here that the combination of Arlt with Borges acquires its politico-economic value through the false attributions made by Kostia or Piglia. Falsification does not bring about only a new literary aesthetic but, by attacking the very principle of the private appropriation of the written, it also attempts to annihilate the foundation that has been the basis of aesthetic judgment throughout modernity.

On an anecdotal level, finally, this destructive operation could even have been inspired by certain ideas from Mao himself. Thus, in a particularly violent moment of the Cultural Revolution, Mao—not without some demagogy—makes the following declaration about the

---

40. Piglia, "Mao Tse-Tung," 22.
41. Ibid.
42. Ibid.

new attitude to be adopted in the universities: "The students should have the right to consult with one another and to cheat during exams. They must be able to present themselves with the name of another candidate. All that matters is that they have good answers and it is a positive thing if these are copied by others."[43] Piglia, the character-editor in "Homage to Roberto Arlt," does exactly that in presenting himself to the exam before his readers, as it were, with the proofs and notes that constitute the bulk of this key story in *Assumed Name*.

Mao in Argentina

Mao seemed to have resolved, from the Great Leap Forward on but espe-cially in the first stage of the Cultural Revolution, one of the problems that worried me and many others, the problem of the relation between the world of letters and the popular masses.

Beatriz Sarlo, La izquierda en la Argentina

The history of Maoism in Argentina still constitutes an obscure chapter in the collective archive of the 1960s and 1970s. This whole era in fact continues to offer a confusing spectacle of revolutionary effervescence. Critical studies on the role of intellectuals in those two decades are relatively scarce. Thus, not long ago, Nicolás Casullo could still wonder: "Why do the '60s and '70s not have any register in the bulk of our critical writing?"[44] It is true that today, aside from collective volumes such as *Cultura y política en los años '60* (Culture and Politics in the 60s), we have at our disposal two classic studies, Silvia Sigal's *Intelectuales y poder en Argentina* (*Intellectuals and Power in Argentina*) and Oscar Terán's *Nuestros años sesentas* (*Our Sixties*). However, as far as I know, there is no comparable document about the 1970s, even less concerning the intellectual role that the thought of Mao Zedong played during that period.

More specifically, the period from the return of Perón until the military coup lacks a serious critical-political study, beyond the merely anecdotal, about the often violent encounter between intellectuals and revolution—in spite of the evident fascination that those years now exert over younger Argentines. As Sarlo suggests in an interview, "There is still something enigmatic in the configuration that goes, fundamentally, from 1973 to 1976 and that has sufficient appeal to explain the passion for history."[45] Among the many signs of this

---

43. Mao Zedong, quoted in Charles Bettelheim and Enrica Collotti Pischel, *La revolución cultural china* (Córdoba: Pasado y Presente, 1971), 227–8.

44. Nicolás Casullo, "Los años '60 y '70 y la crítica histórica," in *Modernidad y cultura crítica* (Buenos Aires: Paidós, 1998), 171. Casullo himself takes up the task of reflecting upon the 1970s, in particular, in "Los años setenta: cultura y política," *Las cuestiones* (Buenos Aires: Fondo de Cultura Económica, 2007), 275–310.

45. Beatriz Sarlo in Javier Trímboli, ed., *La izquierda en la Argentina* (Buenos Aires: Manantial, 1998), 230.

passion, we can mention not only movies like *Cazadores de utopías* (*Hunters of Utopia*), novels such as Luis Guzmán's *Villa*, or Miguel Bonasso's narrativized account of Héctor José Cámpora's role in Argentine Peronism in *El presidente que no fue* (*The President Who Was Not*), but also the ambitious project of a generational history—in the same style as what Hervé Hamon and Patrick Rotman did with *Générations* for May 1968 in France—in the three volumes of *La Voluntad* (*The Will*), written by Eduardo Anguita and Martín Caparrós. Continuing in this same vein, in recent years several recompilations of original documents from the period have appeared, once again with little analysis, in relation to the armed Left's experience among the Montoneros and in the Revolutionary Popular Army (ERP). By contrast, the reader interested in Mao's role in Argentina should be content with the few treatises of Vanguardia Comunista, later called Partido de la Liberación; with the documents of the Partido Comunista Revolucionario, for many years the official organon of Argentine Maoism, at least until the party came out in support of the government of Isabel Perón and López Rega; or with the autobiographical interviews of its leader, Otto Vargas, in *¿Ha muerto el comunismo? El maoísmo en la Argentina* (*Is Communism Dead? Maoism in Argentina*).[46]

With respect to this growing interest in the 1960s and 1970s, something akin to a "new international style"[47] has developed that pretends to write history from below, favoring the collective over the individual

---

46. For studies of the role of intellectuals in the previous decade, see Oscar Terán, *Nuestros años sesentas: La formación de la nueva izquierda intelectual en la Argentina 1956–1966* (Buenos Aires: Puntosur, 1991); and Silvia Sigal, *Intelectuales y poder en Argentina: La década del sesenta* (Buenos Aires: Siglo Veintiuno, 2002). Broader political and historical studies of the following period include Liliana de Riz, *La política en suspenso: 1966–1976* (Buenos Aires: Paidós, 2000); and Tulio Halperín Donghi, *La democracia de masas* (Buenos Aires: Paidós, 2000). Among the many compilations of documents, see especially Pablo Pozzi and Alejandro Schneider, *Los setentistas: Izquierda y clase obrera: 1969–1976* (Buenos Aires: Eudeba, 2000); and, of course, the narrativized three-volume version by Eduardo Anguita and Martín Caparrós, *La Voluntad: Una historia de la militancia revolucionaria en la Argentina* (Barcelona: Norma, 1997), a project that should be compared with Hervé Hamon and Patrick Rotman, *Génération*, 2 vols. (Paris: Seuil, 1987–88). See also Luis Gusmán's novel *Villa* (Madrid: Alfaguara, 1995); and Miguel Bonasso's *El presidente que no fue: Los archivos ocultos del peronismo* (Buenos Aires: Planeta, 1997). For the Ejército Revolucionario Popular, see Daniel de Santis, *A vencer o morir: PRT-ERP documentos* (Buenos Aires: Eudeba, 1998); and Pablo A. Pozzi, *"Por las sendas argentinas": el PRT-ERP, la guerrilla marxista* (Buenos Aires: Eudeba, 2001); and on the Montoneros, Richard Gillespie's classic study, *Soldiers of Peron: Argentina's Montoneros* (New York: Oxford University Press, 1982). Finally, on Argentine Maoism and the Partido Comunista Revolucionario, see Jorge Brega, *¿Ha muerto el comunismo? El maoísmo en la Argentina: Conversaciones con Otto Vargas* (Buenos Aires: Agora, 1997).

47. I borrow this expression from Paul Berman, who speaks of "the international 1968 style," citing Hamon and Rotman as well as Elena Poniatowska, in his otherwise highly problematic book *A Tale of Two Utopias: The Political Journey of the Generation of 1968* (New York: W. W. Norton, 1996), 126–8. See also "Basic Banalities," in Chapter 6.

outlook. This style often privileges the original document over a sustained critical intervention. It is as if the supposed immediateness or naked facticity of the act had defeated the will to interpret its significance, not to mention its possible truth. The success of testimonies is perhaps not foreign to this tendency. Whatever the case, we find ourselves in a paradoxical situation in which, although collections with pamphlets and documents from the era abound, not only do we lack the apparatus for their interpretation, but many of their original authors have also in recent years denigrated their ideological content. Thus, the result of so much editorial work is that the recent past still largely escapes our memory, leaving an empty space that enormously complicates the work of younger generations to reconnect their intellectual debates with the ideas of their predecessors.

Piglia's two essays, "Mao Zedong: Aesthetic Practice and Class Struggle" and "The Ideological Struggle in the Construction of Socialism," here take on more than just an historiographical value, since they constitute one of the rare theoretical sources, in the artistic-cultural field, that can be used to follow the tracks of the Maoist experience of the 1970s in Argentina. In fact, the whole final epoch of the magazine *Los Libros*, in which both essays were published, until its closing by the dictatorship in 1976—and before its editors, challenging the repression through the use of pseudonyms, initiated in March 1978 the publication of its successor, *Punto de Vista*—constitutes an indispensable source for interpreting the passage of Mao's ideas through Argentina. Even more, the work of *Los Libros* ploughed an explicitly Maoist furrow—precisely through Vanguardia Comunista, where Piglia would meet up once again with Sarlo and Altamirano after they had abandoned what they considered the then-rightist ranks of the Partido Revolucionario Comunista.

Even in these cases, however, the significance of the Maoist experience can easily be lost. In the interview from the volume *La izquierda en la Argentina* cited above, Sarlo rejects the idea that there was something in the militancy of those years, as luminous as it might have been, that could be rescued today: "I see no reason to look for elements of identification in something that is closed forever. It would be an impossible task, beyond measure, with results that nobody is looking for."[48] Neither Lenin nor Mao, now considered too rustic or improbable, are saved from this hard retrospective glance. Piglia, for his part, perhaps never renounced his Maoist past; but in a strange omission, the most complete bibliography of his work as a critic and narrator, the one published in Piglia's *Conversación en Princeton*, also fails to mention his two essays about Mao for *Los Libros*, a journal that until its recent facsimile re-edition was already difficult enough to find on its own. Faced with such silences, I insist, it is impossible to undertake the

---

48. Sarlo, *La izquierda*, 234.

sustained work of analysis. On the contrary, many younger or foreign readers, undoubtedly more familiar with *Artificial Respiration* than with *Assumed Name*, will inevitably ignore the ideological context of which this last book is at least in part a product. If this chapter seeks to sketch the generational portrait of a group of intellectuals whose later paths in many cases have never come together again, it is also an attempt to fight against this cursed tendency toward intellectual orphanhood and forgetfulness.

What does Maoism mean in this context? It is evident that no form of politics can be exported without, in some way, altering its essence. Nor does "Maoism" mean the same in China, France, and Argentina. In many cases, we are dealing, after all, solely with the "fables" invented in the West, as Sarlo admits. Even so, it is equally true that there exists a limited number of premises that define what we can call the "rational core" of the Maoist doctrine, to use an expression of Badiou's—an author at that time very avidly read by Piglia.[49] Above all in the realm of politics, but with strong implications for the theory of ideology, Maoism's first innovation with respect to Marxist-Leninist orthodoxy consists in having recognized the existence of internal contradictions in a socialist country even after the initial revolutionary period, and in having responded to this unexpected fact by proposing original tactics and strategies—in particular the famous mass line, the self-critique of the party as form, and the idea of intellectual re-education.

In the period of transition of a socialist country, after the takeover of power and the collective appropriation of the economy, according to Maoism, not only do many of the old habits of the dominant classes still persist, but a new bureaucratic sector is formed with leaders, technicians, and specialists privileged by the party's state apparatus. The old capitalist division of work tends to reproduce itself under socialism, as could be observed at that time in the Soviet Union. This is the meaning of the critique of so-called "revisionism" in China: within the Left, we see the perpetuation or the recommencement of a "rightist" line that, stemming from capitalism, separates the elite in power from its popular bases. "The old capitalist relations persist and tend to reproduce themselves based on the division of labor," Piglia notes in his second essay on Mao. "The contradiction between manual and intellectual labor has as its fundamental effect the opposition between the functions of direction and execution; this fracture is the material base on which the revisionist political line

---

49. See Alain Badiou, Joël Bellassen, and Louis Mossot, *Le noyau rationnel de la dialectique hégélienne* (Paris: François Maspero, 1978). Badiou's most didactic texts on Mao's thought are *Théorie de la contradiction* (Paris: François Maspero, 1975), and, with François Balmès, *De l'idéologie* (Paris: François Maspero, 1976). In a personal conversation, Piglia told me how closely he and his collaborators studied the first of these booklets, which was quickly translated into Spanish as *Teoría de la contradicción*, trans. G. G. Díaz (Madrid: Júcar, 1976). What remains to be written is the history and theory of these international varieties of post-Maoism.

grows and develops that tends to exclude the masses from direction so as to replace them with a technocratic elite that seemed 'destined' to rule."[50] As the Cultural Revolution aimed to show, an adequate answer to this problem can only consist in calling the masses to mobilize in order to exercise political, economic, and cultural power directly, and to eliminate the rightist elements derived from the old social division of work in the midst of the supposed revolutionary Left.

Eliminating the old in order to develop the new, however, is not something that can be achieved through coercion or war. On the contrary, at this point it is necessary to note a crucial difference between external and internal contradictions: if the former typically end up being antagonistic and generally resolve themselves in a military encounter with the enemy, as in the wars of national liberation, the latter do not obey the same logic of antagonism and can only be overcome through an enlarged political and ideological struggle. Theoretically, therefore, another consequence of Maoism is the fundamental redefinition of the role of the different instances or practices that make up a society. In particular, it becomes apparent that the planning of the economy is a necessary but insufficient condition for constructing socialism. It is also necessary to put politics in the command post. According to many Western readers, this is also a valid lesson for a capitalist country tending toward socialism. As Piglia makes clear, "The development of the forces of production, in and of themselves, does not guarantee the transformation of the relations of production. In order to put an end to bourgeois relations one must put an end at the same time to the bourgeois ideological relations. The essential part is the class struggle that modifies the relations between subjects and the productive forces."[51] Two examples of such political-ideological struggles would be, precisely, the critique of private property as the motivating cause that survives at the centre of literary ideology, and the elitist resurgence of the division of labor between the functions of decision and execution at the heart of the party, in the political organization, or in the relations between intellectuals and their allies.

In Argentina, the Maoist experience of which the young Piglia's literary project was a part teaches us that the years immediately prior to the military coup can also be read as a period of crisis for the idea of the organic intellectual. Terán, in *Nuestros años sesentas*, shows how this new type of intellectual had emerged in dialogue with its figuration in the previous decade:

> This description allows one to visualize, first, the figure of the "committed" intellectual, whose predominance in this period should not hide the emergence of the model of the "organic" intellectual. Both types do not necessarily correspond to a temporal sequence, but they can be

---

50. Piglia, "La lucha ideológica," 5–6.
51. Ibid., 6.

superimposed and intertwined, and thus, if the first one speaks to its peers and to society at large while the second rather seeks to address the people or the working class in order to rely on them and to fulfill their mission, between the two structures there appear lines of passage and borrowing which define more complex identities in comparison with those that could be ascribed with greater clarity to one or the other of the purer ideal types.[52]

We can add names to this typology, according to its links with the institutional spaces and theoretical models of two foundational magazines for the history of the 1950s and 1960s in Argentina. Thus, if the group of *Contorno*, with David and Ismael Viñas, Noé Jitrik, and León Rozitchner, among others, represented the ideal of the committed intellectual, following the model of Jean-Paul Sartre in *Les Temps Modernes*, we can identify the idea of the organic intellectual, which is closer to the work of Gramsci, with the group directed by José Aricó around the publishing endeavors of *Pasado y Presente*, the journal and the book series, in Córdoba, Argentina, and later in exile in Mexico.

In his texts and interventions from the period of *Assumed Name*, Piglia adds an important variant to this typology—opening the path to a third, self-critical or split figure of the revolutionary intellectual. In the wider debate about the theme "Intelectuales y revolución: ¿conciencia crítica o conciencia culpable?" ("Intellectuals and Revolution: Critical Consciousness or Guilty Conscience?"), organized in 1971–72 by the Argentine magazine *Nuevos Aires*, a growing tension can be perceived that in my eyes is symptomatic of a deeper falling out between the pronouncements of the young Piglia and the increasingly hostile answers not only of interlocutors such as Jitrik or Rozitchner, but also of militants like José Vazeilles and Mauricio Meinares.

On one hand, Piglia, who in this period was already being presented as the future author of a novel called *Respiración artificial*, insists on something that he also affirms in other forums—namely, the need for the intellectual to link himself through politics to the activism of the masses: "In my opinion, the solution of the problem of intellectuals and the revolution lies in the political realm, in the relation of the intellectual with the revolutionary organizations."[53] Similarly, in a contemporary debate with León Rozitchner and other members of the *Contorno* generation reproduced in *La Voluntad*, Piglia speaks of the field of literature: "The revolutionary writer must unite himself with

---

52. Terán, *Nuestros años sesentas*, 14.
53. Ricardo Piglia, "Intelectuales y revolución: ¿Conciencia crítica o conciencia culpable?," *Nuevos Aires* 6 (1971/72). Without mentioning Piglia's proper name, Sarlo quotes this affirmation, singling out the "exemplary clarity and singular calm" of this view of the leftist intellectual, according to her the "most exasperated" possible, and nowadays utterly "incredible." See Sarlo, "¿La voz universal que toma partido?" in *Tiempo presente: Notas sobre el cambio de una cultura* (Buenos Aires, Siglo Veintiuno, 2001), 206–7. It would not be difficult, of course, to quote even more incredible and exasperated sentences from Sarlo's own Maoist years.

the revolutionary organizations. This is the only way of breaking with the schizophrenia of writer/citizen: bourgeois ideology that recoups a privileged field—literature—as personal product, as private property that one should not socialize."[54] To turn oneself into an organic intellectual, linked to the masses, would then be the only task coherent with the critique of literary ideology. Piglia, like so many intellectuals of his generation, even proposes the construction of a new revolutionary party as the popular instrument for armed struggle: "Nothing can replace the masses as protagonists. The revolution in Argentina depends on the organization of the working class as a revolutionary party, capable of creating the popular army and initiating the war."[55]

On the other hand, however, this model for revolutionary action seems to clash with an insurmountable obstacle, inherent in the class position of the intellectual himself. "What are our essential problems?," Mao had asked rhetorically in Yenan, before responding himself: "In my view, essentially, the problem of serving the people and how to serve the people."[56] Not only does Piglia quote this phrase and others in the same vein, confirming that "to go to the masses, to serve the people, to do productive work, this is for intellectuals both the condition and the outcome of such a point of view" as Mao's; he also, in a text from the late 1960s, anticipates a crucial observation about the ideological struggle in Maoism: "Proposing oneself to go towards the people means, in the end, to confess a bad conscience."[57] To the extent to which he has to go towards the people, the organic intellectual still defines himself by the distance that separates him from them. Only now this distance is no longer the proof of an exceptional destiny, the sign of belonging to a select minority, but rather the mark of a guilty position, the sin of which must be expiated. Bad conscience, as the subjective result of separation, becomes the starting point for the self-critique of the intellectual, who is now supposed to cut the ties that make him an accomplice of the old privileges of his own class. It is this subjective drama that will grant its intriguing intensity to the structure, so deeply split from within, of "Homage to Roberto Arlt."

Even if he accepts the responsibility that comes with his characteristic separation, the intellectual must still confront one last temptation that would paradoxically consist in deflecting his guilt toward a supreme form of good bad conscience. Sartre explains this move very well, speaking of the condition of the intellectual before and after May 1968 in France. Thus, two years before the uprising, he defines the intellectual as a specialist of humanistic knowledge whose commitment

---

54. Piglia, quoted in *La Voluntad*, vol. 1, 498.
55. Ibid.
56. Piglia, "Mao Tse-Tung," 23.
57. Piglia, "La lucha ideológica," 8; and Piglia, quoted in Jorge Fornet, "Un debate de poéticas: Las narraciones de Ricardo Piglia," in *Historia crítica de la literatura argentina*, vol. 11, *La narración gana la partida* (Buenos Aires: Emecé, 2000), 353, n. 12.

inevitably produces a contradiction between the universal goals of his or her search for knowledge and the particular interests that the possession of this knowledge serves. This contradiction between the universal and the particular provokes the typically unhappy conscience of the intellectual that his or her public often interprets as a secret arrogance. The true intellectual, in contrast, takes advantage of this torn nature of his or her being in order to live this bad conscience as the beginning of a possible social consciousness. "The task of the intellectuals," writes Sartre, "consists in living their contradiction *for all* and in overcoming it *for all* thanks to their radicalism (that is, by applying techniques of truth to the lies and the illusions)."[58] After May 1968, however, Sartre begins to glimpse the danger of this programmatic definition for the intellectual. In his interview "L'ami du peuple" ("The People's Friend"), published in 1970, he highlights in particular the risk that the intellectual would become comfortable with his or her unhappy conscience, instead of using it as the jumping-off point for a political intervention. This temptation defines the intellectual that Sartre now denounces as the classical figure: "The classical intellectual," he says with bitter irony, "is the type that derives a good conscience from his bad conscience, thanks to the acts (usually written ones) that the latter allow him to perform in other areas."[59] The only alternative for intellectuals, then, would consist in going against the very foundation of their own existence. "They must suppress themselves as intellectuals," adds Sartre. "Today I understand that the intellectuals cannot remain in the stage of unhappy conscience (idealism, ineffectiveness) but that, in addition, they must attack their very own existence as a problem, or if you prefer, they must negate the *intellectual moment* so as to find a new *popular* status."[60] This is no longer a simple praise of the organic intellectual, but a program for the latter's spectacular self-destitution.

This change of position marks the shift from the classical figure of the committed intellectual, through the bad conscience provoked by the internal division of the latter's organic alliance with the people, toward another figure that we could call self-critical. This is the path that leads Sartre to identify himself with the Maoist line after 1968 in France: "In fact, I followed an evolution that goes from May '68 to my 'entry' in *La Cause du Peuple*. Progressively, I have questioned myself as intellectual. At bottom, I was still a classical intellectual."[61] This is also, I would argue, the context in which figures like Piglia and Sarlo unite themselves around *Los Libros*, as can be read in an editorial from the journal: "It is in this context that we can situate and resolve the problem of science, culture, and intellectuals under socialism, give a

---

58. Jean-Paul Sartre, *Situations VIII* (Paris: Gallimard, 1972), 430.
59. Ibid.
60. Ibid., 467, 343.
61. Ibid., 468.

new dimension and a new foundation to the relations between intellectuals and masses, and create the conditions for overcoming the division between manual and intellectual labor."[62] In its last stage, the journal *Los Libros* in effect proposes a Maoist alternative to projects like those of *Pasado y Presente* and *Contorno*, respectively more linked to Gramsci and to the first Sartre. In the case of Piglia, finally, there is also a biographical note that explains the coincidence with the ideas of Chairman Mao, given that right at the beginning of the period that occupies us, in 1973, the Argentine writer took a trip to China. To a large extent, then, the results of this visit are those that he elaborates both in the essays from *Los Libros* and in the final story from *Assumed Name*.

The Dialectic of Bad Conscience

Of all mistakes, that of good faith is no doubt the most unforgivable.
Jacques Lacan, Écrits

In order to return to "Homenaje a Roberto Arlt," or, better yet, in order to show that in reality we have never left its setting, I wonder why this story—like so many of the author's—has such a strong theatrical character. After the Maoist legacy, this question leads us to what is, without a doubt, the most Brechtian aspect of Piglia's work. In *Assumed Name*, the author not only quotes a line from Brecht that he will subsequently re-use as an epigraph for *Money to Burn*: "What is robbing a bank compared with founding it?"[63] But it is also remarkable to see how easily various parts of *Assumed Name*, without major changes, could be put on the stage. We know, after all, that its author has also made adaptations for film and opera, respectively, of *Money to Burn* and *The Absent City*, not to mention the screenplays, like *Foolish Heart*, for Héctor Babenco. It is evident, then, that there is something intimate that ties Piglia's work to the world of theater and the audiovisual spectacle—in particular, I would say, through the technique of melodrama.

"Luba," the supposedly unpublished Arlt story that in reality is a plagiarized version of Andreyev's "Darkness," offers an extraordinary summary of this melodramatic vision, which could also be used to read the stories related in the first part of "Homage to Roberto Arlt." All these in principle propose the restricted frame of an uneven struggle between two people, in order to see how they mutually transform each other. This structure brings to mind one of the notes attributed to Arlt: "A theme: the pure man and the evil woman in an extreme situation.

---

62. Beatriz Sarlo, Carlos Altamirano, and Ricardo Piglia, "Editorial," in *China después de la revolución cultural*, special issue of *Los Libros* 35 (1974): 3.
63. Piglia, *Assumed Name*, 97.

Enclosed: see how they change, transform."[64] In the case of Enrique and Luba, the conflict is between a revolutionary anarchist and a young prostitute whom he pretends to liberate, but there is a similar duality that marks the criminal story of Lettif and Rinaldi, as well as the struggle for prestige between Kostia and Piglia: "The principal sense of the first part must be: instinctive consciousness of superiority."[65] In all these pairs, as I have pointed out, there is a strong hierarchical division between the good man and the evil woman, between the one who conceives of the perfect crime and the one who executes it, between the professional editor and his imperfect imitation in the drunk poet—or, more generally, between a pure person and the poor victim to whom the former pretends to extend his help in good will. It seems to me that these divisions stage not only the relationship between the writer and his surroundings, but also the position of any intellectual before the masses. Both relationships, then, are subjected to an immanent critique against the superiority of the lettered.

The problem of the superiority of good conscience is foregrounded in Enrique's first reflections, when he enters Luba's room: "He looks around him, full of compassion for the young woman. Everything seems sordid to him; he thinks sadly that this is life and that there are people who live among these things for years and years."[66] This young anarchist thinks in the best tradition of the "beautiful souls" described by Hegel or Lacan. He glorifies himself because of his own good intentions, the purity of which is in reality nothing more than an imaginary reflection of the ugliness of the world that surrounds him. Faced with this anarchist's attitude, the offended prostitute does not delay in responding, as she becomes upset and slaps him in the face: "Coward, son of a bitch," she says, leaning towards him. "You came to make fun of me, so I'd see how good you were. Tell me what you want to do with me? Oh, I am such a wretch. And you dare, to me, you dare, you the pure one, to me who has possessed all the men, all of them. Aren't you ashamed of humiliating a poor woman?"[67] Luba rejects the proud gesture that she detects behind the extended hand. The kindness of her most recent arrival seems shameful to her: "I told you: it's shameful to be good. Didn't you know?"; and she adds: "Yes, my little tiger, it's shameful: it's a betrayal."[68] Behind the gift of total dedication and commitment, she perceives a perverse calculation destined to increase the prestige of the revolutionary hero, while it is precisely the treasure of this inalienable prestige that an authentic revolutionary should be the first to give up. Or better yet, the first thing that any subject of

---

64. Ibid., 107.
65. Ibid., 98.
66. Ibid., 140.
67. Ibid., 141.
68. Ibid., 145.

social change should abandon are the false guarantees of his or her own authenticity.

Here are Luba's reflections in greater detail:

> I just realized it. "What does he want to do?" I thought. "He wants to give me his innocence." And you? You must have thought: "I'll give her this gift and she'll leave me alone." How ingenious, Holy Mary! At first I felt insulted; I thought that you had done it because you're convinced that you are good. You make a simple calculation: "I'm going to sacrifice my purity and with that I will become even more pure." It's like having a gold coin, which can be exchanged; it's eternal and it's always worth the same. You can give it to the beggars, to the poor, but at the end it always returns to your pocket. No, dear, it won't work, I know what I'm saying.[69]

Luba shows an extremely sharp sense of what we might call the economy of revolutionary morality. What is at stake is the surreptitious exchange, which in spite of everything is profoundly unequal, between that which the rebel pretends to give and that which he gets in return. Luba insists on the falseness of this trade-off, denouncing the betrayal it hides and comparing it with the worst paternalism and its baggage of religious pretexts:

> I am not that stupid. I've already seen these kind of merchants: they pile up millions with all the injustices and then they give ten cents to the poor and they think that they've saved their soul. No dear, you have to build the church yourself. Your innocence is not worth anything; you offer it to me because you don't need it; it's worn out, full of filth.[70]

According to Luba, the true attitude for the anarchist would consist in giving that which he would not want to lose under any circumstances. This would be a truly revolutionary act, as opposed to the false appearances that the young anarchist pretends to give her: "You give what has no value. No, dear: give me what is the most valuable. Let's see if you're capable of that: give me, whatever it is, without which you could not live."[71] As long as there is no such act properly speaking, the relationship between the pure man and the evil woman will remain locked in the inertia of a melodramatic non-rapport.

Indeed, what does every melodrama offer if it is not an imaginary conflict between a good conscience and the unjust state of affairs with which, in spite of its pureness or even because of it, this conscience is incapable of engaging? As Althusser writes in *For Marx*, melodrama stages the vacillations of a borrowed conscience. It pretends to bring popular sentiments to the theater, even to elevate them by granting them a higher intellectual and artistic level, but at bottom it continues

---

69. Ibid., 145–6.
70. Ibid., 144.
71. Ibid.

to recognize itself as profoundly distinct from the plebs, whom it evokes with such feigned enthusiasm.

Enrique believes that in the prostitute he has found someone from the lower classes, from the lumpen, both victim of economic exploitation and object of physical and moral degradation. Like Rodolphe in *Les Mystères de Paris*, by Eugène Sue—the master of melodramas whom Kostia quotes in his conversation with Piglia (speaking of "Edgar Sue": another false name? A mixture of Eugène Sue with Edgar Allen Poe, the melodrama and the detective novel as two fundamental matrices to think politics?)—he wants to show himself as being compassionate with the lower classes, making himself one with their poorest and most sordid part. Of course, "Rodolphe neither comes from the 'people,' nor is he 'innocent,'" and no doubt we can say the same of Enrique: "But (naturally) he wants to 'save' the people, to teach them that they have souls, that God exists, etc.—in other words, whether they will or no he gives them bourgeois morality to parrot so as to keep them quiet."[72] The problem is that the intention to "save" the people or to "go to the people," whenever it serves only to leave the intellectual with a tranquil conscience, if not also to lend this good conscience to the people themselves, cancels out the good will that the intellectual vindicates with a fervor proportional to the bad faith that is thus compensated. As Althusser warns elsewhere, "Now there is no other way for an intellectual 'to be of the people' than to become 'people,' through the practical experience of the struggle of that people."[73] Except that even this attempt runs the risk of increasing the level of bad conscience in the exact measure that it seeks to negate it. This is the risk that we have encountered, expressed in different words, in Piglia's critique of the organic intellectual. Those words now sound like a direct echo of Althusser's commentary on Eugène Sue:

> One makes oneself "one of the people" by flirtatiously being above its own methods; that is why it is essential to play at being (not being) the people that one forces the people to be, the people of popular "myth," people with a flavor of melodrama. This melodrama is not worthy of the stage (the real, theatrical stage). It is savoured in small sips in the cabaret.[74]

Is this not the melodrama of Enrique's flirtation with the people and the lumpen in Luba's room?

Luba, however, continues to reject this false relationship with Enrique. In everything she says to her supposed benefactor, beginning with her response to the betrayal that, according to her, hides behind the pretense of a tranquil conscience, she echoes a personal resolution that we also find in the diary of Lettif: "Not to do anything clean or

72. Louis Althusser, "The 'Piccolo Teatro,'" in *For Marx*, 138, n. 4. See also Chapter 2.
73. Louis Althusser, "On Marx and Freud," in *Writings on Psychoanalysis*, 112.
74. Althusser, "The 'Piccolo Teatro,'" 139, n. 4 (translation modified).

hygienic: cleanliness and hygiene are not from this world."[75] Only a
beautiful soul aspires to have clean hands, situating itself in a fantasy
far removed from this filthy world. In doing so, it loses the possibility
of approximating even the smallest truth, not only about the conflicts
that this world obviously encloses, but also about the chains that these
same conflicts project onto the innermost core of its own subjectivity.
Luba, in contrast, as if to rely on some kind of proverbial knowledge,
proposes an imperative of modesty to Enrique: "When truth approaches
you, you have to greet it with humility."[76] This could be a guideline,
even in its very style, copied from one of Mao's maxims: "Every revolutionary worker should be modest, because modesty is a virtue that is
beneficial to the cause of the people."[77] Only a melodramatic vision
can offset the law of the heart of a revolutionary anarchist with the
sordid and degraded world of an impoverished prostitute. Luba herself,
by attacking Enrique, incarnates the first critique of this melodrama
that is the dialectic of the good bad conscience.

Enrique does not take long to learn his lesson: "And he, calm like a
stone upon which life has just spit a new and terrible command,
answers: 'I don't want to be pure.'"[78] Once again it is as if we were
listening to Mao himself: "It is not necessary to be absolutely and
completely 'pure.' Those who have made mistakes too can take part in
work groups, on one hand, in order to facilitate their re-education and
transformation, and on the other, in order to allow that some of them
have a wider understanding of the movement and thus convert themselves into good militants."[79] In the case that concerns us, it is the
anarchist militant himself who seems to initiate a violent process of
re-education and self-criticism: "His will is affirmed in his devastated
soul: he feels capable of demolishing everything and starting anew."[80]
Enrique thus sets in motion a devastating critique and transformation
of the old in favor of the new. The first thing to go in this self-critical
process is the premise of the pure soul imagining that its life alone is
beautiful: "My life was beautiful. It was pure and passionate, my life.
It was like a beautiful crystal glass. But, look: he throws it on the

75. Piglia, *Assumed Name*, 104.
76. Ibid., 145 (translation modified).
77. Mao, quoted in Bettelheim and Collotti Pischel, *La revolución cultural china*, 224.
About his anarchist friends, Enrique also says the following: "I have realized now that they
are not pure: what they do is fight so that the world can be pure and good like a newborn
baby" (*Assumed Name*, 153). I should add, however, that Maoism itself has been interpreted
as precisely such a movement that risks falling in the traps of the beautiful soul. As Guy
Lardreau writes in *L'Ange: Ontologie de la révolution* (Paris: Bernard Grasset, 1976): "The
soul of the Cultural revolution is the 'beautiful soul' as Lacan describes it after Hegel: by
assuming what it knows to be its own folly in the eyes of the world, it also knows that this is
the wisdom of the other, and that it is this world, in fact, that is foolish" (96).
78. Piglia, *Assumed Name*, 149.
79. Mao, quoted in Bettelheim and Collotti Pischel, *La revolución cultural china*, 204.
80. Piglia, *Assumed Name*, 151.

ground."[81] Only a complete breaking-away from his old self—to the point that he speaks of himself in the third person—seems capable of producing the "new man" in Enrique.

On this subject, the story "Luba" proposes a militant didacticism, as if to follow the guidelines of Brecht's new theatre, all the while proclaiming a doctrine similar to Mao's. Enrique, in particular, seems to hear a distant voice that says to him: "How can you doubt that this is the doctrine? For, who is going to make the social revolution if not the prostitutes, the swindlers, the wretched, the murderers, the frauds, all the bastards who suffer below without any hope? Or do you believe that the revolution will be made by the pen-pushers and the shopkeepers?"[82] It fits to compare this doctrine from *Assumed Name* with Mao's version, quoted by Piglia in his second essay for *Los Libros*: "It is the peasants themselves who installed the idols and they, when the moment comes, will bring them down with their own hands; it is not necessary that others do this in their name before this time"; or to use an even more melodramatic variant: "It belongs to the peasants themselves to throw down the idols and destroy the temples to the virgin martyrs and the commemorative arches in honor of the chaste and loyal widows: *it is a mistake for others to do this for them.*"[83] In the case of Enrique, this doctrine still appears with all of the characteristic traits of the voice of conscience, like a calling in his inner self that imposes a ferocious categorical imperative. The story's whole logic, however, revolves around the destruction of individual conscience as such a superegoic point of reference of modern bourgeois morality, surviving even in the midst of the revolutionary ideology.

The strong didacticism of "Homage to Roberto Arlt," which expresses itself with greatest clarity in the story "Luba," has immediate consequences for the role of the critic and the writer. Piglia's aim, once again following the lessons of Maoism, seems to be to destroy the subjective and moralizing criteria with which the intellectual's commitment still tends to define itself: "Mao discredits all voluntarism of the subject (in the manner of Sartrean commitment) and lays the ground for a definition of the relations between literature and revolution in terms of a specific practice with its own connections to ideology and politics within the social structure."[84] It is necessary to rethink the articulation between the three fronts of economics, politics, and culture. Being neither voluntarist nor deterministic, neither subjectivist nor economistic, it is the structure of the class struggle, much more so than

81. Ibid., 151–2.
82. Ibid., 154.
83. Ibid., 98. Curiously, Piglia's own version, quoted in "La lucha ideológica en la construcción socialista," seems less appropriate for the purposes of *Assumed Name*, insofar as it says "in their place" instead of "in their name" (8).
84. Piglia, "Mao Tse-Tung," 23.

the subject's vacillations or the fatality of his class origins, that defines the political character of any literary project. Speaking of popular literature, for example, Piglia suggests that this form "advances in relation to the struggle of the masses and not because of the (good) 'will' of a few isolated writers to reach out to the masses."[85]

There is one figure of the intellectual, in particular, that seems to unite much good will with the bad conscience caused by his separation on the margins of society: the figure of the *poète maudit* as absolute rebel. Piglia, in several of his texts from the 1970s, sets up a combative critique of precisely such politico-literary "Robinsonism," tracing its brief genealogy only in order then to discard it completely, because it would facilitate the idea of an imaginary destruction of bourgeois values, without really abandoning its humanist heritage:

> Faced with the progressive commodification of aesthetics the writer denies the process as a whole: he withdraws himself, tends to consider himself as being ever more separate from society, and thinks of himself as a marginalized individual, that is, free from all social bonds. Inverting the bourgeois ideology without negating it, he takes refuge in an ideal liberty: cut loose in the imaginary from all social relations, he wagers everything on the "human," "expressive" qualities of his work.[86]

Behind this supposed negation, not only is the figure of the beautiful soul cut off from the world around it, but what is more, the politico-economical foundation is also still kept in place that identifies value and rarefication. Property as a basis for the evaluation of the individual ultimately is not put in question. For this reason, the Left's self-criticism must also take apart the whole ideology of the writer as a wild and marginal, eternally misunderstood rebel:

> I mean, we should oppose the petit-bourgeois illusion of "Robinsonism" that tries to define production in individual terms, making of the intellectual (of his "commitment," of his "sincerity") the scene of the whole problem. To decenter this question and to put the class struggle at the heart of the debate means at this point to confront a deep-seated tradition in the criticism of the Left which made us accustomed to see in the texts—instead of a symptom or a network of relations—the result of a free and elected decision, whereby the critic and the writer fought privately over the reason and the place of "meaning."[87]

In this rejection of "commitment" or "sincerity" as the supposed place of inscription of the subject in politics, we can thus discover a much wider process of criticism of the idea of conscience, or consciousness (*conciencia* in Spanish), as an instantaneous gift.

As we read in a note attributed to Arlt, "Capitalism speculates on

---

85. Ibid., 24.
86. Piglia, "Notas sobre Brecht," 8.
87. Piglia, "Hacia la crítica," 7.

good sentiments."[88] In order to avoid the sentimental drama of good
bad conscience, it is still necessary to overcome one last danger that has
to do with the place of the critic, or of the spectator, given that we are
dealing with such a highly theatrical situation. Piglia, as we saw, seems
to adhere to the Maoist doctrine: "Nobody can be the depository of the
consciousness of the masses, because they themselves must learn to
recognize what is just and what is not; nobody can act in their place,
because they must liberate themselves"; or, to put it in another way:
"Maoism denies . . . the false truth with which the unhappy conscience
of revolutionary thinking was covered up."[89] We also saw, however,
that this doctrine implies that no conscience, perhaps not even that
which from the outside lends itself to the masses, can be the absolute
depository of truth, because conscience defines precisely the ground on
which those values of bourgeois thought are erected whose destruction
is sought.

In "Homage to Roberto Arlt," therefore, none of the characters can
really be the proprietor of the meaningfulness of his or her own acts. In
this sense, we can apply to Piglia's story what Althusser writes about
Brecht:

> For him (I am still discussing the "great plays"), no character consciously
> contains in himself the totality of the tragedy's conditions. For him, the
> total, transparent consciousness of self, the mirror of the whole drama is
> never anything but an image of the ideological consciousness, which does
> include the whole world in its own tragedy, save only that this world is
> merely the world of morals, politics and religion, in short, of myths and
> drugs. In this sense these plays are decentred precisely because they can have
> no centre, because, although the illusion-wrapped, naïve consciousness is his
> starting-point, Brecht refuses to make it that centre of the world it would
> like to be.[90]

In Enrique's case, only a distant voice allows him to draw the didactic
lesson from his discussion with Luba. But then, no matter how correct
his conclusion is, he has already converted himself into his own spectator, having fallen into the ideological trap that his moral conscience
tends for him.

It is at this point that Piglia's doctrine about the political and ideological struggle defined by Mao, because of an internal necessity,
requires the new theatrical techniques of Brecht. I am thinking, of
course, of the technique of alienation, or dis-identification, as a

---

88. Piglia, *Assumed Name*, 97. This could be a plagiarism of Marx: "Just as industry
     speculates on the refinement of needs, so too it speculated on their crudity. But the crudity
     on which it speculates is artificially produced, and its true manner of enjoyment is therefore
     self-stupefaction, this apparent satisfaction of need, this civilization within the crude
     barbarism of need," *Economic and Philosophic Manuscripts (1844)*, in Karl Marx, *Early
     Writings*, trans. Rodney Livingston and Gregor Benton (London: Penguin, 1992), 363.
89. Mao, quoted in *La revolución cultural china*, 9–10, 8.
90. Althusser, "The 'Piccolo Teatro,'" 144–5.

decentering of all classical aesthetics. Piglia undoes any possibility for the reader or spectator of identifying himself with a central figure in his stories. Not only is there no centre of consciousness among his characters, but we are also incapable of transferring this centre to the place where we are, as critics or spectators. Ludmer, in her response to the questionnaire in *Los Libros*, had already drawn our attention to this danger: "To refuse to write 'literature' but to continue writing 'criticism' implies withdrawing the former from bourgeois thought but leaving the latter well anchored in it."[91] No one, in other words, can come to fill the empty place of that absolute instance that would hold the truth of the entire situation. Otherwise, the spectator or the critic would give to themselves the privilege of lucidity taken away from the piece they are discussing: "On the stage the image of blindness—in the stalls the image of lucidity—led to consciousness by two hours of unconsciousness. But this division of roles amounts to conceding to the house what has been rigorously excluded from the stage. Really, the spectator has no claim to this absolute consciousness of self which the play cannot tolerate."[92] The critics or spectators are, like the characters, also prisoners of the myth of conscience and its ideological lucubrations.

Here, then, is a possible answer to the question with which we began: Why must there necessarily be a blind spot in the structure of "Homage to Roberto Arlt"? Far from hiding a secret that only a future vanguard reader could decipher, this blind point is precisely the void that allows us to take apart the illusions on which rests the notion of representing a vanguard consciousness, whether in art or in politics. Blindness, then, becomes the starting point for the progressive self-division of any unitary principle of subjectivity. The secret is that there is no secret: thanks to this blank space, the story acquires its narrative effectiveness. In all rigor, the story does not unveil anything but the nothingness that renders visible the false totality of existing ideologies. From there springs the idea that such emptiness can operate as an absent cause whose effects determine the entire structure of the story. The enigma, in other words, functions like an inexhaustible stimulus for the self-criticism of the superiority of consciousness. Better yet, far from inviting an interpretation, the secret imposes the task of a forceful re-education of the intellectual.

Instead of being restricted to purely literary questions about originality, the cult of genius, or the modern invention of the rights of the author, the problematic of plagiarism according to Piglia contains a series of concepts and doctrines—the beautiful soul, purity, sincerity, the abolition of the new and the persistence of the old, good faith and bad conscience, the logic of melodrama, and so on—that, in reality,

91. Ludmer, "Hacia la crítica," 5.
92. Althusser, "The 'Piccolo Teatro,'" 148.

can be read as responses to a question about literature and politics that still remains open in the post-Leninist sequence, the sequence that begins with the closing and the exhaustion of the form of the party and its premise, which consists in standing at the vanguard of consciousness. Like Enrique, it seems that the intellectual must take advantage of the vanishing point of his good bad conscience in order to free himself of everything that separates him from the masses. In order to lose everything that he really has never had, this is his only means of tying himself to those that do not have anything to lose, except their chains, and a whole world to win. "Do you believe in me?" Luba asks Enrique. And he responds: "Yes, because it is only possible to believe in those who have nothing to lose."[93]

---

93. Piglia, *Assumed Name*, 154.

8

BETWEEN FREUD AND
A NAKED WOMAN

Setting the Stage

So please, therapists and analysts, since she is not castrated, even though she may be unsure of her rights and abilities, don't you castrate her.
Marie Langer, From Vienna to Managua: Journey of a Psychoanalyst

In January of 2001, theater-goers in Mexico City were treated to a "scene" worthy of Charcot's notorious seances with hysterics at the Salpêtrière in Paris: On the stage, a young woman called "Dora" is lying naked on an operating table, flanked by two characters called Sigmund Freud and Lou Andreas-Salomé, both of them fully dressed—when the latter announces in an aside to the audience that the doctor has decided to perform "major surgery" and is preparing his symbolical scalpel to "castrate" his patient: "If the illness of the independent woman is an imaginary phallus, we must cut off the phallus."[1] The scene, in which Freud struggles with a woman still boldly talking back at him, even though she now finds herself exposed in the utmost vulnerability of her naked body, comes toward the end of *Feliz nuevo siglo doktor Freud* (*Happy New Century, Doctor Freud*), itself a dramatic rewriting of the famous case of Freud's Dora by the Mexican playwright, journalist, producer, and psychologist by training, Sabina Berman. Directed by Sandra Félix, with superb stage design by Philippe Amand, the play at the time of its opening featured Ricardo Blume in the role of Sigmund Freud, Marina de Tavira as Dora (as well as both Anna Freud and Gloria, described in the stage directions as a 1970s-type feminist, dressed in black and with short hair—I will return to this combination of roles in a single actor, which is the exact opposite of the reduplication of actors for one character that happens in the case of

---

1. Sabina Berman, *Feliz nuevo siglo doktor Freud* (Mexico City: Ediciones El Milagro/ Conaculta, 2001), 65. The play premiered in November 2000 but its longest run, at the Teatro Orientación, started in January 2001. For brief analyses, see Emily Hind, "Hablando histéricamente: La ciencia de la locura en *Feliz nuevo siglo doktor Freud* de Sabina Berman y *Nadie me verá llorar* de Cristina Rivera Garza," *Literatura mexicana* 17 (2006): 147–67; and Nuria Ibáñez, "Sabina Berman y *Feliz nuevo siglo, Doktor Freud*: reivindicación escénica del padre del psicoanálisis," *Revista de literatura mexicana contemporánea* 48 (2011): 69–78.

Freud), Juan Carlos Beyer as Freud 2 (also Herr K. and Otto Rank), Enrique Singer as Freud 3 (also Herr F., a railway worker, and Carl Gustav Jung), and Lisa Owen as Lou Andreas Salomé (also Frau K., Martha Freud, Frau F., Dora as adult, and Ernest Jones).

Berman thus proposes to enter the twenty-first century with a salute to the founder of psychoanalysis. "Feliz nuevo siglo, doktor Freud" is a phrase that in the play is attributed to Dora, at the crucial moment when she abruptly breaks off her treatment with Freud (historically speaking this would have been in December 1900, but once the phrase becomes the title of the play, it can obviously be interpreted as coming from Sabina Berman as well, one hundred years later), just as Freud himself had entered the twentieth century still carrying with him his unpublished "Fragment of an Analysis of a Case of Hysteria." Dora's clinical case history was not officially published until 1905, even though for the most part it was completed in January 1901, and Freud himself describes it as a "continuation" of the 1900 text *The Interpretation of Dreams*—to this day, perhaps, still the single most important founding document for the larger clinical and theoretical project in the history of psychoanalysis.[2] Berman's play, I might add, went on to an enormously successful commercial run in Mexico, and has since been performed abroad as well, including in the United States and Colombia.

An Other Scene

> From Politzer, who talks of "drama" to Freud and Lacan who speak of theatre, stage, mise en scène, machinery, theatrical genre, metteur en scène, etc., there is all the distance between the spectator who takes himself for the theatre—and the theatre itself.
>
> Louis Althusser, "Freud and Lacan"

A series of questions immediately emerge: Why Freud? Why put Freud on stage? Why do so through his only extended case history devoted to a woman, whose real name, we have since found out, was Ida Bauer? And, above all: Why do so now? Or rather, why now, *again*?

Berman is certainly not the first playwright to put Freud on stage, nor is she by any means the only one to do so in Latin America. In Buenos Aires, to give only one example, there is also the case of Juan Pablo Feinman's *Sabor a Freud* (*A Taste of Freud*), which in fact does not present Freud on stage, but a certain Doctor Kovacs, the voice of scientific psychoanalytic reason against the passion of the tropical

---

2. See Sigmund Freud, *Dora: An Analysis of a Case of Hysteria*, ed. Philip Rieff (New York: Simon & Schuster, 1997). For the present reflections, I have also consulted the orthodox Spanish edition, *Obras completas*, ed. James Strachey with Anna Freud, vol. 7, trans. José L. Etcheverry (Buenos Aires: Amorrortu, 1975). For Strachey's notes and timeline of the case, see "Editor's Note," in Sigmund Freud, *The Standard Edition of the Complete Psychological Works of Sigmund Freud*, trans. James Strachey (London: The Hogarth Press, 1953), vol. 7, 3–6.

bolero singer Lucía Espinosa.[3] And this is if we only think of recent examples: were we to look further back, we could quote the example of Arturo Capdevila's 1946 *Consumación de Sigmund Freud* (*Sigmund Freud's Termination*).[4] Furthermore, neither is Berman's play the first one to attempt a feminist reinterpretation of Dora for the stage. Hélène Cixous, most famously, also wrote a play on the same case, *Portrait of Dora*—an adaptation which itself became something of a classic in discussions of French feminism, especially when read in conjunction with the dialogue between Cixous and Catherine Clément as part of their manifesto-like work, *La jeune née* (*The Newly Born Woman*), in which the two theorists argue over some of the case's most stubborn and still unanswered questions.[5] It is even possible—perfectly likely, in fact—that Gloria, the 1970s-style feminist portrayed by Berman, is a direct allusion to figures such as Cixous. In Mexico, finally, *Feliz nuevo siglo doktor Freud*, interestingly enough, was only one in a series of plays that sought to enter the twentieth-first century with an homage, no matter how critical or ironic, to the founder of psychoanalysis. Thus, aside from Berman's restaging of Dora, audiences in Mexico City were also given a chance to see at least two other performances with Freud as their protagonist: we had Carmen Boullosa and Jesusa Rodríguez's 2000 farce *Los hijos de Freud* (*The Children of Freud*) and, shortly thereafter, Ignacio Solares's 2002 *La moneda de oro* (*The Golden Coin*), which confronts Freud with Carl Gustav Jung.[6] Most

---

3. Juan Pablo Feinman, *Sabor a Freud* (Buenos Aires: Norma, 2002).

4. Arturo Capdevila, *Consumación de Sigmund Freud* (Buenos Aires: Sudamericana, 1946). This play is briefly mentioned in Mariano Ben Plotkin's now standard reference work for the history of psychoanalysis in Argentina, *Freud in the Pampas: The Emergence and Development of a Psychoanalytic Culture in Argentina* (Stanford: Stanford University Press, 2001), 58.

5. Hélène Cixous, *Portrait de Dora* (Paris: Des Femmes, 1976). This play is translated as "Portrait of Dora," trans. Sarah Burd, *Diacritics* 13 (1983): 2–32. This special issue of *Diacritics*, titled *A Fine Romance: Freud and Dora* and guest-edited by Neil Hertz, is obviously worth taking up in its entirety. See also Catherine Clément and Hélène Cixous, *La jeune née* (Paris: 10/18, 1975); and *The Newly Born Woman*, trans. Betsy Wing (Minneapolis: University of Minnesota Press, 1986). For the larger context of Dora's feminist reception, see the collection of essays edited by Charles Bernheimer and Claire Kahane, *In Dora's Case: Freud–Hysteria–Feminism*, 2nd edn (New York: Columbia University Press, 1990).

6. Cf. Jacqueline E. Bixler, "Sexo, poder y palabras en *Feliz nuevo siglo, Doktor Freud y 65 contratos para hacer el amor*," in Jacqueline E. Bixler, ed., *Sediciosas seducciones: Sexo, poder y palabras en el teatro de Sabina Berman* (Mexico City: Escenología, 2004), 69, n. 2. Carmen Boullosa and Jesusa Rodríguez's hilarious play, in which Dr. Freud shares the stage with Dr. Scholl, Ana, Sofía and Ernesto Zedillo, has been published as "Los hijos de Freud (*Pastorela inconsciente*)," *Debate feminista* 37 (April 2008): 301–16. For a comparison with *Feliz nuevo siglo doktor Freud*, see Jacqueline E. Bixler, "El sexo de la política y la política del sexo en dos obras 'freudianas' de Sabina Berman y Jesusa Rodríguez," *Teatro XXI* 8 (2002): 8–11. A bilingual edition of Ignacio Solares's play has appeared as *The Gold Coin: Freud or Jung?/La moneda de oro: Freud o Jung?*, trans. Amy Pesola and Timothy Compton (Mexico City: Solar/Ediciones del Ermitaño, 2004). For a brief study, see Rosa María Farfán, "El pensamiento de Carl Gustav Jung en algunas obras de Ignacio Solares," *Revista de*

recently, in October 2009, the Argentine-Mexican psychoanalyst, play-wright, and actor Susana Bercovitch presented her multimedia work *El cuadro (The Tableau)*, devoted to the case of Herbert Graf, better known as the subject of Freud's clinical history of "little Hans."[7] The real question then becomes: What makes Berman's reworking of Dora stand out from these other theatrical elaborations of Freud and psycho-analysis? In what consists the singularity of *Feliz nuevo siglo doktor Freud*?

While answering this last question, it is important to resist a common temptation among interpreters of the Dora case and its successors both on stage and in theory—that is, the temptation to let oneself be drawn back constantly into Freud's original text, "Fragment of an Analysis of a Case of Hysteria," so as either to attribute to one of its many inheri-tors that which is already a feature of the clinical history itself, or else to use the subsequent adaptation only as a springboard for returning to a discussion of Freud's theories. Therefore, if in this chapter I will briefly touch upon questions regarding the theory and practice of psychoanalysis such as the questions of transference and counter-trans-ference, or emancipation and adaptation, I will do so only to the extent that Berman's play and it alone adds new insights to the treatment they have already received elsewhere. At the same time, I would argue that no history of psychoanalysis in Latin America could be complete, if in fact it can ever be, without taking into account these creative—fictive or artistic—developments, beyond the clinical and institutional settings in the strict sense. Such reworkings not only actualize the literary potential already present in Freud's original text—a potential of which Freud himself was well aware, and even proud, despite the disavowals contained in several footnotes and self-reflective asides in Dora's writ-ten case-history; they also allow for speculative elaborations that a purely clinical or theoretical approach might not be able to accomplish with the same ease.

Intervening Doctrines of the Subject

The title I have chosen for this chapter refers not only to a dramatic scene toward the end of *Feliz nuevo siglo doktor Freud*. It can also be read as a triangular composition in which the relations between Freud and Dora, as well as that between Freud and Berman, are mediated by the visible-invisible presence of Marx and Marxism. "Between Freud and a Naked Woman," indeed, is a wordplay on what is perhaps Berman's most successful theater (and later film) production, *Entre*

literatura mexicana contemporánea 19 (2003): 99–104.

7. In addition to Freud's clinical history, Susana Bercovich also relies heavily on François Dachet's book about the historical figure of "little Hans," *L'innocence violée? Le Petit Hans Herbert Graf: Devenir metteur en scène d'opéra* (Paris: L'Unebévue, 2008).

Villa y una mujer desnuda (*Between Villa and a Naked Woman*), itself in turn a diversion (in the sense of a situationist *détournement*) of the title of Jorge Enrique Adoum's experimental "boom" novel *Entre Marx y una mujer desnuda* (*Between Marx and a Naked Woman*).[8] I would thus propose as a larger working hypothesis that we read *Feliz nuevo siglo doktor Freud* from the point of view of the history and theory of what in Latin America, too, has been the long and difficult course of Freudo-Marxism—provided of course that we come to a clear understanding of how this uncanny coupling can be meaningful to begin with.

The point is certainly not to complement Freud's allegedly "individualist" (or at best only familial) perspective with Marx's "social" (or collective) one. Nor is it to oppose, in a combination of stereotypes, the latter's "economism" to the former's "pansexualism." To a large extent this is how the Chilean playwright Marco Antonio de la Parra, for example, stages the war of words between "Carlos" and "Sigmund," the two characters in his hilarious play *La secreta obscenidad de cada día* who may, or may not, be the same as their historical equivalents, but who might also be using the latter's names as pseudonyms in the play, either because they are planning a terrorist attack on the government official visiting a local high school or because they are two pedophiles lying in wait for the schoolgirls to come out, in which case their similar trenchcoats would be hiding something other than a pistol:

> SIGMUND: Look, mister, for your information . . . we all have neuroses . . .
>   All of us!
> CARLOS: Of course we do, as a clear consequence of social development,
>   of the society in which we live . . .
> SIGMUND: Don't make me laugh, whatever determines the presence of
>   neurosis in the individual is the sexual history of each one.
> CARLOS: Not at all, it is a matter of social development.
> SIGMUND: Sexual history, I say!
> CARLOS: Social development!
> SIGMUND: Sexual![9]

All of which culminates, a short while later, in the following exchange of insults:

---

8. See Sabina Berman, *Entre Villa y una mujer desnuda*, which premiered in 1993, and is included in the anthology *Puro teatro* (Mexico City: Fondo de Cultura Económica, 2004), 157–210; Jorge Enrique Adoum, *Entre Marx y una mujer desnuda: Texto con personajes* (Mexico City: Siglo XXI, 1976). As will be clear from previous chapters, my general working hypothesis is enormously indebted to thinkers such as José Revueltas in Mexico and León Rozitchner in Argentina. See Chapters 2 to 5 for further discussion. See also Plotkin's chapter, "When Marx Meets Freud," in Plotkin, *Freud in the Pampas*, 166–90.

9. Marco Antonio de la Parra, *La secreta obscenidad de cada día* (Barcelona: Planeta, 1988), 75–6.

CARLOS: Shut up, you elitist!

SIGMUND: Bolshevik!

CARLOS: Metaphysician!

SIGMUND: Bureaucrat!

CARLOS: Bearded individualist!

SIGMUND: Ugly collectivist!

CARLOS: You despise the power of the masses!

SIGMUND: What advantage do you obtain if you absolutely ignore man's deepest secrets!

CARLOS: Vain! Paranoid! Megalomaniac!

SIGMUND: Narcissist! Egotist! Egocentric!

. . .

CARLOS: Don't talk to me, you know? Don't talk to me . . . I never want to hear from you again, I who thought that we would make a nice couple like O'Higgins and San Martín . . . Like Sacco and Vanzetti . . . like Don Quixote and Sancho . . .

SIGMUND: (sardonic) Like Marx and Engels, no?

CARLOS: Yes, exactly, something like that . . .

SIGMUND: We would have been more like Laurel and Hardy, like Tom and Jerry![10]

One of the reasons why this exchange leads to an extremely comic effect that borders on the grotesque is because its underlying oppositions are misleadingly caricatured and—as is only to be expected in the genre of comedy—based on stereotypes. In any attempt to forge a combination of Freudo-Marxism, the issue is certainly not to couple the psychic and the social into a neat relation of complementarity, but rather to understand how both Marx and Freud are founders of a discourse, whether political or clinical, that is of the order of an intervening doctrine of the subject.

In fact, Freud's radical innovation with regard to the treatment of cases of hysteria such as Dora's consists not only in the power to listen to that which usually falls on deaf ears, but in asserting that in some way there is a truth that speaks through that hysteric young woman with whom fin-de-siècle Vienna prefers to have no dealings whatsoever, except as a pathology to be brought back as quickly and effortlessly as possible into the fold of normality. This truth, in turn, is universal. It is the truth of desire—desire in a universal sense, and not just of the hysteric, even though the hysteric constitutes the absolutely singular and symptomatic site of its appearance. How does this connection between the singular and the universal—between Dora's "case" and the generic "truth" that speaks through her—fare in Berman's treatment of Freud for the stage?

---

10. Ibid., 108–10.

Embodying Transference

The first structural innovation that strikes the viewer of *Feliz nuevo siglo doktor Freud*, in comparison with Freud's original "Fragment of an Analysis of a Case of Hysteria," is due to the inclusion of additional characters who are not present, at least not directly, in Freud's account and who, in some cases, could not even have been present historically speaking. In particular, Berman draws our attention to Freud's daughter Anna as a figure of contrast and similarity to Dora; she adds the fictive character of the 1970s feminist Gloria; and, above all, she makes Lou Andreas-Salomé into a major interlocutor for Freud already at the time of the latter's treatment of Dora in 1900, even though in fact "Frau Andreas" and the "Professor" (as they refer to each other in their correspondence) would not meet until eleven years later.[11] The addition of characters who are technically outside the scope of Dora's clinical case thus allows for a unique syncopation of time, leading to an uncanny superposition of different historical periods or slices of time into an entirely fictive but otherwise not implausible present. It is precisely this simple structural innovation that enables us to take the "happy new century" alternatively as Freud's time or as Berman's, and thus also as our own.

By putting on the stage the character of Anna Freud, furthermore, Berman is able to suggest that Sigmund in some way "learned his lesson" from Dora's treatment, despite its failed and interrupted nature, insofar as he would have transferred onto his daughter the benefits of the insights learned from, yet never applied to, his patient. Witness, for example, the following scene of domesticity—commented upon by Lou in an aside to the audience, as if speaking from a different time frame to an even later moment in history—in which Freud all of a sudden decides to change the hierarchy of the roles of servant and served, child and adult, adolescent girl and elderly man of science:

Anna comes back with a serving of coffee and tea.
ANNA: More coffee? Dad, shall I serve you?
LOU: (*To us.*) And all of a sudden that day Freud did something completely
   contradictory.
FREUD: No, Anna. Come and sit with us, Anna. Have my cup of coffee,
   Lou . . . (*He extends the other recently served cup to the surprised Lou.*)

11. See Sigmund Freud and Lou Andreas-Salomé, *Letters*, ed. Ernst Pfeiffer, trans. William and Elaine Robson-Scott (New York: W. W. Norton, 1972). For a discussion of Lou Andreas-Salomé as an historical figure in general, and of her relation to Freud in particular, see Biddy Martin, *Woman and Modernity: The (Life)styles of Lou Andreas-Salomé* (Ithaca: Cornell University Press, 1991), esp. 191–229.

LOU: Thanks.

FREUD: Or better: let's sit down here.

The three sit down at a little table.

LOU: (*To us.*) And thus Anna, from that afternoon onward, would often sit down with us, even when we talked about clinical cases, as we used to do.[12]

Berman reiterates this lesson at the end of her play, as if the link between Dora and Anna had to be made even more explicit. This is one of the last scenes in the play, when a thirty-two-year-old Dora revisits Freud's consultation room, only to leave even more disappointed than the first time. At this point, on her way out, she crosses paths with Anna:

> *Anna continues on her way to Freud's consultation room and Dora looks at her with a prolonged sadness, as if she saw the woman that she could have been go away.*[13]

This stage direction is actually ambivalent, as the sense of betrayal (Dora was not so lucky to receive the same treatment as Freud's daughter) cannot erase the impression that there has been some vindication (Anna after all seems to benefit from a truth which Freud discovered in Dora).

Even more striking in terms of structural innovation is Berman's clever move in multiplying Freud into Freud, Freud 2 and Freud 3, while at the same time collapsing several other characters into a single actor, as with (the young) Dora, played by an actress who also plays Anna Freud, or Lou, whose part is taken by an actor who also plays Frau K., Martha Freud and (the older) Dora. The case of the three Freuds, though, should not be seen too rashly as an instantiation of Freud's tripartite topologies, whether the earlier (conscious, preconscious, unconscious) or the later one (id, ego, superego). In fact, as far as I can tell, and despite critical opinions to the contrary, there exists no systematic one-to-one correspondence between the three Freuds and the terms of the topologies. The aim of such reduplication, as with the combination of roles into a single actor, is rather to render visible, or literally to embody, the facts of transference.[14]

---

12. Berman, *Feliz nuevo siglo doktor Freud*, 54–5.

13. Ibid., 87.

14. Bixler also suggests this reading in "Sexo, poder y palabras," 72. I should add that a major drawback of this otherwise insightful analysis stems from its selective reliance on Michel Foucault's *History of Sexuality*. Bixler thus repeatedly quotes Foucault's terms regarding the "putting into discourse" of sexuality, and yet there is no trace in her analysis of a willingness to abandon what Foucault criticizes as the "repressive hypothesis"—that is, the common but, according to Foucault, misguided understanding of power as repressive, so that it would supposedly suffice to strip away the power of repression in order to let freedom flourish in all its spontaneous glory. Thus, Bixler writes: "As in *Feliz nuevo siglo*, the paradox

Thanks to this theatrical stroke of genius, in other words, we are given a visual equivalent of the transferential relationships that exist between Freud, Herr K. and Herr F., or between Anna and Dora, and so on. These relationships are not only the topic of didactic meta-commentaries on Freud's part, as in the following instance of transference between Freud and Dora's father, Herr F.:

> FREUD: In a single session Dora passed with me from amorous complicity to hatred, a bond at least as intense, if not more so, than love. It was not for nothing that up to three times she came to say to me:
> DORA: (*While Freud swallows a pill, leaving.*) Yes, you are identical to my dad.[15]

Transference and (the limited recognition of the role of) counter-transference are also discussed by Freud (2 and 3) and Lou Andreas-Salomé (the latter, as usual, in asides to the audience):

> LOU: (*To us.*) And right there I could have stated the obvious; I could have said: but if transference is as you recently said . . .
> FREUD 3: Unavoidable—universal and unavoidable . . .
> LOU: (*To us.*) Then you are also trapped in the transference.
> *The three Freuds, uncomfortable, change position and remain frozen.*
> LOU: That is to say, if Dora saw him—Freud—only through the intimate characters of her psyche, Freud too never saw Dora's story directly but only through his own intimate characters. Perhaps Freud saw Frau K. through his wife Martha, whom he saw through . . . his mother, perhaps; he saw Dora through his daughter Ana and Ana through who knows who; he never saw without veils either Dora or Herr K. (*She coughs. The three Freuds change positions, uncomfortably, and they freeze*). Even more: you who "see" this history now, who "see" me, who knows what you interpret? And through which five or six characters from your past in which the whole culture for you is ciphered? (*Coughs again*). This takes one's breath away, doesn't it? If I had told all this to Freud at that time, he would no doubt have felt positively asphyxiated.
> FREUD 2: What? (*Coughs*) The doctor of the blind is blind too?
> FREUD 3: That is to say: it is impossible to know the truth, only the minuscule point of view of . . . oneself?

---

is conveyed that society, that is to say culture, (re)presents sex as the maximum and at the same time represses it as *the* secret" (83). For Foucault, by contrast, power is (also or above all, at least today) productive rather than repressive: "I do not maintain that the prohibition of sex is a ruse; but it is a ruse to make prohibition into the basic and constitutive element from which one would be able to write the history of what has been said concerning sex starting from the modern epoch." *The History of Sexuality*, vol. 1, *An Introduction*, trans. Robert Hurley (New York: Vintage, 1990), 12. This means both that the mere denunciation of repression is painfully insufficient and that the possibility of resistance poses a challenge of a completely different nature that may as yet remain unexplored.

15.   Berman, *Feliz nuevo siglo doktor Freud*, 25.

The three Freuds cough and move rapidly to different places: Freud to serve himself a glass of water, Freud 2 to lay down on the couch, Freud 3 to a corner: all this while Lou continues:

LOU: If I were to have told him, psychoanalysis as a scientific endeavor would have died right there of chaos and asphyxia. But . . . (*The three Freuds freeze.*) But the mind has some astonishing ways of avoiding its own chaos: not even for a moment did I see the "superobvious" problem—my unconscious bequeathed the problem of counter-transference to subsequent psychoanalysts—and I only said: "One moment . . . ."[16]

The different characters played by a single actor thus represent on the stage the superimposition of images and figures through which they are perceived as a result of transference, in the way this notion is defined in *Feliz nuevo siglo doktor Freud* itself. Through this clever technical innovation, Berman's play gives body to the palimpsest of our psychic apparatus—providing the metaphysics of identification and transference with the physics of their enactment.

In her conversation with Catherine Clément, Cixous had already pointed out the appearance of a merry-go-round in which all the characters in Dora's story seem to be open to exchange and substitution: "Almost all those involved in Dora's scene circulate through the others, which results in a sort of hideous merry-go-round, even more so because, through bourgeois pettiness, they are ambivalent. All consciously play a double game, plus the games of the unconscious."[17] Berman herself seems to allude to this when, rather than repeating Herr K.'s citation of Mantegazza's *Physiology of Love* that appears in Freud's original clinical history as the sexually suggestive book read by Dora, she slips in an apocryphal reference to Alfred Schnitzler's *Reigen* (*La Ronda* or *The Round Dance*) into the conversation between Herr K. and Herr F., as though Dora's sexual fantasies would have been motivated by her having attended a performance of this most popular of plays in *fin-de-siècle* Vienna, which incidentally also serves as the reference point for another of Berman's adaptations, the yet-to-be performed *65 contratos para hacer el amor* (*65 Contracts for Making Love*).[18]

---

16. Ibid., 70–1.
17. Hélène Cixous and Catherine Clément, "The Untenable," in Bernheimer and Kahane, *In Dora's Case*, 278. For a Marxist critique of psychoanalysis, see also Clément's earlier contribution to Catherine Clément, Pierre Bruno, and Lucien Sève, *Pour une critique marxiste de la théorie psychanalytique* (Paris: Éditions sociales, 1973), 11–138; as well as Catherine Clément, *The Weary Sons of Freud* (London: Verso, 1987).
18. For a brief discussion of this new play, see Bixler, "Sexo, poder y palabras," 76–85. Interestingly enough, Schnitzler's *Reigen* had been given another adaptation on stage in Sir David Hare's 1998 play *The Blue Room*, which in its Broadway version starred the same Hollywood actress, Nicole Kidman, who also steals the show in Stanley Kubrick's 1999 adaptation of another Schnitzler original, *Traumnovelle* or "Dream Story," in *Eyes Wide Shut*.

In *Feliz nuevo siglo doktor Freud*, however, there is a stopping point in the chain of transferential substitutions. I am referring, of course, to the actor playing the role of Freud. Unlike Freud 2 and Freud 3, this character is in some way unique and, therefore, bears no number in the role distribution list. The actor plays Freud and Freud alone. We might say that he is, after all, the anchoring point of the transferential chain—the one who gives it its clinical and therapeutic impetus. Without it, there would be no way to stop the effect of sliding identities and, hence, no possibility for a cure; only the patient would be able to put an end to the slipping, just as Dora famously interrupted her treatment. In Berman's play, Freud is the exception who provides the point of intelligibility from where the slippery tracks of transference and counter-transference can be understood in the first place.

The importance of this stopping point—the exception to the structural principles of condensation, reduplication, and substitution already at work in Freud's "Fragment" and brilliantly enacted in *Feliz nuevo siglo doktor Freud*—cannot be overestimated. After all, no subsequent criticism of the Dora case has been able to rely on anything other than Freud's own account of it. Accepting the uniqueness of this reference does not amount to an apology for the obvious shortcomings and prejudices evidenced in the original account, but it does require that we reflect upon the fact that none of these shortcomings and prejudices—which Berman's play also addresses, as can be seen from the passage just quoted—are visible except through Freud's text. In this sense, he is his own harshest critic; all the clues for subsequent emendations are there in his account, in its gaps, its disavowals, and its moments of defensive self-reflexivity—including the denial of otherwise evident literary ambitions that have attracted so many critics and that artists have attempted to turn into a full-fledged reality. Such would be the bitter-sweet lesson to be drawn from the fact that neither Lou nor Anna nor Dora herself in the end can shake the inevitable, almost insidious presence of an unsubstitutable Freud. And ultimately neither can we, a full century later.

Psychoanalysis and Emancipation

This shamefaced misfit of a doctor doesn't know how to "cure" hysterics; half-way down the road towards a new track, one that would enable him to analyze unhappiness and to transform it (and himself), he quits.
        Catherine Clément, The Weary Sons of Freud

But is this "new woman," who has the opportunities her grandmother never even dreamt of, happy?
        Marie Langer, From Vienna to Managua: Journey of a Psychoanalyst

Beyond the question of Freud's undeniable genius, however, Berman's play—like that of many of her feminist precursors such as Cixous and

Marie Langer—also considerably raises the stakes for psychoanalysis in the twenty-first century by confronting the interpretation of hysteria with the possibility of the liberation of women. This problematic becomes particularly evident through the proposed notion of the "new woman" brought up in the play by the half-fictional and half-historical figure of Lou Andreas-Salomé, who uses this expression in another aside to the audience, apparently well aware of its unmistakable echoes of Ernesto "Che" Guevara's manifesto on socialism and the "new man" in Cuba.

In Berman's script, Freud has just compared woman to *un homme manqué*, a "failed" or "lacking" man, to which Lou reacts as follows:

> LOU: (*To us.*) I felt insulted, of course, and highly womanly. As though my whole female body were traversed by a flush. And I had an increasing desire to protest, to tell Freud: that's how it is, that's how it has been for centuries: women are the eunuchs of society, without freedom, without money or power, but it can be otherwise. Why are you, who have seen beyond your own culture in so many respects, why are you here unable to look beyond? What if Dora is . . . ? I mean: we could imagine this, what if Dora is a new woman?[19]

Dora as a "new woman," *una nueva mujer*: here we see that another diverted title for this chapter could have been "Socialism and Woman in Mexico."[20]

In fact, during the entire twentieth century, both Left and Right were traversed by a passion for novelty that included a passion for producing, if necessary by violent means, a new humanity. Thus, as Badiou writes in *The Century*—his attempt to think about how the twentieth century thought of itself in art, politics, and psychoanalysis—"Basically, from a certain point onwards, the century has been haunted by the idea of changing man, of creating a new man"; and it is because of this passion that the early years of the century are so rich in innovations, including the fact, duly pointed out by Badiou, that the year of publication of Freud's "Dora" as well as of his *Three Essays on Sexuality* coincided with that of the failed 1905 revolution in Russia, which Lenin would famously describe as a final rehearsal for the October Revolution:

> Ultimately, and right to its very end, the century will indeed have been the century of the emergence of another humanity, of a radical transformation

19.   Berman, *Feliz nuevo siglo doktor Freud*, 51.
20.   Ernesto "Che" Guevara, "El socialismo y el hombre en Cuba," in *Obra revolucionaria*. Other recent *détournements* or "diversions" of Guevara's text from the point of view of gender and sexual politics include Senel Paz's *El lobo, el bosque y el hombre nuevo* (Mexico City: Era, 1991), which serves as the basis for Tomás Gutiérrez Alea and Juan Carlos Tabío's movie *Fresa y chocolate*; and Daína Chaviano's *El hombre, la hembra y el hambre* (Barcelona: Planeta, 1998).

of what man is. In this respect it will have remained faithful to the extraordinary cognitive ruptures that marked its initial years—though it will have shifted, little by little, from the register of the project to that of the automatisms of profit.[21]

To produce a radical change in what it means to be human, however, also entails that one create not just a "new man" but also a "new woman"—that is, to use Cixous and Clément's expression, *la jeune-née*, the "newly born woman," of which they, too, like Lou in Berman's play, find an example—though perhaps a frustrated or failed one—in Dora.

One of the unsolved mysteries of Dora's case for Cixous and Clément in fact revolves around the question of her status as either heroine or victim. Was she capable, in the end, of breaking with the dominant bourgeois and patriarchal order of her time, to which her hysteria bears witness in a most painfully symptomatic way? Cixous, in this regard, seems more optimistic: "Dora seemed to me to be the one who resists the system," she writes. "It is the nuclear example of women's power to protest. It happened in 1899 [*sic*]; it happens today wherever women have been able to speak differently from Dora, but have spoken so effectively that it bursts the family into pieces."[22] Clément, by contrast, questions the lasting nature of Dora's breakthrough: "The analysis I make of hysteria comes through my reflection on the place of deviants who are not hysterics but clowns, charlatans, crazies, all sorts of odd people. They all occupy challenging positions foreseen by the social bodies, challenging functions within the scope of all cultures. That doesn't change the structures, however. On the contrary, it makes them comfortable."[23] Beyond the particular case of Dora, this productive disagreement points to the thorny issue of the relation between psychoanalysis and emancipation, or between psychoanalysis and politics in general, which in turn harkens back to the earlier discussion of the relation between Marx and Freud.

This much larger problematic regarding psychoanalysis, politics, and the possibility or impossibility of emancipation is brought up in different ways both in the epigraph to Berman's play and in the concluding speech attributed to Doctor Freud himself. The epigraph, on one hand, highlights the radically subversive potential of Freud's revelation. Taken from the famous essay on Leonardo da Vinci, but summarizing a view that receives similar formulations, for instance, at the end of *Three Essays on Sexuality*, Freud's statement affirms the universal and originary disposition toward pathological perversion of all normal sexual activity: "Nadie es tan grande para que no se encuentre sometido a las leyes que gobiernan con igual severidad la actividad

21. Badiou, *The Century*, 8, 9–10.
22. Cixous, in "The Untenable," 285.
23. Clément, in "The Untenable," 286.

normal y la patológica" ("There is no one so great as not to be subject
to the laws which govern both normal and pathological activity with
equal cogency").[24] In asserting this, Freud is not just blurring the line of
demarcation between the normal and the pathological. His observations of so-called perverse dispositions could be called revolutionary
insofar as they allow him to question hitherto unacknowledged aspects
in the universal structure of human desire. Obviously, nothing could be
more unsettling for the continuation of the status quo than this capacity to universalize whatever the social order of the time considers
pathological or perverse.

The final words attributed to Freud in Berman's adaptation, on the
other hand, seem to go very much in the opposite direction, no matter
how great the degree of hesitation we can infer from the points of
suspension: "Una infelicidad . . . general y difusa . . . es el signo . . .
de la buena adaptación" ("A general and diffuse . . . unhappiness . . .
is the sign . . . of good adaptation").[25] In the conclusion to his *Studies
in Hysteria*, Freud had indeed suggested a possible answer to the question regarding the (limited) effects of psychoanalysis on the lives of his
patients suffering from hysteria, by arguing that "much will be gained
if we succeed in transforming your hysterical misery into common
unhappiness. With a mental life that has been restored to health you
will be better armed against that unhappiness."[26] The highest goal of
psychoanalysis thus would be no more than the acceptance of a generalized state of unhappiness.

Such expressions of pessimism, or of modesty bordering on melancholy, with regard to the goals of the psychoanalytic cure—if that is
indeed what is hinted at here—are certainly not unique to Freud.
Jacques Lacan, for one, relies on similar formulations, for instance,
during his mid-1970s lecture tour in the United States: "An analysis
should not be pushed too far. When the analysand feels that he is happy
to be alive, it is enough," and the analysis should not go any further.
"Thank God, we don't make [the analysands] so normal that they will
end up psychotic. That's the point where we must be very cautious."[27]

---

24. Berman, *Feliz nuevo siglo doktor Freud*, 9. See the original quotation in Sigmund
Freud, *Leonardo da Vinci and a Memory of his Childhood*, trans. James Strachey (New
York: W. W. Norton, 1989), 8.
25. Berman, *Feliz nuevo siglo doktor Freud*, 87.
26. Sigmund Freud and Joseph Breuer, *Studies in Hysteria*, trans. Nicola Luckhurst (New
York: Penguin, 2004), 306. Catherine Clément comments sarcastically: "What success—your
misery has been turned into unhappiness. Better yet, common unhappiness, which robs you of
the uniqueness of your body, of your precious disease—Emmy, Katherina, Anna, all you
hysterical women who were listened to by Freud—of the only means you had to tell of your
family oppressions. Common, you are told, and unhappiness," *The Weary Sons of Freud*, 96.
27. Jacques Lacan, quoted and discussed in Badiou, *Theory of the Subject*, 142–3. My
argument here is also indebted to Philippe van Haute, *Against Adaptation: Lacan's
"Subversion" of the Subject*, trans. Paul Crowe and Miranda Vankerk (New York: The
Other Press, 2003).

Finally, one of Lacan's foremost contemporary disciples, Slavoj Žižek, similarly addresses the question of what can be expected from psychoanalysis in relation to that bedrock of the real, or pure negativity, that would be the death drive:

> In this perspective, the "death drive," this dimension of radical negativity, cannot be reduced to an expression of alienated social conditions, it defines *la condition humaine* as such: there is no solution, no escape from it; the thing to do is not to "overcome," to "abolish" it, but to come to terms with it, to learn to recognize it in its terrifying dimension and then, on the basis of this fundamental recognition, to try to articulate a *modus vivendi* with it.[28]

In all these instances it would seem that psychoanalysis, despite its revolutionary insights into the structure of human desire, fantasy, repression, anxiety, and so on, ultimately seeks to avoid giving any subject, patient, or reader the consolation of happiness. It is true that this does not necessarily imply that psychoanalysis proposes an adaptation to the existing state of affairs; rather, in a far more complex and paradoxical move, the end of the cure seems to lie in finding a way to adapt to the radical impossibility of adaptation. But still the fact remains that the final lesson is one of the acceptance or recognition of the human being's essential finitude, rather than an attempt—which by comparison will turn out to have been illusory at best, and disastrous at worst—to overcome the limits posed by it.

Like Berman's play, in the way the script is framed between the epigraph from Freud's *Leonardo da Vinci* and the final words from his *Studies in Hysteria*, psychoanalysis would thus oscillate without end between subversion and adaptation, between emancipatory radicalism and the acceptance of a generalized sense of common unhappiness. The Argentine political thinker and activist Raúl Cerdeiras helpfully sums up this "impasse" at the heart of the psychoanalytical tradition:

> From its origins, psychoanalysis seems to be traversed by an unsolvable conflict. We could state this as follows: *psychoanalysis puts forward revolutionary statements but ultimately gives shape to a reformist clinical practice.* Let us clarify this thesis. Both Freud and Lacan, through the psychoanalytical theory of the unconscious, have managed to provoke a veritable commotion whose effects spread not only through their own domain of mental health but also in the different orders of culture. We might say that the developments of Freud and Lacan subvert the theoretical frameworks and ideas that have by and large been accepted wisdom in the West—so much so that we can talk of a before and an after of the theory of the unconscious. This had the dignity of a rupture, for which in the name of accepted values they suffered the rejection and persecution of the powers that be. This is a history that everyone knows. But do the effects in the clinic with regard to the analysand have the same scope? No. In the end, in what is called analysis there is no other aim except assembling the functioning of a

---

28. Slavoj Žižek, *Sublime Object of Ideology*, 5.

structure. Make function that which did not function, but never produce a rupture within the subject in question.[29]

But Berman's ultimate question in *Feliz nuevo siglo doktor Freud* would appear to be how to reconcile the emancipation of women not just with the deadlock inherent in the theory and practice of psycho-analysis, but with the persistence of gendered biases on both sides of the impasse—the clinical as well as the theoretical. In this sense, the political project behind her stage adaptation could be portrayed as an attempt to inscribe psychoanalysis in a progressive, not to say leftist agenda for the democratization of culture. Berman is, after all, also the coauthor, with the Mexican anthropologist Lucina Jiménez, of a recent book titled *Democracia cultural*, in whose proposal her theater produc-tions would ideally find a place as well. What remains to be seen, however, is whether the inscription of psychoanalysis in a kind of "democratic culturalism" does not unwittingly give up altogether on what potentially remains the subversive kernel of Freud's legacy.

Cultural Democracy: Progress and the Iron Cage of Time

Calling me a genius is the latest way people have of starting their criticism of me . . . First they call me a genius and then they proceed to reject all my views.

Sigmund Freud *in* Fragments of an Analysis with Freud

We can reflect on this final question by returning to the uses and disad-vantages of the syncopated temporalities in *Feliz nuevo siglo doktor Freud*. Berman's bold juxtaposition of Dora, Lou, and Gloria in the fictive present at the turn of the century in fact should not mislead us into believing that their ideas and options are equally available at all times. On the contrary, the play repeatedly affirms the incommensura-bility of different historical periods, each of which is strictly correlated to a system of beliefs, values, and biases that are said to constitute its so-called culture. Ironically, the collapsing of different temporalities

---

29. Raúl J. Cerdeiras, "El *impase* del psicoanálisis," *Acontecimiento: Revista para pensar la política* 13 (1997): 35–6. Interestingly enough, in his contribution to the volume *Psicoanálisis, ¿adaptación o cambio?* (Buenos Aires: Rodolfo Alonso, 1972), the Argentine psychoanalyst Roberto Harari turns his answer into a one-act theatrical play, "Psicoanálisis, ¿ciencia o ideología? (Panel en 1 acto)" (85–133). In this hilarious play Dr Gamma, Dr Agustín Pedro Anker (whose initials spell APA, as in the Argentine Psychoanalytical Association), the Licenciado Harari, and PRT, a.k.a. the Revolutionary Psychologist or Psychiatrist who (almost) does not Work (he is a recent graduate) meet on a panel, not unlike the roundtable in *Memorias del subdesarrollo*, to discuss the compatibility of psychoanalysis and revolution. Harari the character's conclusion is that only an imaginary projection on the part of the would-be analyst, incompatible with Freud's doctrine, can pretend that behind all the mechanisms of repression and distortion there must lie a pure wish for revolutionary change or emancipation.

into a single present thus ultimately strengthens the divide between them, rather than upsetting it in the way that psychoanalysis certainly upset bourgeois morality in *fin-de-siècle* Vienna.

Freud everywhere shows a keen awareness of standing in a relation of critical distance with regard to his own time and place. To insist on the "discontents" of civilization rather than on its proudest achievements could in this sense very well be said to be a question of principle for him, similar to what Friedrich Nietzsche described as the task of an "untimely" or "intempestive" type of thinking—in his case inspired by philology: "For I do not know what meaning classical philology would have for our age if not to have an untimely effect within it, that is, to act against the age and so have an effect on the age to the advantage, it is to be hoped, of a coming age."[30] In Dora's case, the five-year hiatus between the final composition of "Fragment of an Analysis of a Case of Hysteria" and its eventual publication certainly had much to do with the perceived untimeliness of Freud's text. As did perhaps the hesitation on the author's part regarding the actual year of his treatment of Dora: "1899," Freud writes at least twice in the case history, even though Dora's visits to his consultation room happened between the months of October and December in 1900![31] We could almost argue that the founder of psychoanalysis shows his own uncertainty here as to whether this treatment, abruptly cut short by the patient herself, can really be said to hail the beginning of the twentieth century, or whether it is not rather a rearguard survival from the previous one. However this may be, by putting Doctor Freud, so to speak, squarely back in his own time—radically distinct from Lou Andreas-Salomé's no less than from Gloria's or the audience's—Berman may have reduced such symptomatic untimeliness to a seamless contemporaneity, in the sense that each idea, each action, and each prejudice is now assigned to its proper place and time. "It is a sense of contemporaneity that restricts inquiry as it asserts that one can only think what a specific time and place allows us to think," as Jacques Rancière observes in relation to the *Annales* school in the history of mentalities. But to a large extent this trend has become commonplace today in the guise of cultural studies: "To explicate a phenomenon by referring it to 'its time' means to put into play a metaphysical principle of authority camouflaged as a methodological precept of intellectual inquiry."[32] With regard

---

30. Friedrich Nietzsche, *On the Advantage and Disadvantage of History for Life*, trans. Peter Preuss (Indianapolis: Hackett, 1980), 8. Nietzsche further writes: "These reflections are also untimely, because I attempt to understand as a defect, infirmity and shortcoming of the age something of which our age is justifiably proud, its historical education" (8).

31. Cixous, the reader will have noticed, adopts this mistaken chronology, relying on Freud's faulty memory to place Dora's treatment in 1899. Even Berman seems to imply this when she describes Dora in *Feliz nuevo siglo doktor Freud* as a seventeen-year-old, rather than an eighteen-year-old.

32. See Davide Panagia, "Dissenting Words: A Conversation with Jacques Rancière," *Diacritics* 30: 2 (2000): 122. Rancière discusses in greater detail the consequences of this

to Freud's legacy, what I would call the culturalist-progressivist reframing of psychoanalysis, in the very same movement in which it seeks to denounce and ideally overcome past prejudices, in fact risks closing off the possibility of any true emancipation, precisely because the past is merely confirmed in its pastness and the present can feel tacitly authorized to assume that it is at least more advanced, more progressive, or simply more aware than all that. "The celebration of the present is aided by instant history," as Russell Jacoby writes. "Few can resist introducing stock criticism of Freud—be it of the left or right—without the standard observation that Freud was a nineteenth-century Viennese. The endless repetition of such statements suggests the decline of critical thinking; the modern mind can no longer think thought, only locate it in time and space."[33]

The relevant passage from *Feliz nuevo siglo doktor Freud*, in which the underlying presuppositions behind this culturalist interpretation of psychoanalysis are established, comes as part of a dialogue between Lou Andreas-Salomé and Gloria:

LOU: There is something called the principle of authority. Freud was my intellectual father: I could not tell him . . . *no*.

GLORIA: How typical of a woman.

LOU: Look Gloria . . . As human beings we think, that is unavoidable. We don't live the real except through its linguistic translation. And what do we think: we think whatever our culture thinks, nothing more. We are cowards in thought: culture is a house made of ideas and we cannot think anything outside this house. But a genius thinks new things: he adds a room or two to the house. Freud added a whole basement: he discovered the basement of our consciousness: the unconscious. It is a considerable augmentation. But as for women . . .

GLORIA: . . . he did not even add a window.

LOU: This is something we're discussing in another time; when this conversation between you—a feminist from the seventies—and me takes place, Dora is already a famous clinical case and I have been dead for forty years. This is why, in fact, it is only now, in this imaginary discussion, that I can come up with the simile of culture and house—because of a dream that Dora had during her treatment. You recall: a house was on fire and Dora inside the house was asphyxiating.

GLORIA: The house was her culture, you're saying. Dora was asphyxiating in her culture.

LOU: Now I say so. Back then I would never even have considered such a criticism. (*To us, while Gloria leaves.*) None of the brilliant and clever

---

peculiar form of historicism, which he says characterizes the work of Lucien Febvre and Emmanuel Leroy-Ladurie, for example, in *The Names of History: On the Poetics of Knowledge*, trans. Hassan Melehy (Minneapolis: University of Minnesota Press, 1994).
33. Jacoby, *Social Amnesia*, 1.

disciples of Freud, for that matter, thought of it. Except—how strange—
Dora, a seventeen-year old girl.[34]

In short, Berman's play inscribes the discourse of psychoanalysis in the
prison-house of culture of its time, a prison where—perhaps—only the
hysterical woman was able, if not to mount a successful escape, than at
least to point out the heavy bars. The didacticism of this proposal was not
lost on the director of the play at its opening in Mexico City: "One of
Sabina Berman's theses is, if not the misogyny then at least the enclosure
of Freud in his time, the fact that he saw woman according to the ideas of
the end of the nineteenth century. Freud was from a bourgeois Jewish
family, and he was trapped in the Victorian concepts of looking upon
woman," Sandra Félix commented in an interview, before taking up the
script's metaphor of culture as a cage in which Doctor Freud, despite his
genius, remains trapped: "The play itself says as much: he is a genius of
the twentieth century but, like any human being, he also could lose track
of things, or he could have remained trapped in the cage of his time."[35]

In conclusion, I will make two brief comments about what I have
called the democratic-culturalist thesis. Culture, first of all, seems to be
equated with what in another time would have been called ideology. (I
am aware that in saying this, and by adding "in another time," I am
already adopting the culturalist principle—though without its implicit
progressivism—that I am trying to put into question.) This also means
that the ideological debates over leftism and conservatism are subsumed
under this seemingly post-ideological umbrella term of culture, always
deserving of respect if not also, and a bit more pragmatically, of state-
sponsorship. Indeed, if we start from the premise that we all live in the
prison-house of our own culture and time, then the proposal for a
"cultural democracy" would acquire rather ominous overtones, were we
in fact to implement the four programmatic "linkages" or *enlaces*
outlined by Berman in her contribution to the book *Democracia cultural*:

1. Link mass culture, the arts and the private sector.
2. Link culture and tourism.
3. Crucially, link culture with public education of children and adults.
4. Link culture to the phenomenon of globalization.[36]

---

34. Berman, *Feliz nuevo siglo doktor Freud*, 53–4.
35. Quoted in Juan José Olivares, "*Feliz nuevo siglo doktor Freud* muestra los aciertos y
errores de un genio del siglo XX," *La Jornada* (January 26, 2002). Available online at
jornada.unam.mx. Jacoby, in "Social Amnesia," quotes a whole litany of similar judgments:
"Not even a genius can entirely step out of his time" (Karen Horney); "Although a genius,
Freud was in many respects limited by the thinking of his time, as even a genius must be"
(Clara Thompson); "Freud could not surmount certain limitations of his culture and of his
own nature. This was inevitable. Even a genius can do only so much" (Patrick Mullahy); and
so on. Freud's ingenious rebuttal, quoted in the epigraph to this section, appears in Joseph
Fortis, *Fragments of an Analysis with Freud* (New York: Simon and Schuster, 1954), 142.
36. Sabina Berman and Lucina Jiménez, *Democracia cultural: Una conversación a cuatro*

Problems would immediately arise if we were to try to apply this program to the notion of culture implicit in *Feliz nuevo siglo doktor Freud*. In Berman's play, in fact, culture seems to define something more akin to the ideological horizon of one's time, beyond which one cannot think. This definition is hard to reconcile with the desire to integrate culture with everything from primary schools to the state, unless of course we were planning to reinforce the limits of our culture as the limits of our world—which would put us completely at odds with the untimely intervention of Freud himself.

I argued before in favor of the working hypothesis that what defines the innovative force of Freud's endeavor consists in articulating a singular universality. Whether successful or not, his attempt to found a science of the singular defines the tour de force of psychoanalysis—to find a universal truth in the words of a mad adolescent woman, as Freud seems almost to whisper to himself at one point in Berman's play: "A privilege of the youth, still without commitments or terrifying fears: the direct contact with the truth."[37] Democratic culturalism, by contrast, could be said to propose the exact opposite—that is, the absolutization of the particular, trapped behind bars in the iron cage of its proper time and place. No more direct contact with the truth, only languages and cultures are then left, all equally worthy of respect, even though some of them, namely the present ones, seem to be more enlightened about the principle of respect itself than others. Let us recall the following words attributed to Freud 3 upon hearing Lou Andreas-Salomé expand upon the inevitable nature of transference: "That is to say: it is impossible to know the truth, only the minuscule point of view of . . . of oneself?"[38] In democratic culturalism, there is no longer any truth left, only minuscule points of view—and this too is only a minuscule point of view. This conclusion may be consistent with a certain reception of Nietzsche, but is it true to the spirit of Freud?

The fact that psychoanalysis began by listening to the symptoms of hysteria indicated that its anchoring point is not some ideal linkage, but rather an upsetting and untimely delinking. From this tear in the social texture, psychoanalysis did not aim to proceed in the direction of an ever-increasing integration of art, culture, education, and the state

---

manos (Mexico City: Fondo de Cultura Económica, 2006), 78. My discussion of "democratic culturalism" in the final lines is inspired by Alain Badiou's Preface to his major new work, *Logics of Worlds*, trans. Alberto Toscano (London: Continuum, 2009), in which he opposes "democratic materialism" (the idea that "there are only bodies and languages") with the "materialist dialectic" (which adds "except that there are truths"). For a separate translation of this preface, see also Alain Badiou, "Democratic Materialism and the Materialist Dialectic," trans. Alberto Toscano, *Radical Philosophy* 130 (2005): 20–4. For further developments in the turn toward a cultural-democratic understanding of politics, including discussions of the role of melodrama in the moralization of politics, see Chapter 2 and the Epilogue.

37. Berman, *Feliz nuevo siglo doktor Freud*, 48.

38. Ibid., 71..

into the all-round logic of globalization, but rather to strip civilization of its most cherished alibis and mass delusions in order to bring it face to face with its innermost and unsurpassable discontents. Little is left of this heroic effort, however, if its intempestive character is reduced to being nothing more than a sign of the times. This is why all cultural forms of democracy, in their otherwise just and well-founded criticisms of the biases inherent in psychoanalysis, nonetheless risk falling short of Freud's contribution to the twentieth century, or even to the twenty-first. Again, this is not to deny that such biases and prejudices exist and persist; rather, it begs the question of how to redress this situation without falling into the traps of a new, culturalist and progressivist principle of authority which is no longer able to house the discomforting truths of psychoanalysis as voiced, in between the coughing outbursts, by the young Dora.

THE POST-LENINIST DETECTIVE

A Message without a Bottle

We had to take two small steps back, and two forward, like Lenin in Toluca.
We had to remain in the rearguard while the others rode on their horses, to
see them from afar disappear in the dust.
                                        Paco Ignacio Taibo II, De cuerpo entero

Toward the end of the 2000 movie *Amores perros*, written and directed
by the Mexican duo Guillermo Arriaga and Alejandro González Iñár-
ritu, the character nicknamed *el Chivo* ("the Goat")—a one-time
private university professor who turned first into an urban guerrilla
fighter and then into a mercenary killer roaming the streets of Mexico
City, where he also devotes himself to picking up stray dogs and caring
for them back in his home—gives a speech to his only daughter, whom
he never saw grow up. In more senses than one, this is a speech in the
void. Even though the ex-*guerrillero* finds himself sitting on the bed in
the middle of his daughter's room, she herself is absent, so that he is
forced to leave a message on her answering machine with a stolen cell-
phone. Modern technology notwithstanding, the lack of communication
seems insuperable, despite the fact that in his speech, with an honesty
that borders on pathos, the father makes an enormous effort to overcome the gap that separates him from his only child—a gap that is
perhaps less generational than political and ideological. Thus, he
explains to her that, at the time when he held her in his arms for the last
time, he asked her for forgiveness for what he was about to undertake,
but that he felt as though he had more important things to do than to
be with her or with her mother. "Quería componer el mundo para
luego compartirlo contigo o con ustedes," he tells her ("I wanted to
repair the world in order afterwards to be able to share it with you
both"). *Amores perros*, then, is also a story about the loss of this Quix-
otic or Hamletian dream—the hope of righting wrongs in order to
create a universally shared world of justice for all.
     The ex–guerrilla fighter, as a matter of fact, is the only character
who serves as a mediating link between the three parallel episodes of
the movie. He is what we might call a circulating figure, the one
whose function is clearly ideological in the active sense of the term, as
he shuttles back and forth between the different levels of the story
and provides them with a minimal articulation. The other points of

contact are merely quick shoulder brushes, sporadic encounters, or violent collisions that lead alternatively to death or to the loneliness of broken dreams. Compared to the stark separation of narrative levels and social strata that defines each of the movie's three episodes, he is the one who pretends to settle accounts, balance destinies, and, more concretely, save the dogs that are either the instruments or the victims of ubiquitous violence. The moment of truth, at once brutal and melodramatic, comes when one fighting dog brings the violence and internecine strife back inside the home of this old professor, now converted into a coldblooded killer for hire. He had tried to disappear once, as he tells his daughter in the message on her answering machine, but he was unable to stick it out. In a way he died. And now he is back, in search of reintegration, still not capable of disappearing. To the contrary, as he finally says to his daughter: "Soy el fantasma que sigue allí."[1]

Above all, the ghost or phantasm that remains as a figure of the living dead, not only in *Amores perros* but also in other, apparently apolitical blockbuster movies such as *Y tu mamá también*, from the same year, in my view is a legacy of the 1970s—the difficult aftermath of the student-popular movement of 1968 in Mexico. It also reflects the re-emergence of armed struggle, particularly through urban and peasant guerrilla movements that spread like wildfire through Mexico, as they did through much of Latin America and the Third World.[2] But

---

1.　For a brief discussion of *Amores perros* in the context of the post-1968 Mexican Left, see Aurelia Gómez Unamuno, "El movimiento del 68 en el cine mexicano," in Alejandro Bruzual, Antonio Gómez, and Aurelia Gómez Unamuno, eds, *Variaciones sobre cine y política en América Latina*, special issue of *Osa Mayor* 16 (2004): 75–95.

2.　Though by no means comparable to the range of information now available for Argentina, the documentary history of the armed guerrilla movement also has grown exponentially in recent years in the case of Mexico. See especially Verónica Oikión Solano and Marta Eugenia García Ugarte, eds, *Movimientos armados en México, siglo XX*, 3 vols. (Zamora, Michoacán: El Colegio de Michoacán, 2006); Héctor Ibarra, ed., *La guerrilla de los 70 y la transición a la democracia* (Mexico City: Ce-Acatl, 2006); Laura Castellanos, *México armado 1943–1981* (Mexico City: Era, 2007); Carlos Montemayor, *La guerrilla recurrente* (Mexico City: Random House Mondadori, 2007); and Hugo Velázquez Villa and Leticia Carrasco Gutiérrez, *Breve historia del MAR: La guerrilla imaginaria del Movimiento de Acción Revolucionaria* (Guadalajara: Universidad de Guadalajara, 2010). For (auto)biographical approaches, see Alberto Ulloa Bornemann, *Sendero en tinieblas* (Mexico City: Cal y Arena, 2004); and Benjamín Palacios Hernández, *Héroes y fantasmas: La guerrilla mexicana de los años 70* (Nuevo León: Universidad Autónoma de Nuevo León, 2009). For analyses, see Gustavo A. Hirales Morán, *La Liga Comunista 23 de septiembre: Orígenes y naufragio* (Mexico City: Ediciones de Cultura Popular, 1977); Hugo Esteve Díaz, *Las armas de la utopía: La tercera ola de los movimientos guerrilleros en México* (Mexico City: Instituto de Proposiciones Estratégicas, 1996); Jorge Luis Sierra Guzmán, *El enemigo interno: Contrainsurgencia y fuerzas armadas en México* (Barcelona: Plaza y Valdés, 2003); and, especially, the deeply penetrating study by Salvador Castañeda, *La negación del número (La guerrilla en México, 1965–1996: una aproximación crítica)* (Mexico City: Ediciones Sin Nombre/CONACULTA, 2006). The vast body of writing is still waiting to receive a theoretically informed analysis comparable to what Juan Duchesne

the history of this period remains for the most part to be written, because it concerns a forgotten decade, lost somewhere between the radical leftism of the 1960s and the imposition of neoliberalism in the late 1980s and early 1990s. Younger generations thus find themselves in a similar position with regard to this legacy to that of the absent daughter in *Amores perros*. As a young Colombian journalist wrote in 2000 in the cultural magazine *El malpensante*: "The orphans of the Left at this point are somewhere around thirty years old and we still do not understand a great deal of the political past of our parents, but in our memory there are still some of those moments of political fervor— of course, lived in the wake of things."[3] This orphaned time can only be overcome by a work of thought, whether *pensante* or *malpensante*, that is also at the same time a labor of theoretical reflection and historical reconstruction. Such a labor is seriously hampered, however, by the lack of straightforward messages transmitted by the previous generation. As a result, there lies a heritage before us that is almost impossible to interpret, let alone assume. "Ours is a strange generation: it would seem that we have not been able to decipher what we inherited. Perhaps because this generation of leftists did not know how to draw up a balance sheet or how to draft a coherent will," the same journalist continues.

> There are very few books, novels or documents that have taken up the task of exorcizing this period, or that allow the new generations to understand what really happened during those years. To be sure: we have plenty of balance sheets from militants and leftist leaders, but almost all of them relate to those who took up arms, as if these had been the only figures of contestation of the period.[4]

If we do not want the ghosts simply to remain stuck in place—not even so much as figures of protest or contestation (*seres contestatarios*), but as mere answering machines (*máquinas contestadoras*) spewing out their automated messages against the wind—then we surely must find new and different ways of overcoming the curse of oblivion and pseudo-remembrance that constitutes their current state of orphanhood.

Winter offers for the story of the guerrillas in Cuba, Guatemala, and Argentina, in *La guerrilla narrada: acción, acontecimiento, sujeto* (San Juan, Puerto Rico: Ediciones Callejón, 2010).
3. Nicolás Morales Thomas, "Los huérfanos de la izquierda," *El malpensante* 35 (January 2000). See also Rogelio Vizcaíno, "Notas sobre la generación perdida: La nostalgia ya no es como era (hace media hora)," *La cultura en México* 1307 (April 23, 1987): 41–7.
4. Morales Thomas, "Los huérfanos de la izquierda."

One Year in the History of *La Cultura en México*

He felt like a member of an esoteric sect dedicated to the preservation of
ghosts. Maybe that was the problem: he was going at the whole thing more
like a historian or a journalist than as a detective.

Paco Ignacio Taibo II, Cosa fácil

In this chapter—as a modest contribution to the work of counter-
memory that requires not just an effort at historico-empirical
reconstruction but also a vast amount of secondary theoretico-concep-
tual elaboration starting precisely from those blind spots where history
fails to be subsumed into logic—I would like to propose a series of
hypotheses about the new regime of power that emerged out of the
conflict between political militancy and neoliberal capitalism in the
wake of the legacy that the 1970s bequeathed to subsequent generations. To do so, I will begin by turning to a small segment of intellectual
work, a sequence limited in both time and space—namely, to the fifty-
nine issues of *La cultura en México*, the supplement to the magazine
Siempre!, edited for just a little over a year, between March 1987 and
April 1988, by the Mexican polymath Paco Ignacio Taibo II—after
which I will discuss the series of nine novels that Taibo devoted between
1976 and 1993 to his *noir* or hard-boiled independent detective by the
name of Héctor Belascoarán Shayne. In one of these novels, *Regreso a*
la misma ciudad y bajo la lluvia (translated as *Return to the Same*
City), the detective comes back from the dead in order to live through
a slightly telescoped version of those very same years in which Taibo
edited *La cultura en México*: "It would have to be added that, for
narrative reasons, real times have been slightly rearranged," the author
warns in an explanatory note at the start of his novel, "uniting the
student protests of early '87 with the ascent of the Cuauhtémoc Cárdenas campaign of the spring of '88, in a fictional time that could be
situated around the end of 1987."[5] Both projects, in this sense, should
be read in conjunction—with the investigative journalist and the private
investigator joining hands, so to speak, in a single and unique form of
militant writing.

To the public at large, both in Mexico and abroad, Paco Ignacio
Taibo II is no doubt best known as one of the foremost biographers of
Ernesto "Che" Guevara, and more recently of Francisco "Pancho"
Villa. What is less known is the fact that Taibo has written numerous

---

5. Paco Ignacio Taibo II, "Nota del autor," in *Regreso a la misma ciudad y bajo la lluvia*
(Mexico City: Planeta, 1989), 9–10. For a lengthy biographical interview with Cuauhtémoc
Cárdenas, see Paco Ignacio Taibo II, *Cárdenas de cerca* (Mexico City: Planeta, 1994). A
fictionalized autobiography of the author himself appears as Paco Ignacio Taibo II, *De*
cuerpo entero (Mexico City: UNAM/Ediciones Corunda, 1992).

straightforward historical works, including for the Center for Historical Studies of the Mexican Labor Movement. Among such lesser-known works, I should mention his early study of anarchism and syndicalism, *Memoria roja: luchas sindicales de los años 20* (1984); his long out-of-print and recently reissued study of the origins of communism in Mexico, *Los Bolshevikis: historia narrativa de los orígenes del comunismo en México, 1919–1925* (1986, reprinted 2009); and his more recent collection of political biographies—not all of them, to be sure, limited to Mexico, but including cases from other parts of the world as well—in *Arcángeles* (first edition with four biographical vignettes in 1988, expanded with seven more biographies in 1998). Taibo's relatively short-lived time as editor-in-chief of *La Cultura en México*, a job he took over from Carlos Monsiváis, who had served in that position for over fifteen years, should no doubt be seen in the context of this much larger cultural, historical, and political project. In fact, it is no exaggeration to claim that Taibo sees his entire literary, historical, and biographical body of writings as part of a unified cultural front—a shield as much as a cultural battering ram for the counteroffensive—against the ravages wrought by seventy years of political monopoly on the part of the Institutional Revolutionary Party (PRI) and two presidencies under the Party of National Action (PAN). Crossing traditional generic boundaries, it is the art, or perhaps we should simply say the work (the *oficio*—"job" or "occupation") of the storyteller that conspires to produce a fragmented and yet fairly systematic narrative-political history of the twentieth century in Mexico.

As director of *La cultura en México*, Taibo's style is a stark departure from that of his predecessor and successors, including at the graphic level (the artistic layout is handled by Paco's wife, Paloma Sáiz). For one year the supplement thus also looks and reads more like an underground punk magazine than the stodgy museum piece that it would become soon thereafter. Monsiváis, for his part, had ended his last issue as director with a long essay, "25 años de *La cultura en México*" ("25 Years of *La cultura en México*"), in which he traced the history of the official nomenclature of the Mexican intelligentsia. Graphically presented as an angelic cartoon figure on the cover of this transitional special issue, the famous chronicler of the Federal District of Mexico City—"el DF"—ironically appeared here as a fairly traditional defender of freedom of expression and the power of the pen. Under Taibo's direction, by contrast, the supplement became highly politicized and radically internationalist. The worldwide context, of course, made this change inevitable—from the looming election of Carlos Salinas de Gortari in 1988, via the imminent fall of the Berlin Wall, to the run-up to the electoral defeat of the Sandinistas in 1990 in Nicaragua. Other international reference points revisited in the supplement, both contemporary and more recent, include the military dictatorships in Chile, Argentina, and Paraguay; the death squads in

Guatemala; the Carnation Revolution in Portugal; and the Red Brigades in Italy.

Without pretending to evaluate the journalistic accomplishments of this entire output, I would like to focus here on two common threads that in my view exemplify the approach to the present, or the history of actuality, of *La cultura en México* under Taibo's editorship. On the one hand, there is the war of the contras against the Sandinistas in Nicaragua. This struggle provides Taibo with an interpretive key to investigate the "cultural polarities" in his home country—just as the American journalist Marc Cooper, whose work serves as a model of investigative journalism for Taibo and who will in fact make it into one of Taibo's novels, claims that the debacle of Irangate under Reagan brought the war home for the United States: "The war of the *contra* reaches us at home."[6] What this reading suggests is a slight but subtle revision of the usual political historiographies. Instead of marking one of the last revolutionary episodes of the twentieth century, following the model of the Cuban Revolution, the fate of the Sandinistas in the face of overt and undercover opposition made them into a premonition of the whole new logic of war that confounds the respective tasks of the military, the police, and the paramilitary force of the contras—a logic whose effects can still be felt today, with the secret role of private contractors, in the war on terror in Iraq and Afghanistan, and the international tensions surrounding Iran. Here, we seem to enter the terrain of conspiracy theory:

> Those who arrived with their chocolate cakes to give bribes to the ayatollahs, who violated the decisions of Congress and created networks to supply the Nicaraguan contras with arms, are the same ones who have organized the covert actions against Cuba since the '60s, the same ones who directed the secret war in Laos, who created the Phoenix program of assassins in Vietnam, who brought down governments from Chile to Grenada by way of Australia.[7]

---

6. Marc Cooper, "La guerra de la contra llega a casa," *La cultura en México* 1301 (March 5, 1987): 52–3. In response to an article about the culture wars by José Agustín, Taibo admits:

> The lines [*rayas*] that separate us are established and made into frontiers through our support or repudiation of Sandinismo, our solidarity or dismissal of the recent student movement, or our distances from the official breakfasts with politicians. Also wrapped up in the hoopla are the preferences for the cultural magazines we buy or write for, our interest in the European literary fashions, our adherence to Benedetti's poetry or the brutal disqualification of the Uruguayan poet; our support for popular subgenres, our debates about literary elitism or about the fate of the School of Anthropology.

See Paco Ignacio Taibo II, "Las polaridades culturales," *La cultura en México* 1342 (August 20, 1987): 39. However, he refuses to accept Agustín's reductionism: "Something like (and I hope I'm not misinterpreting): Paz + *Vuelta* = neo-PANism + Televisa + more reactionary bureaucacy *versus* Monsiváis + *Nexos* + our cultural supplement (first epoch) + *La Jornada* = cheap neo-PRIism" (ibid.).

7. Marc Cooper, "De los pasillos del Pentágono a las playas de Nicaragua: Instrucciones

Furthermore, Irangate and the contras are read by Taibo and his team as providing a grid with which to scan the cultural surface at home. "*Vuelta*: la voz de la contra desde México" ("*Vuelta*: the voice of the contra within Mexico"), reads the title of an interview taped by Taibo in Cuba with the Nicaraguan poet Julio Valle Castillo, in which the latter significantly raises the conspiratorial tone: "Articles such as the one by Vladimir Rothshuh and others against Nicaragua that appeared in *Vuelta* are the typical writings dictated by the politics of the State Department and President Ronald Reagan against our country."[8]

How, then, do the "páginas negras," the black or *noir* pages, of *La cultura en México* pretend to answer this new war logic? Above all, by mobilizing two popular genres or subgenres in the margins of the literary essay or the experimental novel of the Boom: the *reportaje* and the *neopolicial*. In the first of these subgenres, Taibo reserved pride of place for articles such as the Czech Egon Erwin Kisch's "Investigative Journalism as a Form of Art and Struggle" and the Argentine Miguel Bonasso's piece on "Rodolfo Walsh and Popular Espionage," while the second subgenre, as early as March 1987, brought together the likes of Manuel Vázquez Montalbán, Andreu Martín, and Roger Simon, among others, for an important "Encuentro de escritores policiacos," which could be considered a precursor of the Semana Negra ("Noir Week") that Taibo has organized annually for the past twenty years or so in Gijón, Spain.[9] It is obviously in this context that we should situate the nine novels in Taibo's Belascoarán series. "Investigar un problema es resolverlo" ("To investigate a problem means to solve it"), Mao is quoted as saying in an epigraph from *Días de combate*, whereas in *Cosa fácil* another epigraph is taken from Marx's *Capital*:

para un juego secreto llamado Irangate," *La cultura en México* 1313 (June 4, 1987): 36–8. The story in this piece of investigative-conspiratorial journalism forms the basis for Taibo's novel *Regreso a la misma ciudad y bajo la lluvia*.

8. Paco Ignacio Taibo II, "*Vuelta*: la voz de la contra desde México: Entrevista con el poeta nicaragüense Julio Valle Castillo," *La cultura en México* 1352 (March 2, 1988): 39.

9. Egon Erwin Kisch, "El reportaje como forma de arte y de lucha," *La cultura en México* 1352 (March 2, 1988): 38; Miguel Bonasso, "Rodolfo Walsh y el espionaje popular," *La cultura en México* 1346 (January 21, 1988): 36–40; "Encuentro de escritores policiacos," *La cultura en México* 1302 (March 19, 1987): 36–40. A crucial reference in this context is the interview with Rodolfo Walsh by Ricardo Piglia, "Hoy es imposible en la Argentina hacer literatura desvinculada de la política," as a preface to Walsh's story included in *Un oscuro día de justicia* (Mexico City: Siglo Veintiuno, 1973), 9–28. Walsh famously suggests that the novel, the short story, and fiction in general might be literary forms tied to a type of society in the nineteenth and twentieth century that is now waning:

I believe that it is logically a very powerful idea, but at the same time I believe that younger people formed in different, non-capitalist societies, or in societies that are in the process of a revolution, might more easily accept the idea that testimony and denunciation are artistic categories that are at the very least equivalent and equally deserving as the many efforts devoted to fiction and that in the future perhaps the terms might even be inverted so that what really would be appreciated as art would be the elaboration of testimony or the documentary, which as everyone knows allow for any degree of perfection. (20)

"La investigación debe apropiarse de la materia en detalle" ("The investigation must appropriate the material in detail").[10] Thus, what the hardboiled detective will offer the reader is above all a series of militant investigations, as if written by a participant-observer, into the political history of his adopted country.

Toward a Narrative History of the Left in Mexico

> *He evoked a sentence recalled by Jaramillo that had moved him in his days of struggle; a sentence spoken in 1918, toward the very end of the betrayal of zapatismo by its temporary allies, which reappeared in the seventies as the terrible epilogue to the peasant leader's murder: "Bury the rifles where you may be able to find them again."*
>
> Paco Ignacio Taibo II, *Días de combate*

A few years ago, in a talk at the National Autonomous University of Mexico, in Mexico City, on the occasion of the thirtieth anniversary of the events of 1968, Taibo explained how he conceived of much of his work as part of a "narrative history of the Left in Mexico." This project includes his experiments with the genre of the detective novel, or what he also calls, in a characteristic hybrid, the "new detective adventure novel" ("la nueva novela policiaca de aventuras"), nine of which are united by their main character, Héctor Belascoarán Shayne, a private eye, or, rather, an "independent detective" ("La palabra 'privado' le molestaba y había encontrado el apellido ideal para el oficio" ["He didn't like the sound of 'private detective.' 'Independent' had a much better ring to it"][11]) of proud Irish-Basque descent,

---

10. Paco Ignacio Taibo II, *Días de combate* (Mexico City: Planeta, 1997 [1976]), 173; *Cosa fácil* (Mexico City: Planeta, 1998 [1977]), 37. Marx's line is an allusion to a quote from the Postface to the second German edition of *Capital*, published in 1873:

> Of course the method of presentation must differ in form from that of inquiry. The latter has to appropriate the material in detail, to analyse its different forms of development and to track down their inner connection. Only after this work has been done can the real movement be appropriately described. If this is done successfully, if the life of the subject-matter is now reflected back in the ideas, then it may appear as if we have before us an *a priori* construction. (102)

The militant investigation or survey is also an important component in the ideological work of Maoism. "No investigation, no right to speak," Mao himself wrote in a text from 1930, in "Against the Cult of the Book"; and in his 1947 *Rural Surveys*, which sought to be an example of the proposed practice, he wrote: "Everyone engaged in practical work must investigate conditions at the lower levels. Such investigation is especially necessary for those who know theory but do not know the actual conditions, for otherwise they will not be able to link theory with practice"—included in *Quotations from Chairman Mao Tsetung* (Beijing: Foreign Languages Press, 1972), 230. The quote used by Taibo is also included in the Little Red Book: "When you have investigated the problem thoroughly, you will know how to solve it" (ibid., 233).

11. Taibo, *Cosa fácil*, 116; Paco Ignacio Taibo II, *An Easy Thing*, trans. William I. Neuman (New York: Viking, 1990), 116.

but otherwise completely soaked in the culture, slang, and politics of "el DF."

In Mexico City, as seems only appropriate, one will find Belascoarán's novels on sale almost anywhere, from the supermarket to the book-and-magazine section of the local department store. From the first of the series, *Días de combate*, to the last, *Adiós, Madrid*, all nine novels are now also available in cheap pocket editions that are part of Taibo's collected works reissued by Planeta. As with most of the author's other writings, the large majority of these are painstakingly located in or around Mexico's capital—officially still the largest and most populous city in the world—with only a few occasional escapes to Sinaloa (in *Algunas nubes*), Acapulco (*Regreso a la misma ciudad y bajo la lluvia*), the US-Mexican border (*Sueños de frontera*), Oaxaca (*Desvanecidos difuntos*), and Spain (*Adiós, Madrid*). In fact, Mexico City, or the Federal District, rather than Belascoarán himself, could easily be said to be the real protagonist of these novels. As Taibo himself explains in *Primavera pospuesta: Una versión personal de los 90 en México* (Spring Postponed: A Personal Version of the 1990s in Mexico), "The Federal District is the only possible protagonist for me (Trujillo is making his entry in Tijuana and Hernández Luna, with success, in Puebla) of the Mexican *neopolicial*," to which he adds, "Whoever does not love this city and hate it with the same intensity should not try to govern it; whoever does not enjoy and abhor it should not try to survive it; whoever does not walk its width and breadth in the underground should not narrate it."[12] Representing much more than a simple setting or backdrop, this location also has a decisive impact on the reworking of the detective novel as such. Indeed, the genre's structure and narrative arrangement undergo such a radical transformation that none of its canonical principles will be left standing after passing through the streets, homes, shops, taco and torta stands, factories, schools, and universities of Mexico City.

As literary products, not all of the nine novels in the Belascoarán series should be counted among Taibo's best. The reader would be justified in preferring free-standing detective novels such as *Sombra de la sombra* and *La vida misma*, or others such as *Sintiendo que el campo de batalla*, centered around the woman detective Olga Lavanderos, over the fairly erratic later novels of the Belascoarán series, such as *Amorosos fantasmas* or *Desvanecidos difuntos*. As the series develops, both the plotlines and the volumes themselves become progressively thinner, while nearly all codes of narrative verisimilitude—unity of place, time, and action—are pushed to the limit of tenability. At the same time, it must be said that the narrator, consistent in his attempt to debunk the pantheon of great writers, in many of these texts is the

---

12. Paco Ignacio Taibo II, *Primavera pospuesta: Una versión personal de los 90 en México* (Mexico City: Joaquín Mortiz, 1999), 23, 279.

first mockingly to reject any and all claims to literary or aesthetic value. Thus, in *La vida misma*, the fictive José Daniel Fierro, author of crime novels similar to those of his real creator, postulates:

> For someone from the Third World who wants the novel to eat itself, who thinks that fame and glory depend on his capacity to enchant the metropolis, that is, to fool it, who wants to scare off his own pen and to render the text so obscure that it may seem absolutely transcendent, it is difficult to arrive at the conclusion that what I have always wanted to write is a good adventure novel. A kind of adventurous-socialist-realism, which has nothing realist about it, which is only half socialist and which is totally adventurous.[13]

What interests me in these novels, however, is not, or not only, their willful trashiness, but rather their conscious inscription, as a codified series of genre texts, in the larger project of the writing of a narrative history of left-wing politics in Mexico. Three general questions will guide me in this reading: What is the view of the detective genre that emerges in Taibo's Mexico? How does this highly codified form of storytelling relate to the concept of the political, and more specifically to a politics of the Left? And what is it that makes the detective story— together with the melodramatic imagination with which the genre in its hardboiled variation frequently overlaps—so appealing to the decisively post-Leninist sensibilities of the New Left, tragically inaugurated by the events of 1968 in Mexico, with which Taibo and so many others of his generation identify most forcefully?

A Short Metaphysics of the Detective Story

The distortion of a text is not unlike a murder. The difficulty lies not in the execution of the deed but in the doing away with the traces.
Sigmumd Freud, Moses and Monotheism

Before turning to Taibo's peculiar use of the detective story, I want to recall the genre's structural underpinnings. By this I mean not only the social history of the classical detective story—a history which Walter Benjamin, in some of his most famous pages, devoted to Baudelaire, relates to the rise of anonymous urban masses during the second half of the nineteenth century, creating an explanatory scheme that would be even more coherent if it took account of the multitudes of latter-day Mexico. "The original social content of the detective story was the obliteration of the individual's traces in the big-city crowd," Benjamin writes. "The detective story came into being when this most decisive of all conquests of a person's incognito had been accomplished."[14] In the

---

13. Paco Ignacio Taibo II, *La vida misma* (Mexico City: Planeta, 1995), 75.
14. Walter Benjamin, *Charles Baudelaire: A Lyric Poet in the Era of High Capitalism*, trans. Harry Zohn (London: Verso, 1992), 43, 48.

midst of a nameless crowd, what matters is not that people can hide but that everyone becomes a potential suspect. However, more so than in the history of a person's incognito, whether as a permanent threat or as a rare alibi, I am interested in the well-nigh metaphysical principles that underpin the structural possibility of the detective story, both in its classical form and its revised, hardboiled, or *noir* version. For the purpose of this discussion, I will limit myself to two such principles— one recalling the alleged origins of the social contract and the other pointing to its hoped-for ends, by which, as various thinkers have pointed out, the detective genre has often come to rival the high discourse of philosophy in general and political theory in particular.[15]

Ernst Bloch, in his remarkable essay "A Philosophical View of the Detective Novel," argues that there is one maxim, borrowed from the ancient Roman author Aulus Gellius, that can serve as the organizing principle behind the modern detective novel: "Treat your friends as if they were your future enemies."[16] All trust is thus undercut by the logic of anticipated suspicion. The real threat, however, does not come to us from the future so much as from immemorial times past. The detective's genre obeys a properly metaphysical, or politico-theo-logical, principle according to which, even before the creation of the world itself, there exists an insurmountable share of criminal evil. It is not just a simple, accidental crime that sets the story in motion, but a radical and absolutely prior form of evil—a violent struggle or antagonistic contradiction anterior even to the very first principles of existence: an *Ur*-crime. The late Schelling, of course, would turn this originary violence into the abyssal foundation of a whole new cosmol-ogy, of which the best-known contemporary variant can be found in one of the great antiphilosophers of our time, Slavoj Žižek—not by accident himself a confessed aficionado of detective stories, as well as a fervent admirer of Schelling. "It is important here to refer back to a dreadful primordial event, 'an un-origin' as abyss with reactionary production costs but, on the other hand, curious Oedipal touches of a metaphysical nature," Bloch writes. "Evil *ante rem*—precisely this represents the confluence of the detective form and what is certainly the most eccentric metaphysics."[17] At the origins of society, a crime

---

15. See Elfriede Müller and Alexander Ruoff, *Le polar français: crime et histoire*, trans. Jean-François Poirier (Paris: La Fabrique, 2002). Müller and Ruoff read the *noir* subgenre of the post-1968 crime novel in France as the narrative equivalent of the critical theory of the Frankfurt School. For a general overview of the genre's development, see Ernest Mandel, *Delightful Murder: A Social History of the Crime Story* (London: Pluto Press, 1984).

16. Ernst Bloch, "A Philosophical View of the Detective Novel," in *The Utopian Function of Art and Literature: Selected Essays*, trans. Jack Zipes and Frank Mecklenburg (Cambridge: MIT Press, 1996), 253.

17. Ibid., 258. Žižek, however, insists that the detective story, in both its classical and hardboiled versions, far from recognizing the role of antagonism or the death drive, actually entails a radical avoidance of the real: the first through the fiction of the detective as the "subject supposed to know," and the second through the fiction of avoiding the libidinal

has always already happened. Violence is the repressed but originary truth of every social bond. Or, as Rozitchner writes in *Freud y los límites del individualismo burgués*, paraphrasing the arguments from *Totem and Taboo* and *Civilization and Its Discontents*: "Conscience, and not only moral conscience, begins in a crime."[18] The first organizing principle behind the philosophy of the detective story consists in recovering this impossible point of the real, the unknowable and un-narrated prior "X" that is always waiting in the wings, and that marks the social bond with the terrifying stamp of violence, crime, and antagonism.

Gilles Deleuze, in a little-known short text, "Philosophie de la série noire," recently reissued as part of the posthumous collection *Desert Islands and Other Texts*, draws the reader's attention not to the obscure origins so much as to the lofty ends pursued by the hardboiled detective. In the classical conception of the detective novel, these ends are defined in the strict terms of truth and the rational operations of the mind, which bring the genre once again into close proximity with philosophy. In the hardboiled or *noir* version, however, this emphasis shifts from the metaphysical or scientific pursuit of truth to an entirely different problematic, phrased in terms of justice and restitution. Even aside from the many added ironic twists and botched sexual innuendos, what is new and proper about the *noir* detective is not an epistemological but an ethical and political question. After imitating Sophocles in a police-like Oedipal search for clues to solve the riddle, a social equilibrium—no matter how precarious—must be re-established. As Deleuze writes: "The same process of restitution, equilibrium or compensation also appears in Greek tragedy (but this time that of Aeschylus)," insofar as "these compensations have no other object than to perpetuate an equilibrium that represents a society in its entirety *at the heights of its powers of falsehood*."[19] To correct the originary violence of antagonism, only the power of the simulacrum is available, with the genre's hyperconscious self-parody barely overcoming the temptations of the imaginary. A semblance of justice is what allows society, otherwise on the brink of cynicism, to hide what needs to be hidden, and to show only what it wants to show. After seemingly

---

circuit by rejecting the advances of the femme fatale. See Slavoj Žižek, "Two Ways to Avoid the Real of Desire," *Looking Awry: An Introduction to Jacques Lacan through Popular Culture* (Cambridge: MIT Press, 1995), 48–66. Compare Ricardo Piglia's theory of the detective novel, in "Lectores imaginarios," *El último lector* (Barcelona: Anagrama, 2005), 77–102.

18.   Rozitchner, *Freud y los límites del individualismo burgués*, 224. For further discussion, see Chapter 5.

19.   Gilles Deleuze, "The Philosophy of Crime Novels," in *Desert Islands and Other Texts*, 83. Deleuze's text, originally titled "Philosophie de la série noire," refers to the French collection of hardboiled detective novels, La Série Noire, published by Marcel Duhamel for Gallimard.

embracing the passion of the real as a violent antagonistic origin, the *noir* detective genre thus proposes the power of semblance as its tentative utopian end.

Mexican Variations

In his Decalogue about mystery novels, Chandler forgot to prohibit detectives from getting metaphysical, Héctor Belascoarán Shayne—gun-carrying argonaut of Mexico City, the world's biggest city at its own expense, the biggest cemetery of dreams—said to himself.

Paco Ignacio Taibo II, Regreso a la misma ciudad y bajo la lluvia

How are these two principles—that is, the real of originary violence and the semblance of justice—affected by Taibo's complete revamping of the genre of the detective novel in the context of Mexico City?

Crime and corruption, first of all, are seen as endemic to the existing social order. Instead of being localized and punctual, even as an unknowable prior origin or dark precursor, crime becomes diffuse and omnipresent. For Taibo and so many of its inhabitants, "el DF" is a city of mind-numbing or exhilarating activity, traffic jams, pollution, daily protest marches, and, above all, corruption. It appears almost automatically as the protagonist of a new form of detective writing, insofar as crime in this megacity has everywhere become part of the system. The normal attitude of the "defeño" is therefore a form of righteous paranoia, obviously shared by Belascoarán, which can be summed up in a phrase borrowed from Luis González de Alba: "The police are always guilty."[20] With his characteristic eschatological indulgence, Taibo often refers to this situation as the inverted Midas touch: everything the police touch in Mexico promptly turns to shit. As he writes in *Primavera pospuesta*:

The fact of crime is part of the system, it is incorporated in its logic. The solution of criminality, even if it is a "particular" affair of the passions of common citizens, also enters into this mechanism. I live in a city in which the police produce more crimes than all the organized underworld and marginals, who otherwise are legion.[21]

---

20. Taibo, *Primavera pospuesta*, 23. See also Ilan Stavans, *Antiheroes: Mexico and Its Detective Novel*, trans. Jesse H. Lytle and Jennifer A. Mattson (Madison: Fairleigh Dickinson University Press, 1997), 108–15; Persephone Braham, *Crimes Against the State, Crimes Against Persons: Detective Fiction in Cuba and Mexico* (Minneapolis: University of Minnesota Press, 2004), esp. 81–94; and Alberto Vital, "Paco Ignacio Taibo II, un anarquista moderno," in Miguel G. Rodríguez Lozano and Enrique Flores, eds, *Bang! Bang! Pesquisas sobre narrativa policiaca mexicana* (Mexico City: UNAM, 2005), 133–52. A reading similar to the one I propose here is given for the Brazilian context in Florencia Garramuño, "Moral y política: La dispersión del *noir* en la narrativa brasileña de los '70 y '80," a talk presented at the 2003 Meeting of the Latin American Studies Association (Dallas, March 26–29).

21. Taibo, *Primavera pospuesta*, 23.

As a result, the questions of crime, justice, and punishment are all thoroughly reshuffled. In fact, the solution of the crime is not only absolutely secondary in these novels, to the point of becoming altogether superfluous; what is more, it becomes strictly speaking impossible for the detective to understand, let alone control, the forces that are supposed to operate behind the scenes. Open endings thus abound, with the title of the fourth novel, *No habrá final feliz* (*No Happy Endings*), in which Belascoarán is killed only to be resurrected in *Regreso a la misma ciudad y bajo la lluvia* (*Return to the Same City*), resounding as an ominous reminder of the absurdity of justice, while the overall mood of the remaining novels—particularly that of *Sueños de frontera* (*Frontera Dreams*), the seventh in the series—shifts ever further away from the certitude of paranoia to the melancholy doubts and vagaries of an aimless wanderer, obsessed with the phantasms of his past.

Faced with a state of generalized corruption, the detective in effect can only appear as a parody of himself, whose aims will forever remain frustrated. "It was a joke. Just one hell of a big joke. Thinking that he could be a detective in Mexico. It was crazy. There was nothing else like it, nothing to compare it to," we read in *Cosa fácil* (*An Easy Thing*), the second novel in the Belascoarán series. In *Sueños de frontera*, the brooding narrator adds: "A Mexican detective was by definition a laughable solitary accident."[22] Taibo nevertheless remains faithful to his principled belief in the function of writing and criticism, just as his detective never gives up on his stubborn obsessions. The aim of restituting at least a semblance of justice is not simply abandoned or canceled, as other critics have suggested, but this aim rather turns inward, producing the strange admixture of unabsolved guilt and moral superiority that defines the painful social and political consciousness of Héctor Belascoarán Shayne, independent detective. As he says to himself in *Cosa fácil*: "This social conscience acquired for reasons that stem from an elemental, primitive humanism, from an eminently superficial valorization of the situation, from a political consciousness constructed from within the personal world of the detective, allowed him at least to conceive of Mexico from an acrid vantage point, from a critical position, outside of power and privilege."[23]

Belascoarán having sacrificed his past life as a politically oblivious and well-to-do engineer for General Electric, with wife, house, and a bright future in the comfortable Colonia Nápoles, his adventures in

---

22. Taibo, *Cosa fácil*, 18; *An Easy Thing*, 11; *Sueños de frontera* (Mexico City: Planeta, 1999 [1990]), 20—translated by Bill Verner as *Frontera Dreams: A Héctor Belascoarán Shayne Detective Novel* (El Paso: Cinco Puntos Press, 2002), 8. This English translation also contains an interesting account of the detective's wounds, in "Héctor's Body: A Brief Account of his Scars, Deaths and Resurrections," by Jessica Powers.
23. Taibo, *Cosa fácil*, 26. Inexplicably, this whole passage is skipped in the English translation of *An Easy Thing* (18–19), but it appears in Persephone Braham's careful discussion, *Crimes Against the State, Crimes Against Persons*, 92.

these nine stories in fact amount to one giant or prolonged ethical "act," in the strict Lacanian or Žižekian sense. Not only does he give up his most precious possessions and objects of desire; he also accepts becoming a sheer phantasm or ghost himself—a worthless piece of nothing at the service of a higher cause from which he is barred by definition. "La vida es bella cuando puedes servir. Afila la pistola, caballero andante" ("Life is beautiful when you can be of service to people. Time to sharpen your .45, noble knight"), Belascoarán says to himself, or to his gun, in *Cosa fácil*, and later on:

> He felt a certain uneasiness. The old inertia, that great teacher of the social sciences, had taken hold of him once again, throwing him full force into other people's lives. Again in his job as a ghost he roamed through strange worlds. Wasn't that, after all, what the profession of being a detective was all about? The renunciation of one's own life, the fear of really living one's life, of committing oneself once and for all. Adventure as an excuse to live vicariously. And now, the inertia following mother's death. And the emptiness of living in a country that he didn't understand, but that he longed to experience with intensity. Together these things propelled him into the strange chaos in which he found himself drowning now.[24]

Ultimately, the figure of the detective in these texts appears as a belated reincarnation of the struggling militant, forced to operate at a time when the organization of politics no longer fits the existing forms of masses, classes, trade unions, party, and the state. What is left from past forms of militantism is the unsolved dilemma of "serving the people" while at the same time keeping a "healthy distance" from the corrupt police and military apparatus of the Mexican state. As Taibo writes in *Primavera pospuesta*: "The only possible health is mental health. The only way of preserving it is never to believe the Mexican state."[25] But this conflict between the mental superiority of the lonely detective and the essential corruption of the official ruling apparatuses brings us back in the final instance to the old liberal, or anarchist-libertarian, dilemma of the individual against the state.

Lenin, Guevara, and the Legacy of Political Vanguardism

But you, stubborn purist, you had not excessively varied the original idea, even though perhaps with time passing you had nuanced it; you had softened it. Perhaps you were committing the sin of sectarianism.
                              Paco Ignacio Taibo II, De cuerpo entero

In Taibo's writing, politics becomes above all a question of lived subjectivity. Whence the importance of those moods and affective states that

---

24. Taibo, *Cosa fácil*, 43, 50; *An Easy Thing*, 39, 46 (translation modified to restore passages skipped in the existing English version).
25. Taibo, *Primavera pospuesta*, 222.

a traditional analysis might consider secondary, or simply incidental, to the *noir* neo-detective novel. Héctor Belascoarán Shayne, one-eyed detective in the land of the blind, is defined above all by his stubbornness, his inability to let go, his all-out engagement and fidelity to the principles of justice and equality. In this sense, he is no different from the figure of Ernesto "Che" Guevara that emerges from Taibo's biography, based on the notion of *entrega total*, or total commitment. Politics must then be understood in their interiority—not from the objective or sociological point of view of power, but from within the political capacity of new subjects and movements whose sequences have marked the history of the city and country of Mexico. Among these, the novels directly or indirectly touch upon the ghosts of Zapata and Villa; the anarchist struggles of the 1920s; the (Lázaro) Cárdenas years at mid-century; the peasant rebellion led by Rubén Jaramillo; the railworkers' strike of 1959; the student-popular movement of 1968; the Corpus Christi massacre of June 10, 1971; the years of ideological cooptation under President Luis Echeverría; the re-emergence of syndicalist and armed guerrilla struggles in the 1970s; the astounding popular response to the earthquake in 1985; the new student movement of the CEU in 1987; the promise of a left-wing alternative under (Cuauhtémoc) Cárdenas; the stolen 1988 election that brought Carlos Salinas de Gortari to the presidency; and the rise to power of the Revolutionary Democratic Party, at least in the Federal District—to which we might add, most recently, the emergence of the Zapatista Army of National Liberation, which beyond the Belascoarán series led to Taibo's collaboration with Subcomandante Marcos on the novel *Muertos incómodos* (*The Uncomfortable Dead*). These sequences are more than simply the backdrop of Taibo's stories. They are, in fact, all that really matters—but only if we understand that it is not until history becomes a story, or perhaps even a myth, that the true subjective potential of these political struggles becomes effectively visible. "De-mythifying is not the only option, re-mythifying is the other," Taibo writes. With reference to the myths of 1968 in particular, he adds: "Three hypotheses: 1) A myth is not necessarily a lie. 2) Generally speaking myth is the rumored truth of those who are screwed, while the winners have the national television channel at their disposal. 3) Myths do not always rescue the most beautiful parts of the story to be told, sometimes they pick up on the corniest or the silliest ones."[26] For Taibo, the writing of detective fiction thus seems to involve above all a fidelity to political events which, without such an intervention that gives them the mobilizing force of popular myth, risk vanishing or merely becoming one more of the many ghosts that roam around the streets of Mexico City.

But there is a certain temptation that haunts this use of the detective

---

26. Ibid., 32, 31.

genre as a means of writing the narrative history of the Left in Mexico. This is a risk or temptation that looms up every time a society sees itself only or primarily in terms of endemic corruption, when one is tempted to define politics exclusively in the name of resistance against the condition of generalized crime. The political struggle then becomes more than just a question of mere stubbornness or will power. "He didn't think too highly of himself in general, although he did have a good deal of respect for his capacity for bullheaded stubbornness," we read about Héctor in *Algunas nubes*—something he seems to have inherited from his father, the Spanish resistance fighter who writes similarly about himself in *Cosa fácil*: "I had a reputation for being stubborn and headstrong, and I'm sure I earned it. But I was also known as a man of my word."[27] But this stubborn sense of honesty also tends to assume an air of moral purity that can lead only to self-deception and disillusion in the face of inescapable hardships and losses.

On several occasions, the independent detective arrogates himself the right of becoming the supreme judge of the whole situation, as if to reward himself for the act of having sacrificed even parts of his own body. "I've lost pieces of myself, for the right to be the judge," he exclaims in *Sueños de frontera*: "Shit, for the right to be judge and sometimes even executioner."[28] Taibo, whose historical allegiances are with a certain anarchistic or libertarian kind of socialism, is of course well aware that the complex of moral superiority is part of a most sinister heritage amidst the revolutionary Left. Much of his writing, however, derives its extraordinary force precisely from an individual's fidelity to a number of political events that are attractive above all because of their untainted purity and vanguardism. The figure of Ernesto "Che" Guevara is once more exemplary in this sense, insofar as he can always be contrasted positively with the later corruption of the revolutionary idea under the state socialism of Fidel Castro. But similar observations can be made about the fate of the 1968 student movement, or about the stolen elections of 1988 that kept Cárdenas from reaching the presidency. In a sense, there is always something more to be gained from failure than from success. "Because the failed act, the sharing of absurdity, brings people much closer than triumph," Belascoarán reflects in *Días de combate*, after an unfortunate interruption of the first sexual encounter with his loved one: "Because the absence of the ending to their amorous act did not open the floodgates of doubts, comparisons, regrets. Because adolescence showed up again on the pastures of love battles."[29]

---

27. Taibo, *Algunas nubes* (Mexico City: Planeta, 1993 [1985]), 16—translated into English by William I. Neuman as *Some Clouds* (New York: Viking, 1992), 12; *Cosa fácil*, 157; *An Easy Thing*, 160 (translation modified).
28. Taibo, *Sueños de frontera*, 88–9; *Frontera Dreams*, 92.
29. Taibo, *Días de combate*, 183–4.

Ultimately, what is at issue in this debate is the idea of the political vanguard, in the classical sense defined by Lenin in *What Is To Be Done?* Héctor Belascoarán Shayne is indeed a figure who seems forever on the brink of fully betraying his class origins and joining the ranks of the struggling working class in Mexico. But the subjective type that emerges from his failed attempt remains caught in the mirroring play between a metaphysical understanding of diffuse crime as state-wide corruption, on one hand, and, on the other, a lofty and morally superior rebuffing of all politics-as-usual.

Thus, while Belascoarán in *Días de combate* and *Cosa fácil*, the first two novels of the series, begins to find himself at home in his own country after years of free-floating careerism and comfort-seeking, he nonetheless also continues to oscillate, as though trapped and perplexed, on the threshold between merely betraying his social class and actually committing himself to a political cause. "Because what you are thinking is that you're balancing on the edge of the system, as if skating barefoot on a Gillette. It even produces shivers," his brother Carlos tells Héctor after he takes on his first case as a detective:

> Don't give too much credit to the whole thing about the strangler and the hunting. You are breaking with everything behind you. You are playing a game on the outer edges of the system and you think that it's something else. I feel as though you're hoping that the other will also play on the edge. And that in some vaguely magical way you've created an assassin as idealized as yourself. Outside of the rules of the game. Be careful or you might end up meeting some of the game's artificers.[30]

The fact is that no hardboiled detective can resist the temptation to abandon this dangerous dance on the brink of disaster in favor of a morally reassuring Manichaeism. As Héctor confesses in *Días de combate*: "Maybe in the beginning it was about the adventure, but in committing to the hunt I found a certain love of life and I came back to elementary ideas, simple ones if you want, such as the defense of good against evil."[31] And in *No habrá final feliz*, notwithstanding the fact that this is the gloomiest novel of the entire series, it is again such an elementary moralism that repeatedly gains the upper hand:

> This thing of "the bad guys" wasn't enough. He had to give them names, faces, places, a context. Héctor, who had never exactly thought of himself as a man on a collision course with authority, saw the state as something akin to the witch's castle in *Snow White*, from which emerged not only the Halcones, but other things too, like his own engineering degree, or the crap you saw on Televisa. There were no gray areas there. It was all one big infernal machine that it was best to keep as far away from as possible. Other times he saw it all as a set of characters to be matched up in a series of epic duels. Both ideas appealed to him. In this corner, wearing the black trunks,

30. Ibid., 43.
31. Ibid., 221.

the challenger, Mikhail Bakunin; in that corner, the state. Or Sherlock Holmes vs. Moriarty. In between the two extremes there was nothing, and maybe that was what lay at the source of his grudge match against the unidentified "bad guys." In them, both of these visions came together.[32]

At best, this simplified opposition presents us with a personal diagnosis of the excessive and corrupt power of the state. But aside from the initial subjectivization of this excessive power—a process which usually takes the form of moral indignation, sarcasm, and the wisdom of somehow knowing, against all odds, that all is lost in advance—the detective's stubborn resilience and will power do not engage with actual political struggles. Perhaps, then, the unfortunate result is still only a spectacularization of the post-revolutionary period in Mexico in the name of a mythic-heroic Left in search of an alternative to the party-form of political organization—a form that throughout the twentieth century has been tied, in the capitalist West as much as in the communist East, to the form of the state.

The Belgian Trotskyist Ernest Mandel, in an additional chapter of *Delightful Murder: A Social History of the Crime Story* not included in the English version, but published in Taibo's supplement *La cultura en México* with the title "El asesino es el sistema" ("The Killer is the System"), alludes to this risk as being inherent in the subgenre of what he calls the "revolutionary *polar*" or the "new *noir* novel." In texts of this kind, Mandel suggests, violence remains as the principal feature of the genre, but it is no longer individual or exceptional violence. "What is being denounced is institutional violence, the everyday violence (or, if you want, the terrorism) of the state, to which is opposed a small and feeble mini-violence of those who go their own way."[33] In the face of

---

32. Paco Ignacio Taibo II, *No habrá final feliz* (Mexico City: Planeta, 1989), 102—translated into English by William I. Neuman as *No Happy Endings* (Scottsdale: Poisoned Penn Press, 2003), 135. Compare Gutiérrez Alea's statement about the ideology of identification and the limited opposition between *los buenos* and *los malos*, quoted and discussed in Chapter 4. Los Halcones were a group of paramilitary youth, officially presented as university *porras* or "cheerleaders," considered responsible for the massacre of Corpus Christi on June 10, 1971, under President Echeverría. Taibo offers a narrativized portrait of their actions in this the fourth novel of the Belascoarán series, in which the detective dies. See "Los Halcones," *No habrá final feliz*, 75–9 (*No Happy Endings*, 97–104), a chapter that begins with the same epigraph from Luis González de Alba already mentioned above: "If anyone is suspect in this country, it's the police."
33. Ernst [*sic*] Mandel, "El asesino es el sistema," trans. José María Espinosa, *La cultura en México* 1313 (June 4, 1987): 39. In French, this additional chapter appears under the title "Le 'nouveau polar' et le nouveau roman noir français: 'L'assassin, c'est le système,'" in Ernest Mandel, *Meurtres exquis: Histoire sociale du roman policier*, 2nd ed. (Montreuil: PEC/La Brèche, 1987), 163–71. Already in *Días de combate*, the first Belascoarán novel, the assassin in the end makes the following point: "OK, I have killed eleven times and caused minor wounds. In this same period of time, the state has massacred hundreds of peasants, dozens of Mexicans have died in accidents, hundreds have died in brawls, and hundreds more have expired due to hunger, cold, or curable diseases, and a few dozen even have committed suicide . . . Where is the strangler?" to which Héctor responds: "The Great

daily violence and a war of low intensity, there is no room anymore for the romantic-Quixotic adventure. Nor does triumph seem to lie in wait for the restricted guerrilla action of an enlightened minority to take on yankee imperialism or the all-pervasive corruption of the state.

"Left-wing terrorism and state terrorism, though their motives are beyond comparison, are the two parts of a single grinding machine," Mandel approvingly quotes from a French *noir* novel. "Despair is a commodity, an exchange value, a behavioral model like the cop or the saint."[34] What must be unraveled then is this logic of war which mixes in the same bag the whole spectrum of ideological positions and reduces them to a unique law of terror, rolled out indiscriminately by police and military alike. Otherwise, the only option left would be the seductive anarchism of the loner against the system, which is how politics seems to have been thought in the long aftermath of 1968 in Mexico or France, and after the disastrous years that were the 1970s in Italy, Chile, or Argentina. It is certainly no coincidence, for example, that Aldo Moro's murder was revisited ten years after the facts in the final issue of *La cultura en México*, edited by Taibo.[35] Yet, for Mandel, the reinvention of commitment in the wake of such violence continues to be "a burlesque way of presenting political action as ineffective and condemning it to failure, which renders this literature less 'disintegrative' in relation to the system than it appears at first sight."[36] If we want to prevent the failures, defeats, and heroic nostalgias of those years at the end of the 1960s and in the first half of the 1970s from continuing to produce merely pathetic messages on the answering machines of the next generation, we will also have to go against the grain of this image of the Left, which finds itself absorbed in the total rejection of, and simultaneous fascination with, the logic of war and state terror.

Strangler is the system" (221–2). The long passages from León Rozitchner's *Moral burguesa y revolución*, which Sergio reads out loud in Gutiérrez Alea's movie *Memorias del subdesarrollo* (see Chapter 4), are also introduced with the subtitle, "La verdad del grupo está en el asesino" ("The truth of the group lies in the assassin").

34. Mandel, "El asesino es el sistema," 39.

35. Federico Campbell, "Muerte de un político: El caso Moro, una historia que ya estaba escrita," *La Cultura en México* 1359 (April 20, 1988): 38–41.

36. Mandel, "El asesino es el sistema," 39.

FROM COMPLOT TO POTLATCH

The Right to Paranoia

Paranoids too have enemies!

Ricardo Piglia, Prisión perpetua

In a really globalized world, the truth appears to be on the side of paranoia. From all sides a vague sense of persecution is proliferating, based
on the suspicion of an enemy both global and diffuse. After a moment
of decline, there comes the moment of overcompensation in the invention of secret and clandestine plots, just as the incredulity toward the
"grand narratives" of modernity is followed by an obsessive accumulation of what we might call postmodern "global fictions"—that is,
paranoid stories about the conjuring tricks of the other, which are
reproduced ad nauseam both on the side of ultracapitalists and inside
the new antiglobalization movement. Not only is there a presupposition that the violent process of subsumption under capital obeys the
laws of an implacable logic the deeper structure of which would be as
enigmatic as a nightmare after waking up. What is more, the same
mortiferous coalition of capital, war, and "freedom," which today
conflates into a single act of humanitarian aid with the brutal use of
really existing weapons of mass destruction, also alleges that the true
enemy hides in mysterious networks of terrorism, millenarian conspir-
acies of fundamentalism, and innumerable sleeper cells. Nobody can
deny that we live in a glorious age for conspiracy theorists. We are all
potential suspects; the enemy is systematically the others; and the only
social bonds, permeated by the grayest of affects, are those based on
suspicion, terror, and war.

It should not come as a surprise, therefore, that Ricardo Piglia
devotes a recent essay to "Teoría del complot" ("Theory of the
Complot" or "Theory of Conspiracy"), in which he interrogates the
use of fictional elements on behalf of the state apparatus, secret serv-
ices, and all forms of political capture and control. What else grounds
the social bond, he asks, if not the exchange of stories, rumors and
codes for one gigantic, fragmented, and multitudinous fiction? Does
not the economy, as the allegedly objective base of the total social fact,
depend on such highly subjective factors as the ups and downs of
consumer optimism, moral hazard, and investor confidence? Today,

we may ask in the wake of the most recent financial crisis whether rating agencies such as Standard & Poor's are anything other than instances for transforming such subjective factors into a simulacrum of objectivity and necessity. Much earlier, as we have seen, Piglia had attributed a related phrase to Roberto Arlt in *Nombre false* (*Assumed Name*): "Capitalism speculates with good sentiments."[1] Now what does the market speculate with if not the good or bad sentiments of consumers, mirrored on the opposite side of the fence by the secret anticipations of insider knowledge, whether accurate or computer-simulated? Does this distinction between truth and simulacrum even hold on the stock market? Lastly, in the realm of so-called private life, when does a love relation acquire consistency if not in the act of giving credit to another's words? Are not all our relationships—political, economic, amorous—in one way or another based on the circulation of such "social fictions," to borrow an expression from Fernando Pessoa?

Piglia, for his part, speaks above all about the importance of the complot in order to relate the conspiracy logic to three fundamental questions that have to do with literature, vanguardism, and the economy. He begins by invoking the example that brings together conspiracy and revolution in the clandestine form of the Leninist party, to which we could add the classical example of the Blanquist organization as well as the Cuban model of the *foco*, but rather quickly his attention shifts toward the conspiratorial plot as a politics of fictionalization on the part of the state. Elements of this view can be found in Book V of Plato's *Republic*, a sinister anticipation of "The Lottery of Babylon" by Jorge Luis Borges, all the way to their practical alternatives, the confabulations of counter-power invented by figures such as Pierre Klossowski or, closer to the author's home, Macedonio Fernández—without a doubt the Argentine writer with the greatest influence on this part of Piglia's thought, well beyond that of Borges or Arlt: "The complot, then, would be a point of articulation between practices of construction of alternate realities and a way of deciphering a certain functioning of politics."[2] From the revolutionary prescription, still active in the late

---

1. Ricardo Piglia, "Homenaje a Roberto Arlt," in *Nombre falso* (Barcelona: Seix Barral, 1994), 95. See Chapter 7 for further discussion of this phrase—a likely plagiarism of a line taken from Marx's *1844 Manuscripts*.

2. Ricardo Piglia, "Teoría del Complot," *Ramona: Revista de artes visuales* 23 (May 2002): 4. Piglia's theory can usefully be compared to Fredric Jameson's notion of conspiracy theory as "a poor person's cognitive mapping"—a view first proposed in the famous essay "Cognitive Mapping," in Cary Nelson and Lawrence Grossberg, eds, *Marxism and the Interpretation of Culture* (Urbana: University of Illinois Press, 1988), 356; and then developed, most notably, in Fredric Jameson, "Totality as Conspiracy," *The Geopolitical Aesthetic: Cinema and Space in the World System* (Bloomington: Indiana University Press, 1995), 9–84. The key to Piglia's view, however, can be found in the notion of the complot as a combat against culture, which he derives from Pierre Klossowski, *Nietzsche and the Vicious Circle*, trans. Daniel W. Smith (London: Athlone Press, 1997). On questions of political economy, art, and sexuality, see also Germán García, "La regulación política del goce,"

1960s and early 1970s, we thus move to the time of terror via a paranoid vision of society in the neoliberal era of capitalism. Paranoia would appear to be the far extreme of the irrevocable defeat of that prescription, if it is not a regression pure and simple to the anti-repressive obsession. The state, then, can appear as the only possible subject in a view of politics reduced to sheer management, to the exclusion of anything that would not be the mimetic repetition of one conspiratorial plot against another. Indeed, the answer to the total subsumption of life under capital cannot be the invocation of an impossible outside to this logic; it can only be the production of an immanent counter-conspiracy. As Piglia suggests, "We must construct a complot against the complot."[3] Such would be the task of a new, artistic, sectarian, and conspiratorial vanguard, whose project would converge with the utopian dream of a counter-economy, or an anti-economy, within and against the commodity logic of neoliberalism: "The artistic vanguard clearly deciphers itself as an anti-liberal practice, as a conspiratorial version of politics and art, as a complot to experiment with new forms of sociability, which infiltrates itself into the existing institutions and tends to destroy them and to create alternate networks and forms."[4] In this prolonged war of position, however, the art of the vanguard always runs the risk of doing nothing more than mimic the blind knot between power and conspiracy that is said to shape all social relations within the state.

Power and Counter-Power

How would it be if these insane people were right, if in each of us there is present in his ego an agency which observes and threatens to punish, and which in them has merely become sharply divided from their ego and mistakenly displaced onto external reality?
Sigmund Freud, New Introductory Lectures on Psychoanalysis

The fact that the state would have lost much of its hegemonic role in more recent years—a truism that can easily be advanced against this baleful interpretation of post-revolutionary politics in terms of complot—by no means diminishes the attractiveness of existing conspiracy theories. On the contrary, this change only seems to have increased the latter's power of persuasion, to the point where today their dominance seems to be irrefutable. Perhaps the most powerful conspiratorial theory, in this sense, is the one that may help explain the international success of Michael Hardt and Antonio Negri's bestseller *Empire*, including in Latin America. Combining many familiar ideas

---

Ramona 21–22 (March 2002): 24–34; and César Aira, "La utilidad del arte," *Ramona* 15 (August 2001): 4–5.

3. Piglia, "Teoría del complot." 4.

4. Ibid., 8.

about globalization in a portable encyclopedia of sorts, the book is absolutely sweeping in its capacity of absorption, in spite of the official nomadism of its numerous lines of flight—with its crushing and all-encompassing outlook finding its most immediate precursor not in Marx's *Capital* or even in Deleuze and Guattari's *A Thousand Plateaus*, so much as in Guy Debord's *The Society of the Spectacle*.

The fundamental thesis of the book, like that of any other good complot, is brutally simple, even though its political implications—as the authors readily admit—may not be so clear: the modern concept of national sovereignty, with its logic of imperialist expansion over the past five centuries, has been succeeded in recent decades by a new type of sovereignty that is no longer tied to the nation-state but spreads out uniformly across the globe as an imperial—rather than imperialist—sovereignty. What defines the new regime is something that Hardt and Negri also call "biopower," picking up a notion from Foucault. Late capitalism infiltrates all spheres of human activity, erasing the boundaries between the economic and the cultural, between material labor and intellectual labor—contradictions whose concentration constitutes the political act proper in the orthodox Leninist vision. Today the imperial regime of power directly controls life itself. With regard to this view, we could reiterate what Piglia writes about the lottery in Plato: "It is a total conspiratorial conception: the complot is the social world itself."[5] For Hardt and Negri, the most eloquent image of this new society of control continues to be that of money: "There is nothing, no 'naked life,' no external standpoint, that can be posed outside this field permeated by money; nothing escapes money. Production and reproduction are dressed in monetary clothing. In fact, on the global stage, every biopolitical figure appears dressed in monetary garb."[6] The difference is that earlier imperialism is defined by the occupation and hierarchical disciplining of territories and populations, whereas Empire is characterized by the increasing integration and flexible control of all zones of the globe. On an allegorical level, the diagram of imperialist society takes the panoptic form of a prison, separating the inside from the outside according to the example described by Foucault in *Discipline and Punish*. Empire, by contrast, follows the endless fluctuation of the market, as a network of multiple entry points and lines of flight on the type of map laid out by Deleuze and Guattari in *A Thousand Plateaus*.

---

5. Ibid., 6.

6. Michael Hardt and Antonio Negri, *Empire* (Cambridge: Harvard University Press, 2000), 32. In this section I borrow from my review of Hardt and Negri's book, which appeared under the title "Manifiesto para el ciudadano global" in the cultural supplement *Cultura y Nación* of the newspaper *Clarín* in Argentina (March 23, 2002). Among the plethora of international commentaries on Hardt and Negri's bestseller, I would like to single out the extraordinary critique formulated by the Argentine philosopher and activist Raúl J. Cerdeiras in "Las desventuras de la ontología biopolítica de *Imperio*," *Acontecimiento: Revista para pensar la política* 24–25 (2003): 11–43.

Where Hardt and Negri come closest to Debord's foundational book is in the sensation of placing the reader in the midst of an inescapable and unyielding logic: a global conjuring act in which there is no central culprit, not even the United States. In fact, just as there is no outside to the new imperial order, so too the authors maintain that there is no center. The new form of sovereign not only cancels out all dialectical oppositions between inside and outside, center and periphery, which defined the modern nation-state; it also takes away any efficacy from forms of politics that would still be organized according to such dialectical categories, now considered obsolete. "Empire can be effectively contested only on its own level of generality and by pushing the processes that it offers past their present limitations. We have to accept that challenge and learn to think globally and act globally," Hardt and Negri warn us, adopting the same grammar as Piglia. "Globalization must be met with a counter-globalization, Empire with a counter-Empire."[7]

This diagnostic, perhaps thanks to the peremptory nature of many of its claims, also possesses an uncanny appeal, a mixture of paranoia and jubilation which in my view is not unrelated to the book's international success, including in Latin America. After the crisis of December 19–20, 2001 in Argentina, for instance, a major debate ensued in newspapers and journals around the relevance of the concepts of Empire and multitude in the context of local forms of political mobilization such as the roadblocks of the *piqueteros* or the pots-and-pans movement better known as *cacerolazos*. Sociologists and political scientists promptly responded to these two forms of mobilization by reading them in terms of a typical class analysis—the *piqueteros* corresponding to the working class and the unemployed in the provinces and the *cacerolazos* to the urban middle class which had seen its savings vanish in the banking scandal that was one of the precipitating causes that led to the crisis. The question, then, became once again that of the possible alliance or articulation between these two fronts, embodied in the slogan "Piquete y cacerola: la lucha es una sola" ("*Piquete* and *cacerola*: the struggle is one"). However, such a view of the events of December 19–20, 2001 in Argentina fails to recognize the new type of militancy and ends up reinscribing them into a representational view of politics as tied to objective interests, values, or organizations. By contrast, the most productive approaches to the 2001 crisis in Argentina all take as their point of departure the singularity of the events they are trying to think while at the same time participating in them.

Working in close collaboration with Negri as well as with John Holloway, Horacio González and León Rozitchner, the Argentine Colectivo Situaciones forcefully raises this question about the status of theoretical work—or militant research—in the context of the new social protagonism:

---

7. Hardt and Negri, *Empire*, 206–7.

We need to reflect in the face of the events of the days of the 19th and 20th. What happened? How to go on *being the same* in the face of the power (*potencia*) of those events that we still don't fully understand? How to approach the space of a not yet deciphered signification, that invites us – under the promise of being relevant – to work through its possible meanings? How to dare ourselves to suspend the corpus of knowledges available to us on the social and the political, the certainties referring to "the middle classes," "the excluded," and "the politicians"? How to travel through our contemporaneity under the inevitable (insofar as it is present) condition of the instability of meanings, of the versatility of facts, and the game of evasions that *truth* maintains with us?[8]

The Colectivo Situaciones proposes to begin answering this question by distinguishing between *pensar* and *saber*: "To think is not to know. One and the other—thinking and knowing—constitute two different moments."[9] Whereas knowledge relates events to the pre-existence of an object, class or idea as an external guarantee and source of authority, thinking operates immanently on the basis of the potentials that are already at work from within the situation at hand. This means that there is an excess of thought beyond all available knowledge, or a hole in the presumed totality of knowledge. Thinking functions in a situation only by proceeding from this limit of non-knowledge:

> There is thought in excess. Consciousness does not know all that it would like to know about what it says, about what it wants nor about why it "wants" what it "wants." There is more thought in it than it would have imagined. Thus, perplexed and resigned, consciousness discovers that it thinks when it sleeps. It thinks with the body. Something, of which consciousness is a part, goes beyond what it can control.[10]

Faced with this perplexing situation, however, it is always tempting to attribute the excess of thought to a secret source of knowledge. Paranoia and conspiracy thus come to fill the void in consciousness opened

---

8. Colectivo Situaciones, *19 & 20: Notes for a New Social Protagonism*, trans. Nate Holdren and Sebastián Touza (New York: Autonomedia, 2011), 84. See also the brilliant analysis in Ignacio Lewkowicz, *Sucesos argentinos: Cacerolazo y subjetividad postestatal* (Buenos Aires: Paidós, 2002). I should add that these analyses display an unusual mixture of theoretical and philosophical trajectories—unusual, that is, at least for the Anglo-American reader. In fact, while the authors of Colectivo Situaciones certainly engage with Negri or Holloway, they do so only on the implicit basis of a prior conceptual framework that is completely soaked in the vocabulary and thought of Alain Badiou, so much so that the mention of Badiou's proper name no longer seems necessary. For this reason, the writings of Colectivo Situaciones, which are just now beginning to be translated into English, should always be put in dialogue with the Argentine Badiouians working around the journal *Acontecimiento: Revista para pensar la política*, above all my good friends Raul J. Cerdeiras and Alejandro Cerletti. Conversely, in the "Introduction" to my *Badiou and Politics*, I explain the importance of this Argentine connection for a more dialectical understanding of Badiou.
9. Colectivo Situaciones, *19 & 20: Notes for a New Social Protagonism*, 83.
10. Ibid., 84.

up by the unpredictability of events such as the mass mobilizations of December 19–20 in Argentina.

If in this context Hardt and Negri's *Empire* captivate audiences in ways similar to how Debord did earlier in *The Society of the Spectacle*, this is also due to a curious variation on that figure of the subject-who-is-supposed-to-know, as analyzed by Lacan. There can be no doubt that this is an intrinsic effect of any theory of complot: the almost physical pleasure of knowing ourselves capable of knowing, of being in the know and of understanding the system—all the more so in the case of an almost perverse knowledge that denies the possibility of escaping the very system whose logic it uncovers with such implacable energy. In this way, a certain passion for paranoia may even turn into a machine for the production of irrefutable figures of wisdom. This is not just the wisdom of vulgar common sense, as Paco Ignacio Taibo II suggests in *Primavera pospuesta*: "Once I exchanged definitions of the term 'paranoid' with my friend the crime writer Andreu Martín, and he said that a paranoid is essentially a citizen with common sense; I added that a Mexican paranoid is someone who is certain that they are out to get him and who moreover is right to think so."[11] Rather, paranoia in times of global crisis and terror comes to include a strange kind of surplus knowledge, which can become all the more enjoyable the more it is both all-encompassing and useless. Thus, in a short story by Marcelo Cohen, one character says of the 2001 crisis in Argentina: "Paranoia consists in knowing more than what one can make use of."[12] It is precisely through this supplement of useless knowledge that the intellectual function in times of crisis and terror is capable of spreading itself out uniformly across the globe in a parody of the utopia of the 1960s and 1970s.

At the same time, in the United States, the beginning of the war on terror under President George W. Bush also saw the opposite figure appear—namely, the figure of the subject-who-would-prefer-not-to-know, which frequently comes to support the most arbitrary and unilateral decisions of the military state apparatus. Today, a whole new ideology is anchored in these subjects who are pleased to know that some unknown other does all the knowing that is to be done for them, since this information—which they still ignore—supposedly cannot be disseminated without putting at risk the civil rights of all their compatriots. In addition to the form of interpassivity that Slavoj Žižek has located in the phenomenon of canned laughter, in which a pre-taped soundtrack relieves us of the burden of having to laugh with our daily comedy show, we thus obtain a kind of epistemological

---

11.   Paco Ignacio Taibo II, *Primavera pospuesta*, 190.
12.   Marcelo Cohen, "Un ciudadano en la tormenta," in *Dinero, ficción, política*, a special issue of *Milpalabras: letras y artes en revista* 3 (Fall 2002): 11. See also Ricardo Piglia, "La ficción paranoica," *Suplemento Cultura y Nación, Clarín* (October 10, 1991): 5.

interpassivity, where someone else does the knowing for us. Every subject-supposed-to-know presupposes a subject-supposed-to-enjoy-not-knowing. As the obverse of the paranoid wisdom that one cannot make use of, the obscurantism of this voluntary ignorance thus comes to be a feature inherent in so-called democracy—a new conspiratorial regime the all-powerful tranquility of which would in fact be seriously compromised by the desire for genuine transparency.

What, then, would be the ways to exit the conspiratorial plot, if the new imperial order no longer possesses an outside—no point of critical or dialectical exteriority, as previously assumed? According to Hardt and Negri and their interlocutors in Colectivo Situaciones, the way out of this conundrum consists in coming to grips with the fact that, against the new regime of power but from within its very own operation, as though in a photographic negative, there inevitably arises the immanent specter of the multitude. To be more precise, like any other form of sovereignty, the imperial order from the very beginning is nothing more than an impossible attempt to contain and control the multitude's potential and creativity. The latter's vital constituent force, therefore, must be considered as anterior to any proposal for its mediation on the part of the dominant constituted power, whether in terms of the market or globalization or, previously, in the name of the people or the nation-state. From this inexhaustible fountain of inspiration springs what I would call the unapologetic vitalism and politico-ontological optimism that characterize all of Hardt and Negri's collaborative work and also proved contagious in the midst of the 2001 economic crisis in the Southern Cone: "The creative forces of the multitude that sustain Empire are also capable of autonomously constructing a counter-Empire, an alternative political organization of global flows and exchanges."[13]

There is a relation of both reciprocity and resistance, without dialectical negation, between the multitude and the notion of Empire as developed by Hardt and Negri. The key to understanding this relation in fact stems from Michel Foucault, if not already from Mao Zedong, by way of Gilles Deleuze. This is the idea according to which not only is there no power without resistance, but this resistance is ontologically anterior to power itself. "Moreover, the final word on power is that *resistance comes first,*" Deleuze writes in his *Foucault.* "Thus, there is no diagram that does not also include, besides the points which it connects up, certain relatively free or unbound points, points of creativity, change and resistance, and it is perhaps with these that we ought to begin in order to understand the whole picture."[14] With Negri and Hardt, however, this understanding of power and resistance quickly

---

13. Hardt and Negri, *Empire*, xv.
14. Gilles Deleuze, *Foucault*, trans. Seán Hand (Minneapolis: University of Minnesota Press, 1988), 89, 44.

leads to the conclusion that, even though there is nothing outside of Empire and, hence, all hitherto existing political philosophers have gone astray when they continued to presuppose the existence of such an outside, Empire nonetheless can always at the same time be read as a sign of the potentiality of the multitude. Against the claim that any sort of external aid or extension, such as the Leninist vanguard party, would be needed to guarantee the effectiveness of the current struggles, this logic leads to the almost perverse conclusion that the more power and oppression there is, the better are the chances for resistance and revolt: "Perhaps the more capital extends its global networks of production and control, the more powerful any singular point of revolt can be."[15] Following this logic, to be sure, there is nothing that we cannot hope for nowadays!

At issue is thus a kind of logic of the double signature. Everything that, from the point of view of entities or of constituted power, appears to be a stable identity, can *also* be read as the sign of Being, as the event of virtualization of the actual and actualization of the virtual—that is, in political terms, as constituent power. Colectivo Situaciones describes this as the conflictive coexistence of power and counter-power. "Power and counter-power can live together for quite some time without either one defeating the other," they write. "The principal problem shared in the current class struggles consists precisely in how to assume this conflictive coexistence."[16] Intuitive in an ontological sense, the method for retrieving the potential of this counter-power from within the existing configurations of power consists in following the itinerary back and forth between the two poles, without lapsing into a traditional dialectical contradiction. "From A as entity to B as Being, then from B as Being to A as entity, intuition concatenates thought to things as copresence of a being of simulacrum and of a simulacrum of Being."[17] Everything that exists thus presents itself as doubly signed, depending on whether it is read as entity or as Being, as thing or as event, as identity or as becoming, as power or as potentiality, as Empire or as multitude. This explains the radiant optimism of Hardt and Negri and its contagious effects in much of Latin America, even in the face of some of the gravest economic crises in decades. Indeed, if we adopt the principle of reversibility, not only does the new global order confirm the flexible rule of pure immanence, thus making Spinoza into the quintessential

---

15. Hardt and Negri, *Empire*, 58.
16. MTD de Solano and Colectivo Situaciones, *La hipótesis 891: Más allá de los piquetes* (Buenos Aires: Ediciones De mano en mano, 2002). On the notion of *contrapoder* or "counter-power," see also the interview of Colectivo Situaciones with Toni Negri, in *Contrapoder: Una introducción* (Buenos Aires: Ediciones De mano en mano, 2001), 107–32. For the Argentine reception of Negri's work, see in the same collection Horacio González, "Toni Negri, el argentino," *Contrapoder*, 139–52.
17. Alain Badiou, *Deleuze: "The Clamor of Being,"* trans. Louise Burchill (Minneapolis: University of Minnesota Press, 2000), 36 (translation modified).

philosopher of late capitalism, as Žižek often repeats by way of a critique, but the all-powerful rule of Empire itself, in a sense, also always bears witness to the vitality of the multitude that sustains its rule. To give but one especially eloquent example of this logic from *Empire*:

> From one perspective Empire stands clearly over the multitude and subjects it to the rule of its overarching machine, as a new Leviathan. At the same time, however, from the perspective of social productivity and creativity, from what we have been calling the ontological perspective, the hierarchy is reversed. The multitude is the real productive force of our social world, whereas Empire is a mere apparatus of capture that lives only off the vitality of the multitude—as Marx would say, a vampire regime of accumulated dead labor that survives only by sucking off the blood of the living.[18]

Without mediation or negation, Empire and multitude stand opposed as two signs of a gaze that is no longer dialectical but directly reversible. It suffices that Empire be read in terms of the multitude, and vice-versa. Real change is thereby reduced to a reversal or shift in perspectives. All the interpretive clues needed to understand *Multitude*, the follow-up to Hardt and Negri's bestseller, already coincide, point for point, with the clues that serve to read *Empire*—with both sides, as in a Möbius strip, coinciding on a single surface or common plane, summed up most recently in the third and final installment of the trilogy, *Commonwealth*.

This logic in which the old antagonism is transmuted into a new principle of immanent reversibility explains both the strength and the weakness of Hardt and Negri's project for the analysis of recent events in Latin America. Their enormous force lies precisely in the combination of two equally irrefutable interpretive gestures: by declaring the real subsumption of labor into capital, of life into biopolitics, they are capable of filling the dustbin of history with all those all-too-modern conceptions of politics that still rely on a dialectical contradiction between inside and outside, between old and new, between friend and enemy; but by affirming the reversibility, or the intuitive unity, between power and resistance, between Empire and multitude, they are at the same time capable of overcoming the pessimism of the intellect with the purest optimism of creativity, which is but the ontological name of life itself. In this view, finally, the notion of antagonism does not vanish completely, at least not in name; but it can no longer be understood in the context of older dialectical categories such as the qualitative accumulation of contradictions into an explosive antagonism. Going against "the ABC of revolutionary dialectics," Hardt and Negri thus reject any interpretation of resistance in terms of a theory of the weakest link in the imperial chain: "In the constitution of Empire there is no longer an

---

18. Hardt and Negri, *Empire*, 62.

'outside' to power and thus no longer weak links—if by weak link we mean an external point where the articulations of global power are vulnerable."[19]

Meanwhile, Hardt and Negri's book does not pretend to be the umpteenth messianic version of the passage through purgatory (through the rule of Empire) so as to arrive at redemption (at the potentiality of the multitude). Even so, their work does not always avoid the pitfalls of "the good bad conscience," which I discussed in previous chapters in terms of the dialectic of the Hegelian-Lacanian beautiful soul. Paolo Virno, in his *Grammar of the Multitude*, is less reluctant to recognize the profound ambivalence of the multitude, as being capable of both the best and the worst: "The multitude is a form of being that can give birth to one thing but also to the other: *ambivalence*."[20] By starkly opposing the constituent force of the multitude to its mediation by the constituted power of Empire, no matter how flexible the latter's regime of control is made to appear, Hardt and Negri finally may end up repeating a familiar scheme that contrasts the purity of insurrection and immanence to the equally pure power of transcendence and the established order. The counterposing of Empire with multitude thus appears to repeat previous dualisms, such as those of capital and labor, order and anarchy, power and resistance—or even, at bottom, the old Kantian dualism of necessity and freedom. What this scheme wins in speculative radicality, however, it loses in terms of its specific effectiveness to think through the present political situation.

Conspiracy and Self-Sacrifice

All militant agitation is arranged in waiting for the messianic "leap" that would launch the movement towards the final struggle for power.
    Colectivo Situaciones, 19 & 20: Notes for a New Social Protagonism

In the face of capital's conspiracy there also forms the dream of another type of counter-conspiracy, a plot against the plot of capital: no longer an inverted reading, but a kind of exasperated flight forward into self-destruction and sacrifice. This is the sense in which we might understand the end of Ricardo Piglia's next to last novel, *Plata quemada (Money to Burn)*. The narration of a real story that took place between September 27 and November 6, 1965, between Buenos Aires and Montevideo, the novel reconstructs the tragic destiny of a gang of thieves who, after

---

19. Ibid., 58. Of course, the question is still very much open as to whether the theory of the weakest link was ever meant to be such an *external* point of vulnerability to which the logic of *immanent* resistance could claim to serve as an alternative.

20. See "Apéndice: *General Intellect*, éxodo, multitud: Entrevista a Paolo Virno por el Colectivo Situaciones," in *Gramática de la multitud: Para un análisis de las formas de vida contemporánea*, trans. Adriana Gómez, Juan Domingo Estop, and Miguel Santucho (Madrid: Traficantes de Sueños, 2003), 131.

robbing a bank, die in the midst of a form of collective suicide, their safe-house surrounded by the police—though not without first burning the money bills of their loot and throwing them out of the window, before the incredulous eyes of the multitude of onlookers who have gathered in the streets or in front of their television sets. Far from doing what for many would have been an act of poetic and distributive justice, by returning the money to the poor in the style of a postmodern Robin Hood, the gang thus takes the charge of criminality to its extreme by committing a sacrilegious sin against the supreme value of money itself. "Burning money is ugly, it's a sin. E peccato," says one of the thieves, whereas the indignant crowd in the street indulges in all kinds of rumors that go in the same direction of moral condemnation:

> If the money were the sole justification for the murders they committed, and if what they did, they did for the money they were now burning, that had to mean they had no morals nor motives, that they acted and killed gratuitously, out of a taste for evil, out of pure evil, that they were born assassins, insensate criminals, degenerates.... As it was, everyone understood perfectly well that this was a declaration of all-out war, a direct attack, a textbook case, waged on society as a whole.[21]

It is this "proof of evil and genius" that a fictional Uruguayan philosopher, Washington Andrada, writing in the magazine *Marcha*, takes upon himself to explain, in a set of declarations quoted toward the end of the novel, as "a kind of innocent potlatch let loose on a society with no memory of such a ritual, an act absolute and free in itself, a gesture of sheer waste and sheer expenditure, which in other societies would have been taken as a sacrifice made to the gods because only the most valuable deserves to be sacrificed and there is nothing more valuable between ourselves than money."[22] When the logic of the commodity in its money-form takes the paranoid shape of a conspiratorial plot, then according to this interpretation it would seem that nothing can destroy the fictive power of this plot except an absolutely gratuitous, violent, and fulminating act of self-destruction.

---

21. Ricardo Piglia, *Plata quemada* (Buenos Aires: Planeta, 1997), 189–90, 192. In English, Ricardo Piglia, *Money to Burn*, trans. Amanda Hopkinson (London: Granta, 2003), 156–7, 158. For further analysis, see Michelle Clayton, "Ricardo Piglia: *Plata quemada*," in *Ricardo Piglia: Conversación en Princeton* (Princeton: Program in Latin American Studies, 1998), 45–52. On the occasion of the release of *El vuelo de la reina* by the Argentine novelist Tomás Eloy Martínez (Buenos Aires: Alfaguara, 2002), there also arose a curious debate about the value of art and literature, in which Piglia's *Plata quemada* served as a counterpoint to Eloy Martínez. See Alejandra Laera, "Piglia-Eloy Martínez: Contribuciones a la relación entre realidad y ficción en la literatura argentina," *Milpalabras: letras y artes en revista* 3 (Fall 2002): 47–55; and Daniel Link, "Políticas del género," *Punto de vista* 73 (August 2002): 10–14.
22. Piglia, *Plata quemada*, 192–3; *Money to Burn*, 159 (translation modified in part so as to retain the usual English translation of "expenditure" for the Bataillean notion of *dépense*, or *gasto* in Spanish).

The ritual gesture of the potlatch, both as a humiliating challenge and as the glorious gift of wealth, acquires a double historical valence in this context. In a purely chronological sense, the events narrated in *Plata quemada* are situated at the end of the period of armed struggle, the Peronist resistance, and a rising wave of terrorist activities among urban guerrilla movements that in the late 1960s and early 1970s traverses much of Latin America, including in the clandestine figures of the Montoneros in Argentina and the Tupamaros in Uruguay. As the Argentine Lacanian Germán García observes, "It is a moment during which political violence appears masked, camouflaged in various ways. It is when there exist no criteria to differentiate the zones of exclusion of ideology. The struggle to establish these categories is the struggle for a language in which to define the identity of the actors."[23] Ideologically, though, Piglia's novel rather seems to demonstrate the closure of this entire political sequence, its retrospective exhaustion, if not its defeat pure and simple—while the notion of a revolutionary struggle against a common class enemy is replaced by the paranoia of a conspiracy complete with a tragic ending:

> There was a degree of fatalism in each one of them and no one could imagine the unexpected turn that events were about to take. Those who live under pressure, in situations of extreme danger, persecuted and accused, know that chance is far more important than courage in order to survive in combat. But this wasn't a fight, more a complex movement of dilatory maneuvers, of waiting and procrastination.[24]

In this sense, Piglia's novel is perhaps much closer to the oppressiveness of its contemporary moment in the late 1990s than to the heroic past of the 1960s and 1970s, whose legacy the narrator is otherwise seeking to reconstruct. Faced with the long-term conspiratorial plot of military and police repression that this present seems to uncover, there only remains the fatalism of absolute resistance, without concessions, in a paradoxical art of the escape that prefers dying over giving in—as long as one dies standing up.

Curiously, in a magnificent text from 1922 to which I alluded before, Fernando Pessoa had experimented with the opposite solution, namely, the founding of a bank as a radical anarchist act. Let us recall Brecht's rhetorical question which serves as the epigraph to *Plata quemada* and which Piglia invokes at least as often as contemporary thinkers such as Žižek: "After all, what is robbing a bank compared to founding

---

23. Germán García, *"Plata quemada o los nombres propios,"* in *Virtualia: Revista digital de la Escuela de la Orientación Lacaniana* (available online).
24. Piglia, *Plata quemada*, 98; *Money to Burn*, 78. On complot and tragedy Piglia writes: "The novel has brought politics into the realm of fiction in the shape of the complot; one might say that the difference between tragedy and the novel is linked to a change in the place assigned to the notion of fate, with destiny being lived in the form of a conspiracy" ("Teoría del Complot," 5).

one?"[25] Insofar as both gestures would be equally criminal and radical, Pessoa's "scientific anarchist" may legitimately choose the second option and found a bank, instead of robbing one and burning the loot in despair as the "plotters" or "nihilists" of Piglia's novel do. Throughout Pessoa's story, titled "The Anarchist Banker," the narrator explains to a young interlocutor why he is the only consistent anarchist: "You have compared me with those idiots from the trade unions and the bombs to indicate that I am different from them. I am, but the difference is the following: they (yes, they and not I) are anarchists only in theory; I am anarchist in theory and in practice. They are anarchists and dumb, I am anarchist and intelligent."[26] If the anarchist rebellion aims its force against the injustice of social inequality, then the direct or indirect guideline, whether in action or through propaganda, must consist in destroying the underlying fictions and conventions that support this injustice—from family to money to religion to the state. However, insofar as only a revolution would really put an end to these fictions instead of merely replacing them with others, what the anarchist can do for the time being is nothing more than trying to deactivate all such fictions. "The most important one, at least in our era, is money," he concludes:

> Really, when one flees from combat one is not defeated. But morally one is defeated for one has not battled. The procedure had to be different—a procedure for combat and not for fleeing. How to subjugate money while combating it? How to subtract oneself from its influence and tyranny without trying to avoid its contact? The procedure could be one and one only: *to acquire money*, to acquire it in sufficient quantity so as not to feel its influence.[27]

---

25. Piglia, *Plata quemada*, 9. Brecht's line had already been copied as part of Piglia's "Homenaje a Roberto Arlt" (*Nombre falso*, 95). In what can only be described as a symptomatic coincidence, the same sentence is put in the mouth of a cartoon character after the bank scandal and the crisis of December 2001 in Argentina, in the same issue of *Clarín* in which my review of Hardt and Negri's *Empire* appeared.

26. Fernando Pessoa, *El banquero anarquista y otros cuentos de raciocinio* (Madrid: Alianza, 1995), 11.

27. Ibid., 45. In the struggle for hegemony between poetry and money, artists and bankers, we should also mention two further anecdotes. Piglia quotes the example of Witold Gombrowicz, who would have obtained his post in a Banco Polaco after his boss had heard him lecture "Contra los poetas" ("Against the Poets"). "It seems to me that this relation between the conference against the poets and the Polish bank is almost an allegory," suggests Piglia. "Gombrowicz has managed the perfect gambit, he got rid of the poets and won over a banker" ("Teoría del Complot," 9). The bankers, however, did not wait long to go on the counter-attack. Thus, in the publicity page for an Argentine affiliate of Crédit Lyonnais, we can read the following slogan next to a horrible drawing of Jorge Luis Borges: "In some place in the world, there will always be someone dreaming of Borges"—an obvious allusion to the story "The Circular Ruins," to which the publicists add: "May these dreams multiply themselves the world over. Such is one of our major desires: humankind needs it. And in the universal language of finance, we do our part."

That is to say, it would be equally lucid and radical, if not more so in the eyes of a scientific anarchist, to found a bank rather than rob one.

In the Latin American context, moreover, bank robberies also became a key tactic in certain urban guerrilla groups during the late 1960s. The Uruguayan Tupamaros, especially, justified this type of act by arguing that the struggle against capital would be financed by capital itself: "In this matter, for the urban guerrilla, the principle is the same as the one about arms for the rural guerrilla: to feed off the enemy."[28] In the case of a number of these acts of robbery, assault, and looting, however, the alleged motives behind such acts quickly became the subject of heated debates and moral judgments, as the Tupamaros themselves had anticipated. "There will be no shortage of people who ask: why all this money? What will they do with it?" write the anonymous authors of the influential and widely distributed *Actas Tupamaras* (*Tupamaran Acts*). "Just as there will be no shortage of people who will say: Why aren't the Tupamaros distributing the money among the poor for whom they claim to be fighting?"[29] Because of this moralistic framework in which they risked losing the popular support they were striving to obtain, the Tupamaros finally abandoned the all-too visible tactics of bank robberies and lootings that were not strictly justified by the financial needs of their operation.

What Piglia in *Money to Burn* retains from experiences such as those of the Tupamaros in the 1960s is the pure logic of the deed, or of the act. Perhaps we might even speak of a *passage à l'acte* in the Lacanian sense—without any of the usual justifications in terms of a redistributive justice à la Robin Hood. The tragic and suicidal act of the potlatch performed by the robbers as they burn the banknotes and thrown them out of the window appears to be the final outcome of a search for the perfect gambit that has attracted and trapped numerous radical political experiments since the 1960s and 1970s and continues to be a tempting answer to the deadlock after the crisis of 2001, in Argentina and elsewhere. In the vocabulary of the Tupamaros, this can be described as the desire for precipitating change by leaping out of the present conjuncture altogether. "The *salto*, literally a leap or escalation, was a strategy to be applied (given the appropriate *coyuntura*) immediately before power seizure," the Uruguayan political scientist Arturo C. Porzecanski explains. "The Tupamaros believed that such a mass popular uprising would lead to the establishment of a new social-political order in which the final ideological objectives, which in the past served only as a model for action, would begin to be implemented."[30]

28. Movimiento de Liberación Nacional (MLN-Tupamaros), *Actas Tupamaras: Los Tupamaros en acción* (Mexico City: Diógenes, 1972), 54. Colectivo Situaciones also retrieves the militant legacy and experience of the Uruguayan Tupamaros, in their *Cuaderno Situaciones 2, La experiencia MLN-Tupamaros* (2001).
29. Movimiento de Liberación Nacional (MLN-Tupamaros), *Actas Tupamaras*, 236.
30. Arturo C. Porzecanski, *Uruguay's Tupamaros: The Urban Guerrilla* (New York:

For the Colectivo Situaciones, however, all such dreams of accelerated change remain caught in a traditional and anachronistic political logic of the direct confrontation of power against power, only now brought to the point of its fatal culmination. "The aim is not to politicize or intellectualize experiences. It is not a matter of making the latter take a *leap* so as to move on from the social to 'serious politics,'" they write in a key essay from *Contrapoder*. Later, in *La hipótesis 891*, they explain why they believe that the logic of violent and immediate confrontation, aside from becoming trapped in a mirroring relation with the violence of the existing state of affairs, also remains bound to the dominant vision of political subjectivity based on the question of power seizures: "It is a recourse geared toward power more so than toward potencia. It tends to believe that the conjuncture itself is a unique situation and it subordinates everything in the struggle for power according to this scenario."[31]

The Death and Resurrection of the Spectacle-Commodity Economy

Fire and consummation, this is what our entire life must be, oh you wind-bags of truth!
And the vapor and incense of the sacrifices will live longer than the victims!
Friedrich Nietzsche in Pierre Klossowski, Nietzsche and the Vicious Circle

Another scenario for the collapse of the logic of the commodity is imagined, not in a bank or even in the traditional space of a factory, but in that supreme non-place of the new regime of power, the super-market, which serves as the principal setting for Chilean Diamela Eltit's novel *Mano de obra* (*Manual Labor, or Labor Power*). From its first pages, the text recalls the "enigma" and the "bizarre" or "mystical character" of the famous commodity fetishism described in the first volume of Marx's *Capital*, including all its "metaphysical subtleties" and "theological niceties."[32] Thus, of the consumers, the narrator who works at the supermarket says: "They touch the products as though they were brushing up against God. They caress them with a fanatical (and religiously precipitated) devotion while they become boastful in the face of the premonition of a sacred, urgent, and tragic resentment. Truthfully. I am in a condition to assert that behind this behavior there hides the molecule of a contaminated mysticism."[33]

Praeger, 1973), 24.

31. Colectivo Situaciones, "Por una política más allá de la política," in *Contrapoder*, 39; and MTD de Solano and Colectivo Situaciones, "Doce hipótesis sobre el contrapoder," in *La hipótesis 891*, 162.

32. Marx, *Capital, Volume 1*, 163–4.

33. Diamela Eltit, *Mano de obra* (Barcelona: Seix Barral, 2002), 15. For my reading of this novel, I am greatly indebted to Nelly Richard's interpretation in her essay "Tres recursos

Under the constant surveillance of the panoptic eyes of store super-
visors, disgruntled customers, and treacherous coworkers who do
double duty as sneaks and spies, terrified by an indeterminate fear, the
subject lives in a constant state of emergency. "But what is that fear
that I experience?" the narrator wonders just before summarizing the
dream of a final catastrophe:

> My desire (my ultimate desire) consists in collapsing in the midst of a more-
> than-irreverent noise and thus dragging along with me an endless row of
> shelves so that the commodities may finally be the ones to lapidate me. But
> this is an absurd dream, a demented festival that occurs in the narrow stretch
> of energy still conserved in my head.[34]

The maddening dream of *Mano de obra*, then, consists in imagining the
ultimate demise of the whole commodity logic of neoliberalism itself.
    What is most disquieting about this dream is the fact that it seems
hardly distinguishable from the devastating passage of the mass of
consumers who on a daily basis throw themselves on the merchandise
in the supermarket. Theirs is a sublime, almost mystical movement,
one that the narrator evokes with a mixture of fascination and repul-
sion: "With what voice could I refer myself to this unraveled image of
the treacherous holdup of the commodities when the uncontrollable
crowd devastates the shelves, ruining it all, driven by a violent love and
yet more imperious than the necessary hatred (of the crowd)."[35] The
only answer to the unstoppable onslaught of the commodity, when
there no longer exists any outside to its new imperial or neoliberal
logic, lies in the desperate hope for another complot, one which would
aggravate the effects of loss, frenzy, and defeat without portending to
provide them with a genuine alternative. Ultimately, then, there exists
a relation of extreme mimeticism—an exasperated identification much
more than any old-style antagonism—between the subject's consumption of commodities and the failed act of his or her destructive
self-consummation.
    Eltit throws the lid off the cauldron of "absurd dreams" and
"demented festivals" that boils behind the lavish and uninterrupted
buying and selling of consumer goods, like "the bacchanalia of a
substantial loss that gives pleasure and yet brings a curious consolation

de emergencia: Las rebeldías populares, el desorden somático y la palabra extrema" (author's
typescript). See also Mary Louise Pratt, "Tres incendios y dos mujeres extraviadas: El
imaginario novelístico frente al nuevo contrato social," in Mabel Moraña, ed., *Espacio
urbano, comunicación y violencia en América Latina* (Pittsburgh: Instituto Internacional de
Literatura Iberoamericana, 2002), 91–105; and Jean Franco, "Malas palabras. Sobre *Mano
de obra* de Diamela Eltit," in Antonio Gómez, ed., *Provisoria-mente textos para Diamela
Eltit* (Rosario: Beatriz Viterbo, 2007), 143–52.
34. Eltit, *Mano de obra*, 52, 57.
35. Ibid., 57.

to the multitude."[36] Her narrator, at least in the first half of the novel, dreams of an economy of self-destruction, a counter-economy devoured by the Dionysian drives that lie at the very heart of capital's regime of generalized fetishism. In this properly mythic or tragic economy, the text finds a secret and unavowed foundation of everyday sociability. For instance, there is a moment when the multitude,

> like a sickly prepared chorus, lets loose an irrepressible sea of the worst expressions (insults to the merchandise and its all-powerful management) and the coarseness of the gesture (against the product) that the multitude repeats gives rise to a mystical, divine destruction of everything lying in its pathway. I mean the openly subversive passage of a human conglomerate that strikes out as a single disrespectful body, aesthetically unfolding in the present of an ultramodern gesture that at the same time turns out to be absolutely archaic.[37]

In the aesthetic unfolding of this gesture, in which the absolutely modern coincides with the revelation of an archaic origin, consumerism turns into a willed collapse, accumulation becomes pure expenditure, and the act of buying and selling is precipitated into a gigantic and unproductive waste of energies. The same conspiratorial plot of capitalism in the era of neoliberalism is already somehow a giant potlatch, even though the violence of this archaic origin has been forgotten in a prolonged act of oblivion that is constitutive of our modernity.

To place the potlatch at the bottomless ground of capitalist society amounts to revealing the extent to which looting, waste, and the brutal expenditure of energy are the principal operations of the very logic of capital itself, as a struggle for symbolic as much as economic power. Like Piglia's novel, Eltit's too alludes in this regard to a certain legacy of the 1960s and 1970s: *Plata quemada*, as I mentioned, plays with the proximity of the events of the armed Left between 1965 and 1976 in Argentina and Uruguay, whereas the second half of *Mano de obra* carries the subtitle "Puro Chile (Santiago, 1970)."[38] But there is also

---

36. Ibid.
37. Ibid., 57–8 (parentheses in the original). Eltit continues the discussion about art, literature, and the market in several of her texts included in the anthology *Emergencias: Escritos sobre literatura, arte y política*, ed. Leonidas Morales T. (Santiago: Planeta/Ariel, 2000), 17–40. With regard to the search for a counter-economy in the case of Argentina, see the theses in Miguel Benasayag, "Fundamentos para una metaeconomía," in *Contrapoder: Una introducción* (Buenos Aires: De mano en mano, 2001), 47–71.
38. The first half of *Mano de obra* contains short independent sections or episodes, with dates and titles of labor and union newspapers such as *El Proletario* or *Autonomía y solidaridad* from the 1910s and 1920s in the subheadings. Between the minute quasi-anthropological description of the complete breakdown of the social link in the narrative episodes and the punctual memory of the Chilean labor movement from the beginning of the century, the effect of the juxtaposition is a devastating picture that undoes the socialist dream supposedly encapsulated in the year 1970 at the height of the Allende regime.

another and deeper affinity with the 1970s: *Mano de obra*, with its terse style somewhere between testimony and ethnographical field-work, recalls the controlled, almost clinical style as well as the setting of *L'établi*, translated into English as *The Assembly Line* and into Spanish as *De cadenas y de hombres*—a book about the post-1968 conditions of labor, strikes, and surveillance in a Citroën factory outside Paris by the then-Maoist Robert Linhart.[39] In the displacement from the factory to the supermarket via the bank, that is, from the production of commodities to their unbridled consumption via the hoarding and circulation of money, we also gradually move from the revolutionary prescription in the 1960s and 1970s to its paranoid implosion in the 2000s. What happens is that the utopia of putting an end to the rule of the commodity has turned into the mad dream of a kind of suicidal act at the hands of the consumers themselves, taking up and radicalizing a tendency that already began to take shape during the earlier years and that will only become more frenzied and absolute as time passes. The radicalism of the exit strategy could even be said to be inversely proportional to the sense of closure surrounding the logic of capital under the rule of the spectacle or of Empire.

Debord, for example, dedicates his famous piece on "The Decline and Fall of the Spectacle-Commodity Economy," originally published in 1966 in the journal *Internationale Situationniste*, to the looting of supermarkets that had taken place in the Watts neighborhood of Los Angeles between August 13 and 16, 1965—barely one month before the events narrated in Piglia's novel. The "blacks" of Watts, according to Debord, had taken consumer ideology literally. They demanded the abundance of the goods on display in order to use them up, instantly, thereby negating the exchange value that served as their only motiva-tion and ultimate goal. "Through theft and gift they rediscover a use that immediately refutes the oppressive rationality of the commodity, revealing its relations and manufacture to be arbitrary and unneces-sary," writes Debord. He continues:

> The looting of the Watts district was the most direct realization of the distorted principle, "To each according to his false needs," needs determined and produced by the economic system that the very act of looting rejects. But since the vaunting of abundance is taken at its face value and immediately *seized upon* instead of being eternally pursued in the rat race of alienated labor and increasing but unmet social needs, real desires begin to be expressed in festi-val, in playful self-assertion, in the *potlatch* of destruction.[40]

---

39. See Robert Linhart, *L'établi* (Paris: Minuit, 1978), translated into English by M. Crosland as *The Assembly Line* (Amherst: University of Massachusetts Press, 1981) and into Spanish by Stella Mastrangelo as *De cadenas y de hombres*, ed. Martí Soler (Mexico City: Siglo Veintiuno, 1979).

40. Guy Debord, "The Decline and Fall of the Spectacle-Commodity Economy," *Situationist International: Anthology*, ed. and trans. Ken Knabb (Berkeley: Bureau of Public Secrets, 1989): 155. *Potlatch*, of course, is also the name of the journal of the Lettrist

Is this not the potlatch—the festival of playful self-affirmation and destruction—that we find again some forty years later in *Mano de obra* and *Plata quemada*? The looting and squandering of commodities, rather than pursuing the satisfaction of unmet consumerist needs in a noble act of redistributive justice, would thus mark the realization of the system's logic that coincides with its paroxysmic self-annihilation. Finally, by provoking the reply of brutal repression, the act of robbing the bank or looting the supermarket, as if in a distorting mirror, also renders visible the ultimate principle of reason behind the logic of the commodity form: the police, the army, and the special anti-riot forces behind the legal monopoly of armed violence. Whether they overreact or underreact, the forces of repression cannot avoid laying bare the fact that their excess and their impotence are actually two sides of one and the same coin.

From Expenditure to Anamorphosis

The fact is that a critique capable of surpassing the spectacle must know how to bide its time.

Guy Debord, The Society of the Spectacle

It would be insufficient to conclude that in the notion of the potlatch we can find a form of sociability that is totally foreign to self-interest, an economy of pleasure and waste incompatible with the cold cash nexus of money, or a radical break away from exchange and calculation in capitalist society. Yet this interpretation continues to be quite common among readers of Marcel Mauss's *Essay on the Gift*, or its even more ambitious speculative continuation in Georges Bataille's *The Accursed Share*. The idea is that only a return to a more noble and generous principle of exchange as gift, encapsulated in the potlatch, could save us from the homogeneous avarice of utilitarianism. For example, when in 2007 the Chilean theater director Alfredo Castro prepared an adaptation of Eltit's *Mano de obra* for the stage, Raquel Olea in her presentation of the play quoted the Bataillean notions of expenditure, sovereignty and inner experience, only to conclude with a reaffirmation of the useless utility of artistic creation. "Creation, from the point of view of power, is dilapidation, uselessness, something absolutely unproductive. But therein resides precisely its subversive

International, the precursor to the Situationist International. For a new edition of this journal, which originally was not sold but freely given away, see *Potlatch 1954–1957* (Paris: Gallimard, 1996). For the Argentine and Brazilian reception of the idea of potlatch and other work from the Collège de Sociologie, see Raúl Antelo, *Crítica acéfala* (Buenos Aires: Grumo, 2008). On the lootings after the banking scandal and the insurrections of December 19–20, 2001 in Argentina, see the analysis of the Colectivo Situaciones, "Looting, Social Bond, and the Ethic of the Teacher-Militant," in *19 & 20: Notes for a New Social Protagonism*, 127–44.

power," she writes. And even more concisely: "Art's usefulness consists in this impossibility of serving any purpose whatsoever."[41]

There are at least two reasons why this notion of the potlatch as a useless and disinterested gift cannot but nurture false hopes today. Not only is the anti-utilitarian agenda out of touch with the current moment in the sense that the logic of capital has long abandoned the principles of austerity and frugality of the Weberian Protestant work ethic in order to seek justification instead in terms of risk, incalculable expenditure, and boundless financial speculation. As Jean-Joseph Goux observes, "Bataille did not imagine the paradoxical situation of post-industrial capitalism where only the appeal to compete infinitely in unproductive consumption (through comfort, luxury, technical refinement, the superfluous) allows for the development of production."[42] Far from obeying the image of calculated reason, with its ideals of productivity and austerity for which unproductive expenditure and conspicuous waste would provide radical alternatives, what if capitalism itself were today already a giant potlatch?

Goux specifically refers to the work of one of the ideological gurus of Reagonomics, Georg Gilder, who in *Wealth and Poverty* completely inverts the picture of capitalism and potlatch that authors such as Bataille seem to have inherited from Mauss. Gilder even throws the name of Claude Lévi-Strauss into the ideological mix:

> Contrary to the notions of Mauss and Lévi-Strauss, the giving impulse in modern capitalism is no less prevalent and important—no less central to all creative and productive activity, no less crucial to the mutuality of culture and trust—than in a primitive tribe. The unending offerings of entrepreneurs, investing jobs, accumulating inventories—all long before any return is received, all without any assurance that the enterprise will not fail—constitute a pattern of giving that dwarfs in extent and in essential generosity any primitive rite of exchange. Giving is the vital impulse and moral center of capitalism.[43]

And yet, perhaps the real problem is also of a different nature, beyond the purely historical question of periodization, without our having

---

41. Raquel Olea, "El dolor laboral," in Alfredo Castro, *Mano de obra*/Diamela Eltit (adaptación para teatro) (Santiago, Chile: Editorial Cuarto Propio, 2007), 17.

42. See Jean-Joseph Goux, "General Economics and Postmodern Capitalism," in *On Bataille*, a special issue of *Yale French Studies* 78 (1990): 219.

43. Anthony Gilder, quoted in Goux, "General Economics," 211–12. The title of Gilder's work, *Wealth and Poverty*, incidentally, seems to be a play on Henry George's 1879 *Progress and Poverty*, a book for which José Martí had nothing but the highest praise: "Only Darwin in the natural sciences has made a mark comparable to George's on social science," Martí wrote in 1887, in turn paraphrasing Engels's famous assertion in *The Communist Manifesto* about Marx that the latter's proposition "is destined to do for history what Darwin's theory has done for biology." See Martí, quoted in *Selected Writings*, 425; and Engels in *The Communist Manifesto*, 63. Our study is clearly coming full circle: from wealth to progress, only poverty remains a constant.

entered the late or postmodern phase of capitalism, which it would
have been impossible for Mauss or Bataille to anticipate. Even for
them, the purpose of their investigation after all is not simply to celebrate in potlatch the alternative of a free or gratuitous act detached
from the calculated interests of modern political economy. "Even pure
destruction of wealth does not signify that complete detachment that
one might believe to be found in it," Mauss warns us; instead, we
would do better to redefine, in light of the gift economy and its repercussions today, all our prevalent oppositions of waste and utility:
"These concepts of law and economics that it pleases us to contrast:
liberty and obligation; liberality, generosity, and luxury, as against
savings, interest, and utility—it would be good to put them into the
melting pot once more."[44] The analysis of the gift, in other words, has
above all an heuristic or revelatory function for the present. The
potlatch does not stand outside the conspiracy of capitalist exchange;
rather, it renders visible its most intimate functioning. As Piglia writes
in "Teoría del complot":

> The economy then is seen as producing symptoms and deviations. This is
> where that tension builds between the illusion of a complot that is opposed to
> society without being a political complot in any explicit sense, and the func-
> tioning of a society that naturally generates a type of economic rationality that
> tends to put forward benefit, the circulation of money, and profit as visible
> forms of its functioning, but that in reality hides a network of addictions, fixa-
> tions and fetishes, sacred goods and absolute deficiencies. And this tension
> between two economies cuts across the whole debate about art and value.[45]

This crossing between two economies is the remote outcome of the
persistence of the potlatch in the era of neoliberal capitalism. What this
persistence reveals is the illusory nature of any contractual definition of
society based on consensus or even, in the context of Argentina and
Chile, on the so-called pacts of transition to democracy after the military dictatorships. León Rozitchner, with as much help from Clausewitz
as from Marx and Freud, had already warned us that, behind these
pacts, the transition to democracy conceals the continuation of war
and terror by other means. "The current democracy was opened up on
the basis of terror, not on the basis of desire," Rozitchner wrote in
1986 upon returning from exile to his native Argentina. "Ours is therefore a terrorized democracy: it rose up from defeat in a war."[46] To
begin understanding the condition of democracy, it is the logic of war
and terror that first must be made into the topic of reflection. Piglia
reaches a similar conclusion in his reflections on complot and potlatch:

44. Marcel Mauss, *The Gift: The Form and Reason for Exchange in Archaic Societies*,
transl. W. D. Halls (New York: W. W. Norton, 1990), 73–4.
45. Piglia, "Teoría del Complot," 14.
46. León Rozitchner, "El espejo tan temido," originally published in the journal *Fin de
Siglo* (1986) and included in the collection *Acerca de la derrota y de los vencidos*, 25.

The model for society is the battle, and not the pact; it is the state of exception, and not the law. The vanguard renders visible whatever the dominant ideas deny and it proposes to attack the centers of cultural power and alter the hierarchies and modes of meaning-production. It uses the maneuvers of fraternity and the terror of groups in fusion that Sartre talks about, against the false illusion of the agreement and consensus. It opposes provocation to order, the sect to the majority, and has a decisive politics, both scandalous and hermetic, in the face of the false natural equilibrium of the market and the circulation of cultural goods.[47]

What the investigation into the logic of conspiracy reveals, then, is a radically different image of the political as such. "Conspiracy is so powerful not because it is a metalanguage that defines languages but because it confronts us with the very failure to give the social a foundation. It keeps everything that is well-ordered from speaking properly, without invoking great doubt," Horacio González writes in his ambitious study *Filosofía de la conspiración* (Philosophy of Conspiracy). "I mean the doubt that makes us wonder whether what is destined to *produce the common* is not also that which makes it stumble, striking us with the astonishment that what brings us together is the same thing that leads us astray."[48] For González, conspiracy calls attention to the secret, unknown and obscene underside of political rationality, the side of unavowable opacity that in the eyes of the proponents of transparency—from Marx in his polemic against Blanqui all the way to Habermas against Bataille or Foucault—should never be allowed to occupy the political stage. Militant investigations into the logic of conspiracy thus would amount to inquiries into the hidden rationality of the political, a rationality subtracted from the public sphere, taking place behind the curtains or in the darkness of the night.

To this heuristic capacity of the logic of conspiracy, Piglia in *Money to Burn* adds the conjuring trick of the potlatch as if this were the only resource available against capital, once the ubiquity of the enemy had forced the revolutionary ideal to retreat inward and become paranoid. All of Piglia's critical work during the 1970s, however, consisted precisely in attacking all notions of luxury, waste, and disinterest through which the moral and aesthetic realms have been defined since at least Kant, and which continued to leave their mark on the concepts of art and beauty even among revolutionaries such as Gorky or Trotsky. To read the bonfire of banknotes in *Money to Burn* according to this tradition would amount to falling into a trap denounced by the author himself during his Maoist years around *Los Libros* and *Assumed Name*, when Piglia put into question the value of transgression attributed, for example, to the burning of a secondhand bookstore in Arlt's *El juguete rabioso* (*Mad Toy*): "As a sumptuous act of luxury, in the

47. Piglia, "Teoría del complot," 8.
48. Horacio González, *Filosofía de la conspiración: Marxistas, peronistas y carboneros* (Buenos Aires: Colihue, 2004), 14.

bonfire wealth is negated; this transgression reproduces, in exasperated form, the capital act of society that excludes it: as gratuitous consumption, or sacrifice, one destroys in order to own."[49] Even though such a radical gesture appears to be the dream behind Piglia and Eltit's more recent texts, then, if we take seriously the critique of such sumptuous acts of luxury, the solution cannot consist in merely repeating the marketing plots of gratuitous consumption with an ever-more paroxysmic frenzy of mimicry. Instead, beyond the ethnological interest of the materials brought to bear on the question of the gift in the work of Mauss, Bataille and their followers, we can begin to grasp the profound ambivalence of our current economic relations by underscoring the fact that today a restricted economy, often through war and pillaging, is already functioning as a fragile smokescreen for a violently destructive general economy.

Perhaps we mistakenly believe that we have understood the meaning of the famous "Copernican revolution" between a general and a restricted economy according to Bataille. Perhaps we still fail to understand how this revolution operates by way of a kind of anamorphosis, or shift in perspective, the effects of which never amount to an escape pure and simple from the present conjuncture. The antagonistic violence of the gift and the calculated austerity of exchange and commerce, then, are merely two sides of the same Möbius strip. At a distant remove from the dominant surrealist or neo-romantic readings of Mauss and Bataille, the problem becomes one of rational control, not anarchistic paroxysm. Ultimately this is the goal even for Bataille in *The Accursed Share*: "We can ignore or forget the fact that the ground we live on is little other than a field of multiple destructions. Our ignorance only has this incontestable effect: It causes us to *undergo* what we could *control* in our own way, if we understood how."[50] Today there is perhaps less hope than ever for such control and know-how. At a time when capitalism itself is a gigantic potlatch unleashed

49. Ricardo Piglia, "Roberto Arlt: Una crítica de la economía literaria," *Los Libros: Para una crítica política de la cultura* 29 (1973): 25. See Chapter 7 for further discussion. The different reactions of the so-called Free World to the lootings in Baghdad shortly after the invasion of Iraq are by no means foreign to this logic, which prides itself on preserving the cultural exception by protecting the artistic patrimony of all Iraqis, all the while cynically adopting the lexicon of "popular sovereignty" and "war of liberation" from the revolutionary Left when it comes to oil. There is a certain perverse jubilation in the Western response when Iraqis are seen on television robbing their own banks, when they rip up or burn bills of their national currency turned valueless overnight, or when soldiers of the coalition find millions of dollars hidden behind walls in the presidential palace, as though they were in the midst of *One Thousand and One Nights*. In stark contrast, we hear nothing but indignation on the part of the West when these same Iraqis set fire to the oilfields, or when the art museum is looted even though its treasures will in all likelihood reappear sooner or later on the black markets of the metropolis of the West.
50. Georges Bataille, *The Accursed Share: An Essay on General Economy*, vol. 1, trans. Robert Hurley (New York: Zone Books, 1991), 23.

in the form of war, terror, and the worldwide looting and destruction of both human and natural resources, what principle of hope could possibly remain, if furthermore the sleepless factories of our culture industry almost instantly manage to devour the slightest simulacrum of autonomy?

EPILOGUE:
ETHICS OF LIBERATION OR
LIBERATION FROM ETHICS?

The loser, the one who does not play the game, is the only one to preserve dignity and lucidity.

Ricardo Piglia, El último lector

Those who moralize tend to be the defeated.

Carlos Monsiváis, Mexican Postcards

What, then, are the effects of the moralization of politics that has come up on so many occasions in this book? What significance should we attribute to this ethical turn in the context of critical and theoretical work—some today prefer to speak of militant investigations—in Latin America?

In "The Superstitious Ethic of the Reader," from *Discusión*, Jorge Luis Borges—an author who otherwise makes for an unlikely bedfellow in the context of a book on Marx and Freud in Latin America—attacks what he considers to be a disastrous habit among modern-day readers. He is referring to the habit of mistaking acoustic, metric, and other purely external technicalities for sufficient proof of literary greatness. This sarcastic and seemingly unforgiving attack against "a superstition of style," however, clearly implies that its author believes in the possibility of an "ethics of the reader" that would *not* be superstitious—one that by contrast would be, let us say, truthful, or enlightened, or genuine.[1]

Does this mean that, from this example, we are justified in seeking out an "ethics of Latin American literary criticism" by way of forms of "reading otherwise"?[2] Does this mean that the work of criticism and theory today should focus on ethics—and, more specifically, on an ethics of the other or of the Other? Could this changing focus be part

---

1. Jorge Luis Borges, "The Superstitious Ethics of the Reader," in *Selected Non-Fictions*, ed. Eliot Weinberger (New York: Penguin Books, 1999), 52–5.

2. See the contributions to the collective volume edited by Erin Graff Zivin, *The Ethics of Latin American Literary Criticism: Reading Otherwise* (New York: Palgrave, 2007).

of the reason why Marx and Freud for large portions of today's reader-
ship have become obsolete references, as opposed to the continued
relevance of someone like Borges? Based on Borges's own work, at
least two critics seem to argue in favor of such an assessment. Let me
briefly mention these examples, because they illustrate what I consider
to be two of the most common models for answering the question
about the place of ethics in the context of Latin American literary criticism and critical theory.

The Argentine critic Sylvia Molloy, for one, ends the introduction to
her book *Signs of Borges* with the following suggestion: "Any reading
of Borges should take into account the ethics that sustains it," to which
she adds:

> By ethics I mean the honest conduct and conveyance of a text, seemingly
> deceitful yet aware of its deceptions, admitting to its inevitable traps,
> confessing to the creation of simulacra it does nothing to conceal. If a return
> to Borges, to his entire text, is worthwhile, it is because that text upholds a
> constant and honest disquisition on writing, his own writing, the writing of
> others.[3]

Aside from the brief reference to the practice of confession, as well as
the mention of honesty and self-awareness—two notions we have
certainly come to expect, at least in post-romantic times, from any ethical or moral discussion—the most striking feature of this description
without a doubt involves the role of textuality as a peculiar form of
simulacrum, now made part of a careful disquisition about self and
others. The question regarding worth, if not exactly literary worth in
the older sense of evaluative criticism, thus comes to depend on a new
kind of textual honesty, intrinsic to writing as such: perhaps not all
writing, though this is not excluded either, but at least that of those few
writers to whom a return is worth our while.

No doubt closer to Maurice Blanchot than to Jacques Derrida or
Paul de Man, who in any case are never mentioned by name in the
book, which was originally published in 1979, Molloy's *Signs of Borges*
nonetheless in many ways stands as a high point in a certain deconstructive and more generally poststructuralist tendency in Latin
American criticism and theory. This tendency proves that the textual
turn, despite frequent objections to the contrary, by no means ought to
exclude a turn, or a return, to ethics—whether to an ethics of writing
or, in a subtle slippage that seems to be openly embraced in the lines
quoted above, to an ethics of reading.

From a slightly different angle, but writing within a tradition that is
perhaps not too far removed from the ethics of textual self-reflexivity
promoted by Sylvia Molloy, the Brazilian critic and blogger Idelber

---

3. Sylvia Molloy, *Signs of Borges*, trans. Oscar Montero (Durham: Duke University
Press, 1994), 4.

Avelar turns also to Borges in the quest for what he prefers to call an "ethics of interpretation," in his article "The Ethics of Interpretation and the International Division of Intellectual Labor." Thus, before taking inspiration from Borges's short story "The Etnographer," he proposes to inquire into, and ultimately takes issue with, the common notion that critical theory, particularly of the textual and deconstructive kind in the tradition of what he also calls "post-phenomenological thought," would have entailed a "bracketing," a "demise," or even a total "eclipse" of all moral or ethical concerns. Avelar at the same time goes against the unexamined ethnocentrism of some of our time's most erudite and well-intended liberal critics and moral philosophers, such as Wayne Booth or Martha Nussbaum—authors whose benevolent humanism, according to Avelar, cannot conceal the profoundly unequal and asymmetrical global situation in which their pleas for pluralism and cosmopolitanism risk sounding like a shrill provincialism.

Rejecting the false alternative between the anti-theoretical denial of an ethics of the text and its liberal-humanist reaffirmation, Avelar chooses to rely in detail on "The Ethnographer" as a pedagogical strategy, because it would be "one of the most daring literary texts in its portrayal of the undecidable nature of the ethical encounter."[4] Borges's story, precisely because of the undecidability of its main character's success or failure in becoming one with the Other in the Indian reservation, in fact places in crisis the allegedly universal and value-neutral access to the nature of "the human" that continues to undergird the approach of even as subtle and self-critical a thinker as Nussbaum.

Language, or textuality, and the Other: these are still, I would say, the dominant modes in which, over the last few decades, the ethical turn has become part of literary and cultural studies, as well as of much critical theory today, including in Latin America. We could quibble, no doubt, over minor points that might require clarification in the treatment of these modalities. Among such points I would mention, first, the question of the prior selection of authors, texts, or genres worthy of ethical interrogations to begin with; second, the unclear differentiation between an ethics of writing and an ethics of reading; and, third, the question of knowing whether the ethical experience is wholly intrinsic to literature, or whether this relation between the ethical and the literary is to some degree extrinsic.

Even in the case of Molloy's ethics of language, for instance, there seems to be a set of presuppositions about what constitutes the dimension of the ethical that are not immanently explained through the reading and writing themselves. These presuppositions, while not necessarily extraliterary, are not strictly intrinsic to the literature in question either. And in Avelar's case, a similar separation is present in

---

4. Idelber Avelar, "The Ethics of Interpretation and the International Division of Intellectual Labor," *SubStance* 91 (2000): 92.

the distance between Borges's short-story and the theoretical references to Levinas, Derrida, and Critchley, all of whom are pushed away in the footnotes—not forgetting the overarching but silent figure of Alberto Moreiras, to whom the article is dedicated. Ironically, this "division of international labor" between a literary object from Latin America and theory or philosophy from Europe—a division that is one of the main targets of Avelar's article—is barely compensated for by the mention, in two other footnotes, of the Chilean philosophers Patricio Marchant and Pablo Oyarzún, who thematize precisely the difficulty of redressing this situation of structural imbalance and uneven development.

Most importantly, I would say that both of these approaches remain inscribed in a certain use of literature (which I am reluctant to call "allegorical") as an exemplary instantiation of ethical notions that seem to be available elsewhere, though perhaps not with the same vividness of portrayal. Aside from the qualities of honesty and self-awareness, both modalities rely above all on a certain notion of finitude as the principal key to the ethical experience today—finitude as enacted in and through language, writing, reading. Literature, then, is only one privileged site among others where this experience of finitude is exposed to ethical light as such. Finally, perhaps such exposure is even the very task of criticism and theory today.

The Exposure of Finitude

Regardless of these minor points, it is clear that we are certainly not lacking in ethical models for criticism and theory in Latin America. Here as elsewhere, this region is constantly in dialogue with the larger debates that have inflected the treatment of ethics in other parts of the world. What, then, is the state of this discussion today? Where do we stand in terms of ethics in the current historical and theoretical conjuncture?

In the context of what Avelar calls "post-phenomenological" thought, I would argue that the dominant modes of ethics today are more specifically post-Heideggerian and post-Levinasian—in short, concerning finitude as exposed in and through language and in the face of the Other. Even Lacan's ethics of desire, drive, or the real seems most often to fit this framework, insofar as it too can be summed up in the notion of finitude. In more recent years, however, another tradition has emerged against the current consensus, in the guise of an ethics of truths as elaborated by Alain Badiou and, after him, by the likes of Slavoj Žižek and Alenka Zupančič. Even from a quick glance at the vast production surrounding the so-called ethical turn, it becomes clear that among the thinkers associated with this phenomenon, Levinas and Badiou not only stand out, but are now frequently combined—despite the harsh polemic against, and ultimate dismissal of, Levinas's thought in Badiou's *Ethics: An Essay on the Understanding of Evil.*

This surprising amalgamation of Levinas and Badiou was almost singlehandedly spearheaded some years ago by Simon Critchley, author not only of the well-known *Ethics of Deconstruction*, but also of a number of articles in which he conflates Levinas, Derrida, Lacan, and Badiou into an all-encompassing notion of ethics that remains broadly Kantian in nature. In the context of the "formal structure of ethical experience," as Critchley describes it—which he also calls, following Dieter Henrich, "the grammar of the concept of moral insight"—ethics fundamentally consists in an individual's giving approval to a formal demand or call. How this demand is fulfilled turns out, ironically, to be quite open, not to say indifferent, so that everyone—from Plato to Lacan, and from Saint Paul to Kant to Adorno—somehow fits this scheme. In the case of Levinas and Badiou, for example, the demand of the Other then becomes formally homologous with the call to fidelity to the event. "What Levinas tries to articulate in his work is the experience of a demand to which the subject assents (*tu ne tueras point*), but which heteronomously determines the ethical subject," Critchley writes. And the same formal structure defines the subject's relation to the event in the work of Badiou: "Subject and event come into being at the same time. As I have already shown, in ethical experience, the subject defines itself by binding itself approvingly to the demand that the good makes on it."[5]

Perhaps we ought to revisit some of the reasons why Badiou and Levinas are in fact strictly incompatible. Even aside from specific disagreements over concepts or contents, including the role of religion or the place of heroic figures of the subject, I want to raise the more formal prior question about the very place of ethics in the respective philosophies of Badiou and Levinas. The easiest way to formulate this is to say that almost nothing major is lost in Badiou's overall philosophy if we take away his tiny book *Ethics*, which in any case was written over a few weeks for an audience of mostly high school students—whereas the reader cannot claim to have even a minimal understanding of Levinas's thought without giving an absolutely central role to ethics.

A second discrepancy revolves around the question of the temporality—perhaps better described in terms of sequencing—not just of

---

5. Simon Critchley, "Demanding Approval: On the Ethics of Alain Badiou," *Radical Philosophy* 100 (2000): 16–27. Some of this confusion should have been cleared up by Peter Hallward, both in his response to Simon Critchley titled "Ethics Without Others" and in his translator's "Introduction" to Badiou's *Ethics* itself. "Badiou's book does nothing less than *evacuate* the foundation upon which every deconstructive, 'multicultural' or 'postcolonial' ethics is built: the (ethical) category of alterity," Hallward writes in this "Introduction". He adds: "The whole tangled body of doctrine variously associated with the *Other*—and developed by Levinas, Derrida, Irigaray and Spivak, among so many 'others'—is here simply swept away." See Peter Hallward, "Translator's Introduction," in Badiou, *Ethics*, xxxv. See also Peter Hallward, "Ethics Without Others: A Reply to Critchley on Badiou's Ethics," *Radical Philosophy* 100 (2000): 27–30. This reply, though, could not deter a number of Critchley's followers from becoming reluctant or enthusiastic Badiouians overnight.

alterity and sameness, but also of ethics and politics as such. In one sense, there certainly is a place for a kind of otherness—even for victims and suffering—in Badiou's thought. But it is only the site for a possible event, and an evental site should not be confused with the event itself, which may or may not take place where there are victims. Badiou's dismissal of the logic of victimization is often misunderstood by readers, who are completely taken aback by his notion that the ethics of the other would be nihilistic in reducing us to the role of mere victims, suffering beasts, or mortal or dying bodies: "In his role as executioner, man is an animal abjection, but we must have the courage to add that in his role as victim, he is generally worth little more."[6] This is often read as a brutal indifference toward, not to say a dogmatic exclusion of, those very real victims who populate the dark pages and television screens of history. Badiou's rejection of ethics as a nihilistic framework that reduces humans to the role of suffering animals always portrayed as victims, however, should not lead us to forget that for him, too, an event starts out from the site of the least protected, the most unsheltered, and usually the most harshly victimized part of a given situation—that part which his fellow post-Althusserian Jacques Rancière calls *la part des sans-part*, "the part of those who have no part."[7] The point is that oppression and victimization, which usually do characterize the site of an event, should not be turned into irrefutable reference points of an ethical responsibility that can then be invoked against any and all political effort to right the original wrong. This would keep the site from ever becoming that of an actual event. But this is precisely the operation that, for Badiou, hides behind the self-described radicalism of the ethical turn, which is why we should be wary of all speculative zeal to homologize his thinking with that of Levinas.

The Ethical Turn in Latin America

To underscore this point, we could turn to a Latin American thinker who would seem to be the radical opposite of Badiou. I am referring to Enrique Dussel, who in his lifelong philosophical project, leading up to the recent synthesis in *Ética de la liberación*, has attempted to combine an ethics of the Other with the reinscription of Latin American specificity as a concrete Other of European modernity.

Here, however, I must go against the grain one last time. Dussel himself, in fact, explicitly quotes Badiou in his most recent version of *Ética de la liberación*: not as an opponent, as one might have expected, but in order to support his own argument. More specifically, Dussel

---

6. Badiou, *Ethics*, 11.
7. Jacques Rancière, *Disagreement: Politics and Philosophy*, trans. Julie Rose (Minneapolis: University of Minnesota Press, 1999).

wholeheartedly embraces Badiou's definition of the subject as the
bearer of a truth that results from fidelity to the event: "I call 'subject'
the bearer of a fidelity, the one who bears a process of truth," as Badiou
writes in his *Ethics*. "The subject, therefore, in no way pre-exists the
process. He is absolutely nonexistent in the situation 'before' the event.
We might say that the process of truth *induces* a subject."[8] What
interests Dussel is *el devenir-sujeto de la víctima* ("the becoming-subject
of the victim")—which is why, rather than staring himself blind at the
polemic between Other and Same, victim and subject, he can actually
find an ally in Badiou. From victims and injustice, in other words, we
need to move to subjectivization and justice—that is, to a really transformative act, which Dussel still describes in strictly Marxist or
Marxian terms as the equivalent of revolution: "The 'question of the
subject' (in its inter-subjective, socio-historical sense, as the emergence
of the diverse subjects of *new* social movements in the diagrams of
Power), is thus exactly the problematic of the becoming ethico-critical
of the community of victims."[9]

The potential problem with this ethical turn is two-fold. On the one
hand, the specificity of the ethical experience in this context paradoxically tends to get lost, as the line of demarcation between ethics and
politics seems to have become indiscernible. I see no reason, for example, why Dussel's book could not have been called *Política de la
liberación*, other than to go along with the spirit of our time and its
authoritarian consensus regarding the dignity of the ethical in preference to all potentially illusory, if not purely voluntaristic, political
commitments and partisanships. An alternative effect of this pre-
eminence given to the ethical dimension, in fact, relies on the irrefutable
radicalism of one's openness to the Other in order preemptively to
strike at the dogmatic nature of all processes of political subjectivization. Anecdotal proof of this irrefutability lies in the fact that there
exists no such thing as "ethical incorrectness," since nobody in his or
her right mind would want not to be ethical, whereas the reigning
consensus can at least be broken in an act of "political incorrectness."
On the other hand, both the growing conflation of ethics and politics
and the complete subordination or obliteration of the latter by the
former are themselves the result of an historical process that still needs
to be mapped. This would require a history not just of the ethical turn,

---

8. Badiou, *Ethics*, 43, quoted in Enrique Dussel, *Ética de la liberación en la edad de la
globalización y de la exclusión* (Mexico City: UAM-Iztapalapa/UNAM, 1998), 520. Dussel
has recently expanded this project with *Política de la liberación: Historia mundial y crítica*
(Madrid: Trotta, 2007). In English, see his short book *Twenty Theses on Politics*, trans.
George Ciccariello-Maher (Durham: Duke University Press, 2008). For an excellent analysis
of Dussel's overall philosophy of liberation, see Pedro Enrique García Ruiz, *Filosofía de la
liberación: Una aproximacion al pensamiento de Enrique Dussel* (Mexico City: Dríada,
2003).

9. Dussel, *Ética de la liberación*, 527.

which emerged sometime in the early 1980s—particularly thanks to the renewed interest first in the ethical and then in the political overtones of deconstruction—nor only a history of the various ethical theories that make up the philosophical backdrop for this shift, but rather the historical inscription of various ethical-theoretical frameworks within a specific political situation.

The history of this development, which would amount to a critical genealogy of the ethical turn, still needs to be written. Obviously, I do not pretend to do so in these concluding pages. In each of the chapters of this book, however, I have tried to show how, through both the critique of the logic of commitment or militancy and the crisis of the revolutionary ideal in general, the meaning of ethics and its relation to politics have also undergone a profound displacement.

Toward the Liberation from Ethics

Following Rancière's conclusion in the last chapter of his recent book *Aesthetics and Its Discontents*—a book whose title clearly echoes Freud's *Civilization and Its Discontents*—we could summarize the recent shift as the ethical turn in aesthetics and politics: "The essential aspect of this process is certainly not the virtuous return to norms of morality. It is, rather, the suppression of the division that the word 'morals' implied," and, thus, it is the suppression of politics, since for Rancière "this dividing of violence, morality and right has a name. It is called politics. Politics is not, as is often said, the opposite of morals. It is its dividing."[10]

Using the contrasting examples of Bertold Brecht's theater and Lars von Trier's *Dogville*, as well as the similar contrast between Alfred Hitchcock's *noir* films and Clint Eastwood's *Mystic River*, Rancière describes how morality today, instead of dividing our sense of justice and injustice as it did before, has led, due to a generalized turn to ethics, to a state of indistinctness in which we are all ultimately victims of some originary trauma, witnesses to some radical evil, or subjects of an overwhelming catastrophe. The result is an unprecedented dramaturgy of evil and endless reparation, to which we may also attribute the appeal of the many melodramatic scenarios that we have come across in this book. Unlike what happens in Revueltas's *Los errores* or Rozitchner's *Moral burguesa y revolución*, ethics no longer opens up a promise of radical emancipation beyond the recognition of one's inevitable moral responsibility in the face of history's unfolding. There is no longer a division, for example, between bourgeois morality and revolutionary ethics. Instead, as can be seen in Gutiérrez Alea's movie version

---

10. Jacques Rancière, "The Ethical Turn of Aesthetics and Politics," in *Aesthetics and Its Discontents*, trans. Steven Corcoran (Cambridge: Polity Press, 2009), 109, 114 (translation modified)

of *Memorias del subdesarrollo*, alienation and underdevelopment—also in the structural sense of the film's disjunctions between individual and group, image and sound, action and thought, documentary and fiction—come to define the human condition from which only a criminal lie can promise to liberate us. Art and literature, after the ethical turn, would then be expected to bear witness to this impossibility, the noble philosophical name for which is finitude. In fact, while they are no longer expected to engage in any (narrative or figurative) representation, art and literature are said to respond to the ethical call when they bear witness to a seemingly infinite array of situations of victimhood, from the body in pain to the Holocaust.

In the context of Dussel's work, this shift can be understood if we reflect upon the structural tension—if not exactly an acknowledged discrepancy—between, on the one hand, the strictly ethical theory, and, on the other, the framework of liberation theology and dependency theory. As far as this framework is concerned, Dussel continues to determine his *Ética* in terms of the opposition between center and periphery, or between Europe and its Other, whose exclusion is subsequently covered up in the history of modernity. As I suggested, the vision undergirding this framework of dependency theory might be called political, instead of ethical, insofar as the ultimate aim is a transformative act that collectively would overcome the initial injustice by way of a new and hitherto impossible sense of justice. The ethical theory, however, also risks undermining the political framework, by blocking the occurrence of such a transformative act in the name of an ever higher sense of responsibility toward the Other. Ethics would thus submerge and drown out all politics.

This ambiguity can be seen in the very title of Dussel's book, with its two-pronged orientation: *Ética de la liberación en la edad de la globalización y de la exclusión* (*Ethics of Liberation in the Era of Globalization and Exclusion*). A similar tension, in fact, appears in the title of Avelar's article, with "ethics of interpretation" pointing toward Levinas and the witnessing of the Other, whereas "international division of intellectual labor" begs the question whether the ideal of a revolution, though nowadays mostly unspoken, still promises a way out of dependency and uneven development when approached from the vantage point of Marx and Marxism in Latin America.

In Dussel's case, the origin of this tension may well lie in the qualification of the site of the transformative act as the space of victimhood. In the movement "from . . . to . . ."—that is, "from (injustice, suffering, victim) to (justice, emancipation, subject)," the latter half drops out of the picture altogether once any such attempt at *el devenir-sujeto de la víctima*, or "the becoming-subject of the victim" is seen as entailing the inevitable creation of ever more sacrificial victims. In the name of these new victims, any subjectivization of the process *desde . . . hacia . . .* thus can become truncated from the start. Dussel's project, which in a sense has to be much closer to Badiou than to the general Levinasian trend behind the current ethical turn, nevertheless facilitates this trend by which its ultimate goal, which I believe is still political rather than ethical, ends up being sacrificed on the altar of the general victimization of humanity. For Badiou, by contrast, the task before us is precisely to regain an understanding of the point where ethics ends and politics begins: "Politics begins not when one proposes to represent the victims, which is a project whereby the old Marxist doctrine remained prisoner to the expressive schema, but when one proposes to be faithful to the events in which the victims pronounce themselves."[11]

To illustrate this point once more, we can turn to the contrast between two passages that would have to figure prominently in any genealogy of the ethical turn in Latin America. The first passage frames the analysis of the 2001 economic crisis in Argentina by Colectivo Situaciones and refers the reader to Rozitchner's *Moral burguesa y revolución* in order to define what the group calls the ethics of militant investigation. "The theme of every ethic deals precisely with the moment in which human acts express themselves in a world-defining material action, vindicating the values they promote and doing so amongst those who oppose the existence of this new modality of being," Rozitchner had claimed in 1963, proposing to situate the subject as the nucleus of historico-political truth, at once singular and universal. "In its decisive, and also fleeting, moment, the singular knows that its action is established in the universal, that the course of the world converges in that act."[12] Though written in the midst of the Cuban revolutionary process and in the face of growing US–Soviet nuclear tensions, this definition of ethics clearly resonates with that of the young activists engaged—three decades later—in the militant research into the ripple effects of the collapse of the Washington Consensus for Latin America.

We thus could think of *Moral burguesa y revolución* as another one of those books that were buried in the 1970s and dug up in the 1990s or 2000s, as seen in Marcelo Brodsky's installation *The Wretched of the Earth*. For the members of Colectivo Situaciones, the continuing relevance of Rozitchner's book lies above all in the postulate of the immanence of action and thought: "The classical separation between subject and object is left aside in order to turn thought into another dimension of experience. Thinking becomes a risky activity: it consists not in producing representations of objects, but rather in assuming the theoretical dimension that is present in each situation."[13] Understood

11. Badiou, *Peut-on penser la politique?* 75.
12. Rozitchner, *Moral burguesa y revolución*, 14; quoted in Colectivo Situaciones, *19 & 20: Notes for a New Social Protagonism*, 25.
13. Colectivo Situaciones, *19 & 20: Notes for a New Social Protagonism*, 24.

in this sense, ethics is only another name for the inseparability of subject and object, that is, the commitment to think from within the situation in which actions take place. No theory, philosophy, or sociology can claim to have the power of authority over the immanent potentiality of a given situation; instead, an ethics of knowledge comes to be tied internally to the thoughts and affects with which the situation itself is rife: "This game of passions, reasons and capacities acts as a material base for the ethical process whose goal is that each body experiments for itself what it is capable of."[14]

However, what has happened as part of the ethical turn in the time between Rozitchner's *Moral burguesa y revolución* and its retrieval three decades later by Colectivo Situaciones, risks undermining the continuity of their shared commitment. Ethics, then, no longer founds the internal consistency of a political process within a specific situation but instead becomes a new external point of authority from which all militant processes can be found guilty of dogmatism, authoritarianism, or blind utopianism. Such a complete turnabout in the relations between ethics and politics is anticipated in a passage from *Liberación latinoamericana y Emmanuel Levinas*, in my view still one of Dussel's most compact anticipations of his *Ética de la liberación*. In the epigraph to this little book, the author quotes a convoluted sentence from Levinas's *Otherwise than Being or Beyond Essence*: "The least intoxicated and the most lucid humanity of our time, at the moments most liberated from the concern 'that existence takes for its very existence' has in its clarity no other shadow, in its rest no other disquietude or insomnia than what comes from the destitution of the others."[15] Precisely by recalling the fact that the most lucid and liberated moments of our existence are only the clarity whose shadow is misery, the last two or three decades, in the name of an ethics of the Other, have come preemptively to cancel any attempt to overcome this misery and destitution of the others through a political act of liberation. Especially if we add a note of metaphysical pessimism or melancholy about the insuperably finite human condition, for which we can always find eloquent support in the writings of Freud or Lacan, a superior sense of ethical responsibility and respect toward this human condition thus has the effect of emptying out the utopian promise of politics for which Dussel, like Rozitchner and so many other figures studied in this book, still found an inexhaustible stimulus in the work of Marx. Using proper names as

---

14. Ibid., 30. The reference is explicitly Spinozian but the postulate of the immanence of thought and action, which forces the militant researcher to think politics "from within" or "in interiority to" the situation, is borrowed from Alain Badiou and Sylvain Lazarus. See Chapter 6, above.

15. Quoted in Enrique Dussel, *Liberación latinoamericana y Emmanuel Levinas* (Buenos Aires: Bonum, 1975), 7. The passage appears in Emmanuel Levinas, *Otherwise than Being or Beyond Essence*, trans. Alphonso Lingis (Pittsburgh: Duquesne University Press, 1998), 93.

shorthand notations for a genealogical trajectory from politics to ethics that spanned several decades, we might also say that Levinas has displaced Marx: "The Marx Dussel discovered is what we could call today, of course anachronistically but entirely suggestively and appropriately, a Levinasian Marx."[16] As in the letter-confession by Óscar del Barco, what Rozitchner calls a Christianized version of Levinas's ethical commandment *Tu ne tueras point* ("Thou Shalt Not Kill") has come to put an end to the very possibility of political militancy. In this context, finally, it may seem entirely appropriate and understandable to seek a return to the Borgesian ethics of textual honesty alone, without the impossible pretense of an ethics of liberation. The question with which I would like to end, though, is whether we should not also consider the possibility that today, and for the time being, it might be more urgent to liberate us from ethics.

---

16. Eduardo Mendieta, "Introduction," in Enrique Dussel, *Beyond Philosophy: Ethics, History, Marxism, and Liberation Theology*, ed. Eduardo Mendieta (Lanham: Bowman & Littlefield, 2003), 9. Dussel's reading of Marx covers three volumes: *La producción teórica de Marx. Un comentario de los Grundrisse* (Mexico City: Siglo Veintiuno, 1985); *Hacia un Marx desconocido. Un comentario a los Manuscritos del 1861-1863* (Mexico City: Siglo Veintiuno, 1988); and *El último Marx (1863-1882) y la liberación latinoamericana* (Mexico City: Siglo Veintiuno, 1990). Only the second of these three volumes has been translated into English: *Towards an Unknown Marx: A Commentary on the Manuscripts of 1861-1863*, ed. Fred Moseley, trans. Yolanda Angulo (New York: Routledge, 2001).

SOURCES

Previous versions of chapters or parts of chapters in this book have been published as follows:

Part of the Preface appeared as "Critique of Planned Obscolescence: Marx and Freud in Latin America," *Revista Hispánica Moderna* 64 (June 2011): 23–37.

Chapter 1 appeared partly in a short English article as "Untiming Decadence in Latin America," *PMLA* 124: 1 (2009): 277–80; and partly in Spanish as "Marx y Martí: Lógicas del desencuentro," *Nómadas* 32 (2009): 63–73.

Chapters 2 and 3 appeared as "Marxismo y melodrama: Reflexiones sobre *Los errores* de José Revueltas," in Francisco Ramírez and Martín Oyata, eds, *El terreno de los días: Homenaje a José Revueltas* (Mexico City: Porrúa, 2007), 121–46; and "Una arqueología del porvenir: Acto, memoria, dialéctica," *La Palabra y el Hombre: Revista de la Universidad Veracruzana* 134 (2005): 161–71; in English as "Hegel in Mexico: Memory and Alienation in the Posthumous Writings by José Revueltas," *South Central Review: The Journal of the South Central Modern Language Association* 21: 3 (2004): 46–69; and in French as "Marxisme et mélodrame: Réflexions sur *Los errores* de José Revueltas," trans. Robert March, *ContreTemps: Revue de critique communiste* 5 (2010): 97–117. I offer a more elaborate version of the discussion of Revueltas in the context of the Hegelian legacy and the critique of Eurocentric biases in "Hegel in America," in Slavoj Žižek, Clayton Crockett, and Creston Davis, eds, *Hegel and the Infinite: Religion, Politics, and Dialectic* (New York: Columbia University Press, 2011), 67–90. For the full version, see the online journal *Nessie* 1 (2010); and, in Spanish, "Hegel en América," *Tábula rasa* 11 (2009): 195–234.

Chapter 4 is previously unpublished.

Chapter 5 appeared partly as "Are There Any Saints Left? León Rozitchner as a Reader of Saint Augustine," in Leo Russ, ed., *Cities of Men, Cities of God: Augustine and Late Secularism*, a special issue of *Polygraph: An International Journal of Culture & Politics* 19–20 (2008): 7–22.

Chapter 6 appeared as "Travesías del fantasma: Pequeña metapolítica del 68 en México," *Metapolítica: Revista Trimestral de Teoría y Ciencia de la Política* 12 (1999): 733–68; in English as "The Melancholy Left: Specters of 1968 in Mexico and Beyond," in Cathy Crane and Nicholas Muellner, eds, *(1968) Episodes of Culture in Contest* (London: Cambridge Scholars Publishing, 2008), 74–90; and, in a shorter version, "Mexico 1968: The Revolution of Shame," *Radical Philosophy* 149 (2008): 5–11; in French as "La révolution de la honte," *ContreTemps: Revue de critique communiste* 2 (2009): 63–72.

Chapter 7 appeared as "In the Shadow of Mao: Ricardo Piglia's 'Homenaje a Roberto Arlt,'" *Journal of Latin American Cultural Studies* 12: 2 (2003): 229–59.

Chapter 8 appeared as "Between Freud and a Naked Woman: Notes on Sabina Berman's Dora," in Federico Finchelstein, ed., *Psychoanalysis North and South*, a special issue of *E.I.A.L.: Estudios Interdisciplinarios de América latina y el Caribe* 18: 1 (2007): 41–61.

Chapter 9 is previously unpublished. An abstract for my article "The Usual Suspects: Paco Ignacio Taibo II's Narrative History of the Left in Mexico City," a contribution to a collective volume that never came to fruition, is included in Persephone Braham's discussion of Taibo in her *Crimes Against the State, Crimes Against Persons: Detective Fiction in Cuba and Mexico* (Minneapolis: University of Minnesota Press, 2004), 84.

Chapter 10 appeared in part as "Del complot al potlatch: Política, economía, cultura," in *Neoliberalismo, fabulaciones y complot*, a special issue of *Revista de Crítica Cultural* 26 (2003): 39–45.

The Epilogue appeared in part as "The Ethical Superstition," in Erin Graff Zivin, ed., *The Ethics of Latin American Literary Criticism: Reading Otherwise* (New York: Palgrave, 2007), 10–23.

INDEX